THE SECOND SOPHISTIC

THE SECOND
SOPHISTIC

A Cultural Phenomenon in
the Roman Empire

Graham Anderson

London and New York

First published 1993
by Routledge
11 New Fetter Lane, London EC4P 4EE

Simultaneously published in the USA and Canada
by Routledge
29 West 35th Street, New York, NY 10001

© 1993 Graham Anderson

Typeset in 10 on 12 point Baskerville by
Ponting–Green Publishing Services,
Chesham, Buckinghamshire
Printed in Great Britain by
T.J. Press (Padstow) Ltd, Padstow, Cornwall
Printed on acid free paper

British Library Cataloguing in Publication Data
A catalogue record for this book is available from the British Library

Library of Congress Cataloging in Publication Data
Anderson, Graham.
The second sophistic: a cultural phenomenon in the
Roman empire / Graham Anderson
p.   cm.
Includes bibliographical references and index.
1. Rome–History–Empire, 30 B.B.–284 A.D.
2. Rome–Civilization–Greek influences.
3. Sophists (Greek philosophy)
4. Rhetoric, Ancient.   I. Title
DG78.A63   1993
937'07–dc20   92–47085

ISBN 0–415–09988–9

For Ewen Bowie
πάντοθεν εὐδοκίμῳ

Contents

Preface

This book is an attempt to characterise a cultural phenomenon, or rather a complex of phenomena, that has come to be known as 'The Second Sophistic'. In part it has come about in response to textbook statements so often encountered in studies of individual writers of the Early Empire, that Plutarch or Dio or Marcus Aurelius or any other writer 'belonged to the period known as the Second Sophistic'. Such statements may often be unexceptionable in themselves, but they can also give the impression that the Second Sophistic can be characterised much more specifically than is really the case. The student or scholar who wishes to enquire further will soon find out that it can be very difficult to find out what the Second Sophistic amounts to or implies. The term itself has long been used in standard histories of Greek literature, and is now accepted in dealing with early Imperial history as well. But sophists can be elusive, ambiguous and apparently diffuse both in their interests and patterns of behaviour. Yet there is really no 'book about' the Second Sophistic as such, or the wide variety of perspectives from which it may be seen. While most angles of vision will produce a perspective that will be defensible, it may not always be easy to harmonise with other perspectives to obtain a view of the whole.

For several decades there has been a sustained scholarly interest in the cultural history of the first three centuries AD. The political prominence of sophists has been stressed, and the literary range of the period thoroughly characterised; the archaising outlook of sophists and their associates has also been noticed. But literary and historical activities of sophists have tended to be treated as though they belong to separable domains of 'Greek Literature' and 'Roman History'; sophists' careers have been examined with little reference to their aspirations as sophists; while many-sided figures such as Dio of Prusa or Herodes Atticus can still be accorded biographical treatments that take little account of the cultural attitudes and reflexes which they inherited and transmitted in turn.

In writing I have tried to keep asking how Graeco-Roman aristocrats were conditioned to view their environment through a series of sophistic perspectives. I have attempted to look at sophists first against the general background of the Imperial Greek cities, the working environment in which they so often practised. I have attempted to glance at the long continuity in their activities; and to note some aspects of rhetorical practice and its background in literature and language. I then touch on the sophist's ability to invade the fringes of history, philosophy, the visual arts, fictional literature and religion, and incidentally the capacity of those concerned in these fields to draw on sophistic techniques. I have also tried to remind students of 'Sophistic' how readily it could be conducted with lightness as well as virtuosity, and to look at some texts in which sophists appear in a typical way. Not everything that sophists said or did will excite approval, but we must at least acknowledge that they were there and that they made the most of it; and that sophistic techniques did not stifle literary or cultural creativity, even if they seemed at times to put a premium on an excess of which sophists themselves could be wryly aware.

The scope of ancient evidence and modern scholarship have imposed limitations on the scale of treatment. I have not tried to write a history, still less a textbook of 'Sophistic'; nor have I attempted to do more than remind the reader that sophistic practice does not stop with Philostratus. I have tried instead to create some impression of an ethos or aura through which sophistic habits, tendencies and reflexes can be recognised. This has involved a good deal of primary quotation: sophistic writers are not slow to talk about their world or reveal themselves at least indirectly, and they should be heard. I have included a purely introductory chapter for the benefit of any coming to the Second Sophistic from contexts other than that of the Roman Empire. I have also had to practise a great deal of arbitrary selection among so much, as well as trying to avoid repetition of material from my own previous studies in or around the field, in particular on *Philostratus* and *The Pepaideumenos in Action*, as well as a number of forthcoming studies in *ANRW.*

I am grateful to the many colleagues and friends who have contributed to the making of this book by discussing sophists with me. In particular Donald Russell, Bryan Reardon, Geoffrey Arnott, Christopher Jones, Simon Swain and Michael Trapp have all imparted something of value, often unwittingly, at some time or other. I am also grateful to Suzanne Rothe and Maria Šzarmach for making their own work available to me at the earliest possible moment. I am grateful to Routledge's anonymous referee for many sensible suggestions, to Geraldine Beare who compiled the index, and to Richard Stoneman and his staff for their unfailing courtesy and encouragement; I alone am responsible for what remains. My wife Margaret has been a constant support to over twenty years' work on sophists, even when I seemed in danger of becoming all too like them; while the dedicatee, Ewen Bowie, has generously supported younger scholars in Second Sophistic studies over many years, and I am greatly indebted to him.

Graham Anderson
University of Kent at Canterbury

Abbreviations

AC	L'Antiquité classique
AJPh	American Journal of Philology
ANRW	Aufstieg und Niedergang der römischen Welt
BCH	Bulletin de correspondance Héllénique
BICS	Bulletin of the Institute of Classical Studies
CA	Classical Antiquity
CAH	Cambridge Ancient History
CHCL	Cambridge History of Classical Literature
CJ	Classical Journal
CMG	Corpus medicorum graecorum
CPh	Classical Philology
CQ	Classical Quarterly
CR	Classical Review
CSCPh	California Studies in Classical Philology
EM	Epigraphical Museum in Athens
FGrH	Die Fragmente der griechischen Historiker
GR	Greece and Rome
GRBS	Greek Roman and Byzantine Studies
HE	Historia Ecclesiastica
HSCPh	Harvard Studies in Classical Philology
IE	Die Inschriften von Ephesos
IG	Inscriptiones graecae
JHS	Journal of Hellenic Studies
JÖAL	Jahrehefte der Österreichischen Archäologischen Instituts
JRH	Journal of Religious History
JRS	Journal of Roman Studies
JThS	Journal of Theological Studies
LCL	Loeb Classical Library

LSJ	Liddell-Scott-Jones
MC	Il Mondo Classico
MH	Museum Helveticum
NA	Noctes Atticae
NJklAlt	Neue Jahrbücher für das klassische Altertum
PCPhS	Proceedings of the Cambridge Philological Society
PG	Patrologia graeca
PIR	Prosopographia Imperii Romani
PL	Patrologia latina
RE	Realencyclopädie der klassischen Altertumswissenschaft
REG	Revue des études grecques
RhM	Rheinisches Museum für Philologie
SEG	Supplementum epigraphicum graecum
SHA	Scriptores Historiae Augustae
TAPhA	Transactions of the American Philological Association
VA	Vita Apollonii Tyanensis
VPS	Vitae Philosophorum Sophistarumque
VS	Vitae Sophistarum
WS	Wiener Studien
YCS	Yale Classical Studies

Introduction: Roman Empire and Greek Renaissance

In the year 26 AD, in the reign of the second Roman Emperor Tiberius, a debate took place in the Roman Senate about which Greek city should have the honour of erecting a statue of the Emperor. Among various candidates rejected was Ilium, the traditional site of Troy; the successful candidate was Smyrna, on the basis of past services to Rome itself. Over a century later, there was an outcry when the Greek millionaire Herodes Atticus was allowed by Hadrian to provide a public water-supply for 'Troy': Roman officials in Asia protested at the questionable priority of spending so much on a project of merely sentimental value. But Herodes had his way, and the water-supply was provided with the aid of substantial funds donated by his father.[1]

These two cases offer an interesting contrast: the first takes place at a time when we hear little of the Greek-speaking Eastern Mediterranean in terms of cultural self-consciousness. The second takes place during what historians are increasingly inclined to call 'the period of the Second Sophistic', after a change of attitude by emperors and the Roman world generally towards the whole Greek ambience of the Eastern Mediterranean and beyond. Sophists themselves we should provisionally characterise at this point, though no definition is likely to be ideal: we are dealing with established public speakers who offered a predominantly rhetorical form of higher education, with a distinct emphasis on its more ostentatious forms. But before we discuss 'the Second Sophistic' and what it implied, we should set the scene by looking briefly at some aspects of the Greek world under Roman rule.

The Greek world in historical times had consisted of a welter

1

of independent city-states,[2] whose heyday has been regarded as the era of their resistance to foreign conquest in the fifth and fourth centuries BC: an era of the ascendancy of Athens and Sparta, and of democracy itself in Athens; and an era of cultural sensibility, again most specifically in Athens, where public expression of the arts in literature, especially drama, has still left its impact on world literature, as its visual achievements have on art and architecture. Athens too had taken over the ascendancy of intellectual culture with Socrates, Plato and Aristotle, and had in the late fifth century its first experience of notoriously ambiguous figures who called themselves sophists. The whole basis of this cultural map was changed, and forever, by the Macedonian conquest of Greece by Philip of Macedon at the battle of Chaeronea in 338 BC. Despite the tendency of the rest of the Greek world to regard Macedon as an outsider, it was Philip's son Alexander who offered Greece its most expansive if not its finest hour with an expedition which annexed territory as far as Egypt and India in a series of spectacular military successes. But the political price was already high: the autocracy of a single figure. And this autocracy was perpetuated after the breakup of Alexander's empire into three broad units based on Macedonia, the Asian Seleucid kingdoms and Ptolemaic Egypt. None the less these kingdoms could still include for the succeeding centuries an enormous geographical tract of Western Asia in which Greek language and way of life were perpetuated and superimposed on native cultures as a matter of course. The expansion of Rome's Mediterranean Empire during the late Roman Republic saw the political decline of the Hellenistic kingdoms: the Greek mainland was finally subjugated with the fall of Corinth in 146 BC, and the Ptolemaic line in Egypt ended with the suicide of Cleopatra after the battle of Actium in 31 BC. Greeks had to live under some form of Roman rule comfortably or uncomfortably, and come to terms with the art of accommodating their past glories to it.

The victor of Actium, the future Emperor Augustus, enabled the Greek world to stabilise over the long course of his reign, and Greek-speaking intellectuals were able to continue what they had long been able to do: to travel abroad, to talk, to educate, and to receive acclaim. And as the Mediterranean world recovered from the disruptions of Roman expansionism and civil war, we find an awareness of Hellenism flourishing unhindered in a more favourable climate. The unit of Greek history, the city-state, remained largely intact, and such units were still the standard focus of civilised life, at any rate in the eastern half of the Mediterranean world. A city would expect to be run by its local aristocracy,[3] whatever its relationships with Rome or with the Roman governor of the province surrounding it. And that aristocracy could expect to encourage and partic-ipate in the provision of public buildings, cults, games, festivals, shows and educational amenities, often in a highly competitive spirit, with individual cities striving to outdo their neighbours and those further afield. It is chiefly in these microcosms and their corporate and individual life that rhetoric, literature and intellectual life in the Roman Empire were conceived, and where an often strong sense of continuing Hellenic identity will have been maintained. Rome allowed limited self-government to a number of categories of city to run their affairs outside the jurisdiction of the governor of the surrounding province,[4] and the result was an ethos in which educated Greeks could seek to foster at least an illusion of past glories of the fifth and fourth centuries BC.

CRADLES OF HELLENISM

The fortunes of Athens in the Early Empire[5] certainly attest to a sense of recovery and a more or less characteristic conceit. After little material sign of revival in the first century AD, we find no fewer than three visits by Hadrian[6] in the early second century, two of them as Emperor; we find Hadrian's foundation of the so-called Panhellenion, with its sense of a Greek league and hence a Greek identity; and we note the benefactions of the aristo-cratic Herodes Atticus over a series of reigns in the same century.[7] Even during the Anarchy of the mid-third century we find a defence of the city by a figure, Publius Herennius Dexippus, who would emerge as a littérateur in his own right.[8] In the fourth century once more, in the world known to the sophist Libanius,[9] we find at least the motions of cultural leader-ship of the Greek world when the political realities had centred the Eastern half of the Empire on Constantine's Constan-tinople.

But in the preceding centuries it is most obviously in Asia Minor that Hellenism is flourishing and assertive: in Ephesus for example we can point to fervent politico-religious activity when the silversmiths staged a prolonged protest in the public theatre against the inroads of earliest Christianity at the expense of their native goddess Artemis and her cult-interests; or we can point to the documents of a festival sponsored by a local benefactor with a great pageant to commemorate the city's history;[10] and the remains are still to be seen of a city whose last great surge of building was in the second century itself. Similar portraits could be repeated in Asia and Syria: the picture offered by inscriptions of Aphrodisias in Caria give an important cross-section of the life of a city not in the front rank, but able to commemorate dignitaries and show a sense of self-confidence, while producing one major scholar of Greek philosophy in the person of Alexander of Aphrodisias.

In a number of the speeches of Dio Chrysostom[11] we have a glimpse of lively local politics in the cities of the province of Bithynia, with Dio himself trying to 'improve' his own native Prusa with a portico, generating the kind of controversy comparable to those of developers attempting to provide new town centres in English provincial towns. The repercussions in Dio's case reached Rome, and he was accused by a local rival of embezzlement; Dio himself had nothing to fear, as a friend of the Emperor Trajan, though the governor of the province, Trajan's legate Pliny, showed a keen interest in the matter.[12] Overenthusiastic public spending by Greek cities keen to outdo their neighbours was already Rome's business, and became still more so.[13] And as local aristocracies strove to cope from their private purses with increasingly ambitious development and with the immense cost of festivals and other amenities of civic life, we find a sense of strain and sometimes panic, so that nomination to local offices with their attendant burdens might be ruinous to a wealthy individual or his family.[14] But as these forces worked themselves out, and cities had to adjust to less foreseeable circumstances such as invasion or earthquake, it could not be said that the cities of the East were either uneventful or lacking in liveliness:[15] there was plenty of scope for the able public speaker.

In this context the outward and visible signs of a resurgent sense of the past are a subject in themselves, yet one inseparable from the literary aspect. Pausanias' great *periēgēsis* ('itinerary') of mainland Greece[16] in the mid-second century affords some idea of the richness of both material and associations to be encountered through the regions of mainland Greece, especially in temples and public buildings. And at this stage there was no lack of inclination to continue the adornment: Herodes Atticus in particular seemed to set himself the goal of being as conspicuous as a builder as he could hope to be as a sophist.

It must not be imagined that the frequently costly redevelopments would have caused cities to look as traditionally Greek as they might; distinctively Roman institutions such as bath-buildings and circuses might complement the established Greek agora and gymnasium. At Pergamum we find a Roman theatre, a Roman-sized circus, a temple of Trajan and an amphitheatre,[17] and the catalogue can be readily replicated elsewhere. On the other hand many buildings with a Roman look go back to a widespread Hellenistic Greek adoption of the Corinthian order for opulent or 'expensive' buildings; on the visual aspect of cities, as on their culture, it is often difficult to generalise.

Moreover the economic resurgence of the High Empire was accompanied by a social mobility of a new kind: the availability of Roman citizenship, and of membership of the equestrian and even the senatorial order for prominent provincials.[18] This was a natural concomitant of Roman provincial administration, with its desire to rule through the support of the traditional ruling élites of a locality. St Paul's appeal to Caesar is a celebrated instance of the use of the protection of Roman citizenship in the mid-first century by a Greek speaker from Tarsus in Southern Asia Minor;[19] by the early second century we can point to the consulship of Herodes Atticus in 143 as a high point attainable by the already well-established and ultra-ambitious;[20] though it is worth stressing that in many cases the very nature of Hellenism meant that Roman honours were not sought, or were incidental to a different kind of cultural vocation.

CITIES AND EMPERORS

In a system in which Roman rule was that of the Emperor, either by direct contact with the more priviliged cities or through a provincial governor, significant dimensions of cultural life might depend on the Emperor himself. A city or a province might be dependent on the attitude of an individual Emperor to an embassy sent to him on a particular day. Fortunately for the Greek East, emperors in the first two centuries at any rate were generally responsive:[21] if the embarrassing Hellenomania of Nero was offset by a guarded Vespasian, who revoked the freedom for the Greek cities which Nero had restored, we note too the case of the Greek Games at Vienne in Gallia Narbonensis, revoked by Nerva's body of advisers, as a likely cause of immorality. But the picture from Hadrian to Marcus Aurelius was exceptionally favourable. Hadrian himself showed a genuine and sustained interest in things Greek,[22] and particularly in restoring the material and institutional dignity of Athens; Marcus Aurelius could give potentially tiresome Athenian politicians the time of day even in the midst of a series of hostilities on the northern frontier.[23] Nor was all of this interest a matter of sterile archaism: the famous anecdote of Hadrian attempting to interfere with the designs of the architect Apollodorus[24] shows us an Emperor interested in the innovative use of domes, later seen in his Pantheon and elsewhere. And material rewards came from it: Smyrna needed generous help from the Emperor for rebuilding after serious earthquake destruction under Marcus Aurelius, and duly received it.[25] An aside in Pausanias will give us some idea of the working relationship involved between Greek communities and the Antonines:

> My narrative causes me to mention Pallantium, if indeed there is anything there worthy of record; and to explain why the first Emperor Antoninus [Pius] made it a city in place of a village, and gave its inhabitants their freedom and exemption from taxation. They say that the wisest man and best war-leader among the Arcadians, Evander, son of a nymph, a daughter of the Ladon, and of Hermes, when he was sent to found a colony with a force of Arcadians from Pallantium, founded a city beside the river Tiber. And the part of the present Rome colonised by Evander and his Arcadian followers bears the name Pallantium in memory of the one in Arcadia ... and Antoninus, who made these benefactions to Pallantium, never willingly brought war on the Romans. But when the Moors started one, ... he drove them right out of their country.[26]

Pausanias notes a case where a Roman Emperor has been able to link the legendary past of Rome to that of Greece; money, development and privilege have followed. If he seems guarded about the whole business, he also seems convinced of both the nature and effectiveness of the *Pax Romana*; he goes into a eulogy of the sensible provisions of Pius, and says that the latter deserves a title of Cyrus the Elder, the Persian King who was called the father of humanity. The nuance is subtle: Antoninus is the best type of barbarian, and the present is being neatly translated into terms of the past.

We shall often have the opportunity to note that Roman officials were curiously circumspect about dealing with Greeks. We happen to have a letter of Pliny the Younger giving advice to a friend on how to deal with Greeks in terms of their strong cultural sensitivities, yet when he does so he is not always as tactful as he could be, suggesting that their past is all that these (temperamental and oversensitive) Greeks have to cling to.[27] But Hellenism 'took its fierce captor captive'[28] in the High Empire as surely as it had done in the major injection of Greek culture in the late Republic and under Augustus. Indeed, the very fact of the Greek past as a past invested it with a veneer of antique wisdom at the outset. The tendency of Greeks to persevere in the preservation of things Greek would have provoked admiration from those in search of a complex of historical and legendary traditions longer and more illustrious than their own.

One circumstance in particular underpinned the world as Greeks liked to see it and plausibly could. This is the political fact that a Greek-speaking ruler in the fourth century BC had conquered a huge Eastern Empire, on a scale which Rome had never since been able to emulate in the East itself. The fact that Alexander's Empire[29] did not preserve its unity beyond his own lifetime did not detract from the vast area that had been imbued with Greek culture over a long period, and continued to sustain a good deal of it into the Byzantine era. This meant in effect that over large parts of the East the aristocracies of local cities could see their own cities through a perspective which was un-Roman (though it might still be conveniently favourable to Rome). It also meant that sending an embassy to Rome or to an Emperor on the move was not in itself any more demeaning than sending an embassy from Athens to Macedon had been.

7

It is often assumed that with the advent of the Empire 'real' political activity ceased, and from one point of view this is true. Yet the existence of an Emperor and efficient Imperial defences did not in itself mean the end of lively local politics or inter-city rivalries; rather did it seem to underwrite an often self-indulgent attitude on the part of individuals and cities alike. We can choose to value these activities upwards or downwards, depending on whether we look from a Greek or a Roman point of view. If these are to us empty posturings, they were equally clearly not so to the participants.

THE *PEPAIDEUMENOS* AND HIS WORLD

Renaissance[30] is a term appropriate in some sense to the economic regeneration of the Greek world under the Empire. But it tends to imply some kind of atrophy beforehand, and that is more difficult to prove. There tends, moreover, to be a curious assumption that economic regeneration was responsible for the Second Sophists,[31] but that is not so, as we shall see: rhetorical efflorescence was already there, and fervent cultural nationalism was a continuing trait. What we can say is that increasingly in the first and second centuries AD a flamboyant Hellenism takes on outward and visible signs: the wordsmiths are certainly there to correspond to them.

There is also an overall outlook, and a certain kind of audience, that we should see as receptive to sophists and their values. First come the younger and more impressionable members of local aristocracies, who would constitute the bulk of their pupils; secondly, the citizen bodies of individual communities agog for mass entertainment attending a sophist's more public displays; and thirdly, a class of colleagues and cognoscenti for whom there is a common bond of the cultural standards of *paideia* ('culture').[32] It is as difficult to define *paideia* in this period as it is to define the sophists who are the chief claimants, along with philosophers, to purvey it. Its implications are not just education but the values that go along with it to make men civilised, as in the case of 'the humanities' in English. It presupposes someone who has read the approved canon of classical texts and absorbed from them the values of Hellenism and urban-dwelling man alike, and who applies those values in life.

Much of the culture of the Greek cities was more than just a matter of rhetoric: philosophy, athletics, music, sculpture and architecture were all part of their identity. Yet for all practical purposes higher education tended to represent a choice between, or a combination of, rhetoric and philosophy. And philosophy itself, like rhetoric, might be presented in terms of continuity or revival at will. We note the continuity of the philosophical schools already established soon after the era of Alexander the Great: those intent on a philosophical career would have been as spoiled for choice as they had been five centuries before. At the same time there are at least one apparent revival and one major new development which ultimately converge. A revived Pythagoreanism appears on the fringe of philosophy in the first century AD; in the third Plotinus was able to transform a synthesis of Platonic principles into a new philosophic creed. Nor were other systems idle: even Epicureanism, relatively eclipsed since the first century BC, could be commemorated two centuries later by an extravagant inscription at Oenoanda; for at least some philosophers intellectual life was not necessarily divorced from display – already a sore point for the Stoic Epictetus in the second century.

Rhetoric and philosophy had long contended over the question of which was a more suitable preparation for public life: on the whole the art of speaking effectively could always hold its own in what was properly an unequal debate because of its greater accessibility. It could also expect to be more entertaining; and unlike much of serious philosophy, which might deliberately eschew the attractions of literary style, rhetoric could delight to flaunt it. We should also note that rhetoric and literature were, if not totally inseparable, certainly convergent. We ourselves tend to associate rhetoric with ornament and insincerity, but it cannot always be prised away from notions of good taste and the portrayal of feelings and emotional realities. And with rhetoric itself the principal force in higher education, literature is scarcely to be attempted by those unversed in its techniques.

It has also to be said that life of a rather different kind continued in the shadow of all this brilliance. At the turn of the first and second centuries Plutarch of Chaeronea[33] lived for most of his career as if the Greek Renaissance and Second Sophistic were far over the horizon. He came to terms with

Rome in a genuinely even-handed way, but his whole thought-world has something Hellenistic, as well as anti-rhetorical about it. A few supposedly early works are 'sophistic' in some sense; but Plutarch's whole value-system has little time for sophists. Neither, it has to be said, had that of the Platonist polymath and medical virtuoso Galen in the second century, though he clearly moved in socially elevated circles and mixed with sophists in his own right. The professional and experimental values of a doctor had little time for the world of approximation, equivocation, showmanship and self-proclaimed authority so typical of successful public speakers: a newly published Arabic translation of the treatise *On Choosing the Best Physicians*[34] suggests all too well that doctors who associated themselves with sophistic techniques were just the sort one would do well to avoid.

We shall come across a number of writers who for one reason or another do not seem to have been sophists, strictly speaking, but whose activities clearly lie closer to those of sophists than Plutarch's or Galen's. Pride of place goes to Lucian of Samosata, who succeeds in channelling a philosophical and rhetorical heritage into a clever and often distinctive satire and belles-lettres – and into world literature of the same stature as Plutarch's.[35] Nor is he alone in being able to use the tools of the sophist's trade – which he repudiates a good deal less convincingly than Plutarch himself does. At opposite ends of the scale the miniaturist Alciphron and the encyclopaedic compiler Athenaeus give us a sample of the idiosyncratic repertoire of sophistic learning indulged for its own sake or for purposes of learned entertainment.[36] Still more important, the varied repertoire of sophistic fiction entails putting consummate rhetorical techniques at the service of conventional romantic plots.[37] If the result is not quite 'the novel' as we are accustomed to conceive it, it is still carefully crafted fiction successful on its own terms; and something with a future still more durable than that of the sophistic system itself.

We also note a rather strange phenomenon, the virtual eclipse of Latin literature by Greek in the second century AD till its revival towards the end of the fourth.[38] It might be tempting to speculate that this is because rhetorical performance in Greek has achieved such élan that it has become the preferred vehicle for a now heavily rhetoricised literature. Yet Fronto and Apuleius writing in Latin in the mid-second century still imply a vigorous and vital activity in that language also, in both cases connected with a sophistic ethos.

APPROACHES TO THE SECOND SOPHISTIC

Two basic and sometimes artificially polarised perspectives have served to illuminate sophists and their activities.[39] The first was pioneered by Glen Bowersock in his *Greek Sophists in the Roman Empire* of 1969. Bowersock's goal was to illuminate relations between the Roman Establishment and the upwardly mobile Greeks of the reviving Eastern Empire. His emphasis is on the tracing of career connexions in the broadest sense: we are shown how frequently sophists accumulate honours, recognition and the like, but only incidentally do we catch a glimpse of what they regularly do for a living, or what their professional preoccupations are likely to have been. Reardon by contrast examines the rhetoric of sophists in relation to literary and broadly intellectual currents, but in so doing runs the risk of losing sight of the extra-literary perspective which we have in such measure for sophists during this period. This degree of polarisation still continues: thirteen years after *Courants littér-aires* Reardon reaffirmed that the Greek Renaissance was 'primarily a literary phenomenon, and that in prose'; another five years on and a conference on *The Greek Renaissance* could invite only a single literature paper, and that on verse, devoting the rest to archaeology and institutions.[40] Clearly a more comprehensive set of perspectives is called for. Other approaches and perspectives have made a considerable contribution: Ewen Bowie has stressed the theme of nostalgia for a lost Greek past, while considerably modifying Bowersock's insistence on the political importance of sophists; others have emphasised in various ways the problems of relying on Philostratus' *Lives of the Sophists* for too definitive a view of these intriguing but elusive figures.[41]

I end this introduction as I began, with an illustration. The following anecdote from Aulus Gellius will give us some notion of the ambience of one Greek aristocrat in a Roman context: Aulus Gellius gives us a vignette of Herodes Atticus 'the ex-consul' discussing a moral subject with a group of students.[42] One purports to be a Stoic philosopher and displays his command of suitable jargon. Herodes is able to call for an

11

extract to be read from Arrian's transcription of the *Discourses* of the recent Stoic authority Epictetus, to the effect that scholarly distinctions are among the 'indifferents' – neither good nor evil, but useless out of context in such situations as impending shipwreck or answering an Imperial summons. The Stoic bore is duly humiliated as he applies the moral to himself . . .

We should note the cultural and social mix so casually presented here: a sophist mainly reputed for his public speaking is reading from a book assembled by a fellow Graeco-Roman consular Arrian, on a subject of popular ethics set out by the ex-slave Epictetus – raising the question of a summons by an Emperor. I cite it because it crosses so many cultural boundaries and barriers: between Greek and Roman (and Greek and Latin), between rhetoric and philosophy, between ethics and politics, between narrative and satire. We shall have occasion to cross and re-cross such boundaries more and more as we step from the larger world of Greek Renaissance to that of the Second Sophistic itself. And Gellius' anecdote shows us, as so often, a sophist characteristically on top of any given situation. We must now begin to explore why.

1

Sophists in society

Early in the third century AD the Athenian sophist Philostratus coined the term 'Second Sophistic' to denote the activities of a number of professional speakers, starting in the fourth century BC. In the course of rehearsing the lives of these men, he concentrates on the period of the Early Roman Empire; and it is the one and a half centuries before his own time, from the end of the first century AD to that of the early third, that has most commonly come to bear the title 'Second Sophistic'.[1] In practice Philostratus begins his gallery of sophists far too late, and the Second Sophistic as he conceives it continued long after his own time. But he has given an identity, perhaps an arbitrary or even spurious one, to *something* that flourished, notably in the Greek world, in the early Roman Empire, and it is that something which we must try to characterise.

The very term 'Second Sophistic' implies a 'First Sophistic' beforehand, and some possible resemblance between the two. The idea of a 'First Sophistic' would have evoked the intellectual ferment of the Golden Age of Athens itself in the late fifth century BC,[2] when traditionalist education and civic and religious values were challenged by a new breed of impressively professional outsiders who might claim to teach the skills of public life – including the art of public speaking – for pay. One thinks particularly of luminaries such as Protagoras of Abdera, Gorgias of Leontini, Prodicus of Ceos and Hippias of Elis, flaunting their array of skills and pretensions before impressionable Athenian audiences. Some of the teachings they imported seemed to imply ethical relativism and political pragmatism; the very suggestion that such potentially subversive values could be taught brought about the resistance of Socrates

13

and Plato, and tended to tar sophistic activities with a broad brush of charlatanism. At least one possible sophist, Antiphon, participated in the oligarchic revolution of 411; and debate still continues as to their real place in intellectual history and their contribution to Greek philosophy. But they were a force associated with skill in and teaching of rhetoric and 'wisdom' in general in a bygone golden age. That was enough to justify their being evoked in very different times.

We can go far towards understanding Philostratus' picture if we look first of all at one sophist of the fifth century BC as Philostratus himself chose to see him:

> Gorgias of Leontini was the founder of the older [sophistic] in Thessaly . . . In my opinion he began the art of improvised speech. For making his appearance in the theatre at Athens this man had the confidence to say [to his audience] 'You propose a theme', and he was the first to take this risk with a public announcement, virtually proclaiming that he was omniscient and was willing to speak on any topic, relying on the inspiration of the moment . . . and when already on the threshold of old age, he performed discourses at Athens; it is no wonder that he excited the admiration of the crowd; besides, in my opinion the most distinguished men were enthralled by him, and that includes not only the pair Critias and Alcibiades, who were still young at the time, but Thucydides and Pericles as well, who were already mature in years . . . Moreover, he played a prominent part in the religious festivals of the Hellenes, declaiming his Pythian Oration from the altar; and in acknowledgement a golden statue of him was set up in the temple of the Pythian god; while his Olympian Oration dealt with a most important political theme. For when he saw that Greece was divided into factions he emerged as the proponent of civic harmony and turned them against the barbarians and persuaded them not to think of one another's cities as the prizes of war, but instead the land of the barbarians.[3]

Such is the perspective through which the biographer of sophists in the Early Empire presents the man he sees as the father of 'sophistic'. He is a celebrated rhetorical performer,

14

influential in his friendships and not lacking in serious political concerns or diplomatic skills in the cause of Greek identity.

It is worthwhile to compare Philostratus' notice of Gorgias with the sort of things he chooses to say about one of the most eminent of 'his own' sophists, the first/second century virtuoso Polemo of Laodicea:

> Now when [Polemo] gave an exhibition to the Athenians of extempore orations when he first arrived in Athens, he did not lower himself to pronounce eulogies of the city . . . nor did he make an extended speech boasting about his own prestige, although this style of speech too is to a sophist's advantage in his public exhibitions. But being aware that the Athenian temperament had to be cut down to size rather than inflated, he began like this: 'People say, Athenians, that you are a sophisticated audience for public speeches. I shall soon know.'
>
> When the Emperor [Hadrian] had consecrated the temple of Olympian Zeus at Athens as a great triumph over time (it had been completed at last after five hundred and sixty years), he instructed Polemo too to pronounce a dedicatory hymn at the sacrifice. The sophist fixed his gaze in his accustomed manner on the thoughts that were already assembling in his mind, and then threw himself into his speech, and from the base of the temple delivered a long and marvellous discourse. As the introduction to his speech he declared that it was not without a divine inspiration that he was driven to speak on the theme. (When he spoke at Smyrna, he argued that 'When peace was concluded after the Peloponnesian War, the trophies put up by the Greeks should be taken down'.)[4]

Not much has changed, or so it seems: Gorgias and Polemo both attain the status of a personality cult. They are both 'performers' par excellence. And whatever else had changed, both are urging Greek reconciliation after the Peloponnesian War – in Polemo's case seven centuries too late. But he is a transmitter of what has now become a precious part of Greek cultural tradition and self-awareness: he is able to look back to a period of Greek freedom and independence as if some of its most momentous events were still actually unfolding.

When Philostratus sees fit to enlighten us about the differences between the First Sophistic and the Second, he is content to provide tendentious illustration rather than precise definition: the First Sophistic as he presents it was engaged with philosophic rhetoric, the Second with rhetoric as such;[5] and on the whole his impression has won a good deal of credence. But there is a sense in which Philostratus has performed a clever equivocation: he has applied a term naturally associated with a wide range of intellectual and educational activities to a much narrower range of activities in more recent times; we are left with the impression that the term 'sophist' involves a certain degree of affectation. The problem lies in the flexibility of the word itself. Its basic connexion is with wisdom (*sophia*), and as concepts of wisdom widen its own connotations become treacherously flexible. A useful analogy in English would be the fortunes of the word 'master', whose registers include both the activities of a maestro, a virtuoso performer, and of a person running a school. A Greek sophist during the Empire could generally be expected to perform both functions, by displaying rhetorical expertise and teaching advanced pupils. But neither of the terms 'sophist' or 'master' actually specifies the field of expertise: the word 'sophist' could still be applied, however confusingly or misleadingly, in other fields such as philosophy or medicine, and could still be exploited by any rhetorical performer who wished to affect a knowledge of such fields. Perhaps the best way of looking at it in English is to suggest an expert communicator:[6] or rather, an expert in the eyes of some, a so-called expert in those of others. But it is misleading to look for too much precision: the word 'sophist' is as splendid as it is imprecise, and that is what was simultaneously attractive and repellent about it.

But it is mainly in the realm of rhetoric that Philostratus' exhibits attain their eminence. It should be stressed that even here the relationship between rhetoric and sophistic is a flexible one. It is tempting to say that the distinction is one of quality,[7] that sophists represent the highest echelon of rhetorical attainment and practice – the latter because they were the experts who were expert enough to train the next generation of rhetoricians. There is no specific branch of 'sophistic rhetoric', though again in practice sophists concentrate on 'epideictic' rhetoric,[8] ornamental or display rhetoric for audience entertainment as distinct from that practised in the law courts ('dicanic', or more commonly in its Latin form 'forensic') or in attempting to persuade public assemblies ('symbouleutic'). Here again distinctions between types of rhetoric tend to be blurred, a recurrent problem in the courts themselves. But both these associations tend to converge: sophists tend to run the schools of rhetoric – or at least the more prestigious ones – and display their school rhetoric in public, while 'mere' rhetors practise in the courts. Hence sophists can be called upon to provide the lustre for the great public ornamental occasions, such as delivering an oration at the Olympic Games, or welcoming a visiting dignitary, when they are not actually teaching students; they could expect if they chose to be able to stay out of court-cases or local politics, but they did not always so choose.

In leaving us the lives of some thirty-odd sophists, Philostratus has posed a problem: how do we characterise them as a cultural force, and how do we fit them into the larger cultural framework of the Early Roman Empire? We may simply be content to chart their social milieu by noting friendships, rivalries, networks of pupils and the like; or look as best we can at the surviving declamations and other rhetorical productions that belong to a sophistic context. But neither of these approaches will quite do justice to a sophistic outlook, or to the cultural reflexes that sophists absorbed and transmitted. Two characteristics seem to me to be constant: a determined Hellenism, thoroughly rooted in the classical past (and irrespective of its carrier's origins, which could be Asian or African), and a versatility which can easily border on ambiguity and equivocation. It might be seen as a function of a sophist's identity to be all things Greek to all men; but that did not preclude a considerable degree of personal individuality, as Philostratus' sketches were intended to show.

Philostratus' *Lives of the Sophists* is at pains to present the Second Sophistic as a Renaissance. 'Sophistic', never really defined, is seen as a phenomenon of the Early Empire, a child of the era in which sophists emerged as outstanding cultural leaders, entertainers and participants in the lustre of the Empire itself. They must of course have a respectable antiquity, having been founded by Aeschines, the political opponent of Demosthenes;[9] but the rhetorical achievements after the death of Alexander the Great are glossed over with confident contempt.[10] This would create the impression that the last centuries BC spawned a tribe of mediocre declaimers who were unworthy of the title 'sophist', and that quite suddenly and for no reason offered by Philostratus the lustre of fifth- and fourth-century sophists is recovered. This is patently false, since the popularity of declamation in Rome, and the conflicts between austere Atticism and flamboyant Asianism in the first century BC, testify to lively and prestigious oratorical activity. In Greek practice at least the term *sophistes* was already applied without hesitation to outstanding rhetoricians; some of these also attained to prominence in other fields and could claim the social lustre that Philostratus lavishes on his subjects. Whatever change took place in the aspect of sophists came about early; one might even be tempted to argue that Gorgias himself was a specimen of it, and that there was no real break in the history of 'Sophistic' at all. At all events the notion of a sophist as someone who teaches rhetoric and makes public displays could be said to have definitely emerged by the time of Aeschines and Isocrates. The changed conditions of Alexander's Empire and its successors could arguably have restricted the teacher's terms of reference at a time when political trials or political activity in the manner of the fifth-century Athenian democracy would have been more difficult. The sophist comes to be seen as a specialist teacher and a specialist in ornamental oratory, and this sense itself is implicit in Philodemus' discussions of Epicurus,[11] or in Cicero.[12] Such a relatively narrow concept would obviously not have stopped such figures from practising in courts or assembly as well, or from practising some sort of approach to philosophy or polymathy as part of their curriculum. But the more philosophy was played down, the less it was possible for sophists to avoid the standard Platonic sense of *sophistes* as a figure who only affects to be wise without adequate credentials.[13]

The Greek rhetoricians mentioned frequently by the Elder Seneca as active in the late Republic would serve to confirm the existence of several generations of Greek declamation teachers whose performances and reputation would have comfortably qualified them to be regarded as sophists in Philostratus' or Philodemus' sense. They perform declamation subjects of the kind known in Latin as *suasoriae* ('persuasion-pieces') and *controversiae* ('bilateral debates'), both of which would have been covered by the Greek term *meletē* ('exercise'). They win credit and prestige from their Roman pupils and from Latin declaimers. The names of Hermagoras, Glycon, Dionysius Atticus and Diocles of Carystus stand out among many; and at least some were able to anticipate the role of roving ambassadors and prestigious intellectuals that their Philostratean counterparts are presented as attaining:[14] one thinks particularly of Hybreas the Elder of Mylasa or Potamon of Mytilene.[15] Moreover Seneca's implied dislike of some of their characteristic excesses would certainly anticipate the criticisms and rivalries characteristic of the sophistic lifestyle of later generations.[16] And the key stylistic distinctions between Atticism and Asianism are already implied in at least some of the extracts that have come down to us.[17]

A particularly useful item to confute Philostratus' dubious history comes just at the transition from Roman Republic to Empire. This is the entry on his own namesake, Philostratus the Egyptian. As far as our Philostratus is concerned, this luminary, 'who studied philosophy with queen Cleopatra, was styled a sophist, because he took up a panegyrical and varied style of eloquence, thanks to his association with a woman for whom even the love of letters was a sensual pursuit'.[18] But Plutarch's *Life of Antony* has a different slant, with the claim that after Antony's defeat the Stoic Areius claimed pardon for fellow-members of Cleopatra's circle, including Philostratus, 'the most accomplished of all the sophists of his time in extempore rhetoric; although he wrongly styled himself an academic philosopher'.[19] For Areius' sake Philostratus too obtains pardon. Not without a characteristically theatrical gesture by the Egyptian Philostratus – growing his beard long and reciting the tragic verse

σοφοὶ σοφοὺς σῴζουσιν, ἂν ὦσιν σοφοί.
('The wise save wise men if they too are wise'.)[20]

Such a figure establishes the type only too well: a practised courtier, able to change sides and able to alternate between rhetoric and philosophy, with a formidable reputation at least in the former.

The biographer Philostratus clearly signals the second beginning of 'The Sophistic' as he conceives it with his notice of Nicetes of Smyrna, with a floruit in the latter half of the first century AD.[21] The anecdotal format still leaves the general

19

picture of this paradigm clear enough. He is not necessarily, as Philostratus seems so often to imply, an epideictic orator, but divides his time between courtwork and display, and he is an outstanding civic benefactor of his native Smyrna, though he keeps a low profile in the local assembly. An Emperor takes an interest in his confrontation with authority when Nero attempts to arrange a reconciliation between Nicetes and (most probably Verginius) Rufus while the latter was serving as a legate on the Rhine.[22] Looked at from one angle, Nicetes is an Asianist orator[23] of a traditional and familiar type, moving in high society as we should expect.

Philostratus mentions only one other sophist (or purely such) whose floruit would have fallen comfortably within the first century: the Syrian Isaeus. And here we have valuable corroboration and indeed an eyewitness account from none other than Pliny the Younger, who describes the experience of a declamation performance by him in glowing terms, implying perhaps some sense of novelty about his manner of displaying his virtuosity. But his postscript is perhaps more revealing:

> At sixty he is still only a schoolman [*scholasticus tantum*]: there is no kind of man more genuine, more unaffected, or indeed better. For those of us who are worn down in public business or actual court-cases pick up a great deal of ill-feeling, however much we seek to avoid it. But the school and lecture-hall, with their made-up cases, are less barbed and less harmful, and no less happy for that, especially for the older generation. For what is happier in old age than what afforded the greatest pleasure in our youth? So I think Isaeus is not only the cleverest of men but also the happiest.[24]

Pliny seems to imply that performances in school and in relation to school themes do not take place in the real world, and finds it surprising that Isaeus has not chosen to diversify (by practising in the courts, for example). None the less he acknowledges both the nostalgic appeal of declamation – a fact which would have rendered the system self-perpetuating – and the professional satisfaction to be gained by the speaker. And he goes on to stress the power of the authentic spoken word.

One other luminary, however, fills out the picture all too clearly. Dio Chrysostom (Dio of Prusa) was a contemporary of

Isaeus, and Philostratus accords him a fulsome treatment, while equivocating carefully over his status as a sophist.[25] Here we are aided for the first time by a substantial corpus of extant works, which go far towards corroborating the picture of sophistic writing activity in its broader sense. Aside from a short collection of rather brief and inconsequential philosophical essays, sometimes no longer than extracts, much of his reper-toire consists of short speeches on practical politics in the localities of his native Bithynia, and several much more elabor-ate addresses to great centres such as Rhodes, Tarsus or Alexandria.[26] The latter exhibit a varied and often unpredict-able balance between political advice, or hints of it, and sheer entertainment, a point not lost on Philostratus (who com-mends him for being able to criticise arrogant cities without seeming to be abusive or ungracious). He can also turn to even more obvious entertainment in a speech proving that the Trojan War could not have taken place; or he can produce a panegyric on a city or a dead athlete – or even in praise of hair. The versatile sophist has arrived, and with him sophistic tech-niques of manipulating an audience – as if such techniques had ever been far away.[27] But more important for our present purpose is Dio's not infrequent sniping against enemies he himself regards as sophists.[28] This clearly exposes the highly selective and foreshortened perspective of Philostratus, aware as he is of only two unequivocally sophistic figures in the late first century.

The generations after Dio provide Philostratus with the great efflorescence of his conception of the Sophistic.[29] A series of sophists were able to enjoy the favour, or suffer the disfavour, of Hadrian and the Antonines, while Philostratus' special heroes Polemo[30] and Herodes Atticus[31] are the centre of flourishing networks of pupils. We lack the kind of evidence necessary to prove that sophists were themselves of con-spicuously higher quality than at other times; but we can endorse Philostratus' implication that they had never had it so good, or enjoyed conditions in which exuberant Hellenism as an outlook could have had the freest rein. The provision of further chairs under Marcus Aurelius underlined their status, and the prima donna Herodes could claim the Roman Empire as his sounding board for the often pedantic and trivial quarrels of Athens.

PUPILS AND TEACHERS

In a comment on the Lycian sophist Heraclides, Philostratus lets slip a telling admission:'The tribe of forensic orators is daring and brash, but how could a sophist avoid becoming flustered [by intimidation at court] when he spends most of his day sharing his exertions with mere boys?'[32] In spite of the much-studied social éclat of sophists this central aspect of their activities needs to be kept in view. Sophists owed the demand for their services to pupils, and Philostratus is particularly illuminating on the flourishing sub-culture of academic camaraderie that sophistic teaching and performing evoked. He notes that Scopelian was able to attract to Smyrna not only the immediately accessible students from Asia Minor but others from as far afield as Cappadocia, Assyria, Egypt and Phoenicia, as well as 'the more reputable of the Achaeans and the entire youth of Athens', while Polemo 'made [Smyrna] appear the most populous she had ever been, since the youth surged into her from both Europe and Asia and the islands alike; not some dissolute and indiscriminate mob, but an élite and truly Hellenic company'.[33] And when Heraclides of Lycia was turned out of the chair at Athens he simply attracted the 'Hellenes' of Europe back to Smyrna.[34]

Philostratus seems full of successes; enthusiastic rushings to hear some novelty, as when Hippodromus of Larissa visited Megistias of Smyrna, at first incognito, but 'towards the end of the performance there was a rush by all connoisseurs of culture in Smyrna to Megistias' door, for the news soon spread all over that Hippodromus was on a visit'.[35] Or Herodes himself is hailed as one of the Ten (the established canon of Ten Attic Orators), and in turn proclaims himself better than Andocides,[36] while his exclusive advanced seminar, the Clepsydrion ('water-clocked lecture') helps to generate even more prestige.[37] It is of one of his most highly regarded pupils, Hadrian of Tyre, however, that we have perhaps the most flamboyant image:

> And whenever he had performed he went home an object
> of envy, escorted by a throng of Hellenes from all over. For
> these men held him in awe, just as the tribes of Eleusis
> hold in awe the initiating priest who performs the rites
> with great distinction. He secured their loyalty with games

and drinking-parties and hunts, and by sharing the Hellenic festivals with them. In this way he shared the interests
of young men in this or that activity with the result that
they responded to him like sons to a father who is friendly
and kind, and joins with them in keeping up the revelry
with truly Hellenic abandon. In fact I myself am aware that
some of them actively used to weep when this sophist came
to mind, and that some would try to mimic his accent,
others his way of walking, or his elegant mode of dress.[38]

Such a passage hints at a devotion to teachers which might
amount to a frenzied loyalty, and Philostratus' varied repertoire
of anecdotes catches pupils' aspirations and attitudes in a
variety of situations. The overall impression is one of liveliness
and enthusiasm, not without a certain personality cult of individual teachers. In explaining that Dionysius of Miletus did not
resort to wizardry in teaching the art of memory, Philostratus
explains such a change from the unending pleasure pupils took
in his performances, so much so that the more accomplished of
them would drill themselves in his works by heart, and then
relay them to the rest.[39] Or pupils might be expert at recog-
nising another sophist, faster than their own teacher, as when
one of Polemo's pupils recognised Marcus of Byzantium sitting
in on their class incognito.[40] One characteristic story presents
Hadrian of Tyre in his cups mimicking the style of all the
sophists – except that of his great teacher Herodes, whom he
regards as incomparable.[41] A number of stories show pupils
acting en bloc as an often critical and resourceful claque. All
the Hellenes round Pergamum hang on the oratory of Aristocles
and even Herodes sends pupils to him, as he lends them for a
famous performance of Alexander Peloplaton, of which we
shall hear more.[42] They themselves showed no shortage of
initiative in the downfall of Philagrus of Cilicia: after one of
them was insulted in a chance encounter, they sabotaged his
Athenian début by reading out a previously circulated version
of his pretended improvisation.[43] Aristides seems to find a
claque indispensable for a recitation before Marcus Aurelius.[44]
Such camaraderie could also have an ominous aspect: the
pupils of Hadrian were responsible for the death of a drunken
pupil of Chrestus of Byzantium. Their master was supported in
court by his own entourage;[45] while Heracleides of Lycia was

similarly supported when suffering confiscation for cutting down sacred cedars, perhaps in the role of a high-handed 'developer'.[46] Such fervent loyalties would erupt in regular violence in the student life of the fourth century.[47]

Again, individual pupils no less than teachers can be driven by the urge to excel. Philostratus includes anecdotes about those precocious pupils who earn the qualified admiration of an established master: Dionysius of Miletus allows Polemo 'strength, but not from the wrestling-ground' (i.e. he could do with actual experience);[48] while Herodes allows Hadrian of Tyre's youthful display as 'perhaps the mighty fragments of a colossus'.[49] Or Hippodromus of Larissa humanely refuses a sparring match with his own pupil, the Lemnian Philostratus.[50] But the pressures on pupils produced their share of other problems: sophists might also find themselves as moral correctors, castigating a pupil for excessive boastfulness[51] or ambition,[52] or for partisanship to a previous teacher.[53] We are in a familiar world.

SOPHISTS AND CITIES

Philostratus dilates on the advantages to a city of aristocratic young men from elsewhere:

> So, then, [Heraclides] filled Smyrna with a brilliant company, and helped her too in even more ways besides, as I shall show. A city with a large influx of foreigners, particularly if they are lovers of wisdom, will be prudent in its councils, and prudent too in its assemblies, since it will naturally be wary of being convicted of acting wrongfully in the presence of so many distinguished people; and it will take care of its temples, gymnasia, fountains and porticoes, so as to appear to offer such facilities for such a throng.[54]

An important perspective on the sophistic phenomenon was established by Bowersock's consideration of 'Cities of the Sophists':[55] we are accustomed to view our subjects as a species of urban aristocrat, a characteristic ornament of a characteristic institution of the Empire, as dwellers in and cultural luminaries of their own or an adopted city. Bowersock presents the three most prominent sophistic centres outside Rome as Athens,

Smyrna and Ephesus.[56] The first of these speaks for itself, while Philostratus extravagantly hails Smyrna as holding the pre-eminent position in Ionia like the bridge on musical instruments. And he refers to a succession of sophists – Nicetes, Scopelian, Polemo, Aristides – the first native, the rest illustrious incomers to the city, who maintained its prestige as a sophistic centre.[57] It is not quite so clear that Ephesus could have claimed a comparable reputation: the sophist Bowersock cites as staying there is an indifferent one, Rufinus;[58] a number of others Philostratus high-handedly dismisses;[59] while among those he prizes highly, only Hadrian of Tyre had a spell there and Damianus a permanent residence.[60] We may choose to doubt Philostratus' judgement, but at present we lack the means to refute it. The important papyrus *P.Oxy* 2190 offers the illuminating testimony of a pupil testifying to a shortage of sophists in Egypt in the late first century AD, and the indifferent quality of one teacher who has been foisted on him (lines 18–29). This may well be consistent with Philostratus' avoidance of mention of Alexandria as a sophistic centre.

By the fourth century one notes how far the balance has shifted: Constantinople is now a centre, after the perhaps temporary eclipse of Byzantium under the Severi, and the extravagant refoundation by Constantine of an Eastern Christian capital. But we now hear also of Nicomedia, unmentioned in Philostratus but a happy staging post for Libanius.[61] Antioch too enjoyed the prestige of Libanius, who affords the most detailed view of sophistic practice in any time or place; and he has a very jaded view of Athens, which he finds narcissistic, corrupt and second rate.[62] At the other end of the spectrum, no city at any period in the Empire would have been too insignificant to receive a visit from some sophistically coloured figure: in the first and second centuries we hear of Dio Chrysostom at Borysthenes on the Black Sea, or Lucian at Philippopolis in Thrace.[63]

One theme that runs right through the activities of the sophists is their capacity for intense involvement in the affairs of their native or adopted localities. We are told for example by Philostratus that Marcus of Byzantium reconciled Athens and Megara in a quarrel which included the latter's denying hospitality to the Athenians during the lesser Pythia.[64] Or while Lollianus was hoplite general in Athens, with attendant responsibility for the food supply, he was able to organise private benefaction from his pupils to pay for a consignment of grain which the public treasury could not afford.[65] We hear of Scopelian championing people on trial for their lives in the courts free of charge, and even transacting political affairs just before a declamation.[66]

A recurrent theme in this context is the friction between a sophist and officialdom. Philostratus' very first exhibit of the Imperial period, Nicetes, is already in trouble for snubbing a proconsular official in his native Smyrna (by implication over the interests of the Smyrnaeans), and afterwards they have to be reconciled by no less than the Emperor himself.[67] Three centuries later Libanius is in and out of similar scenarios *ad nauseam*;[68] while Hippodromus of Larissa had risked the displeasure of Septimius Severus by endorsing a politically unpopular win at a festival.[69]

In Philostratus' treatment of Polemo and Herodes Atticus such themes are particularly prominent: as far as the biographer is concerned, the relationship between Polemo and Smyrna is such that he practically owns the place. Not only does he reconcile the geographical divisions within the city between the seashore area and the hinterland:

> besides, Polemo would criticise those who made wrong political decisions, and was often unstinting with his sound advice and proved a great asset. At the same time he routed out all their conceited and insolent behaviour: this feat was all the greater since the Ionians were not inclined to depart from their usual behaviour. He helped them too in the following matters: he would not allow their internal lawsuits to go anywhere beyond the city, but would put an end to them at home.[70]

Polemo evidently performed similar services for his native Laodicea.[71] But such prominence all too often has another side: it is no surprise to learn that Hadrian himself has to clear Polemo on a charge of embezzlement.[72] Philostratus seems almost to choose to minimise the connexion between the lavish building endowments Polemo has secured from Hadrian, the accusation that he has pocketed much of the money, and the expensive lifestyle which causes this sophist to have to toady to a rich patron.[73] We should have been grateful for some independent testimony from Smyrna itself.

The tensions of Herodes are not, so far as Philostratus presents them, directly connected with his fortunes as a speaker or teacher. It is rather his profile as an urban aristocrat and philanthropist extraordinaire that tends to bring him into conflict with other ambitious interests. We have already noticed the *epitropeuontes* (procurators) of Asia complain to Hadrian about the expenditure of 7 million drachmae on the provision of a water-supply for Ilium by Herodes as governor of the free cities of Asia; while his provision of a water-supply at Olympia brings the disapproval of the Cynic Peregrinus.[74] Tensions with the Athenians we find for example over the fact that he could provide them with a Panathenaic stadium – out of funds he had recouped by recalling debts to his father's estate while discharging its largesses to the Athenians in accordance with his father's will.[75] Again, Marcus' henchmen the Quintilii take Herodes to task for the extravagance of putting up statues of his deceased foster-sons.[76] The grand conspiracy among the Athenians involving Demostratus, Praxagoras and Mamertinus is over public policy, though forensic rhetoric is necessarily involved in the course of the dispute and becomes part of the charge. A new testimony on Herodes from a recently edited Arabic translation of Galen has him delivering a sub-standard speech because of the commitments of business in the days before it was made – once more a symptom of the pressures under which sophists could find themselves.[77]

The concern for civic affairs goes on: Herodes' pupil Theodotus was Archon *basileus* at Athens at the time of Herodes' fracas with the Athenians, and supported the faction that opposed Herodes; Antiochus of Aegeae was conspicuous in supplying corn and in restoration work;[78] Aelius Aristides made a moving 'earthquake appeal' on behalf of Smyrna to Marcus Aurelius;[79] Euodianus of Smyrna supervised the actors' trade-guild, the artisans of Dionysus at Rome;[80] Apollonius of Athens served as Eponymus Archon and hoplite general; Proclus of Naucratis came to the rescue of a friend on the point of eviction in Athens.[81] At the same time the avoidance of liturgies by Aristides or Favorinus testifies just as thoroughly to the avoidance of civic burdens.[82] Yet it should be emphasised, rightly, that many of the civic duties of this sort, and the social prominence associated with them, did not come directly out of a sophist's performance as such:[83] rather did it follow from conspicuous aristocratic status, coupled with a particular kind of articulateness and self-confidence. And it is consistent with Bowie's reservations on the 'importance' of sophists that those who are able to put their names to elaborate building projects generally do not do so out of the fees from students, so far as we can make out: Damianus of Ephesus, for example, is singled out as conspicuous for his inherited wealth: he had been lavish in his benefaction even while quite young, so that his philanthropy could not have been the result of his established reputation.[84] In other instances even conspicuously prestigious sophists would seem to act as fund-raisers rather than philanthropists: Polemo was able to enlist the support of Hadrian for a temple, gymnasium and cornmarket (and was himself accused of embezzlement as a result);[85] Dio Chrysostom was similarly involved with municipal funds rather than personal fortune when he was accused of building scandals in his home town of Prusa;[86] while Aristides' 'rebuilding' of Smyrna was as the result of an earthquake appeal.[87] We can draw the conclusion that sophists, like other members of the city aristocracies, could opt in or out of civic involvement at will.[88]

THE SOPHIST AS TRAVELLER

We must complement this urban perspective with another no less important: that of the sophist as a cultural traveller and cultural ambassador. Once again the same kind of generalisation is true: sophists were no more obliged to travel than other aristocratic figures. Yet it is no surprise that we should owe to Philostratus the saying that to the wise man Hellas is everywhere:[89] the sophist might be termed 'the *pepaideumenos* in the world', imposing his particular perspective and personality wherever he goes.[90] Now the lifestyle of sophists in the fifth century BC had indeed tended to include an element of travel. They are often described as travelling lecturers, and memorable Platonic dialogue settings such as those of the *Gorgias*, *Protagoras* and *Euthydemus* present them as plying their wares in Athens as visiting celebrities.[91] The Second Sophistic presents some similarities: Philostratus is at hand with the gossip about the impact of visits of particular sophists, again notably at Athens itself – one thinks of the impressive performance of Alexander Peloplaton, the blunders of the ill-tempered Philagrus,[92] or the calculated condescension of Polemo or Hadrian of Tyre.[93] Undoubtedly some sophists did travel, sometimes in conspicuous style. Polemo's travel arrangements are described in detail by Philostratus:

> when he made a journey he had a long retinue of pack-animals and many horses, slaves and different breeds of dog for different kinds of hunting; he himself used to ride in a chariot from Phrygia or Gaul, with silver bridles.[94]

But the biographer acutely adds, however:

> By this he won great prestige for Smyrna. For just as the market-place and a splendid range of buildings add lustre to a city, so does a thriving household; for not only does a city give a man prestige, but the city itself takes it from a man.[95]

Of Polemo we further know that he enjoyed the right of free travel granted by Hadrian and extended by Hadrian to his descendants; and we should not be surprised to find him in Hadrian's own personal entourage on some of the latter's travels.[96] But a more typical case may have been that of Ptolemy of Naucratis:

> while he visited a great many countries and frequented a great many cities, nowhere did he cause any reproach to his own good name or disappoint their expectations of him; but he passed from city to city, as if journeying on the shining chariot of his own fame.[97]

Sophists might also appear as a matter or course at the great Hellenic festivals, not always or exclusively as performers; the personalities and occasions lent mutual lustre, as they had done in the age of Gorgias.[98]

But there was also an opposite extreme. Several sophists elected to appear at least on occasion incognito or in unlikely attire or both, and could surprise an audience accordingly. Hence the display of Marcus of Byzantium before Polemo, or Hippodromus of Larissa before Megistias in Smyrna;[99] and Dio Chrysostom implies a somewhat similar picture of himself in exile.[100] One notes that not all the journeys by sophists were exclusively or even primarily for lecture tours; we hear often of sophists as ambassadors (Scopelian, Polemo, Marcus of

Byzantium, Alexander Peloplaton),[101] or of travel for more individual reasons: Polemo at Sardis for a court-case,[102] or Nicetes of Smyrna in the Rhineland and Gaul to defend himself against a Roman governor.[103]

Philostratus also singles out a few sophists as conspicuously disinclined to travel, including Aristides, constrained by his illness for many years and ill at ease with crowds,[104] or Aelian, never outside Italy;[105] but the biographer seems to imply that both are exceptions. That still leaves a fair number of sophists who stay in one or more major centres; one suspects that Libanius' well-documented toing and froing between Antioch, Athens, Constantinople, Nicaea, Nicomedia and finally Antioch once more [106] would have been characteristic of many in an age when education was increasingly institutionalised and regimented. Few except the most achevé sophists could have afforded to leave their pupils for too long, unless conceivably they had risen to form part of an imperial entourage, as Polemo, Alexander Peloplaton and Philostratus all did:[107] the attendant patronage would have been expected to ensure its share of prestige in the future.

DISTINCTIONS AND EXEMPTIONS

Two particular signs of Imperial recognition can be noted for sophists: the approval of chairs and appointments to them, and the granting or withholding of immunities from taxation or public services. Vespasian had established chairs of Greek and Latin rhetoric in Rome, and we know of Quintilian as the first incumbent of the latter chair.[108] But it is not till the reign of Antoninus Pius that we hear of a chair in Athens of which Lollianus of Ephesus is the first holder,[109] and in a much-discussed reference a second chair established in the 170s by Marcus Aurelius.[110] The latter chair seems clearly enough an Imperial endowment; the former is ambiguously referred to as ὁ πολιτικὸς θρόνος ('the political/municipal chair').[111] The balance of probability favours an endowed chair funded by the municipality rather than a chair of a different kind of oratory, or one and the same chair at an increased salary. The chair at Rome seems to have paid more than either of the Athenian chairs, and to have been regarded as an upward move.[112] We do not at present have a clear or overall picture of the patterns of chairs; nor, given the subjectivity involved in the process of appointments, are we likely to arrive at one. But it is evident that emperors could take a quite active interest in the incumbencies of such posts,[113] or quite characteristically in the fourth century entrust them to Imperial agents (in the person of provincial governors) to dispose of.[114]

These posts were of such distinction as to generate an anecdotal tradition in Philostratus in their own right; the little that sophists required to operate – skill, reputation, pupils and income – did not depend on such an establishment, but it conferred distinction, sometimes invidious, on a very few, though apparently nothing like the distinction Philostratus confers on Polemo or Herodes without the mention of chairs. Philostratus' information on them tends to be mixed: Philagrus of Cilicia held the chair at Rome, after a most unfortunately mixed impression in Athens;[115] Chrestus does not wish the Athenian assembly to petition on his behalf to succeed Hadrian of Tyre at Athens, arguing οὐχ αἱ μύριαι τὸν ἄνδρα ('the salary of ten thousand drachmae does not make a man').[116] Pausanias of Cappadocia had held both chairs, but had an unfortunate Cappadocian accent.[117] Pollux obtained the chair at Athens from Commodus – after a very mixed notice from Philostratus himself;[118] Euodianus of Smyrna, another incumbent of the Roman chair, furnishes little information.[119] The tenure of the Athenian chair was marred by scandal when Heraclides of Lycia was manoeuvred out of it thanks to the machinations of Apollonius of Naucratis' followers, notably Marcianus of Doliche.[120] Philiscus of Thessaly held it, but was deprived of the attached immunity;[121] while Aspasius of Ravenna is said to have caused resentment by holding the chair at Rome for too long.[122] The litany of criticisms, reservations and resentments may simply mean that there were too few official appointments to satisfy the thirst for recognition of so many able aspirants.

The original sophists had made an impact with their diplomatic activities, in which Gorgias, Prodicus and Hippias all attained prominence. We find that Philostratus is not slow to draw attention to occasions on which 'his' sophists act as ambassadors, and Bowersock has noted some conspicuous cases both of embassies and Imperial secretaryships. But these are only one aspect of the complex and shifting relationships involved. Very often a sophist might be an Imperial *amicus* in his own right, sharing with his Emperor an enthusiasm for declamation as such. In such a case he could have provided relaxation as well as any diplomatic expertise that might be required. Tiberius in Rhodes attended declamation classes and displays (*circa scholas et auditoria professorum*), and even joined in a sophistic quarrel to the extent of taking the field with his tribune's retinue and imprisoning one of the combatants.[123] At least in the mid-second century emperors we are dealing with comparable connoisseurs. We hear repeatedly of emperors either wanting to, or making the effort to hear a particular sophist declaim: the future Emperor Marcus Aurelius, by no means an unequivocal devotee of rhetoric, does listen to a performance by Polemo; his objections are not against a windy rhetorician or an arrogant temperament, but suggest disappointment on purely aesthetic grounds.[124] We also find him wishing of his own free will to meet Aelius Aristides, and at least willing to hear him declaim in Smyrna;[125] or we find him listening to the youthful prodigy Hermogenes as well as testing the appointment of Hadrian of Tyre to the Athenian chair.[126] We are even told that Pollux 'bewitched the Emperor Commodus [with his voice] and obtained from him the Chair at Athens'.[127] We can accordingly note more than one instance where embassy business is diversified by a declamation performance: Heraclides of Lycia loses an immunity after a declamation contest with Apollonius of Athens. It may be that this was the same occasion on which Heraclides is said to have broken down in a speech before Septimius Severus.[128] The second such occasion is under Caracalla, when Heliodorus impresses the Emperor with his presence of mind when he finds himself unsupported by a colleague. The Emperor plays up to the sophist's self-possession by giving him a subject to declaim on the spot, and supporting him in a friendly way.[129]

By contrast, the causes of antipathy between emperors and sophists are rarely connected with public speaking as such: Alexander Peloplaton irritated Antoninus Pius by an abrupt form of address, and by his foppish mannerisms; Philiscus found himself in a similar situation with Caracalla.[130] But most other instances of Imperial disfavour relate to outside causes: Antipater of Hierapolis was too oppressive in provincial administration, and also allowed himself an excessively tactless reference to Geta's murder; the Emperor Hadrian had quarrelled with Dionysius of Miletus.[131] Philostratus does not say so, but we might suspect the hostility of Celer, the Imperial secretary in this case;[132] in that of Favorinus a request for tax exemption in Gaul was somehow involved.[133]

In the correspondence of the future Marcus Aurelius and Fronto we have at least some element of commentary on the problems of the controversial Athenian sophist Herodes Atticus, whom Fronto had to face in a court-case evidently involving Herodes' Athenian enemy Demostratus;[134] Fronto apologises for the minimum rhetorical force the facts oblige him to use against even a newly emerged friend of his pupil. But in general one is struck by the degree of solicitude with which emperors might act as reconcilers of sophists with other interests: Nero sends Nicetes of Smyrna off to the west to make his peace with Rufus (though it has to be noted that the Emperor's intentions appear to be *post eventum* interpretations on Philostratus' part).[135] Trajan had at least to stave off Bithynian criticism of Dio Chrysostom with a rather diplomatic reply to Pliny;[136] Hadrian had twice to rescue Polemo from the results of his high-handed arrogance, once against the Smyrniotes over a charge of embezzlement and once against the likely wrath of the future Antoninus Pius.[137] Marcus, having already had to listen to opposition to Herodes in 143, tolerated excessive abuse from the grief-stricken prima donna in a hearing at Sirmium in the early 170s,[138] and finally compromised with token punishment of the magnate's freedmen.[139]

The role of personality and atmosphere is easy to under-estimate, especially in encounters with emperors. Take the following incident as described by Philostratus. Philiscus of Thessaly had refused to perform liturgies for the Heordaeans; they had gone to court, and when the matter was referred to Caracalla the sophist came to Rome to put his case. He sought the patronage of Julia Domna and obtained from her the chair at Athens. But Caracalla 'was resentful towards Philiscus because he thought the sophist had run rings round him'. The professor was ordered to appear in person:

> And when he made his court appearance Caracalla was offended by the way he walked and the way he stood; his dress seemed inappropriate to the occasion, his voice

33

seemed effeminate, his language arrogant and concerned with anything but the subject in hand. All this alienated the Emperor from Philiscus, so that he kept stopping him all through the speech, both by interposing his own remarks in the time allotted to Philiscus, and interjecting abrupt questions. And when the sophist's replies were not to the point, the Emperor remarked: 'His hair betrays his character, his voice his rhetoric!' And after cutting him short like this a number of times, he took the Heordaeans' side. And when Philiscus said 'You have given me exemption from public liturgies by giving me the Athenian chair,' the Emperor shouted out 'Neither are you exempt, nor is any other teacher! Never would I, on account of trifling, miserable little speeches, deprive the cities of men to perform liturgies!'[140]

Bowersock has noted that

the apparent ease with which Septimius Severus and Caracalla in these cases revoked immunities again suggests the insecurity and impermanence of any such grant. The petulant and extravagant remark of Caracalla implies full awareness of the economic dangers of exempting sophists who were rich.[141]

Other interpretations are also possible. Certainly Caracalla was not lacking in resourcefulness in raising money, as the case of the *Constitutio Antoniniana* shows. But here Philostratus does at least hint at other considerations. The fact that Philiscus obtains the Athenian chair from the Emperor's own mother after he was already in dispute with the Thessalians suggests a patent ploy; and the sophist's apparently arrogant conduct in the Emperor's hearing speaks for itself. So does the fact that the information in this case comes as clearly as any from a source very close to Philostratus himself. He has at least attempted to catch the ethos and atmosphere of the incident: a foppish sophist makes himself insufferable first by underhand manoeuvre, then by something akin to overbearing bad manners. A fit of pique on Caracalla's part is not ruled out either; one thinks of the case of Alexander Peloplaton before Antoninus Pius. But it may also be a matter of more than money: Philiscus had the misfortune to be liable for liturgies by matrilineal succession. He may after all have been liable elsewhere for liturgies on his father's side. On the other hand, Philostratus for his part may have concentrated on the superficial colouring of the incident so as to enhance the prestige of his kinsman, the Lemnian Philostratus; he is not slow to add that Caracalla had seen fit to grant this latter an exemption as the reward for a declamation.[142]

In general sophists and emperors were all too well equipped to withstand one another and generate the kind of *bons mots* cherished by Philostratus.[143] Their professional relationships, as in the case of sophists serving as Imperial secretaries or as tutors,[144] are necessarily less well documented and less public; such appointments carried the same combination of lustre and risk that attends any intellectuals who aspire to be courtiers.

SOME SOURCES OF FRICTION

Bowersock has noted the susceptibilities of sophists to 'professional quarrels',[145] but the profession might be said to invite quarrels on a still broader front. Sophists might indeed fight principally with one another; they might equally well find themselves at variance with philosophers; or they might antagonise officials or emperors, or their own or other people's municipalities. Bowersock enumerates quarrels and notes their prestige value, but in many cases it remains to try to account for the general range of underlying causes.

Some of these do spring, firstly, from the profession as such: sophists were primarily wordsmiths, and did not lightly tolerate those who were not. Those who set conspicuously high standards and then proceeded to cheat them could not have expected sympathy from those who took the trouble – hence the famous showdown in which the pupils of Herodes humiliated the visiting sophist Philagrus for pretending to improvise a speech whose text had already been published. Similarly, Rufinus son of Apollonius of Naucratis was discredited for using his father's material.[146] Philostratus is at pains to point out the envy of those who do not improvise for those who do:

> And it is no surprise if some who would not themselves be able to conceive any great thought of their own or appreciate anyone else who did so, should insult and revile

a man who had the promptest, most daring and greatest style of the Greeks of his time.[147]

Secondly, there were certain natural polarisations: those who cultivated extravagantly 'Asianist' mannerisms could expect suitable reproof from the more restrained of their colleagues. Thus Isaeus would not allow Dionysius of Miletus to deliver his exercises in a singsong, nor would he let another Ionian admire bombastic absurdity.[148] Criticisms levelled at Scopelian (that he was dithyrambic, lacking in restraint, and too heavy [πεπαχυσμένος]) point in the same direction; while Hadrian of Tyre often failed to attain grandeur because he was too lavish with tragic diction.[149] Aelius Aristides dissociated himself from 'those who vomit speeches' (by speaking extempore regardless of consequences);[150] and Alexander Peloplaton's rhythmic self-indulgence was the subject of parody.[151] Stylistic battles could easily spill over into social antipathies.

There was no lack of technicalities on which a sophist could be caught out: one might start a speech ineptly, as Aristides was known to have done, or be put off one's stride in a speech because of a distraction, as Heraclides had been;[152] one could be accused of inept interpretation of a complex political theme, like Ptolemy of Naucratis, or have a weakness in a difficult subject or in a difficult department, such as sustained irony, as Polemo was alleged to have.[153] Or one could transgress the familiar boundaries between the rhetoric of the court and that of the school, as Claudius Severus accused Hadrian of Tyre of doing.[154] The sophist trod a verbal tightrope, and there were always critics and connoisseurs waiting for him to fall off.

Thirdly, sophists had to cope with the constant pressure of pupils. This was not just a matter of class discipline (we hear of Proclus of Naucratis employing special measures to prevent the hissing and taunting of class rivalries).[155] Pupils might readily become overambitious for themselves, so that Chrestus of Byzantium had to take the presumptuous Diogenes of Amastris to task for his 'fantasising about governorships and the court, and the prospect of being next to emperors (as he had been assured by some Egyptian)'.[156] Some pupils might also be overambitious for their own teacher: the same Chrestus had to resist the pressure from 'the Athenians' that they should petition the emperor for his appointment to the Athenian chair.[157] And teachers had their work cut out to resist fomenting rivalries: Herodes took his own outstanding pupil Sceptus of Corinth to task for insulting the performance of Alexander Peloplaton (but was himself accused of listening to the young Hadrian of Tyre 'in an envious and jeering manner');[158] while Hippodromus of Larissa refused to be pressurised into competition with Philostratus of Lemnos.[159]

As regards the rest of mankind, the arrogance which fortified a sophist in his professional life might be felt to serve him conspicuously ill when dealing with the outside world. Philostratus himself recognises 'sophistic' as a profession particularly prone to arrogance and egotism: Polemo's overbearing manner in general, and his actual eviction of the future Antoninus Pius from his house, testify to the degree of highhandedness in question.[160] Sophists were prone to melodramatic gesture, and could lay themselves open to envy or vindictiveness. The stories in Philostratus underline only too well that the sophist might be tempted to patronise where he could, then suddenly find his victim conspicuously elevated. Nicetes had to make his peace with a proconsular governor Rufus;[161] and a sophist might too easily extend his classroom discipline or his reflex of giving orders too far for his own good.

Philostratus sometimes notes the degree of irascibility that might characterise such figures.[162] A sophist might simply take petty offence, or might excite a malicious campaign ending in the loss of a chair. Both Aelius Aristides and Philagrus of Cilicia reacted against lack of enthusiasm in their hearers, the latter to the extent of actually striking a member of an audience who was dropping off.[163] We hear of direct competition in declamation;[164] we hear of petty insults, such as Ptolemy of Naucratis' striking out the 'p' in Heraclides of Lycia's *Encomium of Ponos* ('Hard Work') leaving him with the *Encomium of an Onos* ('Ass') while Philostratus of Lemnos sneered at Aelian for producing an attack on the Emperor Elagabalus only after the latter's death; and Proclus of Naucratis satirised those teaching at Athens, including Hippodromus.[165] The latter incident was countered by politeness on Hippodromus' own part, but personal pique must all too often have escalated into spectacular quarrel. We can only claim to be well informed on one such incident and its ramifications: Philagrus of Cilicia felt himself insulted in Athens in a chance encounter with pupils of

Herodes, and himself slipped up in the process of retaliation
(with a conspicuous solecism); he then brought further ridicule
on himself by the incident of self-plagiarism already mentioned, so that a subsequent performance too was marred by his
anger.[166] But some longer-term animosities seem also to be in
evidence: Philostratus dismisses a rogues' gallery in Ephesus
without explanation: six sophists are listed as 'playthings of the
Greeks'.[167] They may well have been dismissed by Philostratus'
Ephesian informant Damianus, on grounds that are not clear
to us.

Some of the problems involving sophists certainly have
ramifications that are well beyond us. In particular Philostratus'
brief and somewhat grudging notice of Theodotus alludes to
the latter's underhand complicity in producing the infamous
charges got up by one Demostratus and his friends against
Herodes.[168] This seems to be somehow connected (as usual no
thanks to Philostratus' testimony) with Theodotus' tenure of
the chair of rhetoric newly established or newly refurbished by
Marcus Aurelius.[169] The very least we might suspect is that as
part of Marcus' reconciliation of the Athenians in 174/175[170]
the enemies of Herodes rewarded their man with an honour
which he could not under the circumstances have expected to
obtain had Herodes himself been the referee. Given Philostratus' notable bias for Herodes as far as possible, we may not
put too much trust in his verdict: 'Though [Theodotus] never
went so far as any open hostility towards [Herodes], he plotted
against him behind his back, since he was adept at using his
opportunities; for he was really an orator of the contemptible
sort.'[171]

A still more opaque scenario is presented in a dream reported
by Aelius Aristides:

Even before I went into the city [of Smyrna] there were
people to meet me in accordance with the oracle, and the
most prominent young men presented themselves to me
as students. And there was some impression of a lecture
arranged, and the invitation was exactly fulfilled down to
the last detail. And about this time, some insignificant
Egyptian burst into the city and bribed some of the
councillors, and even gave some of the common, ordinary
people to believe that he would play a part in civic affairs

and indulge his amazing ambitions with his fortune – this
fellow somehow broke into the theatre, and the whole city
was seized with such embarrassment.[172]

The passage is perhaps less interesting for its dream than for its
suggestion, outside Philostratus, of the interaction of sophistic
activity and local politics. The interloper[173] seems to have funds
at his disposal. This means benefaction, influence and the
possibility of material enhancement for the city, but Aristides
regards Smyrna as 'his' territory, and sets out to humiliate his
rival at the first opportunity.

It must be said too that the general manner of sophists did
not always fit them to cope with the complexities of aristocratic
family life. Herodes' involvement in the tragic death of his
pregnant wife Regilla is symptomatic of strained relationships
on a wider scale; and the tragic death of two of a freedman's
daughters in a lightning-storm contributed to his tormented
outburst in Marcus' hearing of the Athenian suit against him at
Sirmium.[174] Scopelian's household is riven with intrigue, ultimately over inheritance; while his father's cook is able to run
rings round the sophist himself, though subsequently requiring
his reconciliation.[175] On the other hand a sophist's reputation
might thrive on scandal – Lucian even advises it as a means of
enhancing one's personal status, and it was nothing new in the
world of rhetorical stardom: even Demosthenes had acquired a
reputation for effeminacy because of his dapper dress.[176]

SOPHISTS IN TRANSITION

After the age of Herodes Philostratus himself does not seem to
sense or imply any decline, and his own information is probably
at its best for being contemporary and occasionally that of an
eyewitness. It seems clear, however, that his sophists were
suffering the same pressures as the urban aristocracies with
which they identified. We find under Septimius Severus that
Heraclides of Lycia lost an exemption in Rome as a result of a
contest with Apollonius of Athens; we also hear of the same
sophist breaking down before Severus, in circumstances not
unconnected with the presence of Antipater of Hierapolis.[177]
We hear of sophists having to brave the displeasure of Emperors,
as when Hippodromus awarded a victory at the Amphictyonic

Games to an actor from the disgraced Byzantium; or when Antipater considerably provoked Caracalla by criticising the murder of Geta.[178] We also hear of Proclus of Naucratis leaving his native city by night with his whole portable estate and embracing the tranquillity of Athens to escape from civic dissension and lawlessness at home: we should not be wrong to guess that avoidance of liturgy was somehow in question.[179] But such instances are probably not a basis for generalisation, given that the Severi could elevate sophists such as Apollonius of Athens, Heliodorus or Philostratus the Lemnian just as readily as Hadrian had exercised angry preferences in the past.[180] And since sophistic intrigue and in-fighting is implied in a number of the cases mentioned, we can be even less confident of any trends.

Philostratus is also able to mention close friends or contemporaries of his own: Philostratus the Lemnian, Nicagoras of Athens and Apsines of Gadara serve to imply that the profession was flourishing at the time of writing, still within the Severan period.[181] Thereafter there is a considerable sense of hiatus. The Anarchy produces a lacuna in the history of 'sophistic', as it does in most other areas of Imperial history: one does not expect quite the same call for ceremonial speeches, nor does one look for emperors who are conspicuous patrons of culture; yet the basic drill of rhetorical education would not have skipped a generation, though we can well envisage the compounding of the local difficulties we noted in late first-century Egypt. If Philostratus' *Lives of the Sophists* coincided with the beginning of the disruption, the late third century is the most probable date for one of the most important theoretical offerings on sophistic activity: two treatises *On Epideictic Oratory* attributed to Menander Rhetor.[182] These treatises assume that basic social institutions for speechmaking remain unimpaired: indeed one notices the prominence of speeches for the reception of dignitaries, a far from diminishing activity in the changed world of the Dominate:

The 'formal address' [*prosphōnētikos*] is a laudatory speech addressed to a governor by an individual. It is worked as an encomium, but as a complete one . . . [after praise of the emperor] you follow on to the praise of the addressee himself, saying that the emperors are to be especially admired for their choice of governors ('For what an illustrious man they have sent down to save our people'). You will then proceed to praise the governor himself, especially (as I said) on the strength of his own actions – this indeed is preferable – but if his family is very prestigious and reputable you should briefly allude to the fact, and proceed to actions, especially those in hand, on the present occasion in his present office.[183]

The incidence of the Anarchy did not entail the suppression or disappearance of sophists. By chance Eusebius mentions that the chief opponent of the heretic Paul of Samosata in the struggle to evict him from the church at Antioch was one Malchion, not only a Christian presbyter but a sophist in charge of Greek studies in the city. We also happen to know something of the career of Cassius Longinus,[184] long thought to have been the author of the distinctive treatise *On the Sublime*; he had at some stage taught at Athens and had met and maintained contact with prominent philosophers, including the Neoplatonist Porphyry. He later moved to Palmyra under the patronage of Queen Zenobia, and requested works of Plotinus from his old friend[185] – only to be executed for political involvement when Palmyra fell to Aurelian. Here we have a threefold reminder: of the existence of the rhetorical teacher during the darkest and least documented period of the Empire; of such a figure's interest not only in philosophy, but in philosophy of a novel and contemporary sort;[186] and of the natural involvement of such a figure in the affairs of a *polis*. No less interesting as a reflexion of sophistic culture and heritage is P. Herennius Dexippus, who organised resistance against the invasion of the Heruli of his native Athens and was able afterwards to write a thoroughly classicising account of his exploit.[187] Even in the chaos of the third century, patriotism, letters and action could be effectively interlinked.

THE FOURTH CENTURY AND AFTER

When we find some effort at continuous cataloguing of sophists in the fourth century, the sense of continuity is there but there are some obvious changes to be felt. For one thing the increasingly oppressive authority of the state is matched by a higher level of outrageousness on the part of students, and Christianity has emerged as a force ultimately inimical to the pagan presuppositions and environment of sophistic culture and values.

With the fourth century the sophists naturally reflect something of the irreversible changes that overtook the Empire as a whole. In general the neglect accorded to the period by scholars of rhetoric is compounded by the poor quality of Eunapius' notices,[188] and the sheer bulk of the surviving *oeuvre* of its most important survivor, Libanius.[189] But it must be stressed that in the latter's work in particular we have the most irreplaceable evidence of a sophist's practice, both as a littérateur and as a public figure: indeed we have a picture of sophistic life with a wealth of documentation that is very seldom obtainable for the *largior aether* of the second century.[190]

The changed position of Christianity after the Constantinian settlement did not affect the upper echelons of paganism to the fullest extent; and the phenomenon of the Christian sophist or the sophistically trained Christian father serves to underline the adaptability and resourcefulness of late antique rhetoric and its practitioners.[191] The sudden accession of Julian might indeed have promised a heyday similar to that under Hadrian or Marcus.[192] But Libanius as well as Eunapius reflects a chilling change in cultural climate.[193] His encounter with a governor of Syria, Festus, who knows no Greek, is a sign of the times;[194] and the phenomenon of late antique pagan rhetoric in Greek could not long survive the eventual changes to a Christian Byzantine Empire.[195]

None the less Libanius is able to give a lively account of student life in Athens, including a level of disruptiveness either not reached or delicately suppressed in Philostratus:

I have heard, gentlemen, from boyhood onwards of the wars between the schools in the middle of Athens: of the clubs, knives and stones, the wounds and their resulting lawsuits, the defence speeches, the verdicts on the convicted, and of all the outrageous escapades that students get up to to raise the fortunes of their teachers. I used to consider them noble for the risks they took and not less right than the men who take up arms for their country; I used to pray to the gods that I too should distinguish

myself in this way and run off to the Piraeus and Sunium
and the other ports to kidnap students as they dis-
embarked, then run off again to Corinth to stand trial for
the kidnap; then by giving party after party, run rapidly
through my estate, and then look for a creditor to give me
a loan.[196]

It is not hard to recognise characteristics here that are already
present in the behaviour of Philostratus' sophists and their
pupils: Libanius' *Second Oration*, objecting to the application of
the nickname *barus* ('ponderous') to the author, goes far
towards reflecting the likely reasons for a sophist's unpopul-
arity.[197] Apart from the self-righteous sensitivity that occasions
the speech in the first place, Libanius conjures up accusations
that he is always talking about his prestigious family, and of
success against rivals:

'Ah, but by your own self-congratulation you condemn
other people's performances, good or otherwise,' someone might accuse me. I defeated such and such a sophist,
reduced some other to silence, secured the downfall of
someone else, outwrestled another, and saw another one
off. And I frightened all my rivals in Egypt, and the trio in
Athens, when I was summoned by the council in both
places![198]

Libanius' reply proves the charge:

Haven't you heard this from other people? If they hadn't
reported to you, you would not know of my successes, so
far as I am concerned. And as for the statues of me and the
decrees passed concerning them by cities neither small
nor few, of those you have not yet heard, though perhaps
you will – but you will not hear about them from me.[199]

Of course they have just done so, and Libanius could indeed be
ponderous in broadcasting his successes, as we shall see. From
the viewpoint of such a figure the accession of Julian was hailed
as a breakthrough amid personal and professional problems:

Troubles heaped upon troubles, one thing after another;
one friend died after another, I lost a city I loved, my
mother and her brother had gone, everything that a man
could wish to live for went sour for me, until at last the

man who in the palace loved philosophy better than any philosopher succeeded to the whole Empire unopposed. He brought me back as if from exile, to being once again reconciled to my misfortunes. And so I laughed and pranced about, I composed and delivered my speeches with joy in my heart, the altars had received the blood of the sacrifices, and smoke carried the savour up to heaven; the gods were being honoured with their festivals, a thing that only a few old men survived to remember, the prophetic art once more came into its own, the art of oratory came [once more] to be admired; Romans regained their confidence, and barbarians were either conquered or about to be so.[200]

The phenomenon of Christian sophists is underlined by Julian's attempt to ban them, not without a recourse to the 'philosophic' overtones of the original sophists:

I think it is necessary for those who associate with the young in order to teach rhetoric to be people of [upright character]; since they are expounders of the writings of the ancients, whether as rhetoricians or grammarians, and still more in the case of sophists. For these men aspire to be teachers inter alia not only of the use of words, but of morals as well, and they tell us that 'political philosophy' is their province. Whether this is true or not is a question we must leave aside for the time being.[201]

Julian's question could find no more definitive answer in the mid-fourth century AD than it had done in Plato's time. But the image of the professional sophist could still include the element of training for political success – in however limited a form.

Libanius was not alone in the fourth century in surviving in bulk. An extensive *oeuvre* also remains for both Himerius[202] and Themistius,[203] to say nothing of the sophistically adept Julian himself.[204] And it is possible for Eunapius at least to name enough others to imply the continuity with second-century practice.[205] The strong philosophic colouring of both Themistius and Julian serves as a reminder that this aspect of a sophist's equipment could still be summoned to the fore;[206] and the social eminence of sophists showed no signs of abating, even if their capacity to influence local events in a more totalitarian system could have been much lessened. Libanius boasts of his aristocratic lineage at Antioch,[207] and could still be asked for by an Emperor,[208] while Themistius, already a senator at Constantinople under Constantius in 355, became city prefect and Imperial tutor under Theodosius. The inaccessibility of governors in private could moreover enhance the importance of those required to mediate with them on behalf of cities on public occasions.[209] Nor, it must be emphasised, was their capacity for civic involvement impaired: whatever one might think of Libanius' school declamations, there is no doubting the conviction and skill of his addresses to Theodosius on behalf of the Antiochenes after the riots of 387,[210] even if they cannot have been employed on the actual occasions that gave rise to them; nor can we doubt Libanius' sincerity in championing the cause of the peasantry, or his protesting against the rise of protection rackets.[211] It should of course be remembered that accidents of survival may have contributed to the loss of such speeches on the part of second-century sophists; the activities themselves are well enough attested.[212]

With the unsatisfactory meanderings of Eunapius any hope of continuous history disappears. We cannot mark any formal end to 'sophistic' in quite the way we can point to the dated closure of schools of pagan philosophy; indeed we can infer some further degree of continuity from the flourish of declamation exercise well into the Byzantine era in the works of Choricius and others at Gaza.[213] There are other isolated indications. A sophist Plutarch is epigraphically attested for the fifth century, in the context of a still surviving Panathenaic festival.[214] An inscription from Gönuk commemorates a sophist Longinus in the Byzantine period, and attests to the survival of the title *sophistēs* itself.[215] But a body-blow was dealt to what might have remained of the system by Justinian, who in effect cut off local funding for chairs of rhetoric.[216] Provision was retained from the *Theodosian Code* for sophists[217] in Constantinople and, one infers, Alexandria; similar provisions in Rome were not effective. Yet the immense prestige of the sophistically imbued Cappadocian Fathers in the Christian East serves as a channel of sophistic influence;[218] and one learned Byzantine imitation of the sophistic novel is so thoroughly in the spirit of its original, Achilles Tatius, as to be insensible to the great gulf between the second century and the twelfth.[219] But we do not have sufficient assurance that the concert conditions survived along with the raw materials; and without them one can only anticipate an afterglow, like that of Seneca's tragedies in relation to the state-endowed performances of the fifth-century Athenian festivals. Public performance by pagans in a pagan environment had gone, and Libanius' *pro Templis* is close to being its swansong. With the death of Libanius towards the end of the fourth century the sophists in effect lost the last living voice capable of conveying sophistic values; their last real hope of securing the future of their cultural base had long gone with the death of Julian.

That is as far as we need pursue the outline history of 'Sophistic': it is enough to show the sense of continuity in the sophists' heritage, and the measure of prestige they could indeed attain. But it is also a reminder that their fortunes – and inclinations – were diverse. Patterns can be difficult to sustain with the limited evidence at our disposal; all too often we are left with little more than a sense of the considerable versatility of some very chameleonic figures. How they attained such versatility we can now attempt to examine, through a glimpse at their rhetorical training and practice.

2

Preparation, prelude, performance

So far we have viewed the sophists as they would have appeared to the outside world of Graeco-Roman society at large. We must now take a closer look at the techniques by which they were expected to demonstrate their virtuosity within the context of public or private performance.[1] A system culminating in dazzling displays of extempore rhetoric on anything and everything demanded a great deal of systematic and perhaps over-mechanised preliminary training. Philostratus not infrequently draws attention to the immense efforts sophists had to expend behind the scenes in order to acquire and maintain a seemingly effortless technique,[2] while Lucian could complain about the short-cuts open to the unscrupulous careerist too anxious to get to the top.[3] The following discussion does not set out to offer a history of late Greek rhetoric, but rather to draw attention to aspects of it which are particularly characteristic of sophistic practice.

PREPARATION: THE *PROGYMNASMATA*

One of the most characteristic cultural forces in the formation of a sophist or a sophistic outlook is that of a small group of preliminary exercises, *progymnasmata*,[4] of which we have a steady stream of examples from the second century onwards, some at least by sophists in their own right such as Libanius[5] and possibly Hermogenes as well. Not only do they provide a basic repertoire for the elementary student of rhetoric, they also provide the habits of thought that will preserve or develop it. With minor variation these exercises include essays in narration (*mythos, diēgēma*), description (*ecphrasis*) and basic techniques

47

of argument consisting of proof and refutation (*kataskeuē*, *anaskeuē*), as well as systematic methods of comparison (*syncrisis*), to which we might relate more ambitious exercises such as praise and blame (*enkōmion*, henceforth in its Anglo-Latin form, and *psogos*). These and similar exercises were not seen as an end in themselves, but provide the student with the ability to react to quite basic materials and ways of deploying them.

The trainee rhetorician has to be able to tell a story – which may be anything from a familiar myth, fable or historical tale to a made-up imitation of any of them. 'Hermogenes' illustrates the 'working' of a fable, whose given version is as follows:

> The monkeys assembled and deliberated about whether they should found a city. When they decided to do so, they were on the point of undertaking the work. So an old monkey held them back; he said that they would be more easily captured if they were taken within walls.[6]

The master is then able to illustrate rudimentary extension of the story by means of inserted speeches:

> 'For you see', said one, 'that men are happy because of having cities; each has a house, and they all go to assemblies and the theatre and delight their souls with spectacles and recitations of all sorts'.[7]

It remains to add the inevitable formal decree and the speech of the old monkey. One can see the relevance of such an exercise to a sophistic outlook. The familiar human institutions (city, assembly, theatre, speeches, decree) are all there, but combined in a setting which by its very nature calls for quite whimsical imagination. And the pupil is encouraged to manipulate and think in terms of rhetorical speeches from the start. Moreover there is something thoroughly sophistic about a fable which concerns the founding of civilisation: one thinks of the performance by the sophist Protagoras in Plato's dialogue of the same name.[8]

To illustrate the working of a conventional story 'Hermogenes' processes the Medea legend briefly through a number of figures.[9] Apart from simple grammatical conversion into indirect speech, he provides the same potential for development as before. One can present the story as an *elengtikon* ('cross-examining'): 'What terrible thing did Medea not do?

Was she not in love with Jason, did she not betray the Golden Fleece? Did she not kill her brother Apsyrtus?' Or as *asyndeton* (accumulating statements without conjunctions): 'Medea the daughter of Aietes fell in love with Jason, betrayed the Golden Fleece, killed her brother . . .' Perhaps the most characteristic manipulation belongs to the manner 'Hermogenes' calls *syn-kritikon* ('comparative'): 'Medea the daughter of Aietes fell in love instead of checking her feelings; instead of guarding the Golden Fleece she betrayed it; instead of saving her brother she killed him.' The pupil will have attempted nothing of any originality, but will have acquired fluency in characteristic rhetorical reflexes.

Next in line in the manuals stand the *chreiai*: 'deeds and sayings of famous men'. These are not primarily narrative exercises, but brief moral essays on traditionally elevating material. 'Hermogenes' illustrates with Isocrates' saying: 'The root of education is bitter, its fruits sweet.'[10] Apart from routine statement and paraphrase of the material and commendation of the famous man, there will be moralising development ('the greatest successes usually come from hard work') and extension of the theme ('and successes give pleasure'). This can then be restated by inversion ('Things due to mere chance do not require hard work, and their effect is very unpleasant'). Then a routine simile ('as with farming so with words'); a parallel example ('Demosthenes shut himself in a room, and after much effort reaped the fruit, crowns and public acclamations'). Two quotations are then adduced as traditional authority, one naturally from Hesiod ('The gods have ordained sweat in advance of virtue') and one piece of anonymous wisdom ('The gods sell all good things for toil').

Such an ensemble would not only be important for the elaboration of a moral theme in itself; it also deploys typical basic resources of the rhetorician's *paideia*: the simile, quotation and exemplum which will supply so much of the essential repertoire and texture of sophistic writing. There should be no doubt as to why 'Hermogenes' chose this example: Isocrates certainly stood in an arguably sophistic tradition, as a pre-eminent teacher who produced some of the basic models of epideictic oratory. And the material itself contains an adaptable metaphor once more presented antithetically. It is not surprising to find a substantial emphasis on *paideia* in the repertoire of these exercises: 'when Diogenes sees a boy misbehaving, he strikes the *paidagōgos*';[11] 'Demosthenes, on being asked how an orator is made, replies "by spending more on oil than wine"';[12] 'Plato used to say that the Muses reside in the souls of the good;[13] or that the shoots of virtue grow from sweat and labour.'[14] The pupil will not simply be glib and cultivated: he will have the materials of morality at least on the tip of his tongue.

Perhaps the most characteristic exercises for the future orator were the pair *anaskeuē–kataskeuē* (refutation–assertion). One is expected to refute a myth,[15] for example, by stating that it is unclear when Narcissus lived; unlikely that Arion would have wanted to sing in the midst of adversity; impossible for the same legendary figure to be saved on a dolphin; inconsequential to destroy democracy in order to save it; unworthy for Apollo as a god to sleep with mortal women; and without profit whenever we speak to listen to such things. Such headings are sensible enough in themselves, and they must have increased the pupil's propensity for regarding no proposition as beyond rebuttal. The ultimate extravagance of *anaskeuē* is the thesis of Dio Chrysostom's *Trojan Oration*: that Troy could not have been taken.[16] No truth of Greek tradition is too sacred to be effortlessly overturned.

Scarcely less important for the formation of the sophists' outlook are the *encomium* and *psogos*; and it is to the first of these that sophistic rhetoric might be said to owe its indifferent reputation. The theoretical headings may start with race, city and ancestry, and work through to funeral and children;[17] while the impression is easily given of going through the rhetorical motions in the cause of scoring hollow compliments on contrived official occasions. The handbooks encourage blatant opportunism in encomium in particular: whatever qualities a subject has can be presented as virtues. When 'Hermogenes' is discussing the praise of a plant he advises that:

If it should need a great deal of looking after, you will admire this, if only a little, you will admire that. If a man comes from a great city, that will be in his favour; if from an insignificant one, that will be no less so.[18]

The result is that the urge to praise can sometimes be felt to transgress reasonable bounds: even when Libanius is presenting himself as appealing to Theodosius at a critical juncture on behalf of Antioch, *encomium* and *psogos* are not left out for long, and he will balance beauty and culture against earthquake and invasion.[19] Perhaps the exercise which scholars most readily identify as 'sophistic' as opposed to merely 'rhetorical' is the paradoxical encomium: Libanius can include a bogus encomium of the unworthy Thersites among such obviously worthy subjects as Diomede or Achilles.[20] And he had respectable precedent: Gorgias was able to offer encomia of both Helen and Palamedes.[21]

The *syncrisis*, again, is an exercise with wider implications: a formal comparison ('compare and contrast'). The original sophists had been notable for their inclination to plead for and against, and here is the art of antithesis on its largest scale. To produce a *syncrisis* one could simply juxtapose a pair of *encomia* or *psogoi* in parallel: as in comparing the ancestry, education, deeds and death of Achilles and Hector;[22] or one could produce an equally effective sense of contrast by placing an encomium of Achilles, say, beside that of Thersites.[23] The celebrated contrast of Demosthenes between himself and Aeschines illustrates the technique at its briefest and most effective:

'You did the teaching, I was a pupil; you did the initiations, I was the initiate; you were a small-time actor, I came to see the play; you were hissed off, I did the hissing. All your dealings have served our enemies; mine the state.[24]

Often enough *syncrisis* is seen to underlie some of the most ambitious sophistic ensembles: Dio contrasts Tyranny and Monarchy, Lucian *Paideia* and Sculpture;[25] while Achilles Tatius can even offer a *syncrisis* on homosexual and heterosexual love.[26] And there are the same obviously sophistic implications to such an exercise as for *encomium* and *psogos*: that details may be emphasised or manipulated in the interest of balance rather than truth, sometimes in the most patently artificial way.

The trainee rhetorician of whatever kind had also to be able to handle characterisation, and this might be done by prescribing such a formula as τίνας ἂν εἴποι λόγους ὁ δεῖνος ('What might so-and-so say . . .') in the exercise *ēthopoiia*. Once again it was essential to judicial as well as epideictic oratory to 'play' a character from the inside 'and on all occasions you will preserve the essential character (*to oikeion*) suitable to the given characters and occasions'.[27] Sometimes character as such will predominate (for example in presenting a farmer's first sight of a ship); sometimes emotion (Andromache on Hector).[28] This latter category tends to encourage the use of famous occasions of farewell (Achilles to Deidameia, or over the corpse of Patroclus; Hecuba's lament when Troy has fallen);[29] though Libanius offers an example with amusingly different opportunities: 'How would Chiron have reacted on finding Achilles among the women?'[30]

Perhaps the most unexpected feature in the use of *progymnasmata* is the important application of *eidōlopoiia*, the characterisation of someone already dead in their own person. It is no trouble to a sophistic writer simply to quote the author of his choice. But it is just as easy to bring him on stage, march him into court or cross-examine him with impunity ('and here is Homer, Plato or Demosthenes to say a few words in support of my case'). Hence Fronto summons Socrates to witness that even philosophers need the tools of oratory, or Philostratus can ask his patroness Julia Domna to 'tell Plutarch not to be angry with the sophists', or Dionysius of Miletus can contrive pathos by asking the dead to mourn for Chaeronea: στενάξατε οἱ κατὰ γῆς ἥρωες, ἐγγὺς Πλαταιῶν νενικήμεθα ('Lament ye heroes below the earth; we have been conquered near Plataea!')[31]

The orator has also as a matter of course to be able to handle general propositions ('Should one marry?' 'Does the wise man engage in politics?')[32] The advanced exercise known as *thesis* included such practical issues, as well as exclusively theoretical ones such as 'Do the gods exist?' or 'Do they exercise providence over the universe?'[33] It is here that the rhetor's activity converges with that of the philosopher, or of the original fifth-century conception of a sophist, though in large part the advice from writers of *progymnasmata* consists of facile prompting for subject-division (under such headings as necessity, nobility, or expediency). Once again the side to be taken is immaterial when the point of the exercise was to encourage versatility: 'it does not matter if a person is speaking in this mode, whether one should marry or not, and again, whether marriage is to be chosen or avoided'.[34] Such an outlook is once more thoroughly 'sophistic' in the original sense: the fifth-century sophists had been regularly pilloried for their alleged indifference to truth.

It should be emphasised that the Second Sophistic cannot be dismissed simply because of the existence of such exercises, or because they might be carried to self-indulgent and absurd lengths for their own sakes. Many forms and genres were in fact combined in an experimental way in the literature that has survived, and countless other instances will have been concealed in the literature that is lost. We should note, for example, the degree of both tradition and originality in such an ensemble as Dio Chrysostom's *Euboicus*.[35] Many of the component parts can be classified in terms of one *progymnasma* or another, so that the first section reads like an extended *diēgēsis*, evidently based on Dio's own experience. Shipwrecked and marooned on Euboea, he falls in with a hunter who tells his own *diēgēsis* in turn – containing an idyllic *ecphrasis* of the pastures before his father had turned to hunting.[36] He then continues with a *syncrisis* set in a city, when his squatting on public land leads to enlivened debate: there is not only a *thesis* here (εἰ γεωργητέον, 'should one engage in agriculture?'), but two carefully contrasted *ēthopoiiai*, of a slanderous demagogue who makes out a simple subsistence squatter to be a thief and a pirate, and of the countryman himself,[37] one of nature's gentlemen who naively offers the little he has to the assembly. We are then faced with a dramatic intervention and recognition from a townsman he had once rescued, who guarantees his good faith.[38] A *syncrisis* of the contrasting dispositions of rich and poor follows naturally on the story.[39] The rhetorician's raw materials are all in place, and it is up to the sophistic practitioner to transform them.

PRELUDE: *THE PROLALIA*

We can see the fruits of such exercises most immediately in the prologues which sophistic performers used to preface their more formal displays. These were variously labelled as *laliae* ('chats'), *prolaliae* ('forechats') and *dialexeis* ('discourses'); and it is clear enough that the form was a flexible one.[40] A speaker could humour his audience by telling stories, describing pictures or otherwise parading short extracts from his repertoire, and using them to impose subtle forms of flattery on his audience. Lucian, Apuleius and Dio have all left pieces that are evidently *prolaliae*, while other essays in the form can from time to time be disentangled from the beginnings of longer compositions.[41] And it is often in this medium that sophists are most readily inclined to talk about themselves.

One instance will give us an idea of what to expect. In his *prolalia* Herodotus, Lucian first describes how the great historian read his histories at Olympia and so won attention for them, then describes a picture by Aetion of the marriage of Roxana and Alexander as having been exhibited at Olympia as well.[42] But the main part of the operation is to compare the Olympian audience with Lucian's own current listeners, evidently the élite of Macedonian society:

> You yourselves, then, have already assembled the best from every city, indeed the cream of all Macedonia, in the finest of the country's cities, not at Pisa, I'm glad to say, with not enough space and mere tents and booths, and a stifling climate; and my audience is not any old rabble, more anxious to watch the athletes, most of them regarding Herodotus as a mere sideshow, but instead the most prestigious rhetors, historians and sophists – an important point, for my own arena not to seem much inferior to Olympia.[43]

This judicious final flattery has invited the audience to see itself as superior even to that of the foremost cultural event in the Sacred Calendar, and it deftly manipulates the instructions for praise of a city. Lucian has already been able to disclaim comparison with Herodotus, presumably the first literary figure of note he knew to have attended the games, and he has been able to name in passing other sophistic worthies who attended (Prodicus and Hippias, no less),[44] implying that he is fit to be associated with them; while his description of Aetion's picture allows a lighter interlude, a wedding scene with *erōtes* playing in Alexander's armour.[45] Not only is Alexander a symbolic figure for the Sophistic, as we shall see; for a Macedonian audience he is the local celebrity. Speaker and audience have both been duly flattered and amused, and the performance proper can begin.

Dio needs a still more oblique approach to introduce an elaborate speech on ideal kingship, evidently designed for Trajan. First he tells the story of how Timotheus' music inspired Alexander to a martial mood.[46] The compulsion towards *syncrisis* then leads him to an 'opposite' example: even if Athena herself had performed before Sardanapalus, he would not have responded.[47] It is not music but temperament that counts, and Alexander would have been well served if Timotheus' repertoire had been more varied.[48] The moral can then be readily inferred ('I am able to come to you, Emperor, appealing to your responsive temperament with philosophic advice far more balanced and wide-ranging than any offering of Timotheus – and so you are better served than even Alexander').

The use of this often lightweight material might serve to project the speaker himself in a novel or unexpected light, especially before a new audience: Lucian can have fun working out the implications of being compared to a literary Prometheus,[49] or seeing himself as an ageing Heracles,[50] or as an Anacharsis with a similarly helpful patron,[51] or even as an Antiochus with an army full of surprises.[52] Apuleius could be a good deal less subtle in his self-advertisement, as he compares his own ever-ready eloquence as a philosopher with varieties of birdsong – to his own advantage.[53]

PERFORMANCE: THE *MELETĒ*

It is now time to look at the way sophists conducted themselves in their culminating performance, the formal *meletē* (exercise). Here is Scopelian, arguably Philostratus' first major idol, enacting the ritual entertainment with which the sophistic profession was most readily associated:

> He would appear before [his audience] not with a condescending or conceited air, nor with the manner of someone in fear of them, but as was appropriate for a combatant going into the fray to win reputation for himself and knowing full well that he would not fail. He used to talk from his chair in an agreeable manner, but when he was on his feet for the performance his orations had more polish and vigour. He used to think over his theme neither in private nor in front of the crowd, but would go off only a little and in a short space would review all his material. He had a very melodious voice and a charming diction, and he would often slap his thigh in order to spur on both himself and his audience. Moreover he was also expert in the use of 'figured speech' and ambiguity. But he was still more impressive in his handling of the more demanding

themes, and especially those concerned with the Medes, involving treatment of Darius and Xerxes; for in this department I think he surpassed all his competitors, both in phrasing his allusions and in handing down the technique to his successors; and he used to act out the arrogance and frivolity of the barbarian character. It is said that on these occasions he would sway about more than usual, as if in some Bacchic frenzy; and when one of Polemo's retinue said of him that he beat a drum, Scopelian seized on the jibe and replied, 'Indeed I do beat a drum, but I beat upon the shield of Ajax'.[54]

The remarks from the sophist when seated would correspond to the *prolalia* just discussed. The real drama begins when he rises to speak extempore on a theme, often one of several suggested just beforehand by the audience, whether of students or the public. What stands out from this specimen description is the sense of occasion: the sophist in his own element is a declamatory prima donna, able to transport his public back to the Persian, or even the Trojan War; and able to give them what they wanted on demand. The artifice of the exercise should not disguise its difficulty.

But both at the time, and ever since, it has been possible to denigrate such proceedings as a cheap and dishonest use of techniques of illusion. Here is Lucian's highly critical view of just such a kind of performance:

Whenever it is really necessary for you to speak, and your audience offer themes and points of departure for your speech, you are to find fault with any difficult ones and laugh at them as not at all proper for a real man. But when the audience have made their choice, do not hesitate but say 'Whate'er betide the bad luck of your tongue' . . . on top of everything refer to Marathon and Cynegirus, without which you would achieve nothing. And let Athos unendingly be navigated in ships and the Hellespont trodden on foot; and let the sun be shadowed by the missiles of the Medes, and Xerxes take to flight and Leonidas be an object of wonder; let the inscription of Othryades be made out, and let there be plenty of Salamis, Artemisium and Plataea end to end. And if ever it seems the right time to intone, see that you intone everything and make a song of it. And if ever you run out of material for your intonations, say 'Gentlemen of the jury' in tune and consider the harmony of your sentence complete. You must often cry 'Woe is me!' and slap your thigh, bawl out, clear your throat as you speak, and pace about with a sway of the hips. And if they do not shout their approval, be indignant and take them to task; and if they stand up and prepare to go out in disgust, order them to sit down again; in a word, exercise a tyranny over them ... The lower orders are awestruck at your appearance, your voice, your walk, your pacing about, your intoning, your sandals, and your infamous expression 'whate'ersoever'; and when they see you sweating and gasping they are bound to believe that you are a really formidable opponent in debate ... And afterwards let them form your retinue as you go on your way with your head wrapped in your mantle, while you meditate on what you have said. And if anyone comes up to you, make amazing claims about yourself, go over the top in your self-glorification, and make yourself ob-jectionable to him: 'What was the son of Paian [i.e. Demosthenes] in comparison with me?', or 'Perhaps just one of the ancients can compete with me!' and other things of the kind.[55]

Both these passages serve to convey in some measure the ethos of sophistic performance: the preoccupation with the speaker's mannerisms of delivery, the traditional repertoire of subject-matter, usually with the audience choosing the subject of the main performance on the spot, the frenzy of excitement, and the admiration and criticism of an élite following afterwards. Philostratus' *Lives of the Sophists* depends very largely on string-ing together a whole series of reports and reminiscences of such occasions, viewed with a mixture of the kind of admiration and contempt just quoted. At their best such performances had the power to produce a real sense of evocation in their audience, or they could degenerate into a sequence of hackneyed posturings with hackneyed material. But Philostratus is also able to com-municate a strong sense of the social significance of such occasions. One of his most detailed notices suggests an interest-ing and in some respects elusive interplay between Herodes Atticus and the much less celebrated Alexander Peloplaton of

Cilicia, on the occasion of a rare visit to Athens by the latter.[56] Alexander visited the city during Marcus Aurelius' Marcomannic Wars, when en route to take up an appointment as Imperial Greek secretary *(ab epistolis graecis)*. Taking the opportunity for rhetorical improvisation thus offered, he was astute enough to write to Herodes Atticus asking to 'borrow' the latter's own pupils as an audience. The performance was to take place in the Theatre of Agrippa,[57] but Herodes himself was late in arriving from his country seat at Marathon and the event went ahead without him.

Alexander gave the introductory *lalia*,[58] in this case a miniature Panathenaic oration, an apology for not having made a previous visit; so sensitive an audience would have expected no less. At this stage Philostratus tells us not uncharacteristically of the effect of the sophist's superb appearance, which evidently enhanced the overall effect.[59] The declamation-subject chosen by his audience is reported as 'The speaker encourages the Scythians to resume their previous nomadic way of life, since they are falling ill through living in cities'. Such a subject would have been particularly appropriate to anyone travelling to the northern frontier; it would have given opportunities for the contrast of Greek and barbarian, for the presentation of the Scythian as a noble savage, and for reference to the legend of Anacharsis and allusion to book 4 of Herodotus.[60] Alexander had begun his working when Herodes arrived still in his travelling gear; this gave the speaker his opportunity to improvise a compliment to the master and to demonstrate his skill in variation by rephrasing material he had already used. The example Philostratus gives of these verbal gymnastics might strike us as banal enough; a mildly metaphorical phrase ἑστὸς καὶ τὸ ὕδωρ νοσεῖ ('even water at a standstill is sick') is rephrased much less strikingly as καὶ ὑδάτων ἡδίω τὰ πλανώμενα ('waters are sweeter when they move around').[61] But the facility is a difficult one to maintain for any length of time when thinking on one's feet, all the more so in what was now an artificially literary language to be maintained before an audience of experts. Alexander was able to round off his performance with a dramatic exclamation: ἀλλ' ἀναπέτασον τὰς πύλας, ἀναπνεῦσαι θέλω ('Fling wide the gates, I would breathe the air!'): mannered climaxes were a recurrent feature of such performances.

Herodes was then invited to improvise in turn by Alexander, and duly rose to the occasion on a specific historical subject based on Thucydides 7: 'The Athenians wounded in Sicily beg their retreating companions to kill them.' The result was more melodrama, with the tearfully delivered epigram ναὶ Νικία, ναὶ πάτερ, οὕτως 'Αθήνας ἴδοις ('We implore you, Nicias, you who have been a father to us, may you set eyes on Athens once more!'[If you kill us now].[62] The pathos would have been enhanced by the audience's knowledge of Nicias' real fate along with his men: he was never to see Athens again. We have already been told of the acclamation of individual epigrams in Alexander's own speech: this time he himself exclaimed in honour of Herodes ὦ 'Ηρώδη, τεμάχιά σου ἐσμὲν οἱ σοφισταὶ πάντες ('Herodes, all we sophists are tiny slices of yourself!'). This would not have been such a total self-abasement as it might seem, since Alexander of course alluded to Aeschylus' celebrated acknowledgement of his own work as 'slices of the banquet of Homer'.[63] But Alexander's effusion certainly paid off: Philostratus duly lists the generous gift with which Herodes, ever ostentatious in his generosity, rewarded his guest. But this scenario was not entirely given over to a mutual admiration society. Alexander's showing had not been to everyone's taste: Herodes' eminent pupil Sceptus of Corinth had made a sarcastic gibe on Alexander's nickname Peloplaton ('clay-Plato') by suggesting that he had found the clay but not the Plato; Herodes administered a sharp rebuke and characterised the performer instead as a more sober version of (the flamboyant Asianist) Scopelian.[64]

Here, then, we have a good idea of the performing conventions: a sort of academic debating society with a touch of grand opera – but with a difference: it is as if the prima donna has to improvise the arias as well as the cadenzas, and in the language of Dante for good measure; and if there is not hissing and booing on this occasion there is certainly a hint of backstage backbiting. If the experience is thoroughly alien to us, there is no doubt through Philostratus' narrative of its intoxicating effects on audience and participants alike. To most of the audience, it is implied, this was an illuminating occasion: in spite of a brilliant performance by a visitor at the height of his career, the resident grand master more than held his own, and the honour of Athens itself was maintained.

But not all occasions had their criticisms confined to the witticism of a precocious pupil. Once more Lucian describes a less reputable performance with a wealth of observation and innuendo about what he clearly regards as a 'put-up job':

This fellow who calls himself a sophist . . . once arrived in Olympia, intending to deliver to the people at the festival some speech he had written long before. The topic of his composition was 'Pythagoras, excluded (by one of the Athenians, I think), from participating in the Eleusinian Mysteries as a barbarian, on the grounds that he himself used to say that before the present time he had once been Euphorbus'. As it happened, this speech of his was like Aesop's jackdaw, put together out of borrowed plumes. But of course because he wanted people to think that he was not reciting stale material but improvising what was straight from his book, he asked one of his friends (it was that man from Patras, who is so busy in the courts) to choose Pythagoras for him the moment he asked for subjects for his talk. The man duly did so, and persuaded the whole audience to hear the hoary old speech on behalf of Pythagoras. In the subsequent event he was quite unconvincing in his performance, smoothly reciting of course what he had rehearsed long before and thoroughly practised . . . [while the other] stood by him, defended him to the utmost, lent a hand, and helped in the struggle. And there was a great deal of laughter from the audience: some of them looked from time to time at that man from Patras, and quietly showed that his sleight of hand had not escaped their notice; others recognised the actual words he was using, and all through the performance ended up with this one task, testing one another as to how well their memories could make out which of the sophistic masters of the so-called exercises a little way back each expression belonged to.

Among all these men who were laughing was the very writer of these words. And why should he not have been expected to laugh at an outrage so blatant, unconvincing and shameless? So, somehow being a person who could not control his laughter, when the performer had turned to singing, as he supposed, and was intoning some kind of dirge over Pythagoras, the writer, seeing the proverbial ass trying to play the lyre, burst out into a merry guffaw, this writer of mine, and the other turned round and saw him. That put the two of them into a state of war, and the recent business [an argument over the meaning of the term *apophras*] arose from it.[65]

One notes that this fiasco occurred at Olympia: Lucian's future enemy had chosen the most prominent forum in which to make a fool of himself, and the cognoscenti were there in force. The theme for declamation was relatively unusual, but suitably evocative of a leading religious and cultural institution and its early history. One thinks of an instance in which Epicurus' eligibility as a *dadouchos* (torch-bearer) in the Mysteries was in question in a *meletē* (Syrianus *RG* 4.719). The course of events has a certain resemblance to the much more infamous case in Philostratus, where Philagrus of Cilicia pretended to improvise (with more cause, as the material was originally his own). One notes the complicity between a sophist and a forensic orator; one notes too the reliance on the works of a previous generation of declaimers rather than direct imitation of classical texts, in Lucian a sign of bad taste and short-cutting; though it might just as readily be seen as proof of the formation of a living tradition. In any case serious students of declamation were sufficiently trained memory-artists to be able to detect this sort of fraud. One notes also that the performance seems to have reached a culmination. Rhetors with Asianic tastes in particular could enliven the climax of their performances with intoned recitative (a mannerism which sports commentators still employ to similar effect); Lucian has chosen the best possible moment for his sabotage. The result is once more a sophistic feud, of a kind we have noticed.

It is often taken for granted that the contents of declamations are so stereotyped as to merit dismissal out of hand. Certainly the pull of Marathon or the arrogance of Xerxes seemed as irresistible as Lucian's gibes imply. As late as Himerius in the fourth century one has the impression that themes are being selected to accommodate the inclusion of certain prefabricated situations which lend themselves to the manufacture of facile epigrams, and hence immediate audience applause. We can illustrate from this sophist's fifth declamation:

After the Persian Wars the Athenians vote for a war against the barbarians. On finding this out the King of Persia promises to restore sacrilegious damage if they should put a stop to the war; the Athenians are willing, but Themistocles speaks on the opposite side.[66]

The subject itself is fairly typical: it represents a recreation of what was now regarded as a climax of Greek, and particularly Athenian history: the 'finest hour' of independent city-states against overwhelming barbarian odds. It is not too long before the rhetoricians' standbys, Xerxes' bridge of boats and canal through Athos, are back in action, supplying predictable paradoxes:

Τί πορθμοῖς ἐνοχλεῖς δι᾽ ἐμέ; τί δὲ ὄρη τέμνεις εἰς θάλασσαν; Τί καλύπτεις ἠπείρῳ τὸ ῥόθιον; ἔασον ἑστάναι τὸν Ἄθω, καὶ μὴ πέμπε μοι διὰ τῶν ὀρῶν, ἀλλὰ διὰ τοῦ ῥοθίου, τὸν στόλον;

Why do you trouble with crossings on my account?
Why do you cut mountains through to the sea?
Why do you cover the surge with land? Let Athos stand, and do not send your expedition, I beg you, through the mountains, but through the sea![67]

These and a good many more variations are a prelude to a carefully contrived mixture of metaphors.[68] By divisive negotiation Xerxes now tries to undermine what he has failed to conquer by his expedition, so that the speaker can claim: 'You attack the city from Babylon, and through your heralds you bring siege-engines against us, and by embassies you undermine the city's finest aspirations.'

The much-celebrated Polemo seems to carry such temptations to even greater lengths, by offering what is almost an out-and-out caricature of the medium: the fathers of the fallen war heroes Cynegirus and Callimachus, both killed at Marathon, dispute for the privilege of pronouncing the funeral speech. The father of Cynegirus can use an argument like the following:

Callimachus exposed himself to the enemy missiles falling round him, and because of this he remained at his post, and appeared to be standing because he was unable to fall. The only illustrious thing about Callimachus is that he had the appearance of being alive in a mere corpse [σχῆμα ζῶντος ἐν νεκρῷ σώματι]. But my son Cynegirus left the phalanx, and then, running fearlessly on, made for the very shore where the army was most concentrated and the fighting was thickest and fighting practically naked he went for the sea and was the first man to fight a naval battle from land' [by seizing an enemy ship and having his hand cut off].[69]

But quasi-historical hyperbole is not the only resource for the sophistic declaimer. By contrast, Aelius Aristides goes to the other extreme of providing historically plausible reconstructions of less improbable and extreme situations, as in his pair of Sicilian orations based on Thucydides' account of the Athenian disaster, or the still more ambitious quintet of orations examining the political implications of Leuctra from five different angles. His treatment of an imaginary embassy to Achilles, though based on Epic, is equally sober. Moreover the *meletē* could provide us with an *ēthopoiia* such as the following:

And seeing that the city itself had been ruined by the neglect of its office-holders, because most people were robbing or rather looting the common weal, I revived it by building aqueducts, adorned it with buildings, and strengthened it with walls, while the state revenues I effortlessly increased through the thoroughness of my officials; and I took care of the young, made provision for the old, and kept the people entertained with spectacles, handouts, festivals and public feasts. Girls raped, boys corrupted, wives kidnapped, guards despatched, or any kind of tyrannic threat – I was horrified even to hear about them. Already I was planning to lay aside my power and resign my authority, wondering only how one could safely make an end of it; for being a ruler and arranging for everything already seemed tiresome in itself, and, when exacerbated by envy, a wearisome business. But I was still looking for a means of ensuring that the city would never require such care and attention again. But while I in my old-fashioned naivety was busy with all this, there were some who were already plotting together against me: they were already planning the form their plot and coup would take, orchestrating conspiracies, collecting arms, channelling funds, inciting help from neighbouring cities, and sending embassies to Greece, to Sparta and Athens. What they had already planned to do with me personally, should they have caught me, and how they had threatened to dismember me with their bare hands, and what punishments they had invented for me, they publicly confessed on the rack. For the fact that I suffered no such fate I owe to the gods, who disclosed the plot – especially Apollo, who revealed to me dreams and sent me men to say what they meant.[70]

Without prior knowledge it is impossible to establish until just before the end of the extract that the speaker is anything other than the most benevolent and philanthropic of despots. Only the last sentence would reveal him as the tyrant Phalaris of Agrigentum, anxious to gain the approval of Delphi for his mikado-like regime. The whole passage is contrived as *lexis eschēmatismenē* ('figured speech'), carefully arranged to convey exactly the opposite of what is being said. Only on a careful re-reading is one likely to realise that Phalaris did not like to hear of rapes and the like because he had every reason to cover them up. Philostratus prizes such a mode highly and notes that it is not always sustained successfully. It may have taken a Lucian to bring off this particular tour de force, but it could be done.

MORE *MELETAI*: IN ASSEMBLY AND COURT

Many of a sophist's *meletai* would belong, strictly speaking, to the deliberative rather than the epideictic division of oratory, in the sense that they presuppose a public assembly to be persuaded. But some are quite clearly epideictic, designed for display and entertainment. As an example we might note Dio Chrysostom's *Thirty-Fifth Oration*. This is addressed to the people of Celaenae in Phrygia, on an occasion that cannot be precisely identified.[71] The use of the old name Celaenae as opposed to Apamea, prevalent since Seleucid times, points once more to the characteristic archaism of the Early Empire. Here we seem to have the traditional scheme for the praise of a city (πόλεως ἔπαινος): the audience is to be flattered by means of reference to its own importance, and the speaker is entitled to play on local pride and patriotism, from the advantages of the city's position and benefits of its soil to its being at the source of the Marsyas and the Meander, its position as an international market and assize centre, and its contribution to cult expenses.[72] But, as often in sophistic literature, the traditional 'textbook' topics make way for whimsically creative and expansive treatment. It may be that the speaker does not know or even care too much about the city in question, or deliberately wishes to divert attention from it. But the great bulk of his material is concerned with two other topics: himself and his appearance, and his views on sophists. The first twelve chapters out of twenty-five seem to constitute an unusually extensive *prolalia*, in which the speaker attempts to humour the audience and gain their favour. He uses a 'humility topos': Dio is not the kind of speaker they expect, and he is not to be reverenced for his long hair.[73] He drifts by means of simile, example and allusion into a characteristic attack on sophists and their habits of playing on the gullibility of their audiences, Asiarchs excepted, before returning to the advantages of long hair – a proper fixation of an author who has left an encomium on hair itself.[74]

Dio's other diversion is a description of India; only that land can be said to be more blessed than Celaenae itself, and he launches into the formal description of an earthly paradise, winding up with even more exotic mention of an eldorado: more blessed still are the men who steal gold from the ants that guard it, a quietly ironic envoie.[75] All in all we have here a collection of typically sophistic ploys, amounting to little more than good-humoured and scarcely structured fun.

The sophistic atmosphere in a courtroom can perhaps best be gauged by an item in the correspondence of Fronto. Having found out that Herodes Atticus is his opponent in a lawsuit, and realising that his pupil the young Marcus is a friend of Herodes, he reviews in advance his courtroom gestures:

> But if we conduct the case in continuous speeches, even if
> I do digress outside the case, nevertheless I have to look at
> him quite intently, put vehemence in my voice, and speak
> in stern tones; and at one moment I must make an angry
> gesture, at another point my finger angrily. And this your
> man [Herodes Atticus] should endure with reasonable
> restraint. But it is difficult for him to accede even to that,

for he is said to be fired with a passion for cases [*cupidine agendi flagrare*].[76]

From what else we can gather of Herodes in court, Fronto did well to think hard about his histrionics in advance. When Herodes himself was in the midst of a real murder trial as defendant after the apparent manslaughter of his wife Regilla, he was able to humiliate her prosecuting brother Civica Braduas brilliantly with an epigram about his appearance: (σὺ τὴν εὐγένειαν ἐν τοῖς ἀστραγάλοις ἔχεις) ('your nobility is on the joints of your toes' – i.e. on the senatorial insignia on his sandals).[77]

Such courtroom drama was too good to confine to real cases: no extant ancient novel is without some form of court-case where school rhetoric can be practised with a vengeance. An extreme instance is to be found in Achilles Tatius' novel *Leucippe and Clitophon*, which offers scope for the standard repertoire of private as opposed to historical declamation-subjects, as so often concerned with convoluted cases of adultery, sacrilege, or both. In this case the heroine Leucippe has been sold as a slave and is now claimed by the villain Thersander; she had disappeared and the hero Clitophon accuses himself of her murder. Once he is condemned she turns up; Thersander now claims back his slave (legitimately), but also tries to eliminate his rival by insisting that the sentence be carried out even though the crime has manifestly not been committed and the confession itself has been seen to be false.[78] This is in fact the fourth in a series of speeches which occupy much of the last two books. Thersander devotes an extravagant opening to the *captatio* of his audience, assuring them how confused his speech is going to be because of his indignation, but this leads him to an extravagant and very well-organised parade of paradoxes:

> Whenever adulterers murder other people's housemaids,
> whenever murderers debauch other people's wives,
> whenever pimps break up sacred embassies,
> whenever whores pollute the holiest of temples,
> whenever a man is in the act of fixing the trial date
>   between slave-girls and their master,
> what more could anyone do in excess of this farrago of
>   lawlessness, adultery, impiety and blood-guilt?[79]

The only prop of Thersander's case is his insistence on the carrying out of the sentence ('It was voted that Clitophon should die: where then is the executioner? . . . Quick, administer the hemlock!').[80] But the accuser blatantly omits to mention that the very girl Clitophon has confessed to murdering is still alive. Thersander now turns instead on the priest of Artemis who has protected her, and builds up an innuendo that the priest has taken fugitives into his temple for immoral purposes ('The temple of Artemis is now a house for adulterers and the chamber of a whore'). He then goes on to charge Melite, his own wife, for her association with Clitophon: she had married him, under the genuine assumption that her husband was dead. And he complains that Clitophon, doubly condemned to death for murder and adultery, will only be able to pay the penalty once.[81] There is an overriding irony about all this: the reader knows that the charge of adultery is actually correct, though not for the period Thersander has alleged. It is as if Achilles has contrived a sequence of deliberately self-indulgent courtroom gymnastics in order to misfire.[82] Thersander is so busy contriving sophistically decorated falsehood that the truth slips through unnoticed. But the sophist's salon has invaded the courtroom, in fiction as in fact. One need not argue that irony itself is an exclusively sophistic weapon; yet Philostratus himself makes clear the sophistic taste for such a technique, and the difficulty of sustaining it.[83]

But *prolalia* and *meletē* do not exhaust the sophists' range. A high proportion of a sophist's output, and particularly of his published output, might lie outside it, once more under the catch-all title *dialexis*.[84] The constant homage to Plato produced a long line of works in dialogue and dialogue-related form: a high proportion of Lucian's works are so conceived, but it is also essayed by Dio, Philostratus and others, and in general one notes sophistic tendencies in forms far removed from the school exercise: in the novel, historiography or philosophic discourse.[85] But one notes also a tendency for sophists to experiment: Philagrus of Cilicia won disapproval for an insertion of a lament for his wife into an introductory encomium of Athens;[86] Aelius Aristides has to defend himself for inserting material about himself into a hymn to Athena.[87] And one notes the variety of forms entailed even in the four kingship speeches that open the works of Dio: only the third is an extended philosophic essay incorporating conventional diatribe material; the second and fourth are dialogues between Alexander the Great and Philip and Diogenes respectively; while the first contains an elaborate diptych between essay and first-person report of a telling of the arch-sophistic Allegory of Prodicus. A glance at the Lucianic corpus reveals more hybrids: a *syncrisis* between two encomia presented in dialogue in the pseudo-Lucianic *Demosthenis Encomium*;[88] a mock-encomium presented as a tragic fragment;[89] or an extended *ecphrasis* of a temple in Ionic dialect.[90] Not all such efforts need be uniformly successful in order to show that sophistically educated writers and speakers were prepared to experiment both within and beyond the confines of traditional rhetorical training. Rhetoric, and particularly epideictic rhetoric, provided a means; it remained the province of individual performers to bring about the ends.

We can form some idea, then, of the media available to sophists and very largely under their control; and we can suspect the kind of direction in which literature generated in a sophistic milieu is likely to go. But that only shows us the outward appearance of these godlike figures. We must now take a sample of the ichor that courses through their veins. The literature of the past was the lifeblood of the sophists, and we must now examine how they were able to transfuse it.

3

Communing with the classics

The rhetorical frameworks within which a sophist could be expected to perform offer us only one dimension of his art. At its centre is the preservation of a cultural whole: the world of classical Greece recreated through its literature. In the private fantasies of Aristides' *Hieroi Logoi* closeness to the classics could become a quite literal affair:

> I dreamed that I saw Plato in person standing in my bedroom, directly opposite my bed and me. It so happened that he was working on his letter to Dionysius, and was in a rage. He gave me a glance and said 'What sort of letter-writer do you think I am? Surely better than Celer?' (he meant the Imperial Secretary). And I said 'Shush! Great as you are you should not be talking about your reputation!' And not much later he disappeared, and I was deep in thought. But someone was there and said, 'This man who conversed with you just now as Plato is your Hermes' (he meant the god who has been allotted my nativity). 'But', he said, 'he was in the guise of Plato'.[1]

It might be tempting to attribute this easy familiarity in part to Aristides' personal vanity. But the conscientious Fronto can affect similar familiarity with the past as he sends his pupil, the future Emperor Marcus Aurelius, an imitation of the speeches on Love in Plato's *Phaedrus*:

> My dear boy, this is the third letter I am sending you on the same subject; the first came by the hand of Lysias, the son of Cephalus, the second by the hand of Plato the philosopher, and now this third one is by the hand of this

foreigner, in speech almost a barbarian, but as regards his judgement, I suppose, not totally lacking in sagacity.[2]

What is clear is that such writers saw themselves in a close relationship to their classical forebears. And classical criticism, such as it was, both allowed and expected writers to respect the frame of reference of a classical past.[3] Much of that criticism, to be sure, belongs not to professional literary critics but to teachers concerned with the imitation of authors by those engaged in rhetorical studies. But even in that quarter imitation was distinguished from mere plagiarism, and creative imitation was encouraged and expected. That said, the canon of authors might be deceptively narrow, to correspond to the restrictions of school reading.[4] Homer is ubiquitous and unquestioned;[5] but one might more readily imitate Euripides than lyric poets or Aeschylus, because of the sheer linguistic difficulty involved in the latter.[6] Hellenistic poetry for similar reasons offered less than it might have done.[7] But Plato, Demosthenes and the orators, the Comic poets (New more readily than Old) and the historians Herodotus, Thucydides and Xenophon could all expect to be imitated and recognised. In a revealing set of recommendations to a late learner Dio Chrysostom gives a useful cross-section of the canon, stressing the particular value of Menander, Euripides, Hyperides and Xenophon in their respective fields.[8]

Philostratus' *Lives* should leave us in no doubt as to the imitative capacities of sophists: we hear of Scopelian 'applying himself to all kinds of poetry, but tragedies he absorbed totally in his attempts to rival the magniloquence of his teacher [Nicetes]'; or of Polemo, commending the use of prose-writers '[carried in] on one's shoulders, poets [brought] by the wagon-load'.[9] We find the Imperial Secretary Celer writing an *Araspes*, based presumably on Xenophon's *Cyropaedia*;[10] or we find declamations that look back to specific situations in the orators, such as that of Demosthenes' *in Leptinem*, or in the historians, such as Thucydides' account of Sphacteria or Sicily.[11] Hippodromus of Larissa imitates Plato and Dio in his *dialexeis*,[12] while regarding Homer as the father of the sophists, as Nicagoras had held Tragedy to be their mother; the same spokesman claims Homer as the voice of the sophists, Archilochus as their very breath.[13]

Some indication of the tastes of sophistically educated writers is suggested by the number of full-length paraphrases of classical works under the Empire. Aristides produces a speech embodying book 9 of the *Iliad*, or a pair on the Sicilian episode in Thucydides;[14] Fronto composes a reply to Lysias' speech in Plato's *Phaedrus*,[15] Libanius a speech of Achilles over the corpse of Patroclus, or when deprived of Briseis.[16] It is not hard to see why such individual items have been chosen: 'Epic' crises in which history and tragedy converge have an irrepressible appeal, while the *Phaedrus* passage enables rhetoricians to write paradoxes about love with a veneer of philosophy. A favourite situation is the episode of the Arms of Ajax and its aftermath: we have a pair of *progymnasmata* by Libanius as well as a miniature dialogue by Lucian.[17] Here is a situation that seems to 'have everything': Epic background, potential for *syncrisis* between Ajax and Odysseus (and *ecphrasis*, since the arms themselves can be described), as well as opportunity for character-contrast between the combatants.

Often, however, an author will aim to produce an ingenious pastiche which will have the effect of evoking several classical authors simultaneously; an obvious example is offered by several of Lucian's pieces in which an Old Comic scene is recast in Platonic dialogue, often with significant reference to yet a third author. At the beginning of *Piscator* the philosophers come up from the dead in the manner of the war heroes of Eupolis' *Dēmoi*, uttering tragic and Homeric parodies the while; and Chrysippus actually advises Plato to work in his resounding reference to 'great Zeus in heaven driving his winged chariot', while Diogenes condemns Lucian's use of Menippus as an ally against philosophy.[18]

In a less ingenious or contrived way, the literary texture of a *dialexis* by Maximus of Tyre,[19] for example, will duly allude to a fair cross-section of the classical canon. The fifth *Dialexis* has as its overall theme 'whether one ought to pray' (εἰ δεῖ εὔχεσθαι). Leaving aside the inevitable philosophic commonplaces on providence, we find that Maximus opens with the exemplum of Midas and the Satyr, alluded to near the opening of Xenophon's *Anabasis*; the beginning of the *Republic* provides the reminder that Socrates went down to the Piraeus to pray. The *Iliad* provides no fewer than seven quotations relating to prayer, supported by Croesus' ill-fated consultation of Apollo

71

in Herodotus I.53; Plato provides a Homeric double-quotation στρεπτοὶ δὲ τε καὶ θεοὶ αὐτοί, Menander a less expected tag, while the familiar canon of Cleon, Hipponicus and Meletus as embodiments of injustice belong to the general fifth-century repertoire of exempla. The notion of prayer has been further sanctified by its literary 'endorsements'.

Sometimes a classical framework will serve to evoke the ethos of an author when the imitator is obviously setting himself at variance with his original in some significant way. The point of reference for a symposium would have been Plato's master-piece: few imitators lost the opportunity to flout Plato's careful balance between substance and characterisation, and between elevated discourse and the routine 'events' of a drinking-party; or to observe the content of Plato's *erōtikoi logoi*. Lucian sends in a Cynic philosopher Alcidamas as his uninvited guest to dis-grace the proceedings outright, in clever contrast to Plato's subtle handling of the arrival of Alcibiades.[20] Alciphron seems to be paraphrasing Lucian's symposium in turn, but this time through the eyes of an upstaged parasite;[21] while Athenaeus' symposium is a garrulous orgy of philological pedantry, as we shall see.[22] Lucian's fop Lexiphanes actually claims to be 'counterbanqueting the son of Ariston', i.e. writing a counter-part of Plato's *Symposium*, in the most outlandish (and highly suggestive) jargon.[23] Where there is a notion of a classical norm, there will be an urge to subvert it.

We can take Lucian's treatment of Theocritus *Idyll* 11 as an instance of the resourcefulness of a fair number of imitators.[24] Theocritus' original is essentially a monologue in which the Cyclops Polyphemus laments the fact that the sea-nymph Galatea has turned him down. Despite the handicap of his single eye, he has other compensations – milk and cheese from his flocks, his own singing, or his fawns and bear-cubs. And, less probably, he has 'other offers'. But Galatea, as far as the monologue is concerned, remains unresponsive. Lucian by contrast assumes a relationship between Polyphemus and Gala-tea, discussed by the latter with a more cynical Nereid, Doris. Galatea tries to defend him, referring to the occasion when the Cyclops first caught sight of her, as in Theocritus: his wild hairy look is manly, his eye suits his forehead – and it is her he fancies.[25] Doris rationalises: it's only because of her white skin, and only because he knows nothing but cheese and milk![26] But when Galatea claims he is musical, the full absurdity of the Theocritean love-song is exposed:

> Quiet, Galatea. We heard him singing when he came serenading the other day for your benefit. In the name of Aphrodite! Anyone would have thought it was an ass braying. And the lyre itself – what sort of thing was that? – a stag-skull stripped of the flesh! The horns served as the arms of the lyre; he'd joined them together with a yoke and fitted on the strings, without even winding them round their pegs; his recital was a trifle unmusical and off-key, with him roaring in one key, and the lyre backing him in another.[27]

Doris is able in the send-off to put in a sly hint absent from Theocritus: not only does the Cyclops smell, but he eats meat raw, including visiting strangers.[28]

Here Lucian has found room for retaining more than enough of the given material of Theocritus to establish his model beyond doubt. He has apparently invented or assumed a musical instrument as rustic as its player; one is reminded of the pose of musical connoisseurship that runs through sophistic literature in general.[29] There is also a sense that the action has moved on, at least to the point where Galatea is flattered by the Cyclops and genuinely sympathetic; the throwaway line in Theocritus, that he already has other lovers, is carefully not developed.[30] The situation is further altered through the double change of medium from Doric verse to Attic prose, and from monologue to dialogue:[31] this is a more down-to-earth projection of the situation as it might really have happened. More to the point, Lucian's humour is very carefully calculated to outdo, and undo, that of his model. Theocritus paints the Cyclops as a pathetic love-sick swain: Lucian makes him a nuisance and a laughing-stock to the neighbours. The sophistic imitation might be said to have held its own, and to have proved capable of significant variation in tone.

The short *Fifty-Seventh Oration* of Dio Chrysostom gives a good idea of how well the *pepaideumenos* can accommodate the classics to himself and himself to the classics. Dio opens with a discussion of the famous passage in *Iliad* 1[32] in which Nestor praises the opinion the ancients had of him, and himself gives advice to rulers. The point of course is to justify Dio's own mention of the fact that he is about to deliver a speech previously delivered to an Emperor:[33] he is no more a braggart than Nestor, since in both cases their action is performed for the public good. One feels, as so often, that for the purposes of the argument there is something rather sophistic about Nestor himself:

> So just as Nestor would not have hesitated to run himself down, if by so doing and saying that no one ever saw fit to consult him over anything he were in prospect of persuading Agamemnon and Achilles to obey his advice – likewise if he thought his praising himself would bring them to do this, he was quite right to praise himself.[34]

But there is an obviously disingenuous argument here: the listener who knows his Homer will have to search hard for instances where the boastful Nestor runs himself down, a fact well known to speaker and audience alike.

One particular product of *mimēsis* calls for discussion at length, since the source is clear and complete: in his *Sixteenth Oration* Aelius Aristides contrived to produce a 'version' of the embassy negotiations in *Iliad* 9.[35] In Homer's treatment the principal speeches are divided between Odysseus, who acts as the formal negotiator, and Achilles' old tutor Phoenix, who takes a much more intimate and personal line with his charge, both in his reminiscence of Achilles' childhood, and with a long cautionary tale about Meleager.[36] Faced with the task of translating the situation into sophistic terms, Aristides proceeds as follows. The *presbeutikos* he produces takes the Epic situation as it stands: Achilles is out of the fight, the Greeks are losing heavily and he needs to be persuaded to return; that much is inevitable. But otherwise he does not quite proceed as expected. He dispenses with the heroic characterisation; this is instead an impersonal diplomatic communiqué which takes the Homeric circumstances at their face value.

It goes without saying that Aristides knows the Homeric situation backwards, and comes to terms with most facets of it. He reinterprets elements of book 1 in a somewhat different way: Achilles could have killed Agamemnon if he had wanted to, but he did not.[37] Aristides thus ignores the divine machinery at this point in the action, as Odysseus was bound to do: no one could see Athena's intervention except Achilles himself. Nor does he

take on board the celebrated choice of Achilles between glory at
Troy or ignominy at home.[38] And one looks in vain for excessive
pathos in exclamatory climaxes that characterise so many of the
notices of Philostratus' sophists, for example. Instead, as one
expects from Aristides, arguments are carefully elaborated.
Sententiae there undoubtedly are, but they are not unduly
laboured:

> ὥστε πῶς δίκαιος εἶ περιορᾶν; ὅπως νὴ Δία ἐκεῖνος ἔτι
> μᾶλλον μισοῖτο ὑπὸ πάντων διὰ ταῦτα; ἀλλὰ μάλιστα
> μὲν δέδοικα, μὴ οὐ λειφθῶσιν οἱ μισήσοντες.

(So how are you justified [Achilles], in standing by? So
that, by Zeus, [Agamemnon] should be even more hated
by everyone for this? But I am very much afraid that there
will be no one left to do the hating.)[39]

The overall impression is that Aristides has produced a speech
which would not have disgraced 'Demosthenes before Achilles',
and that is in effect to attain the limits of his chosen medium. It
has to be added that it is actually a more natural medium than
Homer's: a deputation to a Mycenean war-lord might well have
sounded more like Aristides than Homer, and the former's
historical imagination is not so absurd.

TWO TEXTS: THE *ODYSSEY* AND THE *PHAEDRUS*

It might well be claimed that imitation of the adventures of
Odysseus offers a particularly good cross-section of the resources and interests of sophists as such.[40] We should rightly
expect a large accumulation of material: not only does the
Odyssey figure so prominently in the literary curriculum; but the
nature of Odysseus, the cunning, versatile, eloquent and per-
suasive traveller, is very easy to assimilate to the role of the
sophist himself.

Homer is felt to be next door to a teacher of rhetoric in his
own right. It is no surprise to find the speech in which Odysseus
takes leave of the Phaeacian King Alcinous liberally cited as
material for the *Syntaktikos Logos*, the speech of leave-taking, in
Menander Rhetor.[41] And even Nausicaa is not spared the
attention of the rhetoricians: Odysseus' speech to her, when
naked and highly disadvantaged on the Phaeacian shore, can be

made the material even for a Maximus of Tyre: 'When Odysseus recognizes the princess he compares her to Artemis and again to a young shoot; and no one would call him a flatterer on that account'.[42] One notes, too, several situations in which Odysseus' disguise is exploited for rhetorical effect, as when Lucian or Dio sees fit to spring into action with a dramatic change of character: Lucian evokes Odysseus before Irus as he shows new literary vitality in old age, while Dio faces a rebellious army with the tag with which Odysseus prepares to take on the suitors.[43]

It is instructive to compare Lucian's paraphrase of the confrontation between Odysseus and the Cyclops with the two *Ēthopoiiai* on the subject by Libanius. The latter presents Odysseus first in the situation of the cave: he has already fuddled the Cyclops with wine, but has still to hit on the option of blinding his enemy; the soliloquy is brought to an end when he does so.[44] In a second piece he reacts to the Cyclops' eating of members of his crew: εἴθε μὲν οὖν πρῶτον ἔργον ἐγενόμην ἢ τελευταῖος τεθνήξεσθαι ('Would that I had been first rather than last to die').[45] Libanius establishes little more than the fact that he 'knows his Homer' and works efficiently within the given material of *Odyssey* 9. Lucian by contrast has chosen a quite new angle: The Cyclops reports the event to Poseidon afterwards. The *Ēthopoiia* of the Cyclops is more subtly conveyed, through his obtuse reporting of the incident: τὸ μὲν πρῶτον Οὖτιν ἑαυτὸν ἀπεκάλει, ἐπεὶ δὲ διέφυγε καὶ ἔξω ἦν βέλους, Ὀδυσσεὺς ὀνομάζεσθαι ἔφη. ('First he called himself Noman, but when he had got clean away and was out of range he said his name was Odysseus').[46] The whole notion of anthropophagy can now be neatly turned upside down: ἐγὼ δὲ συλλαβών τινας αὐτῶν, ὥσπερ εἰκὸς ἦν, κατέφαγον λῃστάς γε ὄντας ('I caught some of them of course, and naturally I ate them, since they were pirates').[47] Poseidon is at least allowed an aside on the improbability of it all: how odd that the trick worked without any reflex action from the Cyclops! Only Poseidon himself is able to guess the ruse with the ram.[48] Moreover the tables are turned on Odysseus in a natural enough way: being still at sea, he must suffer Poseidon's revenge for his arrogance.[49]

Thanks to such popularity, Odysseus is not exempt from more risqué development. He has an amorous side of which sophistic authors were equally well aware. Lucian refers to a case of *fellatio* where a sophist in a drunken orgy plays the part of the Cyclops, 'swallowing your Noman whole, complete with crew, sails, rudder and all';[50] while a passage in the learnedly lascivious Achilles Tatius delicately implies that the young hero about to deflower his girlfriend has a sharpened stake for erotic purposes: κεῖταί σοι καθεύδων ὁ Κύκλωψ· σὺ δὲ 'Οδυσσεὺς ἀγαθὸς γένῃ ('Your Cyclops is asleep: see that you make yourself a good Odysseus!'). We are in territory close to that of the Homeric *Priapeum* with its obscene interpretation of the naked Odysseus' branch held out before Nausicaa.[51] But more gently romantic development is also possible: in Lucian's *Verae Historiae* Odysseus changes his mind about living with Penelope in the Islands of the Blessed, and sends a love-letter to Calypso, with Lucian as courier:

> When she took the letter and read it over, first of all she wept for a long while, then she invited us in with an offer of hospitality, gave us a marvellous meal and kept asking questions about Odysseus and Penelope: what was she like, and was she really so well-behaved, as Odysseus had long ago been boasting about her? And we gave her the sort of answers we thought would please her.[52]

The fun is not just in Lucian's clever development of the given Homeric material. He also knows just where to break it off: we will never know what his answer was. In a similarly sophistic development we have Odysseus himself doing a deal with Homer[53] to give information about the war in return for the suppression of all mention of Palamedes.[54] Like any latter-day sophist the hero is an astute negotiator.

The sheer variety of Odysseus' career ensured him a place in the repertoire of practitioners devoted to versatility; a similar variety, this time of texture, contributes to ensuring the place of Plato's *Phaedrus*. Why particular parts of this particular text? The celebrated opening, with its walk by the Ilissus, provides a classic *locus amoenus* and a standard 'passport' to a setting for philosophic dialogue: Plato's original has already the potential for paradox, in that it is Socrates, the student of human nature with little time to stray outside the town, who is given the model *ecphrasis* of the scene with its plane tree, grass and cicadas.[55] Apart from the inherent attraction of their subject-matter, the two *erōtikoi logoi*, one attributed to Lysias, the other to Socrates, form a *syncrisis* in themselves.[56] The second speech of Socrates,

its myth of the soul's charioteer, has once more rich possibilities for allegory and *ecphrasis*;[57] while the remainder of the
dialogue offers one of the standard discussions on the role of
rhetoric in civic society,[58] which sophists would be well advised
to be able to answer. Michael Trapp has well explored the use
of the *Phaedrus* in Greek writers as such; but perhaps the most
egregious reworking of the text is not in fact in second-century
Greek literature as generally conceived, but hidden in the
exercises of a rhetorical author writing in Latin: Fronto
switches to Greek to provide his pupil Marcus Aurelius with a
'working' of the theme of Lysias' and Socrates' speeches.[59] Not
only are their language and motifs exploited: as his version
breaks off Fronto is offering to show Marcus a particular flower
'should we both go outside the walls to the Ilissus'. The illusion
is complete.

SOME ASPECTS OF REPERTOIRE

Sophistic writers were expected to be well read in at least the
Greek classics, and to be able to defend their positions with
ancient authority, or adorn the texture of their work with the
décor of a well-defined canon of authors.[60] This is often a
matter of considerable sensitivity, and one notes how often
indignation is a spur to the exhibition of literary erudition.
Aristides has been charged with interjecting praise of himself
into a speech ostensibly in honour of a goddess. His response
is to ransack a wide cross-section of the classics for similar self-
congratulation: not only is the boasting of Nestor invoked, not
to mention Hesiod's claims at the beginning of the *Theogony*,
but Sappho, Pindar and Simonides as well; historians and
orators are also summoned in due course. The more Aristides
cites, the more he is able to imply the ignorance of his critic:

> For I think that, if you have read nothing else by Demos-
> thenes, at least you have read this celebrated speech for
> the proclamation of the Crown. There, then, Demos-
> thenes, a man of whom you admire only the name, says
> . . .[61]

Lucian can be seen to play the same game with a purportedly
less cultivated opponent, who is to recognise his own immoral
practices satirised by the comic poet Eupolis ('Have you read

the *Demoi* – all of it?').[62] The frequent accusations by sophists can always be effectively compounded by the charge that the rival knows his classics less well than the speaker himself.

Displays of erudition could be reinforced by quotation, and in this department the repertoire is subject to certain idiosyncrasies and 'trends'. The writer can take advantage of easily recognisable first lines or commonplace tags, or contrive to place his quotations strategically in his compositions to leave the most favourable impression on his audience.[63] A useful insight into 'quotability' is suggested by a passage in the anonymous *Encomium of Demosthenes*. When comparing rhetoricians, especially Demosthenes, with Homer, his fellow-poet Thersagoras can claim:

> I compare Homer's 'heavy with wine' with the 'drunkenness, dissolute dancing and debauchery of Philip'; or 'One omen is best' with 'the good with good hope in their hearts must . . .', or 'Verily Peleus driver of horses would mightily moan' with 'How loud, I wonder, would those great men who died for glory and freedom lament?' I also place 'Pytho in flood' beside 'Odysseus' words like snow-flakes' and 'should we be destined never to age or die' beside 'For the end to all men's life is death, even if a man shut himself in his chamber and keep watch'; and there are innumerable other passages where they have surged to the same thought.[64]

It is not difficult to envisage the general utility or ornamental value of such materials; the second and fourth pairs are obvious repertoire for the *epitaphios*, the first for the *psogos*, the third for general metaphors on the subject of eloquence.

One notes also how readily quotation overflows from the written works of sophists to their lives. Polemo could stake his claim to have overhauled the reputation of Dionysius of Miletus with the proverbial oracle of Apollo: ἦσάν ποτ', ἦσαν ἄλκιμοι Μιλήσιοι ('Once, ah, once Miletus' men were strong');[65] Herodes chose to insult his teacher Secundus, son of a carpenter, with the Hesiodic parody καὶ κεραμεὺς κεραμεῖ κοτέει καὶ ῥήτορι τέκτων ('and potter with potter doth strive, and craftsman with rhetor').[66] But such parodies could serve more poignant and evocative purposes: Pausanias of Cappadocia could make the transition from the chair at Athens to that in

Rome with Θησεῦ, πάλιν με στρέψον, ὡς ἴδω πόλιν ('Turn me back, Theseus, that I may behold the city') – with of course the implied comparison of Pausanias himself with Heracles, and the city he is leaving with the sight of Heracles' children;[67] while Herodes laments the disasters of his household with comparison of himself to the lone Odysseus: εἷς δ' ἔτι που μωρὸς καταλείπεται εὑρέι οἴκῳ ('One fool alone doth remain, I suppose, in the breadth of the household').[68] The obligation to produce cultured quotation even invades the world of myth. When Homer's Zeus addresses the Olympians, he does so in his own words, even if these are frequently formulaic. But when Lucian's Zeus gathers an assembly, he opens with a pastiche of Demosthenes: the gods want to make a good impression by showing their ability at declamation. But Zeus' stock of Demosthenes does not last very long: an initial flourish for the sake of establishing his *paideia* is all the effort he is prepared to make;[69] even the gods are subject to the same hazards in speechmaking as the sophists themselves.

The practice of *mimēsis* is particularly evident in the use of a repertoire of standard ornaments in sophistic literature. When Nicetes is quoted as using metaphors that are verging on the bacchic and dithyrambic in character, by referring to honey as 'wands of Bacchus' or speaking of 'swarms of milk', he is echoing Euripides' *Bacchae* 710f.[70] Or when Fronto ventures *non vineis neque arietibus errores adulescentium expugnabat, sed cuniculis subruebat* ('he did not lay siege to the errors of youth with mantlets or battering-rams, but sapped them with mines'), he is working a variation on a famous Platonic simile on the assault on the mind by the besieging passions.[71] Moreover rhetorical repertoire would have generated its own imitations en route: Alexander Peloplaton's striking phrase ἑστὸς καὶ τὸ ὕδωρ νοσεῖ is suspiciously like a *sententia* already known to the Elder Seneca in the Roman schools of the Augustan age.[72] Plagiarism of such material would have been rife, as Lucian's testimony has already suggested, and its detection in sophistic circles an art in its own right.[73]

We should ask ourselves why particular features of the repertoire established their place to the extent that they did. The simile of the tragic actor[74] is perhaps the most conspicuous,[75] in some authors an almost compulsive cliché. In Plato himself theatre and chorus imagery is frequent and varied,[76] and that in

itself would have been incentive enough to develop the repertoire further. But we should also note that for sophists the
theatre was an ancient institution with a particular cultural
interest, concerned with stage performance, which was after all
the basic preoccupation of sophists themselves. It also has scope
for very considerable variety: actors can be starving at home
after their performance;[77] or wear masks or elaborate cos-
tumes[78] which call out to be described. Moreover the stage simile
can be easily 'worked up' into a *syncrisis* in its own right,
especially for the contrasting of appearance and reality:

> and already at the end of the play each of them strips off
> that gold-spangled costume, takes off his mask and comes
> down off his buskins and goes around poor and lowly, no
> longer Agamemnon son of Atreus or Creon son of
> Menoeceus, but Polus son of Charicles of Sunium or
> Satyrus son of Theogiton of Marathon.[79]

By this time even the actors' names are as evocative a part of the
literary past as the legendary figures they represent.

A similar success can be claimed for the simile of the ship:
Plato had already elaborated a celebrated comparison between
a political régime and the crew of a vessel.[80] This was worked at
no less elaborate length by Lucian and Maximus of Tyre, both
of whom develop the comparison as a *syncrisis* comparing the
good ship with the bad.[81] One suspects in both cases that the
attraction is not just the air of professionalism about the subject-
matter, but the opportunity for comic incongruity in the
working out of a large number of details. This is the opportunity
to put Sardanapalus on the quarter-deck and consign Socrates
to the bilges. Nor is it the last we shall see of sophists turning the
classical heritage on its head.

Perhaps the most resilient item is the so-called *Allegory of
Prodicus*:[82] at least as old as the fifth century BC, and thereby
sanctified through its use by the archsophist Prodicus, it is used
by Xenophon,[83] one of the most accessible stylistic models, and
itself employs Socrates as the raconteur and Heracles as the
principal character. The further advantage is that it embodies a
built-in *syncrisis* and *ecphrasis* combined: two allegorical figures,
both of whose distinctive attributes can be described. This basic
formula can then be reworked, so that any pair of opposites can
do duty for Virtue and Vice. Lucian's substitution of Sculpture

and *Paideia* in the leading roles in his *Somnium* offers a characteristically sophistic reworking, and we shall encounter others.

With such an *embarras de richesse* to choose from, it seems inevitable that there should have been no shortage of inept imitation: in the context of the schools Seneca the Elder complains that audiences are so lax that a declaimer can pass off even Cicero's Verrines as his own;[84] and Lucian presents an amusing rogues' gallery of imitators *manqués*:

> Then since Thucydides pronounced a funeral speech over the first casualties in the famous war, this historian too thought he should make one over Severianus. For all of them set out to rival Thucydides, who was responsible for none of our misfortunes in Armenia. So having buried Severianus in the grand manner he has some centurion, by the name of Afranius Silo, mount the tomb to rival Pericles. His rhetoric was of the sort (and so much of it too) that I swear by the Graces the tears of laughter just rolled down, especially when our orator Afranius at the end of his performance shed tears and lugubriously lamented the memory of those costly banquets and toasts. Then he capped it all with Ajax: for he drew his sword in a truly noble fashion, as befitted an Afranius, and slew himself on the tomb in full view of everyone – I swear by Enyalios that he deserved to die long before for such a performance. And all the on-lookers, our historian declared, were awestruck and lauded Afranius to the skies. I for my part voted him down on every count for all but reminiscing about the soups and shell-fish and shedding tears when he recollected the pancakes; but this I held against him most of all, that he died without first cutting the throat of the historian who produced the play.[85]

Here we have the dramatic highlights of the sophists' repertoire, the funeral speech and the death of Ajax, rolled into one and trivialised by a nonentity with no taste. And once more the whole scenario is cast as a sort of sophistic performance, complete with the tastelessly admiring audience. The fact that the offender is presented as a historian rather than as a sophist as such only underlines the hold of rhetorical self-indulgence over a wide range of literary activities, as we shall see.

A SOPHISTIC THOUGHT-WORLD

The cumulative effect of life on close terms with the classical canon will not have been without its effect on sophists and their pupils. As Bowie puts it, 'The fantasy of the hypereducated Athenian must have been to walk out into the countryside of Attica and discover that he was in the fifth century.'[86] It is not too difficult to elaborate the illusion from Maximus of Tyre, say, or Dio Chrysostom. It is not so much the world of the fifth century, however, as a world in which the fifth century has been relocated somewhere in the vicinity of the Trojan War, since we still find Homer cheek by jowl with Socrates.[87] If we look at the broad peripheries of this world, we still find Herodotus' Scythians on one side and his Egyptians on the other;[88] Alexander's Babylon and some sort of Indian wonderland enclose it to the east,[89] the Pillars of Heracles to the west.[90] The Homeric Olympus is above, the Homeric Underworld below; but the *Phaedrus* charioteer can take the soul at will from one to the other.[91] And at the centre of this universe is the rhetor or sophist (depending on how he chooses to style himself), receiving the admiration of all and transporting them wherever they ask to go. Communications are direct: he can ask Socrates or Homer directly to put him right on details;[92] he can expatiate on the situation at Thermopylae or describe the cave of Calypso;[93] he can lavish praise or blame,[94] or force comparisons on any of his subject-matter; he can enact new fifth-century or fourth-century laws;[95] and he can 'correct' any part of the tradition as he pleases.

Such a thought-world will tend to produce certain characteristic literary reflexes, especially where there is the prospect of some unexpected display of *paideia*. One typical pose in sophistic literature is for the *pepaideumenos* to be discovered rapt in thought, meditating on some inspiration of his own.[96] One obvious model is the pair of Platonic passages that deal with Socrates' inspiration: in the *Phaedrus* he is moved to verse as he is carried away by the poetic possibilities of love, while in the *Symposium* he is rapt in his own private thoughts.[97] One accordingly finds Philostratus' Apollonius of Tyana at first making no disclosures to his impatient disciple Damis, after his amazing interview with Achilles at the Troad; Lucian's Menippus rapt after his trips to Heaven or Hades; or Lucian himself unable to communicate after his interview with Nigrinus.[98] The scenario provides a means of building up anticipation towards some great cultural revelation; one thinks of the sophists themselves, meditating their proposed themes before leaping into dramatic action.[99]

Especially characteristic of sophistic expectation is the scenario in which a character comes across some paradoxical reminder of the past, and indulges in a cultural game with an erudite but unexpected informant. Such a situation is perhaps most readily embodied in the *mise en scène* of Philostratus' *Heroicus*, in which a passing Phoenician merchant hears of the appearances of heroes of the Trojan War close to the site of their former exploits, with ample opportunity for the correction of Homer;[100] or in Herodes Atticus' encounter with the so-called Boeotian Heracles, able to speak pure Attic uncontaminated by the foreign accents to be heard in Athens.[101] In a similar vein we can find Dio recounting his meeting with a wise woman and local prophetess in the outback of the Western Peloponnese, where he receives a prophecy of the accession of Trajan and his account of the choice of Heracles;[102] or claiming to have met a priest in Onuphos in Egypt, who reveals the 'real' history of the Trojan War, on inscriptions part destroyed and part ignored. One is reminded of the *mise en scène* in Plato's *Timaeus* for Solon's reception of the Atlantis story, a still more ancient theme, from an Egyptian priest.[103]

Such poses do not of course preclude real people from performing real actions: Philostratus is able to tell us how Dio Chrysostom was able to avert a military revolt on the northern frontier after the death of Domitian. But Dio's own account of matters is revealing:

> There you could see everywhere swords, everywhere breast-plates, everywhere spears, and the whole place was crowded with horses, arms, and men under arms. I presented myself all alone in the midst of so many, quite unruffled and a very peaceful observer of war, deficient in body and well on in years, not bearing a 'golden sceptre' or the sacred fillets of some god, and coming to the camp not out

84

of necessity to gain my daughter's release, but wanting to
see men striving together for empire and power, or on the
other side for freedom and their own country.[104]

A sophistically trained *pepaideumenos* has to assure his audience
of the Epic scenario he was *not* enacting at that moment – this
was no embassy of Chryses the priest to brave the wrath of a
mere Agamemnon.

Sophists, then, lived in a world of books – or never too far
away from it. And society expected them to be living on the
closest terms with their authors, as guardians of a heritage. But
this was a heritage in use, which sophists could continually
transform, and by which they themselves could be transformed
in turn. Nor did it stop with literature: it was closely bound up
with the language in which much of that literature was written,
as we shall now see.

4

Atticism and antagonism

The Second Sophistic offers the scenario for a unique lawsuit, when the consonant Sigma brings an action before the Vowels against his fellow-consonant Tau, on thoroughly Thucydidean grounds:

> But this fellow Tau here – for I am unable to call him by a name worse than his own – who would not have been heard on his own, I swear by the gods, unless two upstanding and handsome fellows from among you, Alpha and Upsilon, had come to support him, this Tau, then, has had the nerve to do me injuries beyond any of the previous outrages; he has driven me from my ancestral nouns and verbs, and at the same time banished me at a stroke from conjunctions and prepositions, so that I can no longer bear his amazing expansionism.[1]

Not all of this is fantasy. It reflects the genuine consciousness of Attic forms that characterises the background of Imperial sophistic practice, and well beyond Athens itself. Nor were such matters confined to the realms of *jeu d'esprit*. When Philagrus of Cilicia was about to make his Athenian début he engaged in a heated verbal exchange with Herodes Atticus' star pupil Amphicles, but in the course of it let slip an ἔκφυλον ῥῆμα ('outlandish expression'). On being asked in what author it was found, he told his challenger 'in Philagrus'.[2] The visitor's quick thinking may have retrieved the situation, but in Philostratus' reminiscences he still stands condemned. But Herodes himself may have fared no better: he is quoted as describing a wheel-brake as τροχοπέδη, a word evidently unknown to Attic lexicography.[3] The two stories are symptomatic of an ethos.

86

THE PRESTIGE OF ATTIC

Imitation did not stop at authors or themes: concern for the classical past entailed the restoration not only of its literature but of its language,[4] and Aelius Aristides could accordingly include in his mammoth encomium of Athens a celebration of Attic dialect itself:

> For all the cities and all the races of mankind inclined towards you and your form of life, and your dialect . . . And through you the whole inhabited world has come to share a single tongue. One might see even the Heniochoi, both their herdsmen and the men who live off the sea, and all other peoples, city by city and land by land, holding fast to your dialect and trying to make for your land, like men unable to swim. As for you Lacedaemonians and all other Greeks, I say that every single day this testimony to the city's victory is borne out by you yourselves and especially by the most prominent among you; they have deserted their native dialects and would be ashamed to speak in their ancestral manner even among themselves in front of witnesses . . . not only does this dialect still flourish while all the rest have now almost vanished, but also one might say that all other dialects – to say nothing of those of the barbarians, but only of those of the Greeks themselves – were like mere childish lisping when compared with yours . . . Only this dialect is right for all national festivals, all assemblies and council chambers, and it is also adequate for all times and places and is equally suitable for them. For the first two requirements so to say of language, I mean dignity and charm, only this dialect possesses. In fact who would be able to approach the rigours of the full-scale rhetorical contest, and attain to its pitch, speed and energy, if he brought in some other dialect? Moreover all your poetry is of the highest quality and has reached the peak of its perfection. And if it is necessary to mention Homer's poetry, the city shares in its prestige, not only because his own city was a colony, but also because his own dialect clearly came from here [!][5]

Aristides' claims are to say the least tendentious, at worst transparently false; but there is no mistaking the prestige of

Atticism in the mid-second century, or the capacity of a sophist to make even linguistic purism the subject of a panegyric.

But how is this Atticism to be envisaged? To the unwieldy mass of statistics on the subject assembled by Wilhelm Schmid at the end of the nineteenth century there is now relatively little to add; but something can be offered towards interpreting the ethos of linguistic Atticism and its cultural effect. The object of the exercise (and 'exercise' it must largely have been) was to recreate the literary resources of the fifth and fourth centuries BC in Athens, and in effect to revive the language in which to conduct the kind of literary imitation we have seen. A moment's reflection will serve to show that this simply could not have been done. Not only is there the difficulty of consistently ridding oneself of the modern convenient language of everyday; but having chosen one's special literary period it is impossible to be rigid about defining it. If an English archaising movement were to decide that the language of Francis Bacon were to be the norm, would one be allowed poetic words from Shakespeare and Spenser – and barred from using anything only attested as late as Milton? No one writer encompasses the total linguistic experience of even a single moment in time, and an amalgam of several will produce a slightly distorting effect. To amalgamate the language of Thucydides, Plato and Demosthenes is already to produce one mosaic out of three. Add the usages of Herodotus and the poets from Homer to Theocritus and one will produce a literary mannerism that cannot correspond to 'Atticism' however defined. And the task will be even more difficult if we bear in mind the kind of resources at the disposal of sophistic writers.

A sophist's culture had to be learned from books, and the study of classics from Homer onwards necessarily gave each individual student a differently varied palette of archaising mannerisms. In addition there was a battery of grammatical guides in the form of lexica to guide aspiring purists to avoid the vulgarisms – as they must necessarily have been regarded – of either spoken *koinē* or even the literary language of the post-classical centuries. To write and, more to the point, to speak literary Attic of the fifth and fourth centuries BC in the Early Roman Empire would have been no easy assignment. The student would have had to affect various subtle stylistic choices, such as the doubling of Attic tau for Ionic sigma, the preserving of 'Attic' declension, or the frequent use of the dual, to say nothing of 'purist' declension of such troublesome words as *naus*; he would also have had to purge his language of deviant tendencies such as the lapse into easy alternative -o forms of -mi verbs preferred by the *koine* or on the other hand hypercorrect attempts at restoring the Middle Voice. He would have had to negotiate the syntax of subordinate moods more or less as practised by Plato, Thucydides and the orators; and maintain a correct vocabulary of words used by 'classical' authors (however defined) – preferably with chapter and verse, since sooner or later he would have been likely to be challenged or caught out. Such purification admits of degrees; sophistic writers were free to affect a looser, more relaxed style, especially in syntactical organisation, for narrative and *dialexis*, as opposed to the more demanding conditions entailed in, say, the strictest imitation of the Attic orators.

It is worthwhile to look at the fortunes of our flamboyant panegyrist Aristides when faced with the task of writing the language he was so keen to praise. Of all the Atticists we are able to test he turns out indeed to be the most conspicuously 'purist', and it is small wonder that Philostratus should hail him as τεχνικώτατος ('most skilful').[6] This is the man who knows that δεσμά and Οἰδίπουν are more Attic than δεσμοί and Οἰδίποδα;[7] and who is strict in his preference for -ει over -η forms in the second person present indicative passive or future middle.[8] But still *koine* forms creep in: δυσί for δυοῖν, or middle for passive deponent ἡμιλλήσατο for ἡμιλλήθη.[9] And Aristides uses some *koine* forms side by side with Attic counterparts, as in νεώς or σῶς, and indeed has frequent recourse to post-classical alternatives of the δεικνύω variety.[10] In syntax too there are mannerisms: on the one hand affectation of 'smart' Attic features: obsolete partitive constructions, noun ellipses and the like, and curious use of subordinate optatives in primary sequence.[11] It is rather in matters of vocabulary that Aristides comes across as most conservatively 'Attic': Schmid's (incomplete) statistics demonstrate that over half his wordstock comprises pure Attic prose words, while another fifth come from Homer and Tragedy, but had mostly been adopted already into Attic prose authors and thus 'legitimised'; others again are embedded in verse quotations. This leaves less than a tenth to be accounted for from post-classical prose, mostly technical terms and compounds, and less then one-fifteenth peculiar to Aristides as far as we can judge. His own contribution would appear to be the negative one of avoiding post-classical forms as far as possible.[12] At least in technical accuracy Aristides has probably achieved the best that could have been reasonably expected of someone living in another age.

But several issues have helped to make the perspective of linguistic revival more difficult to place in focus. Firstly a word of caution on the transmission of sophistic compositions. Philostratus occasionally lets slip that the written works of sophists had undergone revision: he notes that Heraclides of Lycia had undertaken a revised edition of Nicetes of Smyrna, and had miserably failed.[13] Presumably the object of the exercise had been to excise excessive Asianism, and the result had been to rob the corpus of its vigour and essential character; we can only guess. But it is more disconcerting when we find pupils of Dionysius of Miletus making more piecemeal revisions of speeches of the master by committing them to memory, then reciting them with alterations of their own.[14] The result one way or another would have been uncertainty over who could have been held as an authority for having said what. On the other hand, we hear of fruitful co-operation and consultation: the grammarian Phrynichus takes his dedicatee Cornelianus to task for using forms with only doubtful classical backing;[15] and he notes that a fellow-grammarian Secundus had missed a certain solecism in a work of Polemo.[16] This seems especially revealing, as it suggests some kind of editorial filtering of formally circulated works.

Moreover the labels 'Atticism' and 'Asianism' themselves, already bandied about in the age of Cicero and the subject of a treatise by Longinus' opponent, Caecilius of Calacte, have given rise to an otiose debate as far as the Early Empire is concerned.[17] Of course there were discernible stylistic poles, of rhetorical extravagance and bizarre effect with a view to inciting mass audiences with theatrical fervour, and these can be loosely labelled 'Asianist'; or a speaker could aim at a purist imitation of the most stylistically sober and reserved Athenian authors, such as Critias, and be called an Atticist.[18] But in practice most performers we can attempt to measure at all can be less easily characterised. Even Philostratus' characterisations tend to be personalised in a cryptic sort of way: a pupil might attend two teachers of different linguistic tendency and temperament, and emerge differently from either.[19]

A second kind of contrast can be seen as slightly artificial: that between 'scholarly' and 'popular' language. Reardon has treated at length the significance of an aberrant εἰ + optative with a main clause in the indicative, well attested in Second Sophistic authors but also down through the hierarchy of writers to the less literary papyri.[20] Is this a non-Attic provincialism,[21] or a confusion of several rare Attic refinements?[22] One story in Philostratus will demonstrate the difficulty of finding out. Herodes Atticus goes into the interior and finds a peasant isolated from the corruption of the city; his 'discovery' speaks the purest Attic.[23] Does Herodes admire such a product because his speech accords with his own notions of Attic, or does he value archaic provincialism on the assumption that Attic is what it must be?

The cause of purism went hand in hand with an industry for grammarians and lexicographers. In fact this had a long tradition behind it, going back to Hellenistic scholarship, but it is hard once more not to notice something of a climax in the second century AD, with two key lexica from which the hosts of others were to derive, those of Aelius Dionysius and Pausanias under Hadrian. The rest of the century also saw, in ascending order of strictness, the so-called *Antiatticista*, Pollux' *Onomasticon*, Phrynichus' *Eklogē* and *Sophistikē Proparaskeuē*, and Moeris' *Lexeis Attikai*. The possible variation and its attendant uncertainties afforded plenty of room for disputes for any *pepaideumenoi* so inclined. It was conjectured early in the twentieth century that the margin of disagreement between the lexica of Pollux and Phrynichus indicated a rivalry for an Athenian chair of rhetoric:[24] Phrynichus dedicated his Ἐκλογὴ Ἀττικῶν ῥημάτων καὶ ὀνομάτων to Cornelianus,[25] the *ab epistulis* of Commodus; Pollux, less 'purist' in his lexical choices and still less pure in his personal style, obtained the actual chair.[26] Such evidence remains circumstantial, but it is at least symptomatic.

Two instances in Lucian shed a more vivid light: some of the tension between individuals must reflect the sheer effort expended on meticulous *mimēsis*. Why bother going back to Plato, Demosthenes or Isocrates for models of stylistic sobriety when success can consist in plundering the arsenal of the declaimers of the previous generation?[27] For Lucian's audience this might well mean anyone from Nicetes of Smyrna to Pollux. The rogues' gallery of offenders stigmatised by Phrynichus himself includes several sophists known to Philostratus. But it has to be said that the grammarian does not always catch out his victims fairly, consistently or indeed accurately. Antiochus of Aegeae is taken to task for using the term μεγιστᾶνες for μέγα δυνά-μενοι;[28] an 'Attic' example in Menander is ruled inadmissible in his defence, but a usage of λιβανωτόν in Menander is recommended against λίβανον in Sophocles: any author is Attic enough when it suits.[29] Similarly Phrynichus censures Favorinus for using σύμπτωμα in the sense of συντυχία, while himself acknowledging an instance in Demosthenes.[30] Other cases can also be questioned. Polemo is criticised for the rare superlative κεφαλαιωδέστατον, doubtless because of the implied pleon-asm: 'chief' should not require a form 'chiefest'. None the less it had had this form since Hippocrates.[31] A few forms moreover have Homeric sanction, which renders them 'classical' though not Attic.[32] Only Favorinus has any serious number of offences recorded against him,[33] including at least a trickle of 'late' forms;[34] but at least three of Phrynichus' dogmatic alleg-ations against him are patently unfounded. The verb ὑστερίζω is constructed with the dative even in Thucydides,[35] while ἀπηρτίζω[36] and ἐξιδιάζομαι[37] are certainly classical in some sense, and it takes very hypercritical canons to exclude them.

At another extreme the movement fosters a curious searching after mannerism, and can draw corresponding ridicule. Lucian offers an illuminating conspectus of abuses, and Philostratus hints at corroboration for many of them.[38] At one extreme a sophist can succeed with the crowd simply by sprinkling a few Attic flosculi in an otherwise indifferent literary texture. A celebrated passage of Lucian refers directly to the temptation confronting extempore performers:

> Select from somewhere or other fifteen, or anyhow not more than twenty, Attic words, practise them carefully, and have them ready on the tip of your tongue: τὸ ἄττα καὶ κᾆτα καὶ μῶν καὶ ἀμηγέπη καὶ λῷστε καὶ τοιαῦτα ['sundry, eftsoons, prithee, in some wise, fair sir and suchlike']. In all your speeches, sprinkle over some of them as a relish. Don't bother whether the rest does not fit

them, but is unrelated and out of key . . . go after obscure,
bizarre vocabulary rarely employed by the ancients, and
heap them up as ready ammunition to shoot off at your
audience. The great majority will look to you in awe and
consider you phenomenal, and far above themselves in
your cultural attainments, if you should call scraping down
'destrigillation', sunbathing 'insolation', payment in advance 'hansel', and dawn 'crepuscule'. And sometimes you
yourself should make new fantastic words and lay down
that a good speaker be called 'fine-dictioned', a clever
person 'sage-minded', and a dancer 'handiwise'. If you
lapse into solecism or barbarism let sheer cheek be your
one and only remedy, and instantly have at the ready the
name of someone who is not alive now nor ever was, either
a poet or a historian, and say that he, a scholar, meticulous
in his expression, saw fit to talk like this.[39]

The other extreme, an overscrupulous concern for Attic forms
at all costs, was just as capable of giving offence, and Plutarch
protests at the preoccupation with presentation rather than
content which is fostered by stylistic purism:

But the man who right from the start does not keep rigidly
to the subject on hand, but thinks that the style has to be
pure Attic and austere, is like the man who refuses to drink
the antidote for a poison unless the vessel is fashioned
from Attic ware, or does not want to put on a cloak in
winter unless the wool shall be from Attic sheep; it is as if
he sits still and does nothing, as if clad only in a finespun
thin covering of Lysias' language. Indeed this sort of
disease has brought about much barrenness of thought
and lack of common sense, much idiocy and childish
babble in the schools, since young men do not keep their
eye on the life, actions or public conduct of the man who
practises philosophy; instead they set store by points of
diction and vocabulary, and good delivery, but what is
being delivered, whether useful or useless, whether necessary or fatuous and redundant, they neither know nor
care.[40]

But this is mild compared with the kind of ultra-purism satirised
by Athenaeus: a Cynic accuses Ulpian of wasting his time asking

κεῖται, οὐ κεῖται; ('does the word occur, or does it not?') and εὕρηται, οὐκ εὕρηται; ('is it said, or is it not said?')[41] The indictment continues:

> You are the one, are you not, who utters that new word *phaenōlēs* not yet accepted by usage – for I assure you, my friend, that *phaenōlēs* is actually masculine – when you say 'Leucus, my boy! Give me that ἄχρηστον [unused, i.e. new, or useless] cloak.'

The locution was perpetuated when the cloak was stolen and caused a further joke at the baths (why search for a 'worthless' cloak at all?).[42] And Ulpian's friend Pompeianus even misapplies ἄχρηστον to someone who has not succeeded in obtaining an oracle from Apollo and can therefore be said to be 'without consultation': 'inconsult'.[43]

Whatever position one took, the simple delight of catching people out was there. Polemo must have made a particularly public blunder when the statue-base of the bronze statue of Demosthenes he dedicated in honour of Asclepius at Pergamum was seen to contain the questionable adverbial phrase κατ' ὄναρ for the more idiomatic ὄναρ (and that in an inscription only four words long!).[44] One is reminded of the case in Gellius where Pompey has to resort to cowardly subterfuge to avoid committing himself between *consul tertius* and *consul tertio* on the inscription on his temple to Victory: even Cicero could not make up his mind on this distinction between 'thrice consul' and 'three times consul'.[45] Or Lucian elaborates on the case of the 'Pseudologist' who fastens on an apparently outlandish application of the word '*apophras*' to himself: to be called a 'nefand' is felt to be at least questionable, even if the word is acknowledged as correct in conjunction with *hēmera* ('an ominous day').[46] As it happens, Lucian is in fact right: there is 'authority', if such be needed, for calling a man an 'ominous' (though with the noun expressed, as in a case in Eupolis).[47] But Lucian ignores it either through genuine unawareness, or because his defence, a searing attack on his enemy, does not admit of such facile solutions. The case illustrates both the inflated pedantry and the genuine doubt of such situations: it is as if one cannot step out of doors in this neoclassical Athens without one's copy of Phrynichus to hand. And there are games to be played against those who are not armed with the same amount of chapter and verse.

LANGUAGE INTO STYLE: SOME SOPHISTIC SPECIMENS

Awareness of language was in the world of the sophists closely related to awareness of style itself. Philostratus furnishes no lack of evidence of the sensitivity of his subjects to matters of diction and rhythm, even if his often cryptic phraseology and not always clearly focused examples sometimes fail to tell us quite what he has in mind. It is difficult to generalise about sophistic rhythms, other than by stressing Philostratus' insistence on their import-ance for the listening public and the degree to which an individual performer could make a preferred rhythmic pattern his own.[48] One notes that Alexander Peloplaton was ridiculed by the parody Ἰωνίαι Λυδίαι Μαρσύαι μωρίαι, δότε προβ-λήματα, where there is a treble cretic ending, no doubt ridiculing the characteristically 'Asianist' double cretic.[49] It is worthwhile to note the preference of Atticising authors for conventionally Asianist clausulae, and also for the strings of short cola which displayed them most prominently. Aristides,[50] Favorinus[51] and Polemo[52] all belong to this category, though once more generalisation is difficult, since Aristides tends to cultivate 'Demosthenic' paragraph organisation in his speeches, yet aims at a much more dithyrambic style in his *Hymns*.[53] The examples collected by Norden from Philostratus' quotations of sophists go to show the very considerable variety of rhythms in a random sample,[54] a variety readily confirmed in the much greater surviving output of Aristides.[55] It should be emphasised that across this same sample the florid euphuism of Gorgias is less often in evidence than one might have expected:[56] sophists were able to conceal their art as well as flaunt or obtrude it.[57]

Another tendency which emerges with some consistency is the technique of using a relaxed, loose and informal manner, *apheleia*, for one's prologue and reserving a more deliberately structured and forceful manner for formal demonstration.[58] Indeed some writers can be generally characterised by their preference for the former (Lucian, Longus, Aelian, Philos-tratus), as for the kind of classical writers on whom such a style tended to be modelled (Lysias or Xenophon, for instance);[59] while a high-flying purist like Aristides will try to pitch his style and subject-matter as close to those of Demosthenes as he can. But such generalisation is often misleading, as sophists could cultivate versatility as a matter of course. The novelists Longus and Achilles Tatius are particularly conspicuous in the contrasts they could produce between deliberate simplicity in ordinary narrative and highly contrived purple passages for dramatic or emotional effects which set out to play every rhetorical trick in the book – anaphora, isocolon, antithesis and the rest.[60] Philostratus offers a reminder when discussing Dionysius of Miletus: this sophist counselled his pupils to restraint in the use of rhetorical special effects, but is able at a suitably emotive point to deliver something more as he consciously evokes the actual persona of Demosthenes with

ὦ Χαιρώνεια πονηρὸν χωρίον . . . ὦ αὐτομολήσασα πρὸς τοὺς βαρβάρους Βοιωτία. στενάξατε οἱ κατὰ γῆς ἥρωες, ἐγγὺς Πλαταιῶν νενικήμεθα.

O Chaeronea, place accursed . . . O deserter to the barbarians Boeotia. Lament, ye heroes beneath the earth: beside Plataea have we been vanquished![61]

Not every assessment in Philostratus is so balanced, however, so that many of his examples seem like no less mannered purple passages which may not represent the total effect of their surroundings: one sophist, Onomarchus of Andros, goes into raptures over a statue:

ὦ κάλλος ἔμψυχον ἐν ἀψύχῳ σώματι, τίς ἄρα σε δαιμόνων ἐδημιούργησεν; πειθώ τις ἢ χάρις ἢ αὐτὸς ὁ Ἔρως, ὁ τοῦ κάλλους πατήρ; ὡς πάντα σοι πρόσεστιν ἐν ἀληθείᾳ προσώπου στάσις χρόας ἄνθος βλέμματος κέντρον μειδίαμα κεχαρισμένον παρειῶν ἔρευθος ἀκοῆς ἴχνος. ἔχεις δὲ καὶ φωνὴν μέλλουσαν ἀεί. τάχα τι καὶ λαλεῖς, ἀλλ' ἐμοῦ μὴ παρόντος, ἀνέραστε καὶ βάσκανε, πρὸς πιστὸν ἐραστὴν ἄπιστε. οὐδενός μοι μετέδωκας ῥήματος· τοιγαροῦν τὴν φρικωδεστάτην ἅπασιν ἀεὶ τοῖς καλοῖς ἀρὰν ἐπὶ σοὶ θήσομαι· εὔχομαί σοι γηρᾶσαι.

Beauty ensouled in a soulless body, what daimon devised you? Some goddess of persuasion, some Grace, or Love himself, the father of beauty? For indeed you have everything – the expression of your face, the bloom of your complexion, the sharpness in your glance, the lovely smile, the blushing of your cheek, the sign that you are listening. You even have a voice always on the point of speech. Perhaps you will actually speak some day, but when I am not there, unloving and baleful woman, unfaithful to a faithful lover. You have allowed me not a word. And so I shall put the most fearsome curse for any thing of beauty on you: I pray for you to grow old.[62]

The phrase κάλλος ἔμψυχον may be an echo of Gorgias' own ἔμψυχοι τάφοι, now supplied with an antithetical phrase; one notes the alliteration of δαιμόνων, ἐδημιούργησεν and πάντα – πρόσεστιν – προσώπου; the long enumeration in asyndeton of στάσις – μειδίαμα, and the *figura etymologica* in πρὸς πιστὸν . . . ἄπιστε. But the whole *mise en scène* is striking in its grotesque way: a lover is smitten by a Pygmalion complex and pleads with the unresponsive statue in rhetoric as bizarrely contrived as it is futile. There can be no doubt that *Gorgieia schēmata*, turns of phrase and tricks of style mimicking the doyen of sophistic rhetoric, were a highly valued and legitimate part of the sophistic heritage: Libanius imports them even into *progymnasmata*. Here is the highly idiosyncratic opening of an *ēthopoiia* – it reflects on the madness of Ajax, who unsurprisingly recovers his rhetorical wits as well as his reason:

Ὦ δύο μεγίστων κακῶν, μανίας τε ἣν ἐμάνην καὶ σωφροσύνης ἣν νῦν σωφρονῶ. δρῶν μὲν οὐκ ᾔδειν ἅ ἔδρων, δράσας δὲ μανθάνω τὰ πεπραγμένα. ἀπέκτεινα μέν, ἀλλὰ βοσκήματα. ἀπέκτεινα μέν, ἀλλ᾽ ὡς οὐκ ἤθελον. καὶ ηὐφραινόμην μὲν ὡς δίκην λαμβάνων, ἐσφάττετο δὲ βοσκήματα, ζῶσι δὲ οἱ πονηρότατοι βασιλεῖς καὶ ὁ κατάρατος Ὀδυσσεύς.

Two of the direst woes must I face, the madness when I went mad, and the return to my senses now that I have returned to them. As I did the deed I did not know what I was doing, and having done it I now learn what I have done. I committed murder, but of grazing beasts; I committed murder, but against my will; and I was glad to be exacting retribution, and yet it was cattle I was slaughtering, while still alive are those worst of all kings and the accursed Odysseus!

But in contrast to this kind of bizarrerie the *apheleis* could strive no less artificially for a studiously casual effect:

Χρυσᾶ τῶν Ἡλιάδων τὰ δάκρυα. Φαέθοντι λόγος αὐτὰ
ῥεῖν· τοῦτον γὰρ παῖδα Ἡλίου γενόμενον ἐπιτολμῆσαι
τῷ πατρῴῳ δίφρῳ κατὰ ἔρωτα ἡνιοχήσεως καὶ μὴ κατασ-
χόντα τὴν ἡνίαν σφαλῆναι καὶ ἐν τῷ Ἠριδανῷ πεσεῖν –
ταῦτα τοῖς μὲν σοφοῖς πλεονεξία τις εἶναι δοκεῖ τοῦ
πυρώδους, ποιηταῖς δὲ καὶ ζωγράφοις ἵπποι καὶ ἅρμα –
καὶ συγχεῖται τὰ οὐράνια.

Golden are the tears of the daughters of Helios; the story
is that they are shed for Phaethon; for in his passion for
driving this son of Helios ventured to mount his father's
chariot, but because he did not keep a firm rein he came
to grief in the Eridanus – wise men interpret the story as
indicating a superabundance of the fiery element in
nature, but for poets and painters it is simply a chariot and
horses – and at his fall the heavens are confounded. [tr. A.
Fairbanks]

Golden the Heliads' tears. Story – shed for Phaethon. This
child of the sun said to have ventured on his father's
chariot through love of riding and not holding the reins to
have gone wrong and fallen in the Eridanus – this to the
wise some sort of excess of the fiery, to poets and painters
a horses and chariot – and the heavens are in chaos.[63]

Here only a ludicrously literal translation, the second, serves to
convey something of the contrived idiosyncrasy Philostratus
seeks to cultivate. Two telegraphic statements with main verbs
to be supplied are followed by a long infinitive construction
broken by a long and asymmetrically balanced parenthesis just
before the end – where we find a change to an indicative verb.
We might well be tempted to apply Russell's label 'arch naivety
and nursery syntax'; but here that is in a sense just what is
needed: Philostratus affects to be conducting a young schoolchild round an art gallery, and a relaxed, inconsequential
manner is adopted. On the contrary, however, an 'Atticist' style
could easily encompass massive paragraphs and ambitious use
of long periods: Aristides' often megalomaniac approach to
constructing vast edifices of neo-Attic verbiage serves all too
often to undermine his case.[64] But we cannot always judge every
effect from the printed page: Marcus is said to have shed tears
over a moment of pathos in the monody for Smyrna.[65]

Two examples will conclude this highly selective overhearing of sophists at work:

Περὶ μὲν οὖν τούτων, ἐὰν ταῦτά τις ἀντίλεγει, τοσαῦτά μοι λελέχθω. ἤδη δὲ λόγον ἤκουσα λεγόμενον, ὅ μοι σημεῖόν ἐστιν ἱκανόν, ὅτι βέλτιστ' ἐστιν, ἀγὼ λέγω τοῖς ἐναντιωσομένοις· εἴπερ ὁ λόγος ἐκεῖνος ἰσχυρότατός ἐστιν, οὐκ ἀξιόν ἔτι φοβηθῆναι. λέγουσι γὰρ ὡς κρείσσων Ἀρχέλαός ἐστι, καὶ τοιοῦτος ὢν πρόσοικος, μᾶλλον ἢ Πελοποννήσιοι· τοῦτον μὲν γάρ, εἰ βουλοίμεθα, δυναίμεθ' ἂν ἀμύνεσθαι, Πελοποννησίους δ' οὐκ ἄν· οὐκοῦν κρεῖσσον στασιάζειν πρὸς ἡμᾶς αὐτοὺς μᾶλλον ἢ δουλεύειν ἑτέροις. ἐγὼ δ' εἰ μὲν ἀνάγκην ἑώρων οὖσαν ἡμῖν ἐλέσθαι δυοῖν θάτερον, ἐβουλευσάμην ἂν ὁπότερον χρή μ' ἐλέσθαι.

On this subject, should anyone oppose my arguments, let all I have said suffice. Already I have heard enough said to indicate that the arguments I am putting to my opponents are best. If their argument offers the best course, there is no need to be afraid. For they say that Archelaus is more powerful, and also a neighbour, while the Peloponnesians are not. For should we wish, we could exact retribution from him, which we could not from the Peloponnesians; and so it is better to engage in a civil struggle against ourselves rather than be slaves to others. For my part if I saw that it was necessary to choose one of the two options, I should consider carefully which I had to choose . . .

Here we are either reading one of the 'real' Attic orators, or a piece of 'designer Attic' prose based on them. The paragraph is 'Attic' and unspectacular: it is perhaps more familiar to historians of the fifth century BC than to Second Sophistic scholars as an extract from the *peri Politeias* attributed to Herodes Atticus himself.[66] If his, it is an unspectacular but virtuoso display of integrity, a piece of *ersatz* Attic so consciously recreated as to be virtually indistinguishable from the genuine article, a supposedly late fifth-century original; if not, its attribution is most likely explained by its having been possessed by Herodes expressly for the purpose of imitation.[67]

One intriguing item still adds a touch of mystery to the linguistic map of the Early Empire: the fragmentary papyrus *P.Oxy* 410[68] purports to be an account of rhetorical proofs in

Doric: it seems to be an account of the methods of Corax and Tisias, the alleged founders of Greek rhetoric.[69] One might well ask why such a production should come to be copied at all in the second century AD, at a time when Doric would have been a very unlikely dialect indeed for literary criticism. We are given a clue by a passage of Lucian, who accuses the Pseudologist – the enemy who does not know the facts about *apophras* – of forging a *Teisiou technē*, a manual by Tisias which he then gulls a collector into buying at an exorbitant price.[70] It is perfectly plausible that Tisias should discuss his own methods in comparison with those of his master Corax – and as a Syracusan, he should indeed do so in Doric. Lucian's accusation testifies to the demand for such an item, as a prized relic of the teacher Tisias himself. Our surviving fragment may be the Pseudologist's very forgery – or the genuine article for which the Pseudologist produced his lucrative substitute.

Enough has been said to emphasise the importance for sophists of linguistic and stylistic awareness. Lines of demarcation are often difficult to draw conclusively, between Atticist and Asianist tendencies, or between styles for court, assembly and salon. What is not in doubt is the degree of conviction with which such distinctions could be pressed. Linguistic ability not only set sophists above the throng of their admirers: the ability to think in language intelligible to Pericles gave them a lifeline to their own past, and we must look next at how they inclined to view it.

5

Hellenic past, Graeco-Roman present

The sophist's expertise in traditional language and literature cannot be isolated from a wider view of the heritage of the past. We can catch a glimpse of one of Philostratus' own sophists enlarging the past of two cities from the following inscription in Argos:

> ... Publius Anteius Antiochus, having stayed in our city with decorum and generosity, has moreover displayed his virtue and his supreme cultural attainment, not least in his zealous disposition towards his native land, having demonstrated our ancient kinship with the people of Aegeae. He said that Perseus, son of Danae, en route to fight the Gorgons, arrived in Cilicia ... and there, bringing the statue of the ancestral goddess ... [rest fragmentary].[1]

The people of Argos express satisfaction at the researches of the famous sophist Antiochus of Aegeae, which emphasise the legendary links between themselves and his own home town. Sophists could bolster the pride of their own and kindred communities by underlining an ancient common heritage. But the view of the past available to them was complex and idiosyncratic, and we must look carefully at the different ways they were able to see it and the use they could make of it.

It is a familiarly accepted phenomenon that in the Early Empire the Greek world looked back with nostalgic self-awareness to the classical era,[2] and that it did so as a reaction against the political impotence of the present. Aspects of this picture are authentic enough, and the general diagnosis is at least partly true. But some modification is called for. It is useful in the first place to note the political realities of the Greek position as seen from the outside. A typical enough Roman perspective is found in Pliny the Younger's letter to Maximus:

> Consider carefully that you have been sent to the province of Achaea, to that very land of Greece that is real and pure, where civilisation and letters, and even agriculture are believed to have originated ... Have respect for their founders the gods and their sacred names, respect their ancient glory and the sheer antiquity which in men evokes respect, in cities reverence. Honour their great age, their mighty achievements and their traditions. Do not detract from anyone's dignity, freedom or even self-importance; always remember that this is the land which gave us rights and provided us with laws, not as conquered subjects, but at our own request.[3]

This tells us a great deal about Roman respect for the Greek past, but what Pliny goes on to say leaves us in no doubt that that was what it was: *recordare quid quaeque civitas fuerit, non ut despicias quod esse desierit* ('remember what each city was, not so as to despise what it is no longer').

It is no less instructive to note how a similar set of instructions might look from the Greek side, as when Plutarch issues advice to an aspiring *stratēgos* in the following terms:

> When you take up any office, you should not only adopt those reflections of which Pericles reminded himself as he took the cloak [of the *stratēgos*]: 'Pay attention, Pericles; you are ruling over Greeks, Athenian citizens,' but you must also say to yourself: 'Even as you rule you yourself are ruled, and you rule over a *polis* answerable to proconsuls, representatives of Caesar' ... You should arrange your cloak more carefully, and from the *stratēgia* cast your eye towards the speaker's platform and not have too much pride or trust in your crown, since you see the Roman boot just above your head.[4]

Plutarch too could be realistic, and he himself could speak from some experience. But one notes the reference to Pericles: every future bearer of the title *stratēgos* could expect to be aware of walking in his shoes.

Among sophistic authors themselves the past could look still more immediate: the sensation of keeping in direct touch with remote antiquity, and in particular its literary canon, is obvious and real, as in the following dream of Aristides:

> And once I dreamed that the poet Sophocles came to my house. When he arrived, he stood in front of the room where I happened to be living. And as he silently stood there his lips of their own accord hummed as sweetly as possible. His general appearance was that of a handsome old man. I was delighted to see him. I rose, welcomed him, and asked 'Where is your brother?' And he said 'Do I have a brother?' 'The famous Aeschylus,' I said, and at the same time I went outside with him, and when we seemed to be at the vestibule, one of our present-day sophists slipped and lay to the left a little way from the door.[5]

The dream seems incoherent enough in itself, yet its pre-occupations are scarcely in doubt. Aristides is the sort of figure that one of the most distinguished of the ancients will deign to seek out in person; but even that is hardly enough for him. As for the contemporary sophist also mentioned, it is not made clear whether his discomfiture is related to Aristides' privileged encounter or not; but we are entitled to suspect as much. One-upmanship is Aristides' way, as it was for so many of his professional colleagues. But above all, such a writer can live in the past and present simultaneously.

AGAMEMNON TO ALEXANDER: THE SHAPE OF THE PAST

Such an illusion was fostered by (for us) a sometimes oddly selective view of Greek History. The archaism of the Greek rhetorical repertoire is almost proverbial, with its cut-off point as early as Alexander the Great.[6] There are two reasons that might be felt to account for this, other than sentimental archaism or political nostalgia. One is that the literary system in the schools would have favoured the use of themes based on school authors: hence Homer, Herodotus, Thucydides, Plato, Xenophon, Demosthenes and Aeschines would have been likely to provide the overall framework of material, and that fact in itself would have encouraged the narrow chronological range of the repertoire. The other factor is the sheer conservatism of that same school system: themes laid down in the age of

Menander did not need to change or be further 'updated' for subsequent generations. To some extent the historically based declamation-themes were supplemented by more general themes which could apply in the present: themes related to magic, adultery, disinheritance and the like are just as much part of the stock in trade of the schools, and they have no time-limits; nor was it beyond the experience of sophists to become involved with disinheritance or even with charges of magic in real life.[7] A sophist could expect to move comfortably between ideal past and fantastic present.

None the less it has to be stressed that Alexander the Great did not always serve to mark the end of sophistic history. In Dio's Kingship orations he has another function, as a relevant exemplum for a Roman patron anxious to emulate the military paragon of world history.[8] And 'ending with Alexander' is not necessarily always to be explained in terms of archaism as such. Cephalion's *Histories*, written under Hadrian, reached as far as Alexander, having begun with Ninus and Semiramis and imitated Herodotus.[9] But such a timescale would be quite natural for a local history of the near East stopping at an obvious terminus. Moreover Arrian, Appian and Plutarch all write on the Hellenistic monarchies, and it is actually quite difficult to isolate much historical work which does stop with Alexander[10] without having recourse to special pleading.[11]

In dealing with periegetic literature, concerned with the touring of historical sites, it may also be tempting to overstate the pressures of the past. The very real difficulty of gathering information for a sustained history of the Greek world in whole or in part encouraged the facile formula of leaping from the legendary past to the present: Criton of Pieria wrote a *periēgēsis* of Syracuse and an account of its foundation.[12] And when Telephus of Pergamum writes a *periēgēsis* of Pergamum, a work on the temple of Augustus at Pergamum and five books on the Pergamene kings,[13] it is not clear whether this really gives us proof of 'archaising tendencies'; it may simply underline the fact that any historical topic will be rooted in the past.

It sometimes seems too easy to oversimplify the relationships of sentimental past and present. In a remarkable provision for a procession in honour of Artemis at Ephesus, C. Vibius Salutaris envisaged a procession which would acknowledge the city's Hellenic past and Roman present as well as its ancient history and earliest association with Artemis.[14] And on the literary plane we should note similar signs of inclusiveness. It is true that Pausanias has a natural penchant for the 'first beginnings' of everything, for the early history of a city-state or region; but that does not preclude his treating recent history when it is necessary to explain the present state of a monument, a city or an area. It may then seem difficult to account for his extended digression on the fortunes of Achaea, including the fall of Corinth, which in another context could well be labelled 'Hellenistic historiography', or for the detailed allusion to the depredations of Sulla or the rearrangements imposed by Augustus, which would properly qualify as recent history. But all these can be accounted for as relevant to the classical past as well: the Corinthian episode is once more symbolic of a last Greek freedom;[15] while Sulla's actions once more serve to evoke the sacrosanctity of a past he failed to respect.[16]

Arrian's work also needs careful interpretation as a paradigm of the Second Sophistic love of the past. While the *Anabasis Alexandri* is not without its tendentious touches, and Arrian may well have fancied himself a new Xenophon, the author's masterpiece can scarcely be written off as a specimen of mere sophistic historiography; and his various *parerga* such as the *Tactica*, *Acies contra Alanos* and *Cynegetica* are in turn quite firmly rooted in the present, notwithstanding their neat correspondence as counterparts to works of Xenophon himself.[17] Moreover Arrian's presentation of Epictetus' *Discourses* testifies to some suspicion of historical declamation: a philosopher's lecture should not be remembered for Xerxes or Thermopylae.[18]

Yet when all the reservations have been made, the general outlook remains essentially the same: we are left time and again with a sense of sifting, so that what is now seen as the Hellenistic dross is only accidentally included with the classical gold; and the emphasis is still overwhelmingly in the distant past, however one interprets it.

THE PROBLEM OF 'SOPHISTIC HISTORIOGRAPHY'

Given the preoccupation with the past, we should also examine the impact of the sophistic ethos on the production of history as such. Philostratus makes it clear enough that some sophists in his canon actually produced historical works, and he shows no signs of regarding such a trait as exceptional. Dio Chrysostom had produced a *Getica*,[19] Antipater of Hierapolis an account of the achievements of Septimius Severus;[20] while Antiochus of Aegeae produced a work of unspecified subject, perhaps including the investigations on the legendary founding of his homeland with which we began.[21] We have to ask in what way, if any, sophistic reflexes and habits of thought threaten to change the way history might be presented. There is not much likelihood that any historian will escape the charge of rhetorical adornment entirely: even when Thucydides had boasted that his work was to be 'a possession for all time, not a prize-essay for the present',[22] he had done so in phrases that Gorgias would have approved. But neither should any given author be assumed to be writing in a sophistic manner simply because he is contemporary with sophists.

At first sight the *oeuvre* of Dio Cassius [23] might promise a case of the abuse of sophistic historiography. Reardon cites the *Roman History* as evidence of *la manière d'écrire sophistique*: 'Everywhere there is drama, commonplace, descriptions (almost *ecphrases*), antitheses, and of course rhetorical displays: the battle of Pharsalia, an earthquake at Antioch, the Sullan proscriptions.'[24] The design is to create a certain emotional climate, not to reproduce particular facts. But to some extent at least this is the consequence of Dio's subject-matter: one does not write a history of the Second World War without Alamein, the concentration camps, the political manoeuvres among the Allies, or the speeches of Hitler and Churchill, against all of which similar objection might be raised. Much depends on sense of proportion, and on the whole Dio is not specially prone to offend, though it is difficult to evaluate crucial stretches where we are reliant on epitome. The one long uninterrupted stretch of the original Dio in the later stages of the *Roman History* offers a narrative from the last of Caracalla through Macrinus to well into the reign of Elagabalus. Given the sensational nature of events at court, with coup followed by counter-coup and the elevation of a bizarre religious pretender, matters could scarcely be made to appear other than melodramatic. Moreover there is a sense in which at least some of the faults can be traced back to mannerisms of Thucydides, of which Dio was undeniably an imitator; and much of the fault lies with rhetoric as such rather than with its more flagrant overindulgence. Hence for example the telescoping of Ciceronian speeches from different occasions and circumstances into a discussion with an unknown Philiscus, intended to encapsulate an ethos rather than act as a historical chronicle;[25] or the use of the infamous speech of Maecenas to embody Dio's reflections on the problems of Empire as they appeared to a courtier of the third century rather than the age of Augustus himself.[26]

Herodian is often felt to be a still more extreme case than Dio.[27] One might reasonably argue that even his choice of subject-matter betrays a taste for the self-indulgently sensational: the period from Marcus' death to Pupienus and Balbinus presents a whole series of coup and counter-coup, palace intrigue and the like, so that extreme dramatic situations at least in the upper echelons of government are difficult to avoid. But in choosing events of his own lifetime, and in writing a βασιλικὴ ἱστορία, Herodian is already committing himself: the historian must not be blamed if events are not to his taste. Nor must we be content to list the items covered by such an author and simply identify them as rhetorical exercises: if Herodian has to mention a battle, a detailed description of it will of course produce 'sophistic history'. But anything that resembles the texture of Sallust or even Tacitus should scarcely deserve to be so described.

On the whole Herodian gets by without too obvious a recourse to the world of declamation, though one suspects that the intended division of Empire between Geta and Caracalla was just too good to miss: there is careful *syncrisis* of the Empire around the Propontis, rendered more momentous by the observation: 'For such, they said, was the division of continents, which the gods had foreseen by their creation of the Propontis that flowed between them.'[28] But once the division is agreed, Julia Domna is made to invite her two sons to divide her as well:

> But how would you divide your mother? And how could I have my miserable body partitioned and cut up between the two of you? Kill me first, divide me, and each bury your part of me in his own territory. That way I could be divided between you together with the land and sea.[29]

Not for nothing, it seems, was the Empress a companion and correspondent of the sophistically inclined Philostratus.

It is in Lucian's pamphlet *de conscribenda historia* that we can most clearly see at least the potential abuse that threatens to emerge from epideictic tastes. Lucian laughs – or purports to laugh – at those who attempt to reshape history in the mould and manner of the past, by importing either literary phraseology or subject-matter into accounts of contemporary events.[30] Such mannerisms include the adapting of the opening sentence of Thucydides, the relocation of the Corcyrean speech in Armenia and the mishandling of the plague at Nisibis, simply stripped of its original Athenian décor.[31] In addition his victims allow incongruities when the material is given Latin names (though Lucian has it both ways and complains of hypercorrection of Latin words into Greek as well).[32] Or they import rhetorical *syncrisis* by comparing the Persian King to Thersites and the Roman general to Achilles.[33] Such décor is no less heinous than the misshaping of history by rhetorical ornament: irrelevant digression, particularly *ecphrasis*, is perpetrated,[34] as is wholesale panegyric,[35] to say nothing of patriotic prophecy.[36] If we cannot always be sure that Lucian's own examples are genuine,[37] there is not likely to be much doubt that the overall situation he describes was real enough. The way was open for rhetoricians and others to turn their hand to history with whatever indulgence they might please.

The worst fears evoked in Lucian's treatise come close to fruition in an almost contemporary work by Fronto, the *Principia Historiae*,[38] in which the former tutor of the co-Emperors Marcus and Verus describes the state of play when Verus entered the Parthian war as follows:

In fact the most demoralised of all, however, were the Syrian contingent; they were mutinous, undisciplined, seldom with their own units, given to wandering in front of their set positions, straggling about like scouts, drunk from one midday to the next, not practised in bearing their arms, and, as from aversion to hard work they shed one item of kit after another, they ended up half-naked like skirmishers and slingers. Apart from this sort of disgraceful situation, their morale had been so lowered by reverses that they turned their tail at the first sight of Parthians and heard the trumpet as if it were the signal for retreat. Such great deterioration in military discipline

Lucius put a stop to as the case demanded, and set up his own energy as a soldier as an example. He himself would march in column, riding no oftener than he wore himself out on foot; he bore the blazing sun as one takes a good day; the dust clouds he took as if they were a mist.[39]

This would be rather more credible if Verus had not written to Fronto in the following terms:

One thing I want not of course to point out to you – since I was the pupil and you were my master – but to suggest for consideration: you will spend a long time on the causes and opening stages of the war, and also on our reverses during my own absence. You will come to my part slowly. Besides, I think it necessary to make very clear how superior the Parthian position was before my arrival, so that it becomes clear how much I myself achieved. So whether you should give only a rapid summary of all that, as Thucydides did in his narration of the Fifty Years' War, or actually go into the subject in a little more detail but avoid the same degree of detail as you would give to my subsequent role, that you yourself will decide.[40]

Fronto has achieved what Plato had in effect foreseen with the first emergence of sophistic training: the artistic adornment of a calculated perversion of the truth.

But it is only at the very end of the fourth century that we can recognise the texture of a history as 'sophistic' – and hence as perverted – as all Lucian's caricatures put together. The continuation of Dexippus' chronicle by Eunapius of Sardis[41] panders to the worst excesses of sophistic taste.[42] The author himself is vain, ostentatiously ignorant and almost unsufferably discursive. He seems to regard it as a great improvement on Dexippus to disregard the annalistic method ('For what contribution can dates make to the wisdom of Socrates or the sagacity of Themistocles? Were these men outstanding only during the summer?')[43] He is prepared to fall back on the rhetorician's facile and anti-intellectual acceptance of ignorance ('When experts disagree . . .'):

For who is so celebrated among all readers and writers as Lycurgus the Lacedaemonian? The god's testimony to him is on everyone's lips, giving him the title divine for his lawgiving. Yet who, when he mentions these matters, agrees with anyone else over the dates of that legislation?[44]

He not unsurprisingly concludes that 'accuracy in recording seasons and days is appropriate for the managers and accountant of the rich, and naturally enough those who gape at the heavens and all the rest who obviously have to do with numbering.'[45] Arguments over historical method or historical fashion one might be tempted to put down simply to indifferent historical judgement. But there must be a strong suspicion that in Eunapius' eyes the sophist is just too elevated to have to care.

In more clearly stylistic matters the author can be all too easily seduced by the temptations of declamatory paradox.[46] Of Constantius' moves against Julian he can say:

> Seeing only his own interest, he lent his power to the enemy, taking what was his own as foreign, if it were to be saved along with his Caesar, and what was foreign as his own, provided it should destroy his Caesar together with himself. So that the war turned into a hidden sore and turned the natural enemy into an ally.[46]

After such a sequence, it is unconvincing when he protests against a battle of Julian's that 'we are setting up and shaping our account not for the purpose of childish and sophistic competition but to attain historical accuracy.'[47] To this end he proposes to skip the details of the battle itself, as well he might; he has protested too much.

Moreover it is disconcerting to find even philosophical mysticism invading the historian's repertoire:

> And just as the Pythagoreans say, when a monad is moved towards a dyad and loses its property as a single number and divides up and multiplies, so when Charietto allied Cercio with himself their activities increased and the number of their allies grew in proportion to their achievements'.[48]

And it is a good deal more ominous still that he should note the recurrence of the same number seven as that of the conspirators of the magi against Darius, and of Arsakes against the Macedonians:[49] one suspects that astral determinism is just round the corner. A *sententia* like οὐ γὰρ ἐν τοῖς μετὰ τέχνης ἀπαντᾷ τὸ παράλογον τῆς τύχης ('For those with skill are not met with unforeseen fortune')[50] sounds again ominously like a reference to divination.[51] Julian is attributed with foreseeing the Scythian disturbance 'either as a result of consulting the gods or by using his power of reason'.[52] The alliance of sophistic rhetoric and superstition is a lethal one.

There is also a texture of banal moralising:

> It seems, besides, that mankind is prone to envy. The soldiers, not having the wherewithal to give due praise to what was being done, 'judged the Achaeans' as they say 'from the tower', each wishing to seem a man of strategy and extraordinary wisdom; and they found evidence to support their foolishness.[53]

Moreover, unconcealed loyalty to Julian makes for a self-indulgently panegyrical style:

> From this point my narrative is concerned with the man who was its goal from the start, and as if feeling some kind of love for him, I am compelled to devote myself to his achievements, though naturally I never saw him or had personal experience of him; for the writer of this history was no more than a child when he was Emperor. But a wonderful and inexorable motivation to love are the common feeling of all mankind for him and the universal reputation he commands.[54]

The fact that he accepts a memorandum from Oribasius of Pergamum, some sort of iatrosophist credited by Eunapius elsewhere with foretelling and contriving Julian's accession, does not inspire confidence either.[55]

Eunapius' concern for the dramatic and pathetic situation is well underlined by a dramatic metaphor:

> Just as in plays, whenever the complications of the plot come to an impossible impasse, the so-called *deus ex machina* is dragged into the midst of things, finishing everything off and manipulating the action to a clearer and more judicious conclusion, so too Julian . . .[56]

The situation itself could have come straight out of a *meletē*: Julian demands hostages from the Chamavi, including the chief's son, whom he already holds. The chief makes a pathetic expostulation, not without its share of *sententiae*: this hostage has already been killed, he supposes by Julian, perhaps unknowingly. Julian himself is then attributed with a speech; it is even more effective to make the almost divine Julian a figure above the drama of life.

None the less Eunapius is capable of achieving some degree of literary effect, as when he describes the bribery which goes on in the time of Pulcheria over the acquisition of provincial governorships:

> Large and small provinces were becoming openly offered to all on the public stalls like any other goods for sale. Anyone who wanted to wrong the Hellespont would buy it and it was his, while someone else did the same for Macedonia or Thrace, or wherever anyone had a craving towards crime or against enemies. It was possible to buy a licence for one's own wickedness with a view to oppressing the population of provinces either individually or collectively; for the vicar or consul could do the latter. And no-one was afraid of the severe statutes which prescribed penalties for judges who took bribes, for they had died with the laws; but the laws themselves were not only, as the Scythian Anacharsis says, weaker and lighter than spiders' webs, but more ready than any dust to be swirled away and scattered. All the households were made penniless by this trick [of extortion], and it was all too easy to see previous governors subjected to confiscations – as the comic poet says: 'the possessions of a former magistrate are in the public domain' (whoever does not know which comic poet is not even fit to read this history) ... The man named Hawk [*Hierax*] was seized, as by an eagle, by the man who had outbid him in bribery, and was now like the nightingale in Hesiod, not able to compete against his superior. And the eagle for his part was no different from the nightingale except insofar as he ended up like the jackdaw of the fable, stripped of his own feathers as if they were someone else's.[57]

At first it is tempting to suggest that Eunapius is simply overloading the texture of historical narrative with literary plunder. But in fact the similes are well chosen, and viewed as satire in the manner of Lucian or Ammianus Marcellinus the piece has an undoubted effectiveness, though Eunapius' puerile pomposity will always out. Yet whatever one may be tempted to applaud, it is difficult to make too firm a judgement on the strength of such fragmentary material. And it is difficult to escape the verdict that overall Eunapius' sophistic repertoire has been too indiscriminately applied to his subject-matter, and that sophistic attitudes and reflexes have served an indifferent historian ill.

Closely linked with questions of 'sophistic' history is the question of the status of Arrian in the second century as a historian of Alexander the Great.[58] That he can he characterised as a child of a sophistic age is a simple historical fact;[59] but how far has he avoided and how far has he succumbed to its influence? Here the balance of evidence seems quite clearly to tend in the opposite direction, and Arrian's press has not been altogether fair to him. The fact that he should aspire to be Alexander's Homer and very clearly emerges as his Xenophon establishes his high literary ambitions, but does not necessarily compromise his integrity.[60] Nor does the fact that he produces a virtual panegyric of Alexander at the end of book 7.[61] A.B. Bosworth draws attention to shortcoming and idiosyncrasy here: the peroration does not totally accord with Arrian's presentation of Alexander in the body of the text, in particular with his presentation of Alexander's drinking in the episode of Clitus' death; there is sophistic manoeuvring in the matter of Alexander's vices, which are ingeniously and artificially minimised and accord ill with the tone and tradition of panegyric; while the general style has some touches of Thucydides, and more of Xenophon.[62] But the material can be viewed in a rather different way. It is both rhetorical good manners and consistent with historical common sense to weigh up the virtues and faults of Alexander. If the results look uneasy, that is again an honest reflection of the subject-matter; even the most superlative admiration of Alexander cannot be allowed to produce a whitewash. Nor is it surprising if a historian should distance himself a little in a very modest number of final paragraphs from the detailed assessment of his text. If Arrian's verdict is less than ideal appraisal, it is no worse than just that.

One rhetorical highlight of the *Anabasis* is the debate at the river Hyphasis as to whether Alexander should be content, or whether he should advance to the Ocean.[63] The sources in general do suggest a debate on the subject; Bosworth argues that Arrian has provided his own rhetorical embellishment.[64] While his arguments are neither conclusive nor overwhelming, it would be surprising if any pagan historian had resisted the temptation to reconstruct a *controversia* at this point; for Bosworth nothing impedes the suggestion that he did so. But here again the evidence of such a subject in the Elder Seneca can be used to suggest an opposite position from Bosworth's: just how little Arrian has been tempted by the meretricious blandishments of a school exercise, such as ὑγίαινε γῆ, ὑγίαινε ἥλιε· Μακεδόνες ἄρα Χάος εἰσᾴσσουσι ('Farewell, earth, farewell, sun; the Macedonians, then, are darting off to Chaos!')[65] And the mere inclusion of anachronistic geography is not necessarily an indictment of the integrity of Arrian: it is simply an attestation of literary propriety, to which writers on India were particularly vulnerable.[66]

Eunapius and Arrian, then, illustrate two extremes: a determined and educated enthusiast of Alexander cannot avoid rhetoric as such, nor can he be exempted from responsibility for questionable judgements; but Arrian does not lurch from one purple passage to the next with a pompous running commentary on his own superiority, as a sophistically intoxicated historian would have done when faced with such tempting material. Nor, on the other hand, are sophistic materials, techniques and attitudes of mind necessarily fatal to historiography: it is the clear over indulgence of the incompetent that is likely to stifle the historian's subject-matter.

SOME SOPHISTIC SET-PIECES

Sophists did not have to attempt formal history as such in order to keep their tryst with the past. How precisely a sophistic figure could 'perform' himself into history is well shown by the two Sicilian speeches of Aelius Aristides.[67] The historical situation envisaged is quite specific: the point when the Athenians have received the report of Nicias to the effect that either substantial reinforcements are required to prosecute the Sicilian campaign effectively, or a withdrawal is necessary at once.[68] Thucydides does not indicate the debate which must have ensued at this critical point (there being little but an update required since he had already given the reasons for sending the expedition in the first place). Aristides in effect supplies it, paying respect to the arguments of Nicias and Alcibiades in the initial debate;[69] Aristides is able to move freely through scattered hints in Thucydides, as on the subject of whether the Syracusans will attack Athens.[70] There is also an element contributed by a second speaker, implying that Nicias was not sincere in proposing large reinforcements – a properly sophistic reflex in viewing the situation – but both speakers in effect refuse to incriminate Nicias.[71] Some more sophistic material is deployed discreetly: 'If on learning of the transformation of Athos or the Hellespont they had at once been terror-struck as on seeing a tragedy . . .'[72] What is perhaps most conspicuous is that Aristides has chosen this point for his debate, as opposed to the end of the expedition, with its obvious opportunities for *ecphrasis* and pathos (one thinks of Herodes' use of it in his declamation before Alexander Peloplaton). Instead reasoned argument with precise historical detail is called for, and Aristides is able to supply it. In effect we seem to have an attempt to recast Thucydides as Demosthenes.

But not all sophistic writing is concerned with straightforward historical recreation of this kind. A good example of the way a historical theme could receive creative and entertaining rhetorical treatment is suggested by Plutarch's showpiece *De Fortuna sive de Virtute Alexandri*:[73] did Alexander owe his success to luck or to his own qualities and efforts? At once the art of ornamental personification is established. Tyche (Fortune) claims Alexander's successes as her own. Alexander is imagined to reply: 'She can claim Darius and Sardanapalus, kings despite their background or proclivities.'[74] The speech becomes a bravado declamation in the first person, replete with that characteristic rhetoricians' purple passage, the catalogue of wounds:

> And my body bears many signs of Fortune as an opponent, not an ally. First, in Illyria, I was wounded on the head by a stone and on the neck with a club. Then at Granicus I had my hand cut open by a barbarian dagger, at Issus my thigh was slit by a sword . . . If Ptolemy had not held his shield over me . . . that nameless barbarian village would have had to be the tomb of Alexander[75].

Plutarch then reverts to the historical situation in the larger sense when he recites the instability at Alexander's accession and the odds against him.[76] We then have the favourite topic of Alexander as the educated prince, not simply equipped by Aristotle and also perhaps by Homer for his leisure hours, but more importantly by philosophic treatises. Plutarch then comes close to the temptation to make Alexander one of those august philosophers of the kind who have written nothing.[77] The real stretch comes when Plato and Socrates are presented as philosophers who have only taken a few pupils, and in their own language; whereas Alexander has taught civilisation in one form or another to so many barbarian peoples. The catalogue of achievements has a specious flavour:

> He trained the Hyrcanians to marry, and taught the Arachosians to farm, and persuaded the Sogdians to support their parents, and not to kill them, and the Persians to respect their mothers and not to marry them. What wonderful philosophy, that causes the Indians to worship Greek gods, and the Scythians to bury their dead, not to eat them![78]

Alexander establishes more than seventy real cities, as against Plato's austere and unrealistic ideal state.[79] But it is only when Plutarch celebrates Alexander's marriage of Persians, Macedonians and Greeks that the sophist in him really comes out:

> For I should have cried in rapture, 'O barbarous Xerxes, such an idiot to spend so much effort in vain on the bridge over the Hellespont; here is how sensible kings join Asia to Europe; not by wood or rafts, not by lifeless and unfeeling fastenings, but by lawful love and modest marriages and the sharing of children do they join the nations together.'[80]

Plutarch now elaborates on the topic of Alexander's adoption of Persian dress, a matter normally anathema to Greek eyes: Persian dress is more modest than Median, and it is appropriate as being in accordance with the custom of the country. And the prince's dicta are those 'of Socrates, Plato, or Pythagoras' – if you take away from what Alexander says of his diadem, his ally Ammon, and his noble lineage! These sayings give Plutarch the cue for one of his favourite means of instruction, a parade of *chreiae*, proving Alexander's modesty and self-restraint.[81] It is against such a specious ensemble that Arrian emerges revindicated. But it is not the last we shall see of the sophistic Alexander.

A further result of the fusion of sophistic interests is the pseudo-Lucianic *Encomium of Demosthenes*.[82] A preliminary dialogue between one Thersagoras and an unnamed interlocutor establishes the former as an encomiast celebrating the birthday of Homer.[83] This leads to a curious *syncrisis* between Homer and Demosthenes, with a certain degree of banter on the methods of encomiasts;[84] but almost half the dialogue is then spent on the reading out of an alleged Macedonian memoir of the circumstances of Demosthenes' death, as he refuses to fall into Antipater's hands.[85] This entails a multi-layered dialogue: at one stage we have Philip talking to Parmenio about his opinion of Demosthenes; this is then reported by Antipater to Archias,[86] by way of establishing how revered an opponent Philip regards Demosthenes as having been. The dialogue ends without a return to the enclosing frame: all attention is focused on the famous last words of the orator, who has taken poison to avoid falling into Antipater's hands.[87]

This historical confection is by no means an artistic success, but we must ask why it should have been written at all. The subject-matter is reminiscent of the kind of *controversia* literature in Latin round such a theme as 'Cicero debates whether to surrender his books to Antony in exchange for his life';[88] and similar historical licence has been taken. The subject comes at a crucial point in the repertoire of the Sophistic, as almost the last event allowable in the 'free' history of classical Greece. Not without effect does Archias fill out the climax: the dying Demosthenes is made to say, '"Come, take this to Antipater, but Demosthenes you will not take, no, by those who . . ."' and I thought he was about to add "who fell at Marathon".'[89] The words are duly taken up in a final tribute from Antipater himself: the ashes of Demosthenes will be an even nobler offering to Athens than those who fell at Marathon.

But the form of the piece is more interesting than its predictable elements. The Macedonian memoir seems to set out to be almost a tragic messenger speech in prose – set out in Platonic dialogue, with the naive encomiastic and sophistic reflexes duly smiled upon, true to Platonic tradition, before being superseded by the serious presentation of the last moment of the last

117

of the Greeks. The author has produced a novel and perhaps not altogether convincing hybrid; but the transition from literary banter to serious dramatic scene of political martyrdom, and the choice of cut-off point, are significant. This was a key moment in the sophistic perception of Greek history, and it is prepared with a carefully calculated solemnity.

But not all historical diversions are for pure entertainment; we have an unusual example of 'rhetoric and history' in action in Fronto's letter to Marcus *de bello Parthico*.[90] This might be termed a *consolatio* for the Roman defeat at Elegeia in 162. First there is a quotation on 'defence of Empire' from Ennius' *Telamon*, on his sons' being exposed to death in the Trojan War; this is imagined, in the mouth of Mars, as applicable to the Romans. Fronto then includes a brief round-up of Roman defeats to which it would have applied.[91] Next comes a transition to humiliations in recent times, beginning with Trajan's Dacian campaign; then, after a fragmentary passage, two *sententiae* on fortune: *haudquaquam utile est homini nato res prosperas perpetuo invenire: fortunae variae magis tutae* ('it is by no means useful to a mortal to find prosperity at all times; shifting fortunes are safer').[92] This is the cue for an extended paraphrase of Herodotus, in the story of Polycrates – excessive prosperity comes to a bad end – after which something of a *non sequitur*. 'but hope for victory soon, for Rome in her affairs has always experienced frequent changes of fortune'.[93] Then there is a forced pun: who does not know that the Empire has been obtained *non minus cadendo quam caedendo* – 'by falling no less than felling' (Haines).[94] After more changes of fortune (submission of those who passed under the yoke, revenge after Cannae), Marcus is to remember that Julius Caesar wrote his *de Analogia* under such circumstances: 'amid the flying missiles he discussed the declension of nouns; he talked about the aspiration of words and their principles of classification amid the calls of bugles and trumpets.' Why should Marcus not find time *inter alia* for syllogisms?[95] Then comes praise of the *pro lege Manilia*: Cicero had secured Pompey's title 'The Great'.[96] The speech contains 'many chapters of reflection suited to advising you in your present state, about the choice of generals, interests of allies, protection of provinces, discipline of soldiers, requisite qualifications for commanders on and off the field . . .'[97]

Fronto has been little greater use, one suspects, than an

armchair compiler of *stratēgēmata* would have been. A handful of Livy, a glance at recent history, a story from Herodotus and 'know your Cicero'. Yet within the cultural parameters available, there is no need to assume that Marcus would have found such advice useless: the conjunction of eloquence and military competence had been unquestioned since Nestor. Marcus might have been as reassured by this specious farrago as we should be depressed.

ATHENS AND ROME: SOME SOPHISTIC PERSPECTIVES

We are seldom left in any doubt that Philostratus regards Sophistic as a Greek phenomenon; and the term 'Hellenes' can be regarded as a virtual synonymn for sophists' students. But the fact of a Roman Empire had still to be faced, and a sophist's versatility could expect to be equal to the task: one finds Aristides speaking as expansively about Rome as about Athens, yet the arguments are necessarily different. How could a Greek sophist respond to the fact of Roman intrusion into Greek history? Much of the background of Graeco-Roman relations is known and understood:[98] not resistance to the fact of Roman political domination, but a sophistic way, or set of ways, to come to terms with it; and indeed to obfuscate or talk it away.

Several factors helped the double-think by which educated Greeks could accommodate themselves to the Empire. The first was the fact that the nature of the principate itself imposed something for their Roman conquerors to come to terms with as well:[99] autocracy was something relatively new to the Roman aristocracy after so many centuries of the Republic. Again, Greece could look back to its subjugation under Philip and Alexander, and make a very great virtue of necessity: it had been the Macedonians, not the Romans, who had first united them. Secondly, the accident that Rome was a city rather than a people or a country in the first instance meant that it was a city among cities; and any such city would always leave open the contest for primacy and the desire to emulate.[100]

There is no doubt of what we might term the sentimental supremacy of Athens in the eyes of sophists. Lucian is even able to laugh at the ridiculous desiderative verb Ἀθηνιῶ ('I long for Athens'); yet it suits the times. And the author of the *Demosthenis*

Encomium illustrates the raptures into which this cultural capital could still send its potential panegyrists:

> But if I could seize hold of Athens, I would use my poetic licence to bring in as well the love-affairs and lawsuits of the gods and the times they spent there, their benefactions and the facts about Eleusis. And by the time her laws, her law-courts, her festivals, her Piraeus, her colonies and her war-memorials for victories by sea and land are brought in as well, 'no-one at all could do justice to them in speech', to quote Demosthenes. Indeed, I'd have a terrific overflow in any encomium, since it is within the rules for eulogies to increase the prestige of the people they are praising by speaking of their countries.[101]

Nor was such material confined to the classical past. The Emperor Hadrian in particular had lavished his personal attentions and his patronage on the city before the dramatic and controversial contributions of Herodes Atticus. Panegyrists could stretch the obvious facts of history at least enough to acknowledge a privileged position for Athens in the eyes of Rome:

> The present Empire over land and sea – and may it be immortal – does not refuse to adorn Athens in the role of teacher and foster-father, but so great is the superiority of its honours that now the city acts differently only insofar as it does not engage in making policies for itself [ἡ πόλις πράττει τὰ νῦν ὅσον οὐ πραγματεύεται].[102]

Under a scheme of history that sees Rome as fifth of five empires (Assyria, Media, Persia, Macedonia, Rome), Athens still has its place:

> Under the Empire that is best and greatest in all respects, the present one, it enjoys seniority [τὰ πρεσβεῖα] over the whole Greek race, and has done so well that no-one would readily long for its ancient state instead of the present one.[103]

Indeed Athens has just been credited with 'all-out' conquest of Persia as well as having been the last to hold out under Macedonia, the Fourth Empire (having begun under the First, the Assyrian, and grown great under the Second, the Median).

In general emperors could endorse these whims of Aristides.

Rather later than these words were written, when Marcus wrote to the city in 174/175, he evinced almost pedantic concern for the correct regulation of its ancient offices – even if he had to use 'Trojan' enemies of his friend Herodes to enforce his constitutional arrangements in the hope of assuaging Athenian complaints against the latter's highhanded behaviour.

None the less Athens could scarcely expect to have everything its own way. Although Philostratus presents the Second Sophistic quite unashamedly from an Athenian point of view, fierce local pride in the great centres of Asia Minor provided a motive energy which sophists did well to harness. Lest it be used as a defence that even the Athenians recycle their statues, as the Rhodians do, Dio Chrysostom quotes recent criticism of the degeneracy of Athens: the Athenians had given the title Olympian to 'some Phoenician not from Tyre or Sidon, but from a mere village or from the interior, not to mention that he has his arms depilated and wears stays';[104] they had honoured a facile poet with a bronze statue, and put it up next to the statue of Menander.[105] And a statue was allegedly given to Nicanor in exchange for the purchase of Salamis; while the Athenians allow gladiatorial shows in the theatre of Dionysus where they erect the god's own statue.[106]

Yet the rhetorical sleights of hand that could be used to favour Athens could be manipulated just as readily in favour of Rome. The key image in Plutarch's *de Fortuna Romanorum*[107] is a patent reworking of that sophistic standby the *Allegory of Prodicus*. This time it is Fortune and Virtue who are seen as competitors in the advancement of Rome:

Virtue treads gently, and looks intently; yet the flush of ambition gives her expression some indication of the coming contest. She walks well behind Fortune, who is in a hurry; bringing her along and guarding her are a mob of . . . men with fronts spattered with wounds, dripping a mixture of blood and sweat, tramp[ing] over battered spoils. Do you want us to ask who on earth these men are? They say they are the Fabricii, the Camilli, the Decii . . . I see also Gaius Marius angry with Fortune, and there Mucius Scaevola displays his burning hand and shouts out; 'Would you thank Fortune for this too?' And Marcus Horatius, the hero of the battle of the river, weighed down by Etruscan shafts and displaying his limping thigh, cries out from the depth of the swirling waters, 'So am I also to be maimed at Fortune's whim?'[108]

In spite of such effusions it can still be remarked how selective Greek littérateurs can be in the treatment of things Roman. It so happens that Philostratus singles out Aelian as a Hellenophile sophist who had never left Italy; such a man's use of traditionally Roman material can be noted with interest. He can mention Aeneas in an anecdote blatantly in favour of the Greeks: they took pity on the Trojans and allowed each free man to take one possession. Aeneas chose his ancestral gods; the Greeks, delighted at his piety, allowed him to take one more thing, his father; so in turn they gave him everything else.[109] It would be difficult to be more divergent from Virgil's picture in *Aeneid* 2; and there is little else in Aelian's repertoire to suggest cultural even-handedness. Lucian is much the same: he shows very little knowledge of Roman history except Numa ranked in a series of ancient lawgivers, or an incidental *bon mot* of Augustus to please an evidently Roman patron; but no real interest even in the standard rhetorician's repertoire of Roman as opposed to Greek history. One idiosyncrasy which goes with such an outlook is a general reluctance even to acknowledge the name of Rome. Even when surveying the world from above in a reworking of the myth of Gyges, Lucian's dreamer Timocles will call in to Italy for lunch, not to Rome as such.[110] And it is interesting that when writing Greek and excusing himself for any possible lapse in Attic, Fronto does not present himself as a Roman or African but as a Libyan, comparable in Greek eyes to a Scythian like the proverbial Anacharsis (i.e. to be regarded as a 'wise barbarian' in spite of his linguistic shortcomings).[111] This master of Latin style exchanges world-views as he exchanges languages: under ideal conditions a Greek outlook will not even notice Rome on the map.

One exemplum is especially interesting because of the double standards it evoked. The position of Nero was bound to challenge the cultural values of Greek and Roman alike. If he had embarrassed both with self-indulgent Hellenophilia allied to barbarism, he had still given Greeks a freedom which Vespasian had subsequently revoked. Pausanias, writing in the next century, can be ingeniously equivocal:

Later on the rulership of Rome came round to Nero, who
left Greece free of all its obligations . . . When I examine
this action of Nero's I think that Plato had it exactly right
when he said that the greatest and most daring atrocities
are not the product of ordinary men, but of a noble soul
corrupted by a perverted education.[112]

There seems to be no atrocity that the right Platonic tag
cannot expiate. Philostratus is perhaps less embarrassed. He
can allow his Hellenophile sage Apollonius of Tyana freedom
to laugh at Nero in the typical gesture of the wise man against
the tyrant: the emperor is like any other *apaideutos* in his
culture, while otherwise he can present the spectacle of a
monster – and hence another convenient opportunity for
sophistic *ecphrasis*.[113]

And yet the picture afforded by Greek sources in isolation
may run the risk of misleading. Even in the highest cultural
circles there is evidence not only of a flourishing bilingualism
but of a flourishing biculturalism as well. Aulus Gellius' presentation of Favorinus' salon performances bears constant witness
to the latter's familiarity with an impressive cross-section of
Latin literature, and his capacity at least for treating it on the
kind of equal terms with Greek that Quintilian attempted to
prescribe.[114] Favorinus is able to compare Pindar and Virgil on
volcanoes, or to discuss barbarisms or colour-terms or words for
winds in either language;[115] he is equally at home in settling
questions of Plautine authenticity or comparing the styles of
Plato and Lysias.[116]

One curiosity of bilingual culture emerges from the eighteenth of Apuleius' *Florida*: Apuleius promises as his main
performance a hymn in both Greek and Latin in honour of
Asclepius; this in turn is to be prefaced by a bilingual dialogue
between Julius Persius and Sabidius Severus, in contention over
the praise of Carthage. A similar hybrid is mentioned in *Florida*
26: Apuleius had delivered the previous part of his discourse in
Greek, and it continued in Latin. This seems to be in deference
to two different segments of audience;[117] but there is in both
cases, one suspects, a strong element of tour de force about the
whole business. The sophist as *desultor litterarum*, a literary
acrobat, is able to demonstrate his ability to leap from one
language to the other.

Yet even in a bicultural milieu one can at least sense that opportunities to trump Roman philistinism will be taken:

> When a fellow by the name of Polybius, absolutely un-educated and uncouth in his speech, said, 'The Emperor has honoured me with Roman citizenship', 'Oh, if only he'd made you a Greek instead of a Roman', replied Demonax.[118]

Such an anecdote pointedly stresses the element of cultural one-upmanship in which the cultured Greek can cut the philistine Roman down to size. The ever-conservative Apollonius of Tyana objected to the fashion for Roman names in Asia Minor: those who once bore the names of Greek naval heroes and lawgivers now style themselves Luculli and Fabricii;[119] while the philo-sopher Nigrinus in Lucian's dialogue of that name does not hesitate to locate traditional ills of society in the city of Rome itself.[120]

The final perspective should perhaps be given to Aristides. It is easy to regard him as accommodating to the reality of Rome, and evoking perhaps the most generously optimistic picture of the *Pax Romana* to have survived in literature. But for all its apparent pro-Romanness the Εἰς Ῥώμην might almost be termed a tour de force of how to write convincingly about Rome with almost no evidence whatever of expert knowledge of the Roman past:

> All men praise the city and will continue to do so. Yet their praises achieve less than if they had never spoken them . . . their speeches detract in most cases from her wonders. It is rather as if someone were to want to describe the size of an army like that of Xerxes when totally awestruck by it. He would tell of seeing 10,000 infantry here, or 20,000 there and this or that number of cavalry, but in describing what excites his wonder he would fail to report so much as a fraction of the whole.[121]

In fact the speech as a whole might seem to draw its information much more readily from the Persian Empire than it does from modern times. And the elements of contempt for an overblown barbarian enterprise might have been arguably similar. It is nothing to Greeks that they are currently mastered by infinitely greater force. Even when describing the distinctively Roman war machine Aristides elects to do so in Homeric terms:

[The wall of troops] is a barrier of men who have no thought of flight . . . They have adjusted themselves to one another in the harmony by which Homer says the Myrmidons[122] did when he compares them to the wall I mentioned, with all the instruments of war: their helmets are so close together that an arrow cannot pass between them; the shields are raised above their heads that would provide a race-track in mid-air, so much stronger than those made in the city that horsemen could race over them, and the famous phrase of Euripides 'a bronze plain' you will then truly say you see.[123]

In an ethos where rhetoric could present the world as stable and unchanging, it is worthwhile to stress that the balance was quietly slipping away from Rome as the centre of Empire. The coming of age of provinces and provincials in the first century set off a chain reaction which culminated in Rome's eventually reverting to that living on past glory so fervently practised by Athens. The Empire came to be centred where the Emperor was, long before the division into Eastern and Western halves. In Aristides' world-view this is scarcely a visible trait: any city he deigns to praise on any given occasion will be presented as superlative for the purposes of the moment. But in Philostratus the incidental occurrences of Rome in the world of an Imperial courtier may not be due solely to a snobbish Hellenism. Under the Severi Rome was already ceasing to matter, and the 'levelling-down' of Italy had begun.[124]

When the fourth century produced a Hellenophile Emperor in the person of Julian, the past continued to loom large. Even in answering an appeal of Argos against taxation by Corinth,[125] the Emperor begins with the city's achievements in the Trojan War, with a brief rehearsal from the return of the Heraclidae down to Macedon and Rome, speciously noting the Argive ancestry of Alexander and Philip and its alliance with Rome.[126] On the issue in question, the burden on Argos of its contribution to the traditional Nemean Games is noted, whereas contribution to Corinthian Games would be unjustified ἄλλως τε οὐδὲ πρὸς Ἑλληνικὴν οὐδὲ παλαιὰν πανήγυριν ('especially as the contribution is towards a festival neither Hellenic nor ancient'):[127] doubtless he means wild beast shows and similar entertainments at Corinth. Julian promises for his part to exhort the Corinthians not to be more ambitious than their fathers, and not to bring about the end of the customs which their fathers had sensibly maintained for the cities of Greece.[128]

The ultimate accolade is for a Hellenophile Emperor to make the Romans honorary Greeks:

And [Apollo] has civilised most of the inhabited world by means of his Greek colonies, and so prepared it to obey Romans more readily. For they themselves are Greek not only by race, but even their sacred ordinances and their pious belief in the Gods which they have laid down and maintain are all Greek from beginning to end. And in addition their state constitution is not inferior to that of any of the best-governed states, if it is not actually superior to all the others that have been put into practice. For these reasons I myself recognise that the city of Rome is Greek, both in ancestry and constitution.[129]

Julian's own sophistic reflexes have been put to use.

The Second Sophistic, then, had much to do with history and with coming to terms with it. And in both cases it is history as presented through the eyes of sophists. To someone who could issue orders to Xerxes to whip the Hellespont harder, or tell Alexander to take a rest at the Ocean's edge, there were no real barriers, and nothing to prevent history from turning in any direction one might wish to turn it. In a sense sophists were in the forefront of now-fashionable 'heritage history'. And yet Aristides' *Roman Oration* remains a world apart from his *Panathenaicus*; one could not make Greek sophists take more than a peripheral interest in Roman history, and no one seems to have tried.

SOPHISTIC BIOGRAPHY: FROM PHILOSTRATUS TO EUNAPIUS

It remains to ask how adequately sophists could relate themselves to their predecessors. There are only two surviving works that might claim to deal systematically with the biographies of sophists; a contrast between them is illuminating, since it can at least serve to show the difference between a writer who was a master of sophistic techniques for better or worse, and one who has been mastered by them, inevitably for the worse.

Philostratus[130] was well equipped to write about the milieu of sophists: he had been a pupil of Proclus of Naucratis, and knew current sophists well. His teacher was a luminary of the movement who had migrated to Athens;[131] and Philostratus, from the Athenian dependency of Lemnos, could claim to have held high civic office in Athens itself,[132] and to be able to view sophists from the very hub of their own universe. A place in the Empress Julia Domna's circle gave him a courtier's perspective as well,[133] and the combination of the two was not uncharacteristic of his age. For the benefit of a consular Gordian, himself to become Emperor,[134] he took up from a conversation in the temple of Apollo at Antiochene Daphne a subject which had not yet found its historian.[135]

Philostratus never quite loses the impression of casual reminiscences appropriate to a conversation of that sort. He gives the impression of being extremely well informed in a somewhat nonchalant way; it is often as if the general background is far too well known to require more than an occasional hint, even if on some specific points the record has to be set straight.[136] And Philostratus can often seem pretentiously patronising in his capacity to do just that.

It is worthwhile to note his performance on a single sophist close to his own time, Hippodromus of Larissa.[137] First there is a somewhat formal indicator of rank: Hippodromus is not to be deemed inferior to Philostratus' previous candidates, and in a somewhat contrived antithesis τῶν μὲν γὰρ βελτίων φαίνεται, τῶν δὲ οὐκ οἶδα ὅ τι λείπεται ('he seemed better than some, and I do not know how others surpass him'). Then there is the often telegraphic assignment to a city and parentage, complimentary where possible: Larissa is εὖ πράττουσα ἐν Θετταλοῖς ('prosperous among the Thessalians'), while Hippodromus' father Olympiodorus is the leading horsebreeder in Thessaly. Given the prominence of horse-breeding as such in the local economy, this is as one might expect: Philostratus' subjects will have an illustrious pedigree mentioned where possible.[138]

Then, as often, comes social and financial distinction. Hippodromus has been twice president of the Pythian Games; the lavishness of his provisions for the occasion enhances his standing still further. This is the point on which to hang an anecdote about his umpiring of a contest: Philostratus has him uphold the victory of one Clemens of Byzantium in tragic recitation, after judges at other festivals had rejected the latter's skills on political grounds (Septimius Severus was currently besieging Byzantium). The sophist confronts the Amphictyonic Committee, which is about to take the same line. We are told that ἀναπηδήσας δὲ ξὺν ὁρμῇ ὁ Ἱππόδρομος, οὗτοι μὲν, εἶπεν, ἐρρώσθων ἐπιορκοῦντες τε καὶ παραγιγνώσκοντες τοῦ δικαίου, ἐγὼ δὲ Κλήμεντι τὴν νικῶσαν δίδωμι (Hippodromus sprang vigorously to his feet and declared 'Let those men prosper by breaking oaths and refusing to recognise what is right, but I give victory to Clemens').[139] As so often, we can have a good idea why Philostratus should have chosen this anecdote. It has a 'cultural' setting second to none. And Hippodromus carries off a quite courageous gesture with a sophistic flourish. The scene could indeed have corresponded to a genuine declamation subject ('The Delphians exclude x from the Games because of the anger of Philip', or the like).

We are then given a *chreia* on the modesty of Hippodromus himself, in the form of a quotation in which he could identify himself with Odysseus (τί μ᾽ ἀθανάτοισιν ἐΐσκεις; 'why liken me to the immortals?'). While dismissing any attempts by others to compare him with Polemo, '[by this answer] he neither deprived Polemo of his superhuman reputation, nor did he allow himself to be compared with so wonderful a man.'[140] We are reminded of just how much sophistic comment is concerned with the perpetual fascination of grading and ranking. On the other hand one notes Philostratus' often protective attitude towards his idols: he can criticise them on occasion himself, but will allow few others to do so.

Hippodromus' reputation is further enhanced by his refusal to hit back at a satire by Proclus of Naucratis; instead he produces a eulogy on speaking well of people, using the peacock as an illustration.[141] One sees here Philostratus' admiration for *ecphrasis* and the sophistic reflex to praise. Another story follows: teaching a former pupil of Heraclides of Lycia, too fulsome in the latter's praise, Hippodromus decides to teach him how his idol should really be praised and delivers a model encomium.[142] Then come two anecdotes about his fatherly character towards up-and-coming sophists: grief at the death of a precocious youth, Diodotus, not a rare occurrence in the sophists' profession,[143] and generosity towards Philostratus' own kinsman, Philostratus of Lemnos. Hippodromus not only gives him help in panegyric before his début in extempore performance, but refuses to take him on in competition merely to provide a spectacle.[144] Once more a situation is subsumed in a melodramatic *bon mot*: 'When the Hellenes expected Hippodromus to come forward himself without delay, to compete with his pupil, he replies, 'I will not strip for action against my own flesh and blood' and he accordingly postpones the date of his own performance. This section on what we might call the humanity of Hippodromus is rounded off with a brief flourish: 'Let this, then, suffice to show that he was a man of genuine culture [*pepaideumenos*], humane and gentle in disposition.'[145] However equivocal some of Philostratus' accolades, he has served this contemporary well indeed.

As the most informative source on sophists, Philostratus none the less fails all too often to tell us enough; and where there is copious detail, as in the reviews of Polemo and Herodes Atticus, the biographer seems too often to be mesmerised by his subjects, in the latter instance perhaps in deference to his patron's connexion with Herodes.[146] Yet he has left a medium which is second to none for the evocation of sophists in action, and for the conveying of their self-importance.[147]

The sophists of the Early Empire are not entirely happy in having Philostratus as their chronicler, invaluable as he may be for both detail and ethos. But Eunapius is many times worse,[148] yet for all that his faults once more reflect the vanity and vulnerability of the fourth-century sophists themselves. It is almost Eunapius' first gesture to imply Philostratus' failure to do justice to philosophers;[149] he more than rectifies the matter with his attention to Neoplatonising theurgists, but it is on the measured mile of bona fide rhetorical sophists that he is particularly unrestrained. He is evidently far too close to his own master Prohaeresius not to be blinded in his attitude to the latter's would-be rivals, such as Epiphanius and Diophantus.[150] The fact that he is more often an eyewitness than Philostratus tends to mean that he concentrates less on the flosculi of the sophists in their performances than on the moments of grandiose gossip that characterise the society of the sophists as much in the fourth century as in the second; hence we are liable to be told on the authority of an eyewitness how a proconsul acquitted Prohaeresius after the rival faction's case against him collapsed through a procedural problem.[151] Eunapius preserves the

sophist Julian's witticism to the proconsul ('through the overriding exercise of your justice you have turned Apsines into
Pythagoras', i.e. you have reduced him to silence) and adds a
not very striking epigram by Prohaeresius himself; but beyond
illustrating the passionate involvement in factional violence
characteristic of fourth-century students, the biographer has
succeeded in saying next to nothing.

It is not too long before we find Eunapius smothering his
subjects with similes: 'pupils made off full of enthusiasm to
Iamblichus, with a view to filling themselves full as if from a
spring that bubbles over its limits.'[152] Or Alypius and Iamblichus
'chanced upon each other or met in their courses like stars, and
the audience was seated round them in a circle as if in some
great palace of the Muses'.[153] And vainly ponderous comparisons between Sopater and Socrates as victims of intrigue are
to be expected.[154] Exuberant banality is the order of the day.

In Eunapius one senses much more than in Philostratus the
element of pretentious affectation which so often lurks in the
background of sophistic activity. Much can be told from his very
first sentence:

Ξενοφῶν ὁ φιλόσοφος, ἀνὴρ μόνος ἐξ ἁπάντων φιλο-
σόφων ἐν λόγοις τε καὶ ἔργοις φιλοσοφίαν κοσμήσας (τὰ
μέν, ἐν λόγοις, ἔστι τε καὶ ἐν γράμμασι, τὴν ἠθικὴν
ἀρετὴν γράφει, τὰ δέ, ἐν πράξεσί τε ἦν ἄριστος, ἀλλὰ καὶ
ἐγέννα στρατηγοὺς τοῖς ὑποδείγμασιν· ὁ γοῦν μέγας Ἀλέ-
ξανδρος, οὐκ ἂν ἐγένετο μέγας, εἰ μὴ Ξενοφῶν), καὶ τὰ
παρεργά φησι δεῖν τῶν σπουδαίων ἀνδρῶν ἀναγράφειν.

Xenophon the philosopher, a man unique among all
philosophers in having been a credit to philosophy in
word and deed alike (for he writes not only about moral
excellence both in his informal conversation-pieces and in
his formal works, while he excelled too in his actions, but
also generated leaders of armies by the example he
offered; for example the Great Alexander would never
have become great had there been no Xenophon) – he, I
say, tells us to record even the incidental affairs of
outstanding men.[155]

Eunapius cultivates eccentricity from the start: a tendentious
encomium of Xenophon 'the philosopher' is used to herald a

trivial claim. There is already some bias in the characterising of Xenophon as the only philosopher to combine words and actions – one has only to think of Socrates' retreat from Delium. More extraordinary is the claim that only Xenophon made Alexander great. The stylistic effect is no less tendentious, with Xenophon as subject rather than incidental parenthesis, and an overloaded digression on his inspiration of Alexander. We are in for a tastelessly overblown sophistic muddle. And that is only a beginning: with the same pretentiousness as in the *Histories*, the author now tells us that if Xenophon thought the trivia important enough, he, Eunapius, is going to record their real achievements.[156] And he has the nerve to shift blame on to his sources, claiming credit for giving fixity to unstable oral tradition (while preserving written material with integrity).

Eunapius' notice of Julian of Cappadocia[157] offers a sample of his treatment of a sophist not directly involved in philosophical or medical diversion. It is said at the outset that he ἐτυράννει γε τῶν ᾿Αθηνῶν ('tyrannised the Athenians'). One is reminded of Lucian's exhortation to the would-be rhetorician to make his performance into a tyranny.[158] Julian has an enthusiastic following, a favourite theme of Philostratus; one notes, as often in Eunapius, an almost religious tone: ῥητορικῆς ἕνεκεν τὸν ἄνδρα καὶ μεγέθους φύσεως σεβαζόμενοι ('they held the man in awe for his rhetoric and the greatness of his nature').[159] Eunapius wishes, again characteristically, to make his subject out to be a superlative one: 'But Julian surpassed them all by the greatness of his genius, and whoever was second to him was second by a long way.'[160] His four most distinguished pupils include Prohaeresius, who will figure as an even greater star in due course.

Next Eunapius praises Julian's house in Athens, but immediately finds himself in two minds: he wants it to be small and humble and a temple redolent of Hermes and the Muses; but when we find it containing statues of his pupils and equipped with a miniature theatre we may be rather more sceptical.[161] The reason for a private auditorium is given as the factional strife between town and gown:[162] Eunapius all too ineptly invokes a comparison with ancient times when wars rather than internal quarrels were the rule.

Eunapius' one and only anecdote about Julian results from this factionalism: he recounts in great detail the courtroom incident already noted between the factions of Julian and the rival sophist Apsines of Gadara. Julian's faction had been prosecuted, and the proconsul had ordered Julian to be arrested as well. Apsines himself attempted to make a speech for the prosecution, but was barred by the proconsul, a man of culture; but the latter insisted that one Themistocles, the instigator of the affair, should do so instead, having spoken at the original hearing; he is tongue-tied, and Prohaeresius makes a moving speech for the defence, to the acclaim of the proconsul.[163] But despite Julian's witticism about Pythagoras, there is no real attempt at reproducing stylistic extracts as Philostratus does as a matter of course.[164] It is easy enough to be hard on Eunapius; but one is left with the suspicion that he has set out to emulate Philostratus without anything like sufficient information at his disposal; while the inclusion of philosophers has only rendered his limitations all the more apparent. This time there is just not enough of a framework on which to hang the adornments. Had Eunapius proved himself the lively raconteur that Philostratus or Libanius turns out to be, it might have been possible to sympathise with the work's possibilities as literary diversion; but once more Eunapius' materials are so stifled with the verbiage he sets out to flaunt that they defy easy interpretation.

In biography as in history, then, the sophist has to he treated with care. He can bring the past of his fellow-professionals alive, but he cannot always resist the temptation to adorn it as well; his success or failure will depend on his being able to strike a balance between the two.

6

Cookery and confection: sophistic philosophy, philosophic sophistry

One of the distinctive features of intellectual life in the Early Roman Empire is the continued co-existence, peaceful or otherwise, of rhetoric and philosophy as the main pillars of the educational system.[1] What interests us here is the middle ground which both sides could claim and attempt to fortify against their rivals. Sophists could not ignore philosophy, or the fact that they had now to all intents parted company from it; and they had to protect themselves with arguments to enable them to come to terms with it all the same.

Throughout the period of the Empire there was certainly no lack of philosophy with which to come to terms. In the first two centuries the familiar cavalcade of Hellenistic schools were all in varying degrees still available. Stoics and Epicureans had long joined the ranks of the successors of Plato and Aristotle (Academics and Peripatetics), and the decidedly less social Cynics. A revival in two extremes was also apparent: Neo-Pythagoreanism and Pyrrhonian Scepticism experienced an upsurge, and the very success of the latter in undermining the rational basis of the dogmatic schools favoured the eventual collapse of rationalism in favour of mysticism. It was to be the Platonists who acted as carriers of both into late antiquity, with the new synthesis of Plotinus in the third century. And whatever the profusion of doctrines (and the suspicion and distaste they engendered) there was scope for a healthy philosophic life: Stoics, Epicureans and Cynics could all claim to seek a life according to nature but interpreted their goal in radically different ways, so that Stoics came to be caricatured as pedantic paradigms of social correctness, Epicureans as pleasure-seekers and Cynics as boorish radicals. It was the task of rhetoricians at all levels to be able to hold their own against philosophers in an intellectually respectable way.

There is no lack of cases in real life where we know of an individual who applied himself to both rhetoric and philosophy, and finally declared himself for one or the other.[2] Lucian works in a number of variations on conversions to or from philosophy, including at least the claim that he himself made the transition;[3] Philostratus quotes a couple of cases en passant; association between sophists and more philosophically inclined intellectuals would have been commonplace, as in Herodes' friendship with 'Lucius', or Polemo's with Timocrates of Heraclea.[4] Moreover, the Stoic Dio Chrysostom and the Peripatetic Favorinus were quite clearly sophists in their own right, however Philostratus saw fit to present them (as only apparently so). And one need only think of the case of Marcus Aurelius, whose correspondence with Fronto and *Meditations* conveniently mark the rhetorical and philosophical sides of his formation.[5] In the fourth century Themistius can produce Platonic and Aristotelian paraphrases, but is capable also of defending philosophy with the techniques and repertoire of the sophist.[6] The two professions were never totally divorced from one another, either socially or intellectually; it should be no surprise that Marcus Aurelius entrusted the appointments to newly endowed philosophical chairs to Herodes Atticus.

During the heyday of the first sophists, it might have been argued that a single intellect could easily accommodate both rhetoric and the study of human concerns: and figures such as Protagoras and Gorgias could easily imply that they were simultaneously thinkers and communicators.[7] But in Plato's reaction to the death of Socrates there is already a fully articulated hostility to rhetoric as an end in itself: the tools of an art of communication are far too dangerous, especially in a democracy, to be allowed to fall into the wrong hands, and the concern of philosophy with truth betokens a distaste for the arts of effective expression,[8] to say nothing of mercenary concerns such as teachers' fees or star performances. Against this attitude, specialists in the teaching of rhetoric could at best stress the responsibility for the effective expression of truth, and insist on a sense of moral responsibility in the ideal orator;[9] but the danger of mob oratory admitted no rebuttal.

Such is the situation as it already stood by the time of

Isocrates: by the Second Sophistic period as Philostratus presents it, the picture has changed in only one essential: the high
degree of specialisation both possible and necessary to fulfil the
highest professional demands of either rhetoric or philosophy.
The proliferation of schools since Plato meant a bewildering
array of potentially conflicting claims, amusingly satirised in
Lucian's *Vitarum Auctio*; in particular the more extreme expressions of Stoicism, such as the paradoxes or the claims of the
ideal Stoic sage, contained a series of preoccupations easy for
the layman to regard with ridicule. On the other hand serious
rhetorical training itself now involved a degree of regimentation
and abstruse nuancing that left little room for more than a
smattering of philosophy.

Yet channels of communication there remained: the common
heritage of Plato, as accomplished a prose littérateur as a
philosopher;[10] a place in the rhetorician's curriculum at least
for the exhibition of *paideia*, with room for parading not only
knowledge of doctrines but of lives of philosophers; and in turn
a tendency towards 'display philosophy' in some sense. Lucian's
teacher Demonax ridiculed a 'Sidonian sophist' who had
boasted 'If Aristotle calls me to the Lyceum, I shall follow him,
if Plato to the Academy, I shall be there; if Zeno, I shall spend
my time in the Porch; if Pythagoras, I shall be silent.'[11] Whatever
his philosophical allegiance, if any, he certainly knew how to
construct verbal parallelisms. And even in the Platonising
Plutarch, who in all but a few works practises what he preaches
and regards literary artistry as secondary to subject-matter, such
a tendency can still emerge. At the outset of 'How to tell a
flatterer from a friend'[12] we are assured that flattery 'does not
follow after people who are poor, obscure, or unimportant, but
makes a pitfall and a pestilence in great houses and important
affairs, often overturning kingdoms and governments'.[13] Plutarch does develop an abstract argument of a kind: the flatterer
attaches to a victim who is vulnerable through self-love; he
operates by imitation and can be detected inter alia by his
inconsistency. None the less the reader cannot help noticing
the frequency of images, in particular similes, used to illustrate
what might as readily have been presented as a rhetorical *thesis*:
flatterers go for the best people as bore-worms for delicate and
sweet-smelling woods; they are like blood-sucking lice in the
speed with which they desert their juicy victims; friends should

be pre-tested like currency; the flatterer imitates the pleasant and attractive aspects of a friend like fake and counterfeit imitation of gold.[14] And he inevitably plays the friend's role as a tragedian, while flatterers and friends are mixed like wild seeds and genuine wheat.[15] Even they use outspokenness to their own ends, 'just as skilled chefs employ bitter extracts and austere flavourings to take away the excessive sweetness';[16] they are difficult to detect, like animals able to change colour;[17] their victims are like animals at pasture, and so easy to associate with; unlike the ape, the flatterer is not captured by imitating but does his own capturing that way; his changes are like those of the cuttle-fish, or the chameleon who can assimilate himself to any colour but not to white.[18] The sheer length of such a catalogue may hint at a genuine interest in natural history on Plutarch's part, but it also suggests the possibility that illustration in a philosophic essay is close to becoming an end in itself.

Such tendencies in philosophic writing did not go unnoticed by the apologists for rhetoric. An obvious ploy is to make out philosophers to be accomplished rhetoricians despite themselves. With Plato this is easy enough, given the speeches on Love in the *Phaedrus* and *Symposium*. But Fronto goes further:

> Wake up and listen to what Chrysippus himself wants. Is he really content to teach, to explain the subject, to offer definitions and explanations? He is not: instead he expands as much as he can, he exaggerates, he anticipates objections, he repeats himself, he postpones topics and returns to them, he asks questions, supplies descriptions, divides his subject, introduces imaginary characters, puts his own words in someone else's mouth . . . Do you realise that he handles almost all the orator's armament? And so if Chrysippus himself has shown that these are to be used, what more can I ask, except that you should not [use] the mere [words] of dialecticians, but rather [the eloquence] of Plato?[19]

Even on such sophistic subjects as style and vocabulary, it is unsurprising to see proponents of rhetoric and philosophy elaborating on the same basic metaphor of the 'War of Words'. When Fronto tells the young Marcus Aurelius how to array his expressions he employs an extended military metaphor: he is discussing

On what principle words should be doubled, sometimes
trebled, occasionally drawn up four deep, often arranged
in fives, or even extended to still larger groups . . . Just as
in war, when a legion has to be recruited, we do not just
collect the volunteers, but also hunt down the men of
military age who are lying low, so when we need to call up
word-reinforcements, we must not only make use of the
volunteers who offer themselves, but tease out the less
obvious [*latentia*] and hunt them down to put them under
orders.[20]

All this might be legitimate illustration for a teacher of rhetoric;
but we find Plutarch resorting to the same material in order to
condemn excesses of sophistic wordage:

For [Isocrates] did not grow old sharpening a sword or
whetting his spear, or polishing his helmet or going on
campaign or taking the oar, but in glueing together and
placing contrasting pairs, units of equal length, and
expressions with similar endings, all but smoothing down
and balancing his periods with chisels and files. How could
this person avoid being afraid of the clash of arms and the
clash of phalanxes, a man who was afraid to allow vowels to
collide, or to come out with a phrase out of balance by a
single syllable?[21]

The easy interaction between rhetoric and philosophy is perhaps most readily noted in the *dialexeis* of Maximus of Tyre. Of
forty-one short pieces no fewer than ten have an obvious literary
interest in the titles alone, in that they deal with materials that
have a reference to either Plato or Homer as literary texts: 'Was
Socrates right to have refused to make his defence?'; 'What was
the Demon of Socrates?' (two speeches);[22] 'Was Plato right to
ban Homer from his state?'; 'What is Socratic Love?' (four
speeches); 'Is there choice in Homer?'[23] Others still have an
obvious rhetorical potential: 'Are soldiers or farmers more
useful to a city?' (two speeches, on opposite sides); or on the
goodness and security of pleasure (two speeches).[24] The philosophical *controversia* has arrived.

If we take Maximus' performance on the most obviously
cultural subject, Εἰ συμβάλλεται πρὸς ἀρετὴν τὰ ἐγκύκλια
μαθήματα ('Whether the Arts Curriculum contributes to

Virtue'),[25] we can soon see the author's preoccupation with facile presentation. First let us take two vignettes – Socrates at the Piraeus discussing the Republic, then the Athenian stranger of *Laws* I.624Aff. – and an easy transition from one to the other: Εἰ δὲ βούλει, τὸν μὲν Σωκράτην ἐῶ· τὸν δὲ Ἀθηναῖον παρακαλῶμεν ξένον ἀποκρίνασθαι ἡμῖν ('If you like, let us leave Socrates, and ask the Athenian stranger for his reply'). He informs us, unsurprisingly, that philosophy is the best πολιτεία τῆς ψυχῆς ('Republic of the soul').[27] This evokes a picture of Philosophy herself brought on as a lawgiver, summoning the liberal arts as her helpers (not excluding Rhetoric as the messenger of the thoughts of the soul, ἄγγελον τῶν τῆς ψυχῆς διανοημάτων).[28] Music is singled out for special treatment – largely, one suspects, because it has a ready supply of 'Platonic' echoes, particularly in the *Republic* and *Laws* once more; while the Sybarites are cited as a facile example of the corruption of Dorian music.[29]

Not only is Maximus in full control of the cultural décor of philosophy; he can arrogate to himself all the mannerisms of the sophist in preparation for an entertaining volte-face:

And so I for my part kept silent towards all men up to now about my attainments, having said nothing arrogant or excessive either in private or in public, but think that now it will be to your advantage for me to speak in a very arrogant and boastful manner. This array of speeches, young gentlemen, has arrived before you abundant and varied, and offers you everything; they are directed towards all listeners, all dispositions, the zealous pursuit of knowledge, and every kind of cultural instruction; they are a generous gesture, free of charge, lavish, and there for all who are able to take advantage of them. If someone is a lover of rhetoric this is a convenient course to supply all his needs, easy to take, elevating, amazing, complete, powerful and unflagging. Or if a man is a lover of poetry, let him come along, after acquiring no more than his metres elsewhere, and let him receive all the rest of his equipment here: the dignity, the magnificence, the distinction, the fertility, the divine inspiration, the restraint, the sense of drama, the lavish diction, the perfect harmony of composition. But do you come without knowledge of your

fellow-citizens and the senate? Then you have actually
found out the heart of the matter: you see the people, you
see the senate-chamber, the speaker, the act of persuasion,
and the power of rhetoric.[30]

At this point Maximus changes sides and in a cleverly abrupt
syncrisis emerges as an advocate of 'true philosophy' after all:

But is there one who sees over the top of these things,
welcomes philosophy, and honours truth? At this point I
climb down, I suppress my boasting, I am not the same
man: the subject is a lofty one, it requires a champion of
more than the rabble-rousing sort, by Zeus, and not
someone who crawls along the ground or hangs onto the
disposition of the crowd.

Now, if a man believes that philosophy consists only in
this – verbs and nouns, or the techniques of speaking, or
refuting opponents, raising contentions, creating sophisms and spending all one's time on these topics – it is not
a hard task to find a teacher. You can find plenty of
sophists of that sort everywhere; they are easy to come by
and do not take long to appear; and I would confidently
say that this sort of philosophy has more teachers than
students.

But it is all too obvious that Maximus has been able to execute
a large stretch of sustained irony (*lexis eschēmatismenē*) and pull
off a glib rhetorical trick. Yet if called to account, he could
easily have pointed to Socrates' first and 'pretended' speech on
Love in the *Phaedrus*. The philosophically inclined could indeed
manipulate the resources of rhetoric to their own ends.

Maximus at least believes that he is still in the province of
philosophy. Apuleius by contrast is well aware that he has a foot
in both camps, and crosses between them with equal ease.[31] The
eighteenth piece in the *Florida* illustrates in short compass the
facile way in which a façade of philosophy can be maintained
against 'sophistic' when Apuleius' real priority is the reverse.
First he gives a flourish for an occasion: the philosopher
speaking before an audience in the theatre must put out of his
mind the splendid building and purely theatrical diversions – as
good an excuse as any for describing them.[32] The moment he is
back to his subject he decides to transport his audience with the

help of two verse quotations to the senate-house or library of Carthage.[33] Now he hesitates to address a familiar crowd – a cue for an extended autobiographical notice, including his own student days at Athens, and the fame of his own books.[34] He will give the crowd what Thales got away without asking, what Protagoras stipulated but never received. This cryptic formulation leads to stories about both: Protagoras is mentioned for a celebrated *aporon* ('insoluble') over a court-case with his pupil Euathlus: the sophist asks for a high fee if the latter wins his first court-case. Each man claims that either by the verdict of the jury or by the terms of the bargain he himself is the winner.[35] Apuleius rejects the problem – an ideal *controversia*-subject in its own right – and tells the story of a philosopher instead: Thales' reward for teaching Mandraytus of Priene his theory of the sun's revolution is to have it duly credited to himself.[36] The implications are clear. The story of the sophist and his student bickering over a fee is deftly contrasted with the story of the true natural philosopher who has a trusting relationship with his pupil. And yet by *praeteritio* Apuleius has still entertained rather than edified in a thoroughly sophistic manner.

A different approach to 'sophistic philosophy' is shown in Aelius Aristides' vast ensemble Πρὸς Πλάτωνα ὑπὲρ ῥητορικῆς ('Against Plato, in Defence of Rhetoric').[37] The staggering scale of this work is some indication of the importance Aristides attached to the defence of his vocation and the passionate belief he had in it. He is also concerned to produce more than mere vindication of Rhetoric's position by exhibiting a mastery of the tools of philosophy against their acknowledged master Plato. The key passage of Plato's *Gorgias* in which Socrates relates Gorgias' art to cookery and flattery is itself quoted at great length,[38] and Aristides spares no accumulation of argument, real or so-called, to refute it. The offensive claim is Socrates' assertion that 'What the art of beautification is to that of gymnastics, so is sophistry to law-giving; and what the art of cookery is to that of medicine, so is rhetoric to justice.' Aristides immediately and rightly exposes the unwarranted assumption relating oratory to cookery.[39] He then moves tangentially – and laboriously – in, for him, a familiar religious direction. Medicine, greater than cookery, is still inferior to cures from Delphi, while human legislation is inferior to divine constitutions obtained from oracles, and poets make inspired declarations without art: if prediction comes through the agency of Apollo and poetry through that of the Muses, why should oratory not be a gift from Hermes? [40] Plato takes refuge with the Pythia in the *Laws*, and resorts to divine madness as a basis for poetry,[41] while Socrates had no skill, yet the Pythia claimed him to be the wisest.[42] In like manner the rhetor in turn can be seen as free to luxuriate in divine inspiration as well.

But the argument can also be conducted on a more direct and personal level. Towards the end of the *Republic* Plato had been able to address Homer directly, and ask him what state had been better administered thanks to the efforts of Homer the legislator. Aristides is able to repay Plato in kind:

> Now then, Plato, did you ever lead the Athenians or any other people, Greek or barbarian, towards the noblest goal? Any one of those men would be glad to put the question. You could not say that you did. For you did not lead them at all. And what about your teacher and comrade Socrates? Neither did he.[43]

As so often the sophist is in his element in an imaginary court, winning hands down against his long-deceased but remarkably resilient rival.

On a no less ambitious scale Lucian sees fit to contrive the slow demolition of dogmatic philosophy on the grand scale in his *Hermotimus*: the interlocutor who gives his name to the dialogue is a 'Platonic' dupe, actually a Stoic, subjected to standard sceptic tropes and condemned to face the fact that a single lifetime is not now sufficient to allow satisfactory testing of all the available schools: the alternative is the happy but ignorant life of the layman.[44] It is as though both Lucian and Aristides, as far divorced by temperament from philosophy as they are from each other, nevertheless have to prove to themselves as much as to some section of their public that they have the wherewithal to confute their opponents at will.

A less expected and less comfortable role is offered by the rhetor's facility to produce panegyrics of philosophers as readily as of rulers or officials. In the *Nigrinus* Lucian produces a curious hybrid, packaging some clichés of moral satire within a rather overgilded Platonic frame;[45] while his *apomnēmoneumata* (memoirs based on *bons mots*) of his own teacher Demonax[46] are less pretentious and contrived, and afford a much less theatrical presentation of a philosophic mentor. But it is the biographer of sophists, Philostratus himself, who provides the most ambitious synthesis of philosophy and rhetoric in his bizarre presentation of the first-century sage Apollonius of Tyana. The 'life' of a sage who seemed to make only fugitive appearances in the eastern cities, Athens and Rome, and to be famed for his laconic utterances, might have been unpromising material for a sophist, whatever ingredients Philostratus' real sources may have offered.[47] Yet the biographer has produced a romantic panegyric which not only makes full use of a sophist's resources but also exploits the coincidence between sophist and sage.[48] There are spectacular contretemps with the social and political élite of the Empire and indeed outside it;[49] and no lack of rhetorical display and sophistic drama from a figure who is persistently presented as above such things. But out of it all emerges a hymn less to neo-Pythagorean[50] revival than to Hellenism itself, and on an enormous scale.

The sophists of the Empire, then, were able to continue the feud between philosophy and rhetoric which was already emerging in the activities of their fifth-century predecessors. They borrowed enough of the philosophers' tools, and even of their literary décor, to be able to hold their own ground and share uneasily some common territory. This sense of accommodation should at least help us to explain why Eunapius is able to present his fourth-century sophists in terms so similar to his descriptions of his Neoplatonic sages. Of his own teacher Prohaeresius Eunapius is prepared to say:

> His powers of speaking were at such a peak, and he so held together his weary body by the youthfulness of his soul, that the writer of this account considered him ageless and immortal, and paid attention to him as if to a god who had manifested himself with neither summons nor ceremony.[51]

In the case of those philosophers he does treat, often at great length, eloquence tends to rank next only to miracle-mongering in their assets, and Eunapius tends to be attracted to what one might call sophistic displays of theurgy, in particular on the part of Maximus of Ephesus.[52] The synthesis of rhetoric and philosophy possible in the hands of the first sophists approaches a reality once more. Nor should such assimilation be too hard to account for. Throughout the Empire the literary and spiritual bonds of the thought-world of the fifth and fourth centuries BC was still vital to both rhetoric and philosophy. It still mattered to Maximus of Tyre and Libanius alike what arguments Socrates had used in his defence; and it meant something to both to mobilise all the rhetorical resources at their command to improve on them.[53]

7

Some sophistic scene-painting

We have already witnessed a sophist going into raptures over a statue which refused to come to life in spite of the cascade of words so lovingly lavished on it. We have also seen that the sophists' world was able to witness not only a wealth of survivals from the great art and architecture of the past, but also a great deal of new building and artistic activity in the economic resurgence of the Eastern provinces. Sophists themselves participated in the patronage of the arts: Herodes Atticus was noted, and in a number of cases derided, for what his contemporaries saw as excessive enthusiasm in this direction; and we find Damascius, at the very end of antiquity, captivated by a statue of Aphrodite provided by Herodes himself.[1] In such an environment we expect some verbal response on the part of sophists to the visual world. And as in the case of history or philosophy, it will not always be quite the response we might expect.

It was taken for granted that part of a sophist's skill was to be adept in the presentation of verbal pictures in the broadest sense, as opposed to simple description of works of art. When Apollonius of Tyana is to stand trial before Domitian, a sophistic flourish invites us to 'picture the scene':

> Let us go to the court-room to listen to our hero making his defence in the case, for already it is sunrise and the doors are open for eminent persons to enter. And the imperial retinue declare that the emperor has not even had a taste of food, doubtless absorbed in the details of the case. For they say he has to hand some scroll which he reads at times in anger, at others less so. And we should

imagine him as a figure enraged at the laws, since they have invented law-courts.[2]

However improbable the proceedings that follow, Philostratus has succeeded in getting his readers into the courtroom. Indeed he was a practised hand at formal description (*ecphrasis*), as the author of two books of descriptions of paintings. Handbook recipes for this technique tend to emphasise its role as a school exercise. '*Ecphrasis* is a descriptive work [*logos periēgēmatikos*] which clearly puts the object before one's eyes', announces Theon drily; and he goes on to illustrate descriptions of characters, events, places and seasons. Its chief advantages are clarity and vividness that almost make one see what is being reported. But irrelevance has to be avoided, and description accommodated to the character of the subject-matter; it has to be florid if the subject is florid; and if it is sordid or horrific the description must not detract from such aspects.[3] However, beyond such standard precepts sophistic authors were able to impart some distinctive nuances to description and to find their own uses for it.

Ecphrasis had been a natural component of Greek literature from its beginnings, whether or not recognised as such:[4] the Shield of Achilles or the sketch of Socrates by the Ilissus entails conscious ornamentation. Other specimens do not: Herodotus' description of the valley-formation of Thessaly is scarcely conceived in such a way, yet would still offer an effective tableau in its own right:

> They say that long ago Thessaly was a lake – on the grounds that it is surrounded on all sides by very high mountains. To the east it is shut off by Pelion and Ossa, two mountains which share a common base; to the north is Olympus, to the west Pindus, to the south Orthrys. In the centre of all these mountains is the low-lying plain of Thessaly, so that a number of rivers pour into it, of which the five best known are the Peneus, Apidanus, Onochonus, Enipeus, and Pamisus; these collect their waters from the surrounding mountains and flow into a single channel, and find their outlet to the east through a single narrow gorge. The moment they join the name Peneus prevails, and the other names accordingly disappear. The story goes that long ago, before there was a gorge or an outlet

for the water, these rivers, which in common with Lake Boebeis were as yet unnamed, poured down from the hills as much water as they now do, and so made the whole of Thessaly a sea. The Thessalians themselves say that it was Poseidon who made the gorge which forms the outlet of the Peneus, and their account is a reasonable one; for if one accepts that Poseidon shakes the earth and so is responsible for the chasms caused by earthquakes, then one would say on seeing this region that it is Poseidon's work. For it seemed to me that the cleft in the mountains was the work of an earthquake.[5]

Herodotus' description amounts to little more than enumeration of natural features and an attached *mythos;* the subject-matter does not call for undue elaboration. In the second or third centuries AD such a scene is still a natural subject for description, and no doubt thanks to Herodotus a traditional one as well. But sophistic techniques tend to call for elaboration. In his sketch of the vale of Tempe in the *Varia Historia* Aelian may well have set out to avoid or to complement the simple grandeur and mythological reference in Herodotus' account; but it is at least clear how seriously the whole business is now being taken, and to what different ends:

The place offers a variety of delights of every kind: these are not the work of human hand, but of nature unbidden, ambitious for beauty at the time when the place had its beginning. For there is a profusion of ivy, which comes into fruition in a rich luxuriance, and has come into bloom and like well-bred vines creeps up the high trees and has embraced them; and a great deal of bindweed runs towards the slope and overshadows the rock. That for its part escapes notice, but the whole blossoming growth is visible and offers a great feast for the eyes. And in the low-lying places there are a variety of groves and a sequence of bowers, which also gladly afford refreshment, in the summer season a very pleasant retreat for travellers. And there flow through it a great many springs, and streams of cold water very sweet to drink. It is said that these waters are very good for bathers and contribute to their health. And birds sing scattered one here one there, particularly the song-birds, and they feast the ears and deliver their

146

songs unforced and gladly, taking away the weariness of
the passers-by.[6]

It is not that Herodotus' interest in remote origins or implication of elemental grandeur is foreign to sophistic tastes; but
Aelian has fallen victim to the temptation of reducing the
subject to a prettified set piece – and one which he himself
would not have seen, if Philostratus is right in telling us that he
never left Italy.

It is not too hard so see how the taste for such purple passages
can be overindulged or misplaced. Lucian satirises descriptions
after Thucydides that have 'gone wrong':

He described in the most vivid and striking way every city,
mountain, plain and river, or so he supposed. I wish
Heracles the Averter of Evil would make all this rebound
against the heads of the enemy, there was so much frigidity
there, more than all the Caspian snow and Celtic ice! Take
the emperor's shield: it took a whole book for his meticulous description of it, the Gorgon on the boss, with its eyes
in blue and white and black, and its girdle all the colours
of the rainbow, not to mention the serpents coiling and
curling. As for Vologesus' trousers and his horse's bit –
Good God! – how many thousands of words for each, and
what Osroes' hair was like as he was swimming the Tigris,
and the description of the cave where he took refuge,
which had ivy, myrrh and laurel all enmeshed together to
make it totally dark. Think how indispensable this is to
history: without it we should not have had an inkling what
happened there![7]

The parody is not too far from the tendency to *ecphrasis* that
bedevils Fronto's contemporary *Principia Historiae*:[8] once the
facility is there, it is difficult for the rhetorically trained practitioner to learn economy.

Much of the sophistic repertoire of description consists of
representation of mythological scenes: we have two books of
Eikones ('Pictures') by one of the Philostrati – most likely the
author of the *Lives of the Sophists*[9] – and another two, rather less
resourceful, by a grandson of the same name; a set of descriptions of statues by Callistratus,[10] and a collection of exercises in *ecphrasis* by or attributed to Libanius,[11] bring the total

to well over a hundred items in all. These can be supplemented by a host of single examples in the novels and the literature of *dialexeis*, including a number of *prolaliae*. We might be tempted to ask what the relationship was between the visual arts, contemporary or otherwise, and such a cavalcade of descriptions. The answers are fruitful up to a point, then frustrating. It has been relatively easy to relate Philostratus' expertise to that of Hellenistic and Roman Imperial wall-painting in general, without its being possible to 'prove' beyond doubt that the gallery at Naples he claims to be describing is a real one. And in particular his description of Chiron and Achilles[12] has been compared to the stern Chiron and rather resentful Achilles depicted in a wall-painting from the basilica at Herculaneum now in the Museo Nazionale at Naples. The suggestion in modern times that this is the work of the so-called 'Herculaneum Master' brought from Naples might well strengthen the case for the 'real' existence of the original Neapolitan location. But in general sophistic descriptions do not resemble art criticism as we take it for granted. Anything resembling scholarly classifications of paintings in schools or styles is not seen as important, any more than the systematic description of colour schemes, ornamental surrounds, architectural vistas or technicalities of perspective. That is not to say that any one such topic is absolutely excluded: it is rather a warning that littérateurs see literary subject-matter and are uncomfortable with the technicalities of a medium whose practitioners were not generally held in high regard. Artists in themselves might be mentioned because they themselves serve to evoke the Golden Age, such as the perpetually symbolic Phidias, or because they happen to appear in anecdotes figuring Pericles or Alexander the Great. Lucian's piece devoted to the description of paintings in a real hall relegates them to a mere catalogue at the end, while the real substance of the piece is a rhetorical debate on whether they detract from the performance of the spoken word in the auditorium – a topic naturally dear to any sophist's heart.

Seldom in any of these cases is the author content with simply describing what is (or purports to be) in front of him and leaving it at that. Instead the sophist's approach to art tends to show a distinct penchant for the paradoxical. The selection of themes in the Elder Philostratus, for example, shows a recurrent interest in themes connected with Pan and Dionysus, unusual births, collections of little people, and paradoxography itself.[13] One notes too that Achilles will appear as readily with Chiron or among the women of Scyros as on the field at Troy.[14] And accumulations of paradox can also be achieved by describing the more unusual aspects of a familiar scene before illuminating it with an affectation of *paideia*. One such ensemble is Philostratus' description of Dionysus and the pirates. The immediate sources are familiar: the change of the pirates into dolphins is told in the *Homeric Hymn to Dionysus*;[15] an additional artistic source is always conceivable. But the sophist's narrative technique is different. He presents the scene as a mysterious spectacle: one ship is presented as a revel, the other as going mad; so what, the reader must ask, is the painting about? Dionysus' crew can be presented as an unlikely rout reported to the pirates.[16] Then Philostratus offers a *syncrisis* of the two paradoxical ships: the pirate ship is monstrous enough, but nothing to the *teratologia* exhibited by Dionysus' own vessel, where pirates are already changing shape before their change of character into philanthropic dolphins.[17]

The taste for paradoxical pictures could all too easily be allied to a characteristic rhetorical taste for portraying extremes of cruelty and suffering: the theme of Prometheus' punishment was well suited to supplying both. Libanius' *ecphrasis* on the subject illustrates a wide range of approaches. No suffering is too extreme for antithesis: (ἡ μὲν φύσις τὴν κόμην, τὴν δὲ ἀκοσμίαν ἡ τιμωρία πεποίηκεν ('Nature has contrived his hair, punishment its disordered appearance')[18]. There is much detail and wordplay on the agony evident all over the Titan's body, but relative restraint at the vital point ('the eagle . . . approaches the liver itself and seems to have stretched the incision it has made . . .').[19] But any restraint here had not been felt by Achilles Tatius, whose preoccupation with the probing of privacy is second to none:

Next came the painting of Prometheus: [the Titan] is bound by iron and rock, and Heracles is armed with bow and spear. The bird is feasting on Prometheus' belly, and stands ripping it open, or rather has already done so, and has dipped its beak into the wound, and is evidently digging about inside, looking for the liver, only a little of which can be seen, just as far as the painter has opened the incision of the wound; and it is pressing the sharp tips of its claws into Prometheus' thigh . . . Prometheus' expression is filled with a mixture of hope and fear: he has one eye on the wound, the other on Heracles; he wants to look at the hero, but the pain drags his attention back to the wound.[20]

Clearly such a promising source of bizarrerie was too good to confine to mere *ecphrasis,* and we find the subject of Prometheus invading the *meletē* as well with a further twist. Seneca records a *controversia*-subject with some Greek declamation-fragments:

> The Athenian painter Parrhasius bought an old man from among the Olynthian captives whom Philip of Macedon had put up for sale, and brought him to Athens. He tortured him, and used him as a model to paint Prometheus; the Olympian died under torture. Parrhasius put the picture in the Temple of Minerva. An action is brought of harming the state.[21]

It is not hard to see why such a grotesque business should have found its way into the repertoire. It offers the opportunity for an *ecphrasis* of Prometheus' sufferings and those of the old man; the familiar antipathy of the Athenians to Philip; an artistic or cultural theme paradoxically perverted; and some sort of disquisition on sacrilege and the state. Nor was Prometheus the only subject to offer such possibilities: the Oedipus theme could be pressed into the plot of a declamation subject, then recycled into a series of bizarre vignettes which Himerius 'orders' a painter to paint.[22] Or Libanius could put words into the mouth of a painter trying to paint Apollo on laurel wood when the surface refuses to accept the colours out of loyalty to its former self Daphne![23]

In the case of Lucian and Philostratus on centaurs we have an opportunity to look at two sophistic writers on almost exactly the same subject, and we have some notion of its range of possibilities.[24] First we can note the nature of the subject itself, doubly paradoxical: not a centaur as such, but a family including a female centaur and her young. The centaur is an acknowledged freak; no less freakish is the idea that it can have a gentle side. Both writers comment in different ways on the join. For Philostratus 'the tenderness of their female form acquires sturdiness when the horse is seen blended with it' (ἡ γὰρ τοῦ γυναικείου εἴδους ἁβρότης ῥώννυται συνορωμένου αὐτῷ τοῦ ἵππου),[25] while for Lucian,

> The fusion and junction of bodies as the horse part is merged with the woman part and bound to it is done through gradual change, not as an abrupt one; so that the subtle transition deceives the eye as it passes gradually from one to the other.[26]

So far little to choose. Both writers also comment on the nature of the baby centaurs:

> Some gambol underneath their mothers, some embrace them as they kneel down, and this one is throwing a stone at his mother, for already he is too cheeky . . . some show a little shagginess as they leap about, and are sprouting manes and hooves, even if these are still tender.[27]

For Lucian, 'as for the young, their infant nature is wild and in their gentleness they are already fearsome.'[28] The parallel working out of possibilities seems predictable enough, and one sophist again much like another. But beyond this point Philostratus is inclined to delight in parading unconventional information. Pelion is 'a very pleasing home; for I think you would not weary of Pelion and the lifestyle there with its growth of ash nourished by the wind: this furnishes spear-shafts that are straight and do not break at the spearhead'. And there is a chance for still more paradox (a white female centaur growing out of a black mare).[29] This is the sort of material Lucian is able to avoid: as so often, a greater degree of success may consist in knowing when to stop.

None the less Philostratus' tendencies point to a general trend: the painter, like almost anyone in the sophist's world, must be invested with *sophia*.[30] Hence we find the application of *paideia* to the visual arts in a number of topics of abstract aesthetics which tend to recur in sophistic writing. These again did not require any detailed knowledge of artists or their work, but turned on the repertoire of problems already familiar to Plato and his contemporaries.[31] This allows the possibility of Platonic 'authority' and ornament.[32] When discussing the portrayal of the gods, Apollonius of Tyana is made to defend anthropomorphic images before Ethiopian sages used to gods in animal shape:

'So artists like Phidias,' said [Thespesion], 'or Praxiteles, went up to heaven, did they, took a mould of the forms of the gods, and then used their art to reproduce them? Or was there some other factor which governed their creation?' 'There was indeed,' said Apollonius, 'and something replete with wisdom.' 'What sort of thing,' said the other, 'for I do not think you could name any except imitation?' 'It was imagination,' replied Apollonius, 'that produced these works, a more subtle creator than imitation; for imitation will only create what it has seen, but imagination will also create what it has not seen. For it progresses fearlessly to the end it has set itself.'[33]

Philostratus has taken the opportunity to allude to the celebrated discussion of imitation in *Republic* 10, but as it were to go beyond Plato in introducing an instinct that surpasses imitation (in fact it amounts to the Aristotelian conception of imitation already outlined in *VA* 2.22). It is not uncharacteristic of Philostratus to set such a discussion in an exotic spot in the Egyptian desert, where the Hellenic philosopher Apollonius can be made to rout his barbarian opponent none the less. If a sage cannot find Hellas everywhere, he will proceed to import it.

Plato can also supply the sophists with suggestions for how imagination can produce artistic creation. He can present Socrates as proposing to fashion an image of the mould of the tyrant that will turn out a single shape of a manifold and many-headed monster with a circle of heads of both tame and wild beasts, and is able to change them and grow from itself all these growths:

'That would be the work of a skilled artist,' he replied, 'but nonetheless, since words are more plastic than wax and other things of the kind, let us assume that it has been fashioned in this way.' 'Then fashion one other form, that of a lion, and a third, that of a man, and let the first be by far the largest and the second one second in size.' 'That is easier,' he said, 'and has been done.' 'Join together the three in one, then, so as somehow to coalesce.' 'They have been so joined,' he replied. 'Then mould around them on the outside the likeness of a single creature, that of a man, so that to anyone who is not able to look inside but who can only see the outside sheath it has the appearance of a single living creature, the man.' 'The sheath is moulded round him,' he said.[34]

It is an easy matter for a sophistic writer to turn this 'no-sooner-said-than-done' comedy from the portrayal of a tyrant's soul to that of an emperor's mistress' body:

> So, then, let us invite along Polygnotus and our old friend Euphranor, and Apelles and Aetion. Let them divide the work, with Euphranor colouring the hair the way he painted Hera's; and Polygnotus doing the majestic brows and the faint red glow of her cheeks, the way he did Cassandra in the Lesche at Delphi . . . and Aetion must do her lips like Roxana's. But wait – here is Homer, the best of painters, even beside Euphranor and Apelles. The colour Homer applied to the thighs of Menelaus when he likened them to ivory with a tinge of crimson – it must be like that all over; and let this same artist portray the eyes and make her 'ox-eyed'. And the Theban poet, too, shall take part in the work, and give her 'violet brows'. Yes, and Homer shall make her 'a lover of smiles' and 'white-armed' and 'rosy-fingered', and altogether he shall liken her to golden Aphrodite far more appropriately than he did the daughter of Briseus.[35]

Lucian elects to turn the painting of Lucius Verus' companion Panthea into an elaborate tour de force of *paideia*, characteristically skipping when he can from artistic to literary 'authority'.

Second Sophistic writers had a particular penchant for cultural topics dealing with the artistic achievements of the classical period. But it is noteworthy how often the treatment of such material is either contrivedly incongruous or paradoxical, and concerned less with technical discussion of the art in question than with the urbane manipulation of its background. Anecdotes about artists well illustrate the nature of the repertoire. When Parrhasius loses a competition with his painting of Ajax, then Ajax can be said to have been defeated twice; or when Zeuxis charges money to see his Helen, she can be described as a courtesan.[36] By another paradox, the most unlikely agents can emerge as connoisseurs, as in the following anecdote in Aelian:

> When Alexander saw the picture of himself in Ephesus painted by Apelles he did not praise it according to its merits. But when his horse was brought in and neighed at the horse in the picture as if it was a real one, 'Your majesty,' said Apelles, 'it seems that the horse is much more artistic than you.'[37]

The ultimate in games with *ecphrasis* is to make the artist a sophist in his own right. Even this had Platonic sanction: in the discussion of imitation at the end of the *Republic* it can be claimed that 'the *cheirotechnēs* is able to produce among much else all that is in heaven, and that makes him a marvellous sophist.'[38] It is not too far from this to a literal development in Dio Chrysostom, who brings Phidias himself into court to deliver a speech in defence of his conception of Zeus. Sophists have a penchant for expertise, and the ultimate expertise is that of the orator: 'if in your eyes I am held to be at fault for my handling of the statue's features, you would not be too hasty in being angry first with Homer'.[39]

With Phidias' speech the artist's atelier has become the sophist's salon, just as easily as sophists might see their exhibition halls as art galleries. Art was as much an organ of Hellenism as literature, and for that reason alone sophists had every reason to find ways of annexing it. It will be clear that 'description' in sophistic hands was more than a mere literary exercise. Like so much else it was an extension of cultural experience and a way of seeing the world. But as often as not it did not presuppose any commitment of sophists to art as such, as opposed to the literary opportunities provided by its subject-matter; yet here as elsewhere the sophist is the arch-illusionist, and no field is too remote from the impression of his expertise.

We might make the transition from image to novel through one final example. When Clitophon, the hero of Achilles Tatius' novel *Leucippe and Clitophon* is drinking with his beloved, he describes a distinctive drinking-cup:

> The whole piece was hollowed out of solid crystal: there were vines wreathing round the rim in a crown, growing out of the vessel itself; and the clusters were festooned all over. When the cup was empty, the grapes were unripe; but once you pour in some wine, the clusters turn dark red, and cause the unripe grapes to ripen.[40]

Achilles' choice of subject accords neatly enough with the generally Dionysiac flavour of the wine-party of which it forms a part. But it also has a very specific reference to a rare type of luxury artefact, an *allassōn*, in which the colour of the surrounding vessel changes with the presence or absence of light. The most celebrated surviving example belongs in fact later than Achilles: the so-called Lycurgus cup, again with a Dionysiac reference, dates from the fourth century. But there is more to this than artistic reference: this rare and strange object underlines the penchant of sophistic writers for the paradoxical. And we can also note an individual touch of a kind at which Achilles is adept. Clitophon is about to look more sensuously at Leucippe, and we are about to be told that wine is the sustenance of love; it is not too hard to see an erotic symbolism in the wine filling the vessel from the bottom upwards. In the hands of sophistic writers artistic description can be used as the ally of erotic fiction, and to that we shall now turn.

8

Logos Erōtikos: the sophist as storyteller

From the very first exercise in the *progymnasmata* sophists could expect to be trained in the art of telling stories as such, and some sophists at least would have made successful raconteurs in their own right. The *prolaliae* to sophistic performances frequently entail inserted stories for the purpose of relaxing the audience; and we hear that Hadrian of Tyre used marvellous accounts of the practices of magicians,[1] to the extent of actually being mistaken for one. Lucian's *Philopseudes* and Apuleius' *Metamorphoses* would testify to a similar talent; and we have already seen how far the world of the *progymnasmata* is reflected in the extended narrative that begins Dio Chrysostom's *Euboicus*. It is time to consider sophists as narrators in their own right.

The reflexes of telling a simple story in elaborate form can perhaps be seen to best advantage in a predictable tale such as that of a holy man raising a patient from the dead. In the story of Jairus' daughter as it appears in St Mark's Gospel we have such an account in almost its simplest possible form:

> And they came to the house of the leader of the synagogue, and saw the hubbub, and a great deal of weeping and wailing. And [Jesus] went in and said to them, 'Why are you making a row and weeping? The child is not dead, but is sleeping.' And they laughed at him . . . and taking the child's hand he said . . . 'Girl, I tell you, wake up.' And she immediately got up . . . and immediately there was great rejoicing.[2]

When Apuleius tells a similar tale about the healing powers of the doctor Asclepiades, we have the chance to see such a scenario in sophistic hands:

When he came into the city and returned to his own quarter from the country, he saw within the boundaries of the city a huge funeral and a great throng of people who had come for it standing around, all very sad and dressed in the most mournful clothing. Already all the unfortunate man's members were covered in spices, already his mouth was filled with fragrant ointment; already he was embalmed; already he was almost ready for the fire. But Asclepiades observed him carefully, paid close attention to certain signs he noticed, and as he gradually inspected the man's entire body he observed hidden signs of life. Immediately he exclaimed that the man was alive: so they were to throw away their torches, take down the pyre, and return the funeral meal from the tomb to the table. Meanwhile there was a murmur: some said they should believe the doctor, some actually laughed at him. Finally against the will of even the dead man's relations – whether because they already had their hands on his estate, or because they still had no confidence in the doctor – Asclepiades none the less succeeded with great effort in the difficult task of obtaining a brief respite for the dead man, and sent him home. Thus wrested as he was from the hands of the undertaker as if from the jaws of death, Asclepiades immediately restored his spirit and with certain medicines immediately revived the life hidden in the recesses of his body.[3]

Pleonasm, antithesis and alliteration run riot here: even the banal business of getting Asclepiades into town seems to call for arguably unnecessary verbiage (*is igitur cum forte in civitatem sese reciperet et rure suo suburbano rediret . . .*), and there is much more decoration of the kind, as in the fourfold accumulation of alliterating but carefully asymmetrical cola in the scene-setting (*iam miseri illius membra omnia aromatis perspersa, iam os ipsius unguine odoro delibutum, iam eum pollinctum, iam paene rogum paratum*). But the story's momentum is not diminished by individual detail or verbal artifice: the two aims can be readily integrated (*murmur interea exortum; partim medico credendum dicere, partim etiam inridere medicinam*). And we are also left with the intriguing suspicion of foul play: legacy-hunters (*captatores*) wish the funeral to go ahead with indecent haste. But above all the whole business has become something of a performance, like so much in sophistic literature.

It is in the writing of full-blown novels, however, that sophistic storytelling finds its most characteristic expression: the Early Empire reveals a flourishing industry of prose fiction based on stereotyped plots of love and adventure.[4] Two of their writers, Chariton and Xenophon of Ephesus, emerge as relatively unpretentious narrators. Three other more ambitious writers have rightly been regarded as 'sophistic'. That is not to say that sophists in Philostratus' canon actually wrote novels; but the whole intellectual equipment they acquired and transmitted is characteristically reflected in surviving productions. And a sophistic novelist can cleverly present Eros himself in a sophistic context. Achilles Tatius makes him an αὐτοσχέδιος σοφιστής ('a sophistic improviser') when a hero is unexpectedly seduced by an attractive woman even after his own fiancée has reappeared, and the lovemaking itself is felt to be none the worse for having been improvised.[5] In Achilles at least one has the sense that the boudoir is about to turn into a sophist's classroom.

The completely extant sophistic romantic novels as generally understood are Achilles Tatius' *Leucippe and Clitophon*, Heliodorus' *Aethiopica* and Longus' *Daphnis and Chloe*. Papyri have steadily moved the date of Achilles back into the second century; Longus must still be tentatively assigned to the second or third century, Heliodorus to the third or fourth. Two further second-century productions, Apuleius' *Metamorphoses* and Lucian's *Verae Historiae*, will qualify rather as comic confections of the sophistic period; while Philostratus' own *Life of Apollonius* has a good deal of the sophistic romance about it. But these latter three are best considered as individual works on their own terms. For the present we must be content to ask ourselves what is 'sophistic' about Achilles, Heliodorus or Longus. It should not be regarded as simply a matter of date, as productions of possible or actual second-century date might well be excluded (in particular Xenophon of Ephesus' mediocre and possibly abridged *Ephesiaca*).

Some control on the sophistic element might be sought by comparing similar situations in novels that are generally felt to be 'non-sophistic'. I choose two versions of a familiar enough romantic impasse: the hero and heroine have been reunited after long separation, and the hero now recriminates with a

rival who has turned up in the interval. First Chariton, an
unpretentious writer generally assigned to the first century BC
or AD:

> When men are rivals in love, they are usually ready to go to
> war. And for these two the sight of the prize excited their
> rivalry all the more; so that had it not been for their
> respect for the king's presence they would have laid
> violent hands on each other. But they went only as far as
> words. 'I am her first husband,' Chaereas exclaimed; 'but
> I am her more reliable one,' rejoined Dionysius. 'I didn't
> put away my wife, did I?'; 'But you buried her.' 'Show me
> the deed of divorce'; 'I can show you her tomb.' 'Her
> father gave her away to me'; 'She gave herself to me.' 'You
> are unworthy of Hermocrates' daughter'; 'You're even less
> worthy – you were Mithridates' prisoner.' 'I demand
> Callirhoe's return'; 'And I am keeping hold of her.'
> 'You're taking another man's wife'; 'You killed your own.'
> 'Adulterer.' 'Murderer.'[6]

This is undeniably a rhetorical treatment, with neatly organised
accusations carefully contrived between the contending parties.
But the whole business is kept almost daintily under control.
Here by contrast is Achilles:

> [Thersander shouted] 'You have also a slave-girl of mine,
> a loose woman mad about men; make sure you keep her
> safe for me!' When he called her a slave and a loose
> woman, I was very hurt, and could not bear the wounds his
> words had inflicted, but while he was still going on I broke
> in: 'As for you, slave three times over, you're a sex maniac,
> while she is a free-born virgin, worthy of the goddess
> [Artemis].' At this he exclaimed: 'Are you slandering me,
> you a man in chains already condemned!', and with that
> he hit me hard on the face and followed with another
> blow, so that my nostrils were streaming with blood, as
> there was all the force of his fury behind the blow. But
> when he hit me a third time without looking where the
> blow was going, he accidentally hit his hand against my
> mouth, full in the teeth, and hurting his knuckles badly he
> shouted out and with difficulty drew back his hand; and so
> the teeth avenged the violence done to the nose, wounding

the fingers that had struck the blow, and the hand suffered what it had inflicted ... I put on a theatrical display of high-handed rage, and filled the temple with my shouting: 'Where is there left to go to escape such violent men? What is to be our refuge? To what other gods are we to turn, when Artemis has failed us? In her very temple we are being beaten; we are being struck at the very veil of the sanctuary ... Are not these the sacrifices barbarians and Taurians offer?; and is not this the Artemis of the Scythians? Only there is the shrine drenched with blood like this. You have turned Ionia into Scythia, Thersander, and in Ephesus blood flows as it does in Taurus.'[7]

This too is rhetorical, indeed a great deal more so. And it is learnedly and grotesquely so, with its exotic reference to human sacrifice among the Taurians. What is more, it is not only the author who knows it, but the character, as he tellingly admits that he has laid on a melodramatic speech when all the injury he has sustained is a trifling nose-bleed, already atoned for by his opponent's mishit. We should have been tempted to say that Clitophon's rhetoric was gratuitous; however, he tells us that himself, so that it is no longer so but contributes a clever twist to his character. It would not be unfair to suggest that Achilles has gone over the top, but that he has done so knowingly. This is indeed virtuosity in the use of rhetoric, and marks a sophistic resourcefulness. Part of the distinction between these two treatments is in ambition and scale, part a matter of the particular preoccupations of craftsmanship. But part is also a matter of cultural ethos and attitude of mind, both of the writer and of the society his characters reflect.

Such an ethos entails a fairly distinctive repertoire of sophistic erotica which turns up in any rhetorical context. It is required for example by the author of the second treatise attributed to Menander Rhetor, when illustrating the procedures for epithalamia:

And if we were athletes and had to compete at the Olympic or Pythian Games against other men, there would have had to have been a prize on offer, a herald at the scene, a judge to establish the winner, and a race-course open to the public. But since what is being performed is the rite of marriage, with Eros as umpire, Hymen as herald, and the bedroom as your racecourse, you must be sure not to suffer the fate of cowards in battle, to fear being routed even before the engagement begins. Reflect instead that on one side your attendant is Desire, while Marriage stands on the other, and Love is the judge, and Hymen cries 'Go and fight in a manner worthy of your ancestors.'[8]

It is hard to keep the sophist out of the bridal suite, and not a little of his repertoire in such quarters will be supplied from Platonic treatment of Love, perhaps best illustrated by the author of the pseudo-Lucianic *Amores*.[9] The anonymous author of this fourth-century text has done little more than reshuffle some Platonic parts and rearrange Platonic 'furniture': the *Phaedrus* plane-tree, the mixture of fun and seriousness, or the affectations of surprise at the eloquence of another speaker.[10] One notes, however, several extensions of Platonic paradox: it is the non-lover, Lycinus, who is appointed judge of the contest of lovers – a new variation on the point of Lysias' speech. And despite the elevated tone of the speakers there is a new physical element with Platonic décor and propriety focused on admiring the buttocks of a statue of Aphrodite – once violated by a human lover, as it turns out;[11] while after the speeches and arbitration, a final speech dwells on the physical delights of intercourse, and the physical relationship of Socrates and Alcibiades.[12] This is an essay in the elegant scholarship of sex. And that is one of the traits which sophistic writers will be tempted to incorporate into their views of the romantic plot.

In scale neither Achilles nor Heliodorus errs on the side of brevity: they presuppose a readership with as much leisure for private reading as Aristides' audience would have needed for the proper study of his speeches.[13] They contain and indeed flaunt an ornament of theme as well as style which is not totally essential to the standard romantic plot. In matters of style they find room for the same degree of sententiousness as the standard rhetorical exercises themselves. This will be evident from Achilles' handling of an εἰ γαμητέον; ('should a man marry?'), delivered with considerable bias by the homosexual Cleinias to his cousin, the hero Clitophon:

Why, the magnitude of the evil can be conjectured from the very preparations for a marriage, the whistling of the flutes, the banging of doors, the carrying of torches;

anyone who sees all the disturbance would naturally say: 'How wretched is a bridegroom – he looks to me like one being sent off to the wars!' If you were one that were uninstructed in the examples of poetry, you might perhaps be unaware of women's doings; but as it is you know enough even to teach others the kind of stories with which women have filled the stage – Eriphile's necklace, Philomela's feast, Sthenoboea's false accusation, Aerope's wicked stratagem, Procne's murder . . .[14]

But in a wider narrative context it is possible to follow up such an outburst. The homosexual lover who pronounces it soon finds his boyfriend killed in a riding accident for which he himself has been in part responsible. It is not an exercise for its own sake, but integrated – cynically – into the plot.

Heliodorus is no less resourceful in his techniques of incorporating the stock in trade of the *meletē* into his cleverly convoluted story:

'But in this present case I am asking from you one single item of our booty: this foreign girl here. Although I could give her to myself, I think it better to take her by common consent; for it would be foolish to take the prisoner by force and so be seen to act against the will of my friends. But I do not ask this favour from you for free. In compensation I shall take no further share of the spoils. Since we priests have no regard for mere sex it is not for physical pleasure that I have decided to make her my own, but to continue my family line.

And I want to give you the reasons. First of all she seems to me to be of high birth. I infer this from the treasure we found with her, and the fact that she has not succumbed to her current misfortunes but maintains a spirit in accordance with her original status. Secondly I guess that her soul is good and chaste: for if she excels all other women in her beauty, by the modesty of her looks she induces respect from all who see her: surely she must inspire the highest estimate of herself, and rightly. But my most important point is this: I think she must be the priestess of one of the gods. At any rate she thinks it quite wrong to remove her sacred robe and fillets even in her dire misfortune. And so, my friends, what more fitting marriage could there be than that of a high priest who marries a consecrated priestess?' They all cheered him and wished him an auspicious marriage. 'I am grateful to you,' he went on, 'but we should also act correctly if we were to ask the young lady how she feels about this.'[15]

The paradoxical character of the speaker Thyamis offers a clever variation on that standby of the rhetorical schools, the prostitute priestess: here we actually meet our first priestly pirate-chief. His credentials of priesthood are impeccable and he will in due course succeed to his rightful office, from which he has been only temporarily excluded. He goes to any length to establish that he is no lustful ravisher, but we are not obliged to believe for a moment that physical attraction is not the primary motive for his wish to marry the heroine Charicleia; such patently disingenuous rhetoric is duly frustrated by events.

Some at least of the foregoing situation could have been produced as readily by a 'presophistic' novelist such as Chariton, though we should have expected his treatment to be less complex and subtle. But with Achilles' production in particular we are conscious of an ethos of smartness and cynical sophistication. We are dealing not with a lover in the Sicilian street, but with a lover straight out of a Tyrian declamation school. Clitophon is physically as well as intellectually experienced;[16] there has been sexual experience for a start, and a distinctly academic approach to sexuality: the scene in which the hero debates the comparative merits of homosexual and heterosexual fulfilment seems as much in place here[17] as it would have been out of place in *Chaereas and Callirhoe*.

The three so-called sophistic novels respond in quite different ways to the challenges and opportunities of 'sophistic' manner and material. It might not be unfair to suggest that Achilles Tatius is the author who presents a sophistic face to the world with the least apology or inhibition; in particular the materials of the *progymnasmata* are quite obtrusively present, at any rate in the first half of the romance. *Ecphrasis* is particularly prominent,[18] both of landscapes (Sidon and Alexandria)[19] and of a series of works of art which prefigure points in the action,[20] of paradoxa including the hippopotamus, phoenix and crocodile,[21] and of 'erotic psychology'.[22] But that is perhaps of less consequence than the general atmosphere and the presentation of the character of the hero; one feels, and is meant to feel, that he is a product of a sophistic academy, whose resources he has committed with gusto to the service of love and seduction.[23] One could argue that the author knows no other idiom than school rhetoric, and that it is applied all but indiscriminately;[24] yet that is not wholly true, and the sheer exuberance of Achilles' *epideixis* is restrained as the plot itself gathers momentum.

The important feature is that Achilles is able to manipulate and control the sophistic resources at his disposal, and so to arrange them as to assist rather than hamper the plot. He does allow himself a lengthy paradoxical *ecphrasis* of the Nile:

> Their river is land, sea and lake; and it is a strange spectacle to see together the boat and the hoe, the oar and the plough, the rudder and the winnowing-fan; it is the place where sailors meet farmers and fish meet oxen. Where you have just sailed, there you sow, and where you sow the sea is being farmed.[25]

But there is nothing rhetorically strained about the description of the robbers' haunts, and little encumbrance in the elaborate ruse, ambush and battle which follows,[26] yet Achilles cannot resist some indulgence: 'there are strange misfortunes – so many shipwrecks, yet not a ship in sight; both happenings were strange and paradoxical, a land-battle in the water and ship-wreck on land.'[27] Yet when he chooses he can produce as exciting a battle scene as any historian with a sense of vividness (*enargeia*):

> There were scouts watching what was going on from a distance. The *boukoloi* [marsh-pirates] had disposed them in advance, with orders to cut down the river-dyke and unleash the full force of the water against the enemy should they see them crossing . . . everything happened at once; the old men facing them suddenly stood apart, while the rest raised their spears and ran forward. And the water was on them already.[28]

Moreover, the most idiosyncratic descriptions are disposed in a manner which makes them more than merely ornamental: an Egyptian commander is presented as talking to the heroine about the hippopotamus and elephant, thus both showing off and revealing himself to be an inept bore.[29] By contrast the hero Clitophon also woos the lady with *Naturwissenschaft* – thus demonstrating adolescent ineptitude in his accumulation of rhetorical overingenuity.[30] Indeed Clitophon cannot even experience his first sight of Leucippe without having his ineptitudes subjected to careful rhetorical organisation:

> As soon as I saw her, I was lost, for beauty wounds deeper than an arrow and floods down through the eyes into the soul; the eye is the passage for the wound of love. Every emotion took hold of me at once – admiration, amazement, fear, shame and shamelessness. I admired her height, I was amazed by her beauty, I showed fear in my heart; I shamelessly stared at her, but was ashamed to be caught staring. I kept trying to take my eyes off the girl, but they refused to obey me; instead they dragged themselves back, attracted by the pull of her beauty, and at last they won.[31]

At first sight Achilles seems to be saying nothing out of the ordinary: 'Love at first sight,' 'I couldn't take my eyes off her,' and the like. But at the same time he is establishing a web of imagery which is both recurrent and characteristic: wounding, eyes and the conflict between modesty and lust. All of these topics will receive a good deal of variation and development through the purple passages of the story, as when Achilles describes the prospect of drowning, for example:

> A slow death at sea anticipates suffering before it actually happens. For the eye takes its fill of the huge ocean, extending the fear beyond all bounds, so that those who die that way suffer greater misfortune; for the fear of death is as immense as the sea itself.[32]

Such touches collectively amount to a good deal of self-indulgent rhetorical mannerism in Achilles' case: there is an almost Ovidian self-indulgence in rhetorical excess for its own sake. But what Achilles is well able to show is that the texture thus created does not detract from the equally mannered chain of incidents that make up his plot. Rhetorical grotesquerie is well suited to events that include three *Scheintod* (pretended death) scenes for the heroine: melodrama is no less effective for being cleverly mannered. Achilles has succeeded in establishing and sustaining a strong literary personality, and one quite different from that of his fellow sophistic narrators.

For a novel of even larger scale, Heliodorus' *Aethiopica* at first sight looks less preoccupied with the display of sophistic resources as such. The plot itself is particularly long on sheer romantic adventures, and indeed on such techniques of manipulation of narrative viewpoint as commend themselves to the readers of modern fiction. It is however in this latter respect that sophistic technique is itself most prominent. The long narrative of the Egyptian priest Calasiris which controls the action is an extended exercise in presentation of the same facts from different points of view: he seems to make it clear to the reader that he has heard the facts of the heroine Charicleia's parentage from the Queen of Ethiopia when he has really heard them from Charicles, the priest at Delphi, and had them confirmed by the Ethiopian belt left among his recognition-tokens;[33] and the plot as a whole has much in common with the sophistic atmosphere as characterised by Eunapius' *Lives of the Sophists*. Calasiris himself has the air of a philosophic iatro-sophist throughout: it takes the best part of a page for him to explain to the credulous Charicles how the latter's foster-daughter Charicleia has been infected by the evil eye[34] – either through malevolent exhalations or simply unintentional ones – in order to conceal the fact that she is in love, as Charicles himself had correctly suspected, so that he himself can go on to arrange an elopement. Resourcefulness and narrative skill are well to the fore, as they must be for any sophist.

Moreover, much of the ethos has a markedly sophistic touch, as when the antiquarian credentials of the hero Theagenes, on an embassy from the Aenians, are reviewed.[35] The overall atmosphere of the Delphic festival shows the same preoccupations as for example Philostratus' *Gymnasticus*, with its concern for the athletic glories of the past.[36] As in Achilles, we expect a parade of readymade rhetorical devices – in particular *ecphrasis*;[37] but the texture is rarely flat or entirely predictable and it is carefully integrated by a sense of context. We can see Heliodorus in his element in one of several climaxes to the action:

> Once they sped round the walls in this way, then a second time; but as they were nearing the end of their third lap, Thyamis was already brandishing his spear against his brother's back and forcing him either to stand his ground

or be cut down, while the whole city stood round the walls and watched as if adjudicating a theatrical performance – it was just at that moment that somehow some divine power or some fortune presiding over human affairs interpolated a new scene in the tragedy, as if bringing on the beginning of a different play to offset the first one. It brought on Calasiris at the very hour of that very day to join in the race, and to be an ill-starred spectator of his own sons locked in mortal combat. He had by now endured many sufferings and engineered every means – he had even banished himself and imposed on himself exile abroad, in the hope of averting such a dreadful sight. But he was totally routed by destiny, and driven to look at the shift the gods had foretold to him long before; and although he first caught sight of the pursuit from a distance, none the less from all the prophecies he had heard he realised that they were his own sons, and forced himself in spite of his age to run faster than his years so as to forestall their fight to the death. And so when he had caught up with them and was already running alongside them, he kept calling over and over, 'What is this, Thyamis and Petosiris?'; 'What is this, my sons?' he kept on repeating. But for their part they still failed to recognise the sight of their father, for while he was still wrapped in his beggar's rags, they were totally absorbed in their contest, and they dismissed him as a mere vagabond or some other sort of madman. But some of the spectators on the walls were amazed at the way he took no thought for himself but tried to throw himself into the fray, while others thought he was out of his mind, and laughed at such a vain struggle.

But when the old man realised that he could not be recognised because of his shabby appearance, he cast off his disguise of rags, let down his priestly locks, threw away the pack off his shoulders and the staff from his hands, and stood facing them, a noble sight in his sacral magnificence. Then he slowly went down to his knees with his hands stretched out in supplication. 'My children,' he wailed through his tears, 'Here I am! Calasiris, your very own father. Stay still and stop this madness that fate has forced on you. Receive your own father and show him the honour you owe him!'[38]

In isolation, much of such a passage has the flavour of a straightforward declamation exercise: 'A father, advancing in years and disguised as a beggar, pleads with his sons disputing over a priesthood,' with its possibilities of melodramatic exclamation. Philostratus, like Seneca, leaves us in no doubt as to the excitement such outbursts might engender. Moreover the sophistic flavour is enhanced by several theatrical metaphors: the audience as judges of a dramatic performance, the notion of Calasiris *ex machina* and the superimposition of one drama on another.[39] Heliodorus seldom loses an opportunity to stress the sense of sheer spectacle inherent in a given situation. At the same time we can point to *mimēsis* of not one but two favourite Homeric passages: not only Achilles and Hector outside the walls of Troy;[40] but the situation in *Odyssey* 18 when Odysseus strips off his rags to reveal his heroic stature in the fight with the beggar Irus.[41] If we are in any doubt about the latter, the words about Calasiris ('many ordeals had he endured and everything contrived', πολλὰ μὲν ἀνατλάντα καὶ πάντα μηχανησάμενον) would have served as a reminder.[42] Heliodorus has a much greater emphasis on drama as opposed to melodrama than Achilles, and a still more expansive scale and manner. In both cases there is a strong sense of the overall control of proliferating elaboration, in this case with strongly religious interests as well; we could well have envisaged that had Aristides seen fit to compose a novel it might have looked rather like this (though without Heliodorus' often cleverly wry undertones and whimsical touches).

In spite of its different scale[43] and quite genuine emotional effect, Longus' novel *Daphnis and Chloe* is no less rhetorically contrived than the rest.[44] If we look for an *erōs sophistēs* we shall find it here as well,[45] in the ironic speech by a parasite with designs on the hero, remonstrating with his patron:

I who up till now was in love with nothing but your table, who used to swear in the past that nothing was more attractive than an old wine, who declared that your chefs were superior to the lads in Mytilene – I now consider only one thing of beauty, and that is Daphnis. I cannot taste expensive dishes, although every day there is so much meat, fish and honeycakes being prepared; but I should gladly become a goat and eat grass and leaves, listening to

Daphnis' pipe and having him graze me. But you must rescue poor Gnathon and conquer unconquerable love. But if not, I swear to you by my own god [Dionysus] that I'll take a dagger, and after filling my belly with food I'll kill myself in front of Daphnis' door. And you'll never call me your dear little Gnathon any more again, as you always used to do when you were having a laugh.[46]

Not surprisingly further outpourings in this vein cause the revolting Gnathon's patron Astylus to observe that love makes great sophists:[47] Gnathon blatantly misuses the eloquence of the *polis* to ends that are morally unacceptable (at any rate for the needs of the plot), and to no effect. But the lovers themselves have eloquence of a different order, as when Chloe wants an oath from Daphnis as their relationship deepens:

'Daphnis,' she said, 'Pan is an amorous god and I don't trust him. He fell in love with Pitys; he fell in love with Syrinx; he never stops making a nuisance of himself to the Dryads and pestering the nymphs in charge of the flocks. If you neglect your oaths to him, he'll neglect to punish you, even if you go after more women than a pipe has reeds. Swear to me, by this herd of goats and the very she-goat that suckled you, not to abandon Chloe, so long as she remains faithful to you. But if she does wrong by you and the nymphs, run away from her, hate her, and kill her like a wolf.'

Daphnis was delighted at being distrusted, and he stood in the middle of the herd, held a she-goat with one hand and a he-goat with the other, and swore to love Chloe as long as she loved him. And if ever she preferred another man to Daphnis, he swore to kill not her but himself. She was delighted and trusted him: she was a girl, and a herd-girl at that: she thought the goats and sheep were the proper gods for shepherds and goatherds.[48]

Here we have Chloe's adolescent insecurity translated into a game of lovers' oaths. The artifice corresponds to that of a couple of teenagers carried away by the melodramatics of first love; but the author's gentle humour adds a measure of genuine insight when Daphnis transfers the death sentence to himself. Once more in the tradition of the *Phaedrus* an author can show himself the master of false and truthful *erōtikoi*.

Longus' literary personality is different again from that of Achilles and Heliodorus: here we have a delicate miniaturist smiling at the naivety of characters set in a much smaller world, that of rural Lesbos. The traditional melodramatics of the plot with its pirates and kidnappings are offset by a genuine insight into the development of adolescent sexuality, observed in a very different way from that of the voyeuristic Achilles, as Daphnis and Chloe discover their feelings and synchronise with the rhythm of the seasons. We are made aware that Longus' own sophistication and his ability to smile at his characters does not inhibit a genuine sense of warmth and humanity. Like Dio in the *Euboicus*, Longus serves to show that the basic cleverness that goes hand in hand with superb rhetorical technique can be used to create a gentle country world away from the school and the theatre auditorium.

There is no doubt, then, of sophistic influence on the novel. Whether it was uniformly beneficial or not is another matter; but no sophistic novel fails in the way that the non-sophistic Xenophon of Ephesus so obviously does, with a melodramatic mishmash lacking judgement in almost every respect. And even the self-indulgent Achilles knows what he is doing and is able to carry it through. It was the rhetorically highly educated who made something more of romance than just another love story. The sophistic Eros is not just quiver and arrows and a bare bottom; there is a satchel crammed with *progymnasmata* as well.

9

Adoxa paradoxa: the *pepaideumenos* at play

So far we have noted those activities of sophists which in one sense or another are predominantly serious. But a sophist could strike other poses that were much less so, and attitudes that fostered a more light-hearted literature could influence the main body of his output. It is worth exploring this seldom discussed aspect of sophistic activity as a force in its own right.

'THINGS WITHOUT HONOUR': THE WORLD OF THE *ADOXON*

In the course of his travels Apollonius of Tyana meets a conceited composer of an panegyric on Zeus, and wryly acknowledges him to be an expert in encomium:

> 'And for that reason,' the young man replied, 'I have composed an encomium of gout as well, and of blindness and deafness.' 'And why not of dropsy into the bargain?' said Apollonius, 'and you mustn't deprive catarrh of your talents, if you really must praise those sorts of things. And while you're about it, you would do even better to attend funerals and rehearse encomia of the diseases the victims died of; for the fathers, children and close relatives of the dead will feel less pain if you do.'[1]

It is this kind of activity, the writing of so-called *adoxa*, or praise of things normally disreputable or worthless,[2] that has brought the Sophistic itself most quickly into disrepute in the past. There is felt to be something inscrutably perverse or stupid about a society whose most learned members expend their energies on the praise of, for example, hair or baldness, as Dio

171

and Synesius did.[3] Nor are those productions isolated: Lucian contributed the encomium of a fly,[4] Fronto examples on sleep, smoke and dust, and negligence;[5] and we know of a piece by Favorinus on quartan fever.[6] Philostratus felt that he had to justify at least Dio's production of such works: μὴ μικρὰ ἡγώμεθα, ἀλλὰ σοφιστικά ('let us not regard them as trivia, but as sophistic works').[7] Indeed Gorgias' *Helen* and *Palamedes* and his pupil Isocrates' *Busiris* attest to the prestige and ambition of such exercises; while Philostratus himself shows every evidence of having practised such techniques, and it is important to notice how pervasive their influence was on the modes of thought of any sophist. Fronto offers a working formula:

> In the first place the writer has to please. For this kind of discourse is not for the purpose of defending in a capital trial, nor to pass a bill, nor to encourage an army nor to inflame a meeting, but for *jeu d'esprit* and fun. But it should be handled in every instance as if the subject-matter were consequential and brilliant, and tiny things should be likened and compared to great ones. In a word the greatest merit in this sort of speaking is an air of solemnity. Tales of Gods or men should be brought in as the occasion demands; so too, relevant verse quotations and suitable proverbs and cleverly conceived falsehoods.[8]

A standard technique of the *adoxon* is to reduce the scale of everything to microcosm. Virgil's 'Battle of the Bees' is a familiar example,[9] and perhaps a pointer to intermediate tradition: the mock-Epic *Battle of the Frogs and the Mice* (Batracho-myomachia) is likely to have been a product of the Hellenistic world.[10] A less familiar example, from a sophistic hand, is Philostratus' *ecphrasis* of Heracles and the Pygmies:[11] despite the tiny scale of their operations (they assume that grains are trees), they try to lay siege to the sleeping giant. The opportunities for wit lie in the rational organisation of detail in an absurd situation: 'two companies assault the right hand, a single phalanx the left: the king takes command of the assault on the head, and brings against it all the apparatus of a siege'.[12] Again as in Virgil, there is mixture of humour and pathos: instead of the handful of dust to settle the conflict, Heracles sweeps them all into his lionskin to take back, one imagines, to Eurystheus.[13] But much of the playful use of *paideia* is not to be found within the narrow bounds of *adoxa,* nor will the *adoxa* themselves serve to explain a much broader attitude of learned relaxation: we find Philostratus picturing Favorinus and Herodes amusing themselves as they listen to the bad Greek of their oriental slave Autolekythos; while Lucian establishes at the beginning of *Verae Historiae* that relaxation is necessary after serious reading and so sets his audience or reader a tour de force of source-hunting.[14]

We can scarcely underestimate the importance of Plato for this aspect of the sophists' output. Here was a classical prose artist who afforded great prominence to sophists themselves (or to persons who called themselves by that name), and who struck a balance between serious philosophical exposition and elegant literary diversion in prose. He is the writer who above all embodies the polite learning of the educated in a charming way – in settings which emphasise relaxation, be it at the wrestling school, the harbour or the symposium. Plato is the patron of the scholar on holiday. Hence his Socrates can be made to discuss the Great King whose son is prince of Asia: if Socrates and Lysis prove to be better cooks than his son, will they not have the privilege of making the soup and throwing in the salt?[15] And as we shall see, few factors change the nuance of a situation so quickly as references to cookery. The *mise en scène* of the *Symposium* or *Phaedrus* promises more wit: wise men in their cups, or taking a leisured stroll in an unfamiliar environment.

But Plato will not explain entirely the lighter side of a sophist's interests. Many habits of thought were ingrained at the elementary stage of school training. A rhetor's technique was developed early and entailed dealing with a repertoire at least adapted for children. Fables, myths and proverbs belong to a naive world; and the development of techniques entailed in expanding them joined ingenuity to absurdity.[16]

The selection of material that might interest a sophist can be illustrated in short compass from Apuleius' *Florida*: among over twenty extracts there is an *ecphrasis* of a parrot and largely anecdotal treatment of Crates, Pythagoras, the Indian Gymnosophists and Thales, side by side with tales of the pipe-player Antigenidas and the poet Philemon.[17] We are in a world of exotic titbits and gossip about the great. Moreover, the world had moved on since Plato. Alexandrian literature had reflected the development of systematic scholarship and research by

establishing the taste for learned trifles. The learning of at least
some sophists was far from contemptible: one only has to think
of Favorinus or (by report) Herodes Atticus himself. History too
had moved on. If Imperial Greek sophists tended to stop not
long after Alexander, they could at least acquaint themselves
with the early history of the Hellenistic kingdoms and the new
vistas they opened up. The results might often be contemptible
in both literary and scientific terms: manuals of *Variae Historiae*
and *Mirabilia* were at best the scrapbooks, and at worst the
scrapheaps, of the educated.[18] But pedantic trivia could acquire
an entertainment value of their own.

HOMERIC HILARITY

The basis of literary education in Greece was still Homer,[19] and
he remained a correspondingly central source of diversion. It
was a task for sophists to transmute the questions of Homeric
scholarship into belles-lettres. Here again there was a chance to
contrive the maximum of absurdity within a framework of
familiar literature. The makings of sophistic attitudes to Homer
are ready to be taken over from Plato; Socrates can still affect to
give instructions to Phaedrus to tell Homer what the nymphs
had told both of them to tell him about the presentation of
truth.[20]

There was already Platonic 'authority' for criticising Homer
and for presenting criticism in an urbane manner. In an age
when Epic was less fashionable than prose, it was possible to
imitate the master in a way which was both scholarly and novel
by rewriting the canonic material in prose. When Homer's
Odysseus encounters Ajax in the Underworld, the narrated
action is presented as follows:

οἴη δ' Αἴαντος ψυχὴ Τελαμωνιάδαο
νόσφιν ἀφεστήκει, κεχολωμένη εἵνεκα νίκης . . .
. . . τοίην γὰρ κεφαλὴν ἕνεκ' αὐτῶν γαῖα κατέσχεν . . .

ὣς ἐφάμην, ὁ δέ μ' οὐδὲν ἀμείβετο, βῆ δὲ μετ' ἄλλας
ψυχὰς εἰς Ἔρεβος νεκύων κατατεθνηώτων.

The soul of Telamonian Ajax stood alone apart from the
rest, still angry because of my victory . . . such a figure the

earth now held because of the arms . . . Such were my words, but he made no reply, but went off with other souls of the dead corpses to Darkness.[21]

In Lucian's hands such a passage can be turned to very different effect, when Agamemnon asks:

τί αἰτιᾷ τὸν 'Οδυσσέα καὶ πρώην οὔτε προσέβλεψας αὐτόν, ὁπότε ἧκεν μαντευσόμενος, οὔτε προσειπεῖν ἠξίωσας ἄνδρα συστρατιώτην καὶ ἑταῖρον, ἀλλ' ὑπεροπτικῶς μεγάλα βαίνων παρῆλθες;

Why do you blame Odysseus, and why didn't you look him in the face the other day, when he arrived looking for an oracle, and why didn't you see your way to talking to your companion and fellow-soldier, but stride right past him with your head in the air?[22]

The *eidōlopoiia* involves a slight alteration in time and speaker, and a less formal medium; but now Ajax has the air of a bad-tempered spoilsport instead of a tragic hero.

Such a game can also be played by making Homer some sort of liar and manipulating the clichés of his biography. Because his life was already a popular mystery, there is a natural opportunity to disguise knowingly absurd theories as scholarship. In Heliodorus' *Ethiopica* the rather dubious Egyptian priest Calasiris claims Homer himself as an Egyptian on the ground that he was nicknamed ὁ μηρός ('the thigh') because of a divine mark of hair there left by his real father Hermes. His dupe Cnemon is convinced of this, because of the 'Egyptian' combination of mystery and pleasure in this poetry, as well as his divine genius![23] Dio Chrysostom's *Troicus* is the most sustained effort to assail the falsehoods of Homer.[24] His contradictions of the poet require little comment. Paris legitimately married Helen; Hector killed Achilles; Troy did not actually fall.[25] A recurrent reflex is to focus attention on the obscure characters in Homer. We know of at least five encomia on Thersites; while Philostratus centred his *Heroicus*[26] on Protesilaus, who of all Homer's characters played the shortest and least successful part in the fighting.[27] And Dio set himself the task of constructing a character sketch of Chryseis, the cause of the quarrel between Achilles and Agamemnon, but totally unobtrusive in her own right.[28]

The extreme development of these tendencies is 'Homer the head chef'. Such a conception was not entirely new in the second century AD, but the whole *Tendenz* of sophistic literature undoubtedly encouraged it. The length and breadth of the *Iliad* and *Odyssey* can be made to yield a considerable number of meals and scenes of relaxation, eagerly forced into Homeric 'teaching' on cookery and the arts. Athenaeus naturally seizes on Nestor's cup – and cleverly twists the sense of Νέστορα δ' οὐκ ἔλαθεν ἰαχὴ πίνοντά περ ἔμπης ('the roar of battle did not escape Nestor even as he drank') to mean that Nestor was drinking even at the height of battle, rather than that the battle reached the ears of Nestor when he had no reason to be expecting it.[29] But the *locus classicus* is Odysseus' reply to Alcinous:

οὐ γάρ τι στυγερῇ ἐπὶ γαστέρι κύντερον ἄλλο
ἔπλετο, ἥ τ'ἐκέλευσεν ἕο μνήσασθαι ἀνάγκη.

For there is nothing more shameful than a wretched belly, which forces a man to be mindful of it.[30]

And sophists were quick to remember that the shamefulness of it had been endorsed – and liberally practised – by Odysseus himself.

SOME SOPHISTIC SYMPOSIA

The natural setting for learned relaxation was the symposium, in life as well as literature.[31] Both Plato and Xenophon had laid the foundation for a genre of donnish humour, with scope for any amount of variety. And by nature it promised that learning was going to be paradoxically applied to food. The most conspicuous and bizarre example is the *Deipnosophistae* of Athenaeus,[32] the ultimate development of paradox and *paideia*. It is difficult to find the measure of this work, with its mixture of tedious recitation of recherché facts broken by recherché wit. It is not intended as a cookery-book, but rather as an extension of Platonic possibilities to the limit – if not well beyond. A curious accident of second-century interests made the genesis of such a work all the more likely. Sophists and their kind were interested as a matter of course in rare words, and such words for everyday things were to be sought in the Comic poet Aristophanes and

his contemporaries. The results frequently verge on the ludicrous: this is the place to find learned academic discussion of the
vessel the Cyclops drank from,[33] or even an inventory of the
duels fought at banquets.[34] And there is much of the pot calling
the kettle black: the polymath Ulpian interrupts Myrtilus'
recitation of lovers to ask whether 'tigris' is masculine – to be
confronted with suitable testimony; the man who knows obscure
facts about courtesans and flute-girls is accused of not knowing
the names of all Odysseus' companions, or of the men inside
the Trojan horse;[35] and the redoubtable Ulpian, of all people,
objects to the obscure cookery authorities who carry the names
of the great: Chrysippus of Tyana on breadmaking, Harpo-
cration of Mendes on honey-cakes.[36]

In Plato's *Symposium* food and drink had been of no account:
Agathon and his friends had not felt like drinking to excess, and
the choice of food had been left to the servants.[37] Already there
had been a hint of paradox: the host Agathon appoints himself
a guest, the waiters his hosts.[38] Imitators were able to develop
the implications in a facetious way. Cooks and chefs can now
become the centre of attention, and paradox and *paideia* are
most ludicrously at variance in the scholarship of cookery.
Athenaeus cites no fewer than eighteen authorities on *opsar-
tutika*;[39] and the title 'deipnosophist' itself is a facetious formation ('High Table at All Haddocks'; 'Fellows of the Royal
Gastronomical Society'). Here cookery is invested with the same
academic apparatus as literature or philosophy: hence special
reverence for Archestratus, the Hesiod of the dining-hall.[40] This
pretence allows some pseudo-scholarship on Hesiod himself:
any knowledge of cookery he possesses must be reattributed to
a master chef (how could the poet of rustic Ascra know about
the delicacies of Parium or Byzantium?).[41] There is even the
hint of a Socratic chef in Alexis, made to boast that he does not
teach his recipes for pay;[42] while as a matter of course Archestratus anticipates Epicurus, and cooks are illiterate if unversed
in the authorities on pleasure, Democritus and of course
Epicurus once more.[43] The concept of gastric philosophy has
arrived.

The author and his characters are well aware of the bizarrerie
of such a work. It is the only banquet to my knowledge whose
Epic scale actually enables it to possess its own catalogue of
ships.[44] The erudition of individuals is repeatedly admitted to

be excessive; when Cynulcus condemns Myrtilus' virtuoso performance on beauty contests, he himself cannot condemn
useless knowledge without citing Timon, Heraclitus and Hippon
to make the point.[45] Even the cook (Sophon, significantly)
rebukes an uninvited guest (*aklētos*) from Eubulus' *Auge* and
Antiphanes' *Lover of Thebes*.[46] Accusations of verbal dining and
verbal diarrhoea are both made and justified.[47]

The deipnosophists' erudition is extraordinary and difficult
to characterise. The scale can perhaps be measured by the
amount of information offered on the subject of water. And
individual diners are prepared to go to amazing lengths of one-
upmanship: Plutarch of Alexandria claims to have read Hege-
sander's *Commentaries* for no other reason than to find references to citron; or Ulpian is given an instance of *galeagra* ('sea-
weasel') in Hyperides – and told to look it up for himself![48] A
recurrent feature is the use of Plato as an authority on matters
he disapproves or condemns as luxurious. *Gorgias* 518B appears
in a list of testimonia from comic poets on breadmaking; Plato
appears no less unexpectedly in matters of hunger, thirst, tables
and even bedding.[49] And the *Deipnosophistae* specialises in one
particular learned paradox: the ridicule of the behaviour of
intellectuals at banquets.[50] We are even offered the lines from
the *Bacchae* with which the founder of Stoicism, Zeno, had
snatched back part of a fish someone had filched from him;[51]
and a recitation of philosophic set texts on banqueting does not
inspire confidence. This is the place to find Socrates on kissing,
with of course due authority in Xenophon.[52] Philosophers'
hypocritical misdemeanours are a cliché of imperial rhetoric
and satire, and Athenaeus' Myrtilus duly catalogues their expul-
sions.[53]

As to the conversation itself, Plato had allowed a limited role
for questions of language and style, including Agathon's parody
of the language of Gorgias.[54] In Athenaeus' hands, however,
there is scope for detailed treatment of linguistic eccentricity in
the form of the Ulpianist controversy, the degeneration of neo-
Attic purism into the mere tracing of exotic words.[55] A recurrent
paradox is the idea that the whole business of dining is a kind of
heroic warfare in its own right. Naturally a long Epic parody
from Matron is quoted, beginning δεῖπνα μοι ἔννεπε, Μοῦσα,
πολύτροφα καὶ μάλα πολλά ('Dinners rehearse me, O Muse,
much-nourishing and very many'), parodying the opening line

of the Odyssey, Ἄνδρα μοι ἔννεπε, Μοῦσα, πολύτροπον, ὃς
μάλα πολλὰ, and particularly ingenious in its change of only a
letter from *polytropa* to *polytropha* ('of many wiles', 'of much
nourishment').[56] And a tag requiring no alteration was of
course available in Homer (νῦν δ' ἔρχεσθ' ἐπὶ δεῖπνον,
ἵνα ξυνάγωμεν Ἄρηα – 'now go forth to the dinner, that we may
engage in the battle').[57] Alexandrian dinners are presented as
noisy and brawling affairs, those of Philip or Ninus as actual
wars.[58] It is not surprising to find even the host Larensis as the
Asteropaeus of Athenaeus, a formidable warrior on the field of
Dinner.[59]

Some sophistic banquets took place on a more elevated
plane. Lucian includes a symposium in the Islands of the
Blessed, with Plato predictably excluded[60] but Aristippus and
Epicurus in attendance, Aesop as jester and Diogenes, now
married to the courtesan Lais, dancing and making a drunken
fool of himself. Philostratus for his part can have Apollonius of
Tyana dining with the Indian gymnosophists – in a fairytale
landscape, with the local king as the statutory drunken disturber
who mocks philosophy and Tantalus somewhat surprisingly
honoured as a benefactor of mankind;[61] while Dio Chrysostom's *Thirtieth Oration* includes an elaborate banquet of life,
to which mankind is invited by the king of the gods.[62] This
richly ornamented allegory is a serious variation conflating the
Platonic *Symposium* and *Phaedo*. Perhaps because of the implied
frivolity of the motif of banqueting, Dio has ascribed it to an
unnamed peasant, who is allowed to describe the seasons as
waiters and the tables as meadows.[63] The texture of *spoudaio-
geloion* (serio-comic entertainment) is well understood and
assiduously cultivated, and not just by Lucian.

Such themes are developed with great panache at the expense
of Plato himself. The *Deipnosophistae* is the greatest *antisym-
posiasmos* of the master and so sets out to discredit him on a
corresponding scale, often using the techniques of Plato's own
attacks on Homer and the sophists. A motley crew of gossip-
mongers is assembled to present Plato as an unpopular egotist,
suspected as much by Socrates as by Gorgias.[64] But hypocrisy is
the main charge: Plato criticised Aristippus' attentions to Dionysius, while falling victim to his own criticisms;[65] and the arch-
critic of Homer is made to derive his doctrine of the soul's
immortality from that very source.[66]

PAST ABSURD: MARATHON AND ALL THAT

It is well established that the Second Sophistic had a cult of the Greek past.[67] But that too had its lighter side. The more familiar and accepted the facts of formal history, the more exposed it is to affectionate trifling. English history has long had its '1066 and all that', a bogus gloss on the history that every schoolchild knows and has been made to learn. Greek history has a similar repertoire of the improbable, and a sophistic ethos encourages the will to assemble it. The celebrated miseries of the Athenians at Syracuse can be made to look very different when adjusted into a rhetorical reversal (*adynaton*):

> It would have been the easiest thing for Thucydides with a single flimsy pen to overturn the counter-fortification at Epipolae and sink Hermocrates' trireme, to run through that confounded villain Gylippus as he was blocking off the roads with his walls and ditches, and end by throwing the Syracusans into the quarries and having the Athenians sail around Sicily and Italy as Alcibiades had hoped in the first place.[68]

Lucian was not, as we might assume, alone in such *jeux d'esprit*: Athenaeus is prepared to tell us what recitation the Athenians were listening to at the moment when the news of the Sicilian disaster was brought; and it is cited not as an illustration of 'stiff upper lip' but to show that Athens had a place among 'peoples devoted to luxury'.[69] This is the likely place to find those subsidiary details that must accompany the giant steps for mankind – such as the sacrifice of a hecatomb offered by Pythagoras to celebrate the discovery of his theorem.[70]

From the anecdote-books we can construct a little canon of trivial or paradoxical history. Sometimes this is a matter of context: the somewhat staid and snobbish Philostratus can legitimately single out the bizarre *bon mot* of Python of Byzantium before the Athenian Assembly:

> Why do you laugh, Athenians? Because I am so big and fat? My wife is much stouter, and when we agree the bed is big enough for both of us; but when we fall out even the house is too small![71]

In its proper place this *chreia* seems merely an unusually light-hearted illustration of political harmony (*homonoia*); it acquires

180

a different perspective when included in Athenaeus with tales of amazing fatness and thinness.[72]

Certain preoccupations emerge besides the merely amazing. Most striking perhaps is the class of anecdotes which deal with the petty foibles of tyrants. The mighty are cut down to size by presentation in their least dignified moments. The tyrant Agathocles has a wig which the Syracusans dare not tell him about;[73] Philip of Macedon pushes the dice-board under the couch when Antipater arrives;[74], or Demetrius Poliorcetes goes to the courtesan Lamia in full armour.[75] In particular Dionysius the Elder of Sicily emerges as the butt. Lucian offers quotation from his unbearable tragedies,[76] or presents Plato as his parasite,[77] while Athenaeus offers illustration of his horrific syllogisms,[78] or reports that his squad of flatterers goes so far as to imitate his own short-sightedness at dinner.[79]

There was a particular fascination with the Greeks who confronted barbarian luxury. Hence Athenaeus' detailed description of the great bed sent by the Great King to Entimus; or mention of the athlete who eats a whole Persian banquet (plus a table-leg shaped like a lentil)[80] while a guest of Ariobarzanes; or of Timocreon, who when invited to the Persian court, fills himself with food, then still conquers any number of Persian opponents.[81] Nor it is surprising to find a *syncrisis* of Persian and Spartan banquets – as seen through the eyes of the Sybarites: Spartans would rather die a thousand times than behave as they do.[82] And sophistic history is much concerned with royal gourmets and dinners of the great.

Military history too had its own set of paradoxes. A host of unlikely characters could be put in the front line. There are amateur generals such as Phrynichus, chosen for his marching songs in the theatre; or Timotheus, so effortless that he sleeps while Fortune drags the cities into a net.[83] Even the most celebrated commander can be put drunk into the fray: Philip drinks all night with his boon companions before going to revel with the Athenian ambassadors.[84] There is also a dossier of exotic accompaniments to battle: Lydian panpipes and flutes, Spartan flutes, Cretan lyres.[85] The most pointed paradox is perhaps that of the philosopher in battle, hence the interest in Athenaeus in examining the historicity of Socrates' bravery at the retreat from Delium,[86] for which the deipnosophists predictably suspect the sole testimony of Plato.[87] A related paradox was

181

that of the army of lovers contrasted with that of non-lovers;[88] it is not surprising to find Alcibiades as a dandified general, with a shield inscribed with Eros carrying a thunderbolt for his javelin, and Timandra, mother of Lais, and Theodote the courtesan on his campaign.[89] One tale most fully encapsulates sophistic taste: Sybarites teach their horses to dance to the flute at feasts; the men of Croton have flautists play the dance tune and cause them to desert in battle.[90] The tale incorporates ancient luxury, dancing animals and a paradoxical stratagem; there are variants, including Longus' ludicrous stratagem against the pirates, in which a troupe of musical cows capsize their ship on hearing a herdsman's pipe.

THE 'ALTERNATIVE' ALEXANDER

As arguably the most striking single figure in Greek history, Alexander acquires the lion's share of trivialising scandal and learned fun. We find jokes on his drinking, his being sexually out of condition, or his kissing Bagoas at the theatre[91] – not to mention his carousing in a chariot drawn by asses.[92] There is an inventory of his various charades, as Artemis, Hermes or Heracles. Or we are reminded that he re-enacted a scene from Euripides' *Andromeda* at his last dinner.[93] There will even be catalogues and cast-lists of the trivia of his luxuries – not excluding the international roll-call of artistes at his marriage in Babylon.[94] A similar series of stories emerges on the positive side: Alexander does not accede to a flatterer who attributes a thunderbolt to him; he rejects the idea of being a god who has to take medicine;[95] or he refuses to have a mountain carved in his image.[96] One story sums up all such *asteismoi*. The courtesan Phryne offered to restore the walls of Thebes in return for the inscription on her tombstone: 'Alexander destroyed them, Phryne rebuilt them.'[97] A sophistic mentality will seize on the paradox that Alexander is inferior in achievement to a courtesan.

The most standard features of Alexander's biography can be elegantly twisted to accommodate the thesis of a declamation: Plutarch's Alexander in the *de Fortuna Alexandri* turns out to be a philosopher: like Socrates he wrote nothing, but then his pupils turned out better![98] In this vein Alexander's luxuries can be added to the catalogue of his virtues; he could even claim that through him the gymnosophists will come to be aware of, and he of them. Alexander's moderation can be advanced with such pleas as 'who was it who mingled banquets with wars, who expeditions with revels, who orgies and marriage celebrations with sieges and military reviews?'[99] The fictions of declamation enable Alexander to be playfully represented as pleading with Fortune that she should claim Darius instead;[100] and it is more than faintly ridiculous that he should be made to provide a melodramatic catalogue of his wounds in the first person.[101]

Lastly, Alexander's immortality is a natural subject for satire: the Spartans propose a comic law, to the effect that Alexander should be a god – if he wants to be.[102] Lucian has Alexander defending himself on this score ('even if I did seem like a god to men, they could be pardoned for believing something of the sort about me in view of the magnitude of my achievements') – but the defence is conducted in Hades.[103]

History, then, could continue seriously in the second century, in the hands of Arrian; but round him is a world in which Alexander spends his time issuing drinking orders to the Macedonians while Socrates and Alcibiades man the front line. It is tempting to see in all this a kind of escapism.[104] The world was now in other hands; none but emperors could emulate the glorious deeds of Alexander; but he is always good for an erudite laugh. A convergent explanation, however, lies in the academic frame of mind. Not all academics are wholly serious all the time. We have already noticed the occasion when Bucephalus was declared a more discerning art critic than Alexander.[105] And it may well be that the dedicated biographer of Alexander joked with Marcus Aurelius about his going too late to school, when 'his' Alexander died at thirty-two.[106]

HISTORY INTO LUXURY: PARASITES AND COURTESANS

Sophists were specially interested in the revival of classical Athens: it is perhaps a surprise to see the presentation of parasites and courtesans against a scrupulously contrived background of the fifth and fourth centuries BC. With the decline of drama these characters become detached from their natural place in Comedy and can stand independently in *ēthopoiiae*.[107] And there they illustrate the sophistic quality under discussion: because they are the character types least likely to epitomise the genuine cultural heritage of classical Athens, there is a certain perverse sophistication in allowing them to do so. There were, however, precedents in classical literature for such types. The classic case is Socrates' interview with the courtesan Theodote:[108] Xenophon presents the dialogue as if the two meet on equal terms, and as if the courtesan's techniques of attraction constitute a *techne* in themselves, on a par with the wisdom of Socrates. Plato could contrive an equally wry treatment of Aspasia.[109]

A similarly paradoxical *paideia* could be attached to parasites. Athenaeus reports Athenian γελωτοποιοί ('laughter-makers') facetiously styled the Sixty – i.e. double the Thirty Tyrants.[110] There had been much insistence (in Comedy) on investing the parasite too with a *techne*; he could claim for example to be a λαρυγγικός, ('throat-specialist'), or a γελοιαστής ('laugh-artist'),[111] of course sharing much of his expertise with the chef, in whose smoke he is an expert.[112] The catalogue of absurdity extends to making him a loyal friend, soldier, hero and patriot: hence Podes the parasite of Hector, wounded in the belly by a Spartan, or parasites invested with the same prizes as Olympic victors, public maintenance.[113] All such jokes are well subsumed in Lucian's brilliant mock-encomium in *de Parasito*, where Odysseus and Plato are both shown to be practitioners of the art and the parasite can even be transformed into the ideal war hero.[114]

The clearest opportunity to combine paradox and *paideia* comes in the dialogue of philosopher and courtesan. Athenaeus' deipnosophists can summon a small inventory even of the courtesans kept by philosophers.[115] The likely outcome of such associations will be a dialogue such as that between the Cynic Nikion and a courtesan, inter alia over digestion.[116] The epistolographer Alciphron elegantly develops such a theme in short compass, as we shall see.[117] There is corresponding attention to learned 'research' on courtesans: for a short stretch Athenaeus has become a sort of erotic Pausanias, as he details the lore of a courtesan like Lais, ending with her tomb.[118] Indeed his whole inventory is presented as a rather unlikely 'Catalogue of Women';[119] while the conventional title of Hesiod's classic *Catalogue*, its puzzling first words *Ē hoiai*, are still more improbably passed off as the name of Hesiod's girlfriend.[120]

But parasites could provide several different lines of diversion.

Alciphron tends to concentrate not on the intellectual paradox of the scrounger but on his virtuosity as a picturesque scoundrel – and his discomfiture none the less. His parasite epistolographer Trechedeipnus is planning to 'fix' the gnomon on his patron's sundial, since the latter never dines before the appointed hour.[121] Such an operation is advanced as a 'ploy worthy of Palamedes', the very deviser of dinner-hours and therefore an innovator in such matters, unlike his stuffy master who 'has no radical ideas' (οὐδὲν φρονεῖ νεώτερον).[122] And the wit of several sketches lies in the parasite's detailed account of his ignominious escapades in the first person: Psichoclastes at the hands of Smikrines, apparently his dissolute young master's paedagogus, or Oenochaeron at the hands of Cleaenetus, his dissolute mistress' grim father.[123] And, as in Athenaeus, this learned world of Old and New Comic textures and expressions revolves round dinners and dining.

PHILOSOPHER-COCKS AND JACKDAW-SOPHISTS: ANIMAL ADOXOGRAPHY

With the treatment of courtesans we begin to notice the emergence of wisdom ascribed to people further and further down the social scale. And there is a tendency in sophistic diversions in general to assign great truths to unlikely sources. Anacharsis the Scythian can be presented as an unlikely authority on the folly of Greek athletics,[124] or Philetas the herdsman as an authority on Love as lord of the universe.[125] From their respective vantage-points above the crowd the Boeotian Heracles and Pan himself dismiss the follies of mankind: the former laughs at athletes' pretensions,[126] while Pan is indignant to find philosophers with beards like his own.[127] And such scenarios reflect the taste for popular philosophy, particularly with a Cyno-Stoic bent.[128] It is not too difficult to descend a little further again and see animals as the properly qualified commentators on human affairs.

The animal world is prominent in its own right in the Stoicising Aelian or the Platonising Plutarch: animals are instances of the working of Providence, and souls are subject to animal transmigration. The potential of animal material for paradox and *paideia* is no less clear: dubious curiosities about animals are already near the border-line; animals as learned interlocutors are over it. The pathetic fallacy was an ideal device for the exercise of donnish wit. A typical example of animal adoxography is found in Philostratus' *Life of Apollonius*: Philostratus decorates the purveyor of simple animal stories with pretentious Platonic apparatus, by adapting the myth of Epimetheus to account for the origins of fable. Aesop does not tell shameful myths (of the kind Plato had condemned); instead he was given the gift of telling farmyard stories when Hermes ran out of gifts. Philostratus is thus able to present even Aesop's fables as a special kind of sophistic creation: it was, after all, the first wisdom Hermes himself had learned when the Hours had told him the story of the man, the earth and the cow before his raid on Apollo's cattle.[129] This idealisation is reinforced in the *Imagines*, where Aesop is depicted surrounded by fables, with the fox as his chorus-leader.[130]

A common source of sophisticated amusement is the paradoxography relating to animals. It is scarcely surprising to find the garrulous Apuleius expatiating on the curiosities surrounding the voice of the parrot;[131] while Socrates' researches into the trumpeting of the gnat in Aristophanes' *Clouds* are nothing to the creature's boast in its own person in Achilles Tatius: σάλπιγξ δέ μοι καὶ βέλος τὸ στόμα· ὥστε εἰμι καὶ αὐλητὴς καὶ τοξότης ('My mouth is both trumpet and weapon, so that I am both musician and archer').[132] One notes also the verdict of the sages in Plutarch's *Banquet of the Seven Sages*, when faced with a newly-born centaur. Thales facetiously suggests that it is a portent requiring expiation – but adds that Periander should either not employ such young men as ostlers, or should give them wives![133] Such a company will readily discuss any other animal in a paradoxical way, such as the mule impressed by its reflection into behaving like a horse till it remembered its father, or the ass's musical bones, or even the dolphin who carries Arion, here unexpectedly reported as having performed in the very recent past.[134]

It is an easy matter to modulate from fable to *progymnasma*. Hermogenes demonstrates a standard school treatment of the monkeys and their city. The nuance of the exercise is changed the moment animals are allowed to make speeches; any animal which begins ὦ ἄνδρες πίθηκοι ('gentlemen of the monkeys') confers bogus sophistication, and a bunch of monkeys becomes a *Boulē*.[135] Achilles Tatius' fable of the lion and the gnat carries this technique well beyond textbook precept: the gnat delivers a tendentious *adoxon* on its own endowments before attacking the lion – only to fall victim to a spider. Small wonder that the servant Satyrus who delivers it has to acknowledge that he heard his version from a man of learning.[136]

The scope of delightful animal narrative can be gauged from the two contrasting handlings of the tale of Arion's rescue by Plutarch and Lucian. The former has carefully embellished the version of Herodotus with vivid realistic detail, which in turn reinforces the paradoxical nature of the story: the dolphins take turns to carry their charge, while Arion himself contemplates the nature of providence and sees the stars as the eyes of justice. The event is carefully contrived as just having taken place, so that it can be reported to Periander's Banquet of the Sages, to the amusement of Aesop ('You make fun of my jackdaws and crows if they talk to one another, and yet dolphins do silly things like that').[137] This is an invitation to confirm the Arion story with equally unlikely stories of the dolphin which conveyed the corpse of Hesiod; dolphins are musical and playful, and need only ever be punished like badly behaved children. Lucian for his part also presents the rescue of Arion as having just taken place, but this time even more playfully in the mouth of Poseidon, congratulating the dolphins on their philanthropy.[138]

The two classic cases are Plutarch's *Gryllus* and Lucian's *Gallus*. Both their respective central characters, the pig and the cock, turn out to be Homeric critics of distinction and indeed first-hand experience as well; the former had been transformed by Circe while the latter had been in action at Troy as Euphorbus, and is not above exaggerating his prowess; small wonder if he should confess that while he was Pythagoras he was a sophist as well.[139] By contrast Aelian is frequently content with retailing information in a mechanical way. But he can also choose to elaborate on the human qualities of his creatures, or their superiority to humankind. Military comparisons are frequent, as are Homeric ones:

> [of the dolphin] and just as in a military phalanx some serve as guards in the front rank, others in the second or third – what, my fine Homer, would Nestor be able to say to that, the Nestor you sing of as the best tactician of his day?'.[140]

Such topoi are easily inverted: it is just as easy to discover animal barbarians. Dio Chrysostom presents an 'Aesopic' fable in which among the other animals dogs listened to Orpheus and practised by themselves; transformed into humans as Macedonians, they were settled by Alexander in Egypt, and now survive in the harpists of Alexandria.[141] Or animals revert to type: hence the evident popularity of the tale of performing monkeys in disguise, which forget their human roles when nuts are thrown.[142] The moral is different in such cases: the fool cannot disguise his lack of culture. Two further instances suggest the propensity for such stories to acquire 'cultural' significance in addition to their entertainment value. When the Sybarites want to buy monkeys, Massinissa, King of Mauritania, asks them whether their women don't have babies.[143] The authenticity of the tale is perhaps less important than the reasons for its selection in Athenaeus: it offers an instance of the bewildered barbarian and noble savage, and yet another of the scandalous behaviour of the Sybarites, who prefer monkeys to men. There is also the *adynaton* of a whole city where monkeys will be brought up as men. A still more sophisticated instance is Apollonius of Tyana's rebuke of the rich fop who trained birds without himself having an education: the result is that even the birds will fall short of Attic purity.

Sometimes the pathetic fallacy is pushed to extremes: Aelian, who appears to be genuinely convinced of the moral sincerity and superiority of animals, feels free to present the flies as voluntarily absenting themselves from the Olympic festival (and in this particular superior to women, who have to be barred from it), then returning afterwards in the manner of exiles.[144] However, as often in matters of paradoxography, the palm goes to Achilles Tatius, who has the phoenix on its funeral pyre pronouncing its swansong; but of course as this must be a speech, the bird itself is an ἐπιτάφιος σοφιστής, 'a sophist pronouncing the funeral oration'.[145] And in the *Life of Apollonius* Philostratus sets such material in a much more pretentious setting: it is part of Apollonius' wisdom to recognise the wisdom of elephants crossing a stream with the smallest first, or surrounding their wounded like doctors round a patient.[146]

A TYPICAL BLEND: ALEXANDER ON THE DIET OF KINGS

A good idea of the lightness of cultural sophistication is offered by Dio's *Second Discourse on Kingship* (*Or.* 2): Philip of Macedon and Alexander are imagined in conversation at the Olympic Festival at Dium, obviously in an atmosphere of some relaxation, since they see fit to discuss the reading material suitable for a King. Why, asks Philip, does Alexander have such a preference for Homer? Only he has the sentiments suitable for a King, so that Alexander has not only no time for other poets but does not tolerate any metre other than the hexameter. Philip advances the claims of Hesiod, only to be told that he had suitable advice only for shepherds, carpenters and farmers. Rather than admire the much-quoted lines of Hesiod on the rising of the Pleiads, Alexander even prefers 'Homer on farming': this unlikely treatment turns out to be a simile in which Greeks and Trojans butchering one another are compared to two rows of reapers cutting barley or wheat.[147] Homer lost in the *Contest of Homer and Hesiod* – because of course the audience was not one of kings but of farmers: Homer therefore portrayed the Euboeans as effeminate in vengeance for the affront.[148] Philip introduces the opportunities for a *syncrisis*, by asking whether Alexander identifies with particular heroes. He wants to be better than Achilles, since Philip is not inferior to Peleus, nor Macedon to Phthia, nor Olympus to Pelion – nor Aristotle to Phoenix, who had the stigma of exile. Moreover, Achilles had to take orders from others and was not even in command of the Trojan expedition.[149]

Alexander is shown thus far in the unlikely role of a literary critic – and a very bad one, falling for the notion so well exposed in Plato's *Ion* that Homer has an expertise and that a narrative poem is really a textbook. 'Homer on farming' is an obvious *paignion*, and Alexander is patently perverting the poet: one might be tempted to compare Dio's similarly playful treatment of the boyhood of Achilles himself.[150]

It is no surprise after such a start that the qualities Alexander actually goes on to admire in Homer's heroes are extempore rhetoric – like the good sophist so many ancient worthies have now become. Philip has to speak in opposition to a good orator like Demosthenes,[151] so Alexander admires Phoenix, Diomede,

Odysseus, and especially Nestor.[152] In particular he points out
that the rescue from retreat at Troy was due to Odysseus and
Nestor, the orators: disingenuously, since he omits the fact that
on this occasion Odysseus actually made a physical attack on
Thersites as well.[153] We soon find other unlikely emphases: on
Achilles the musician, or the relative asceticism of Homeric
kings, to say nothing of their not eating fish.[154]

It is difficult to define the relationship between paradox and
paideia in the intellectual life of the early Empire, and perhaps
wiser to accept the sheer diversity of its patterns. In the first
place we must accept the enormous variation in the taste or use
of paradoxical *paideia* by individual writers: Dio Chrysostom can
free himself from the straitjacket of such a repertoire when the
occasion demands; Lucian and Philostratus are less able, or
rather less inclined, to leave it behind. In other cases our
evidence is sometimes less adequate, but we can reasonably
suspect that Favorinus' ten books of *Pyrrhonic Tropes* left rather
less room for erudite surprise than, for example, his lost
Encomium of Quartan Fever. The least engaging writers are those
who either indulge academic wit grudgingly, like Aristides, or
those who often seem unaware of the real potential of the basic
ingredients, and combine sophistic materials with naive moral
platitude, as in the case of Aelian or Maximus of Tyre. Yet the
impression remains that paradox and *paideia* embody quite
basic reflexes of the Second Sophistic.

THE ART OF THE MINIATURE

Adoxa are very often the more effective for being short works;
and the Second Sophistic produced a wide range of pieces in
various forms which can be treated together conveniently as
'miniatures'. For most of them this would certainly not be the
only possible label, and much of the literature on a good
number of them is devoted to 'Epistolography'.[155] I have preferred a description that enables us to look at, say, the shortest
dialogues of Lucian as part of the same literary phenomenon as
the *Letters* of Aelian or Alciphron. We should be asking what it
could have been that possessed sophists or *pepaideumenoi* to
write *Dialogues of Courtesans* or *Letters of Parasites*, and what
opportunities such art forms could have provided.

In the first place we might notice that the *progymnasmata*

themselves were miniatures by nature, even if they were capable of quite elaborate development. If their length was determined in the first instance by their role as preliminary literary tasks in the schools, they had a length none the less that sophists might well wish to use as a norm for the *prolalia* before an *epideixis*. We might also suspect that when such and such a kind of miniature was felt as a literary end in itself, then uses might also be found for it in the context of more ambitious compositions.[156]

Epistolography in miniature has been variously interpreted. Reardon has characterised the work of Alciphron as literary *pointillisme*;[157] others have been less charitable and condemned such products as little more than third-rate pastiches of classical material in the work of more accomplished sophists, in particular because of the suspicion that Alciphron draws both on Comedy and on Lucian.[158] But again much of the eccentricity of these works can be illuminated if we regard them once more as learned paradox contrived to make its point in the shortest possible compass. While the begging letters of parasites and love letters of courtesans are a natural kind of fiction, those of farmers and fishermen seem distinctly unlikely and affected: hence the farmer of Aelian's last letter can claim that 'If all this addressed to you is too clever for the resources of the countryside, do not be surprised: for we are not Libyan or Lydian, but Athenian farmers.'[159]

Miniatures offer a natural opportunity for literary variation; they can be readily worked in series. The accumulation of no fewer than nineteen *Letters of Courtesans* and fifteen *Dialogues of Sea Gods* by Lucian, or sixty-six *Imagines* by a single Philostratus, affords some idea of the fascination of the form, at least for the writer himself. And within each of such groups there was often scope for smaller sequences in turn: an amorous farmer and a reluctant courtesan; correspondence between Menander and Glycera,[160] different developments of Aphrodite and Eros,[161] or an Alexander-suite.[162] Some such compositions seem ingenious compressions of a variety of traditional forms and motifs: Aelian is able to find room for a fair impression of the substance of Demosthenes' *against Callicles* in a matter of sentences, in which he has been able to include a Hesiodic tag for good measure.[163] And in the seventh of Alciphron's *Letters of Courtesans*, we find Thais remonstrating with Euthydemus[164] about his ostentatious attendance on a sophist who is pestering her himself; she threatens to grant the latter the favours Euthy-demus is now refusing. Then follows a comparison of courtesan and sophist: the inspiration may well be the famous exchange between the courtesan and Socrates in Xenophon's *Memorabilia*.[165] Here however the paradoxes are more compressed: courtesans are more religious than sophists, as well as more moral;[166] and their clients do not dream of tyranny or revolution:

> We educate young men just as well as they do. For you can, if you like, judge between Aspasia the courtesan and Socrates the sophist, and work out which of them trained the better men. You will find that Aspasia had Pericles as her pupil while Socrates had Critias.[167]

Thais then reverts to a personal note with deliberate ambiguity: Euthydemus is to come 'so that we can have a little drink and then give each other a demonstration of that noble end, pleasure'. She herself is *sophē*, a wise woman, and believes in *carpe diem*.[168] In a sophist's world it is difficult to get too far away from expertise, even in so short a compass.

A similarly clever kaleidoscope is presented against a background of Comedy.[169] The author takes no more than a matter of lines to establish the scene: the father Euthydicus ('fairplay') has sent his son to town to sell farm produce, but he has fallen into the hand of the Cynics and has turned his back on his parents. What a turn-up! There should be a law against it! Such a piece might well be seen in terms of the *progymnasmata*, as a brief *diēgēsis*, though in fact there is only a minimum of action, which in any case the teller would be unable to recount. All he can know is that his son has set eyes on one of these men, and is now a follower. We have *ēthopoiia* here:('what words a farmer could say about a Cynic'). The detail is actually quite carefully controlled: few words on the familiar farming tasks, sending the son to sell wool and barley for 'brass'; but much on the revolting antisocial habits of the Cynics as they appear to the farmer; a touch of *ecphrasis* and *psogos* – for them the son is not the product of parents but a mixture of elements; money, farming and decency are all lost on him. The scenario itself is authentic enough: a simple generation gap and a popular antipathy to intellectuals. There are two important literary hints: the description of enthusiasm for philosophy compared to the bite of a mad dog is Platonic, and it has added point when applied to an attack by Cynics (*kynes*). And Euthydicus condemns the *Phrontistērion* of these philosophers, a clear enough allusion to the scenes between Strepsiades and Pheidippides in Aristophanes' *Clouds*;[170] (other allusions make it perfectly clear that Alciphron knew the passage). Having invited comparison with Aristophanes, how does Alciphron succeed? He does so in a Terentian rather than a Plautine way: a Greek comic model is naturalised, and ingeniously adjusted just far enough to be both ancient and recognisably 'modern'. Lucian correctly complains of Cynicism as a current phenomenon;[171] but it had still gone back to Diogenes' floruit, the fourth century BC.[172]

The double effect of compression and erudite wit can also be seen to advantage in Dio Chrysostom's paraphrase on Achilles and Chiron.[173] The young Achilles refuses to learn archery, as he regards the bow as cowardly, by implication condemning the characteristic weapon of the centaur who is teaching him; and he objects to being taught the lyre or how to dig (medicinal) roots.[174] Thus far this is a civilised conversation between tutor and a precocious but wayward child. Then comes an important break in the dramatic illusion: Chiron asks whether Achilles likes riding and gets the answer, 'No, nor do I like somebody like you, τοιοῦτος ὤν,[175] (with the implication 'you horsy creature'). Only very delicately does Dio hint at the absurdity of the mythical situation. But when Achilles goes too far and suggests that Chiron himself is better equipped for running away, the centaur reveals his true nature, φρίξας τὴν χαίτην ('shaking his mane'). Achilles gets a talking to: his parents have spoiled him – Peleus will have boasted of the gods who attended his wedding. And the child will never be a warrior: while others rule he will be bribed by gifts and silly compliments to risk his life and be killed. He will not even leave corpses unmutilated, but behave in a childish way. And he will die not at the hands of any noblemen but at the hand of ἀνδρὸς φρονίμου καὶ πολεμικοῦ ('a man skilled in the technology of warfare'), without even seeing him.[176]

Dio's little scene produces an ingenious compression of the *Iliad*, or rather an *Achilleid*, into a matter of sentences. From Chiron's point of view Achilles will make a childish adult, and the whole tragic sequence of the embassies persuading Achilles to return can now be seen in a new light: he will lose his life thanks to praises and bribes. But the mainspring of the dialogue lies in the fact that the real point is unstated, though it can just be inferred at the very end. Achilles will perish by the bow – and will not have the medical skill for a cure. What is it about all this that is 'typically sophistic'? Surely the clever moral twist that turns Paris into a man of science: missile technology is what beats Achilles, and he cannot foresee it. The traditional amorality of fifth-century sophists is just hinted at: Paris is ignoble, but that does not affect his weaponry. Not for nothing does Achilles in his childish banter call Chiron a sophist.[177]

One miniature in particular comes close to encapsulating the values of a good many previous chapters: Lucian's *Twenty-fifth Dialogue of the Dead*.[178] Hannibal disputes with Alexander the Great in front of Minos as to which of them had been the greater general. The accounts are sufficiently well balanced to suggest virtual equality: both are inclined to be almost equally specious on the subject of their respective military careers. Hannibal argues inter alia that Alexander was fighting against mere cowards in the Medes and Persians, Alexander that he invaded Asia with only a few men and that it was pardonable for people to think him a god in view of the magnitude of his achievements.[179] But the matter of *paideia* looms large: Hannibal has learned Greek in the Underworld (where it is tacitly assumed to be the international language of the dead); he had not had the benefits of being able to recite Homer, as Alexander had had; nor had he been educated by Professor Aristotle.[180] The matter is resolved when Scipio, the victor over Hannibal, acknowledges the superiority of Alexander, allowing Minos to place Hannibal a respectable third.[181]

Here we have an episode created out of little more than a single *chreia* from the voluminous folklore on Alexander.[182] The standard version concerned Hannibal in conversation with Scipio ranking Alexander before Pyrrhus, then himself; Scipio asks where Hannibal would have ranked himself if he had defeated Scipio, and the answer is 'first'. Lucian has reshaped the material considerably, not least in transferring it to the Underworld, where the precedent best known to him may well have been Aristophanes' *Frogs*, in which the competition was literary, not military.[183] One might say that he has mixed two types of *progymnasmata*, to produce *syncrisis* between two encomia – all within the framework of *eidōlopoiia*. There is also an unusual concession to the 'Roman' subject; but Scipio is duly made to grant the palm to Alexander, as readily as Roman emperors might have been asked to do:[184] Philostratus' 'Lucius' reminded Marcus Aurelius that he was still attending classes, while 'Lucius'' Emperor Alexander had died at thirty-two. The fun lies in having these two world-class rulers turned into practitioners of *meletae* on their own behalf; the values of the Second Sophistic make it possible for Hannibal to have a war of words with Alexander – and lose. And we also have a characteristically sophistic scene in which the *pepaideumenos* must triumph over the *apaideutos.*

In sophistic literature the idea of miniature should also be seen as a relative term. Longus' novel *Daphnis and Chloe* can fairly be claimed as such in relation to the rest of the genre.[185] Had it been very much shorter it might have qualified as a mere novella (though the terminology of both is foreign to antiquity). One has the sense of a complete and in some respects complex love story scaled down; single cases of *ecphrasis* of a sophistic sort are incorporated,[186] but on a scale scarcely larger than that used by Alciphron. Where larger forces are used, as in the Methymnaean expedition against Mytilene, they are rejected as irrelevant (a little hard-headed diplomacy and common sense renders them pointless).[187] The youthfulness of the hero and heroine is much more emphatically dwelt on than elsewhere: they are still little more than children, as they have to be to remain as sexually naive as they do. And they are 'little people' in terms of their social status for most of the tale.

Much of the detail is focused on tiny objects: the cricket that has to be rescued from Chloe's breast; the little child who could effortlessly harvest grapes from the tiny vines of Lesbos;[188] or the little boy Tityrus who brings Philetas' pipes.[189] And the slightness of Eros himself is stressed: the Hellenistic *putto* found in Philetas' garden turns out to be lord of the universe. There is a strong sense here too of the world of the *adoxon*:

> Love . . . is a god, young, beautiful, and winged. That's why he delights in youthfulness and pursues beauty and gives wings to people's souls. And he has greater powers than even Zeus. He has power over the elements, he has power over the stars, he has power over gods like himself – not even you have so much power over your goats and sheep.[190]

The last observation reminds us how tiny Daphnis' universe is at this point, for his powers of comparison to be so limited.

FANTASY AND PLAYFULNESS[191]

Often sophistic outlook will produce an alliance of fantasy and wit.[192] Declamation-subjects themselves can verge on the facetious, as when Libanius has a parasite accuse himself when the horse he is riding mistakes a post at the host's house for the turning-post of a racecourse, and so deprives his rider of a meal by carrying him off again.[193] And not all declaimers are blind to the results of excessive melodrama. When a pupil praised Nicetes of Smyrna's bombastic phrase ἐκ τῆς βασιλείου νεὼς Αἴγιναν ἀναδησώμεθα ('Let us bind Aegina to the King of Persia's ship'), Isaeus was able to ridicule him with ἀνόητε, καὶ πῶς ἀναχθήσῃ; ('Madman, and how will you get under way?')[194] Some of the epigrams seem to verge on self-parody, as we find in a declamation-fragment which is probably the work of Hadrian of Tyre. The mercenaries divert the river against the enemy and demand their reward in their plea before the Amphictyonic court:

> We did not waste any time on the war, but proceeded straight to victory ... what an amazing feat of ours this was. A whole army struck by a river, swept away by a land wave and flooded by a hand-made storm. To think that we not only did not fight on foot, but even fought a naval battle without ships ... to think we have commanded not only men, but rivers![195]

The context of this fragment is missing; but it clearly evokes yet another paradoxical battle where idle ingenuity and clever claims have replaced such troublesome chores as fighting.

The fantastic ingenuity called for by the school themes is similarly shown in Lucian's summing up of a claim by a would-be tyrannicide. Having failed to find his victim, but killed only the tyrant's son and left the sword in the body, he claims the inevitable reward for tyrannicide when the tyrant returns and kills himself with the same sword:

> In fact it was I who destroyed the tyranny in its entirety; but the roles had been distributed over a number of actors as in a play. I played the lead, with the tyrant's son as my

supporting actor, the walk-on part was played by the tyrant himself, and the sword served as the prop for all of us.[196]

Both the last two passages achieve their effect by incongruous crossing of the themes of declamation with the apparatus of drama: the mercenary is a *miles gloriosus* without raising a finger; while Lucian's tyrannicide characteristically combines his role with that of tragic actor.

What Bompaire called 'fantaisie barbare et exotique' is also for sophistic writers an important ingredient of both the literary and the philosophical repertoire.[197] 'Talk about things in India or Ecbatana' says Lucian ironically, but he is perfectly capable of doing so himself.[198] Beyond the thin crust of self-confident Hellenism is another world, where all things are topsy-turvy but where something is either Greek or even better than Greek. Dio gives his Alexandrian audience a laugh at the Scythian visitor who imagines that the ointment used by athletes at gymnasia is a drug which drives them mad till they scrape it off again. And Lucian devotes a whole dialogue, *Anacharsis*, to seeing the Greeks through the eyes of a rational and therefore uncomprehending barbarian.[199]

Lucian's small-scale dialogue *Charon* gives some idea of the scope of a learned imagination that combines sophisticated paradox with the simplest themes of moral philosophy. Charon has obtained shore-leave from Hades himself to see the upper world and why it is that men are so sorry to leave it.[200] The exercise of *eidōlopoiia* dealt with words spoken by those returned from the Underworld, but the examples we have tend to use men of bygone days;[201] Charon is a character not likely to have any special interest of his own. As his guide, Hermes arranges a vantage-point: Pelion piled on top of Ossa piled on Olympus should give him a good view, and special vision is arranged to allow him to use his vantage-point effectively – by means of suitable tag-lines from Homer.[202]

By a further paradox, Charon himself turns out to be not only an expert ship-handler but an expert in Homeric recitation, having picked up lines literally thrown up by Homer, seasick on the crossing! The direct source of this idea may well have been a picture by Galato known to Lucian's near-contemporary Aelian;[203] but the tone also recalls the vulgarity of Old Comedy. None the less we are left with the notion of even a boatman as *pepaideumenos.* The result of all this comic scene-setting is that Charon is privileged to 'listen in' on a conversation between Croesus and Solon, and hear the fates of Cyrus, Cambyses and Polycrates of Samos.[204] Finally we are confronted with a sophisticated allegorical conundrum: a crowd of shapes hovers unseen around the cities of men where the humans are like wasps; the shapes are revealed as embodiments of Hope, Fear, Ignorance and the like, while the Fates hold the destinies of men on threads, mostly already entwined. Charon offers to relieve their ignorance, but is discouraged.[205] We should note the resemblance of such material to the imagery of the celebrated allegorical *ecphrasis* of pseudo-Cebes, the *Pinax*:[206] Lucian has an eye for the stock in trade of popular philosophy and for whimsical ways of reworking it.

And indeed the palm in sophistic fantasy must go to Lucian, not so much for the accumulation and clever recycling of exotic details, but for the deft application of *paideia* to what might otherwise have been a tedious catalogue of marvels. If one might single out a passage of *Verae Historiae* that best illustrates sophistic technique in fantasy, it might well be Lucian's consultation of Homer in the Islands of the Blessed:

> Scarcely two or three days had elapsed when I went up to Homer the poet (we both had time on our hands), and started asking him questions, particularly about his place of origin: 'Where do you come from? For this point above all is under investigation to this day back in our land.' He for his part acknowledged that he was not unaware that some people thought he was from Chios, others from Smyrna, and a good many from Colophon. But his story was that he came from Babylon, and that the people there called him not Homer but Tigranes. But later on, when he was a hostage [*homēros*] in Greek lands, he had changed his name.' And I went on to enquire further about his authorship of the bracketed lines, and he laid claim to every one of them; so I found the grammarians Zenodotus and Aristarchus guilty of a high degree of pedantry. And since he had given me satisfactory answers on these counts, I asked him next just why it was that he had begun with the Wrath of Achilles; and he said that it had just come into his head that way, without any special effort. Moreover, I

wanted to know the answer to this problem as well: had he written the *Odyssey* before the *Iliad*, as most people say? He said this was not the case. And as for the fact that he was not blind either – they say this about him as well – I realised that at the outset: it was simply a matter of observation and I did not even need to ask. Often too at other times I would do this any time he had time to spare: I would go and ask him something and he would be glad to give me the answer, especially after the court-case he won; for a charge of defamation had been brought against him by Thersites because of the way he had made fun of him in the poem, and the case was won by Homer, with Odysseus for his lawyer.[207]

Such a passage requires little comment. But it does emphasise how well equipped *pepaideumenoi* were to play games with a complex sophistic heritage. From scholarly trifles to whole fantastic novels, the Sophistic can offer a lighter side – and one in which its creative efforts were perhaps best suited to flourish.

10

Piety and *paideia*: the sophist and his gods

We have already encountered Polemo claiming divine inspiration when he spoke at the inauguration in 131 AD of Hadrian's newly completed Olympieion. Elsewhere we find the same sophist 'conversing with the gods on equal terms', and even making witty remarks at the expense of a health prescription from Asclepius.[1] Nor was he alone in such company: Philostratus assures us that Asclepius used to converse with Antiochus of Aegeae even when he was awake, and thought of it as a fine achievement of his art to protect this sophist from illness; and we have also seen Antiochus depositing his researches on Perseus in the temple of Apollo Lykeios at Argos.[2] A relationship with the Panhellenic and local festivals meant as a matter of course the involvement of sophists in religious occasions; and the lavishness of such occasions could reflect the splendour of the sophists themselves. Herodes Atticus served as curator of both the Panhellenic and Panathenaic festivals;[3] Philostratus digresses on the latter with its ceremonial pageant in which the robe of Athena was conveyed in a ship mechanically drawn from the Ceramicus to the Eleusinium – a suitably grandiose setting for this prince among performers. Sophists can have relationships with the gods, and we can explore them further.

Speakers of widely different talent and complexion could claim divine support for their endeavours; the classic case has always been Aelius Aristides:

> I seemed to be addressing some audience and giving them a rhetorical display when in the middle of my performance I called on the gods like this: 'Lord Asclepius, if in fact I am an excellent orator and a virtuoso, grant me health

200

and make those who envy me burst.' I happened to have
seen all this in the dream, but when it was day, I took a
book and read it. In the book I found the very words I had
said.[4]

The connexion between the sophist and his god could be even
more practical: Asclepius commands Aristides during his illness
to improvise; he demurs until his fellow-worshipper Sedatius
Severianus realises that the exertion involved may contribute to
the health-cure Aristides is seeking. He duly improvises on
Demosthenes and Alexander.[5] But we find Apuleius no less
pious – if in a much more superficial manner – and proclaiming
the benefits of initiation into the mysteries of Isis and Osiris for
his hero Lucius' career as a rhetorician:

> And so when all the preparations had been made, and I
> had once more abstained for ten days from animal meats,
> and also shaved my head, I was initiated into the nocturnal
> ceremonies of the chief of the gods, and attended his
> divine services already full of confidence in the related
> cult of Isis. This gave me the greatest peace of mind in my
> travels, and also provided me with a richer means of living
> – for under the favouring breath of fortune, through my
> pleading in the Latin language I was nourished by my
> winning in the courts.[6]

There was moreover a means of expressing gratitude quite
directly to the gods. Aristides cultivated the prose hymn as more
than a literary genre,[7] though it had become just that by the
time of the first pseudo-Menander treatise *peri Epideiktikōn*,[8]
with its characteristically mechanical division of hymns into
klētic ('invocatory'), *apopemptic* ('valedictory'), *physic* ('scientific') and no fewer than five other categories, with the insistence that even in this field Plato is the master among prose-
writers. Socrates' invocation of the Muses in the *Phaedrus* is
cited as an instance of a *klētic* hymn, his prayer to Pan as a
specimen of the category *euktikon* ('precatory'). In the Men-
andrian divisions the hymn is treated as a panegyric of a god;
but this is not to rule out such a form as a vehicle for genuine or
at any rate convincing portrayal of religious sensibility.

There is an obvious sense in which the grandeur at the
disposal of sophistic writers could be used to evoke a religious

atmosphere. One notes in particular the preoccupation of Heliodorus with just such an effect,[9] as in the sacrificial rite at which Theagenes and Charicleia are to meet one another in Delphi itself:

> So then, Cnemon, when the line of the procession had circled three times round the tomb of Neoptolemos, and the young men had ridden around it three times, the women gave a loud cry and the men raised a loud shout; at this, as if at a single prearranged signal, they began to sacrifice sheep and goats, just as if a single hand had been carrying out the slaughter. On a huge altar they first heaped countless twigs, then on top they laid all the choicest parts of the victims, as was customary. They then asked the priest of the Pythian god to begin the libation and light the fire on the altar. Charicles declared that it was his duty to pour the libation, 'but it is for the leader of the sacred embassy to light the altar fire, holding the torch that he has received from the acolyte. This is the custom as laid down by ancestral laws.' With this he began the libation, while Theagenes was ready to receive the fire; and at that moment we became convinced, Cnemon, that the soul is divine and akin to the celestial. For the moment they set eyes on one another, the young couple fell in love, as if the soul recognised its counterpart at the first encounter and ran to meet that which was rightfully its own. First in their elation they stood motionless; then ever so slowly she handed him the torch and he received it, and all this time they fixed their gaze unflinchingly into one another's eyes, as if somehow recognising one another and recollecting some previous sighting. Then they each gave a short furtive smile, only apparent as a slight relaxing of their expressions. And then, as if they were embarrassed at what had occurred, they blushed, and next – I suppose as the passion actually touched their hearts – they turned pale.[10]

Heliodorus has provided a rich and carefully observed religious background for the Platonic language of soul-recognition with which he disguises 'love at first sight'. As we should know to expect, there is room for a certain sophistic wryness in the treatment of religious décor, serving as it does a conventionally amorous business. But that does not prevent the author from revelling in religion.[11] We should not of course posit any common standard of religious belief for sophists any more than for any other social category during the period: we have only to compare the religious profiles of Aristides and Apuleius to underline how difficult it would be to generalise. But any sophist or sophistically educated person would have had the resources to embody genuine piety or literary reflex as required.

JUDAEO-CHRISTIAN ADAPTATION

Sophistic resources proved no less flexible in the hands of educated and eloquent Jewish and Christian performers. The Alexandrian Jew Philo was already playing the traditional sophistic role of ambassador to the Emperor Gaius before Philostratus proclaimed the second beginning of the Second Sophistic with Nicetes. And Philo's later account of the embassy is certainly not lacking in sophistic panache:

> All these [demi-gods], Gaius, were admired and are admired even now for the good works which they began, and were considered worthy of worship and the highest honours. So tell us yourself, about what similar works do you have to brag and swell with pride? Let me begin with the Dioscuri: did you imitate them in brotherly love? No, you cruelly murdered your brother and fellow-heir in the first bloom of youth. Did you imitate Dionysus? Have you been the discoverer of new blessings, as he was? Did you fill the whole world with well-being? Can Asia or Europe not suffice to contain your gifts? You certainly did invent new arts and sciences, but you invented them as a total destroyer and murderer . . . But did you emulate Heracles as well by your unremitting efforts and unflagging virtue? Did you fill continents and islands with law and order, prosperity, plenty and an abundant supply of those other blessings created by profound peace? You ignoble villain, you low coward, you have emptied the cities of all that produces stability and happiness, and made them full of all that produces disorder and disturbance and abject misery![12]

Philo's techniques entail the equivocal acceptance of the traditionally Hellenic demi-gods as benefactors of mankind so that
Gaius can be shown to fall short of each of those with whom he
aspires to identify. The gods serve as the cast-list for bitterly
sarcastic sophistic *psogos*. Of course there is every reason to
assume that such a speech could not have been delivered as it
stands; one thinks of the sophistic practice of writing sabre-
rattling invectives after the victim's death, as in the case of
Aelian's attack on Elagabalus. But the resources were certainly
in place.

As in criticism of an emperor, so in paraphrase of scripture:
sophistic techniques of amplification can be let loose even on
traditional Old Testament tales:

> My child, it is not your dying which causes me grief, but its
> manner. If you had been buried in your own land, I should
> have consoled you and cared for you as you lay ill, shared
> your farewells as you died, closed your eyes, wept over the
> body when it was laid out, given you a costly funeral and
> left out none of the customary rites. But even if it had been
> in a foreign land, I should have consoled myself: 'Listen,'
> I should have told myself, 'Do not be downcast, now that
> nature has taken away her own that was due to her.
> Different lands are a matter for the living; every land is the
> tomb of the dead . . . But now you have become, as they
> say, a rich feast for savage, flesh-eating beasts who have
> tasted and feasted on my own flesh and blood.'[13]

This is not, as it might so easily have been, the lament of a father
for the heroine of some fragmentary Greek novel. It is Philo's
version of Jacob's lament for the missing Joseph, on seeing the
coat of many colours stained with blood. It gives any proof that
might be needed that the stock language of the *epitaphios logos*
(complete with likely reminiscence of Thucydides) transfers
effortlessly to what in the Book of Genesis is a simple folktale.
No less characteristically, sophistic technique is lavished where
the reader already knows it is not appropriate: Jacob laments,
like Achilles Tatius' Clitophon and other romantic heroes, over
what will of course turn out to be a *Scheintod*. And when Philo
comes to mention in due course that Potiphar is a cook, we have
the cue for a Platonic flourish against cookery:

Yet it is very appropriate that [Moses] calls him a head chef: for just as a cook cares for nothing but the unending, superfluous pleasures of the stomach, so does the throng in the city care about the charms and pleasures of the ears, by which the taut strings of understanding are loosed and the nerves of the soul somehow relaxed. And who does not know the difference between doctors and cooks?[14]

The Jewish assimilation of the techniques and outlook of the Hellenistic schools would already have had a long history by Philo's time. Likewise, in the first four centuries of the Christian Church sophists were familiar figures; and it was no less inevitable that any educated Christian should find himself either using or reacting to the tools of the sophists' trade. Where there was Christian rhetoric, one could expect an element of 'Christian Sophistic',[15] of cultural or ornamental display in the service of Christ.

It might at first seem paradoxical that Christianity should have come to espouse the pagan heritage of sophistic rhetoric at all. The ethical teachings of Jesus Christ were perceived as emphasising humility, self-sacrifice and unpretentiousness, qualities which seem antithetical to the kind of values one might expect of a sophist. And the social context in which such teachings were offered did not presuppose a highly educated audience. Indeed, as early as its first surviving documents, the correspondence of St Paul, Christianity harboured a suspicion that anything which could be regarded as worldly wisdom was foolishness in the sight of God.[16] And with good reason: revelatory religions must reserve the right to a highly selective use of the resources of reasoned argument if they are to fortify themselves with a climate of faith. Even Roman persecutors might not fail to note the simplicity of the community of which they disapproved: Pliny the Younger was aware of the uncomplicated and ingenuous nature of the Christian worship he set out to examine. But none of this prevented a gradual attempt at accommodation. When Paul himself preaches on or to the Areopagus in Athens the Luke-biographer invests his discourse with quotation from Greek poetry: he must meet the wisdom of the Greeks on its own ground. Moreover there was an unexpected cultural convergence in the pagan perception of the founder of Christianity at a relatively early stage. When Lucian makes brief allusion to Christ in connexion with his own enemy Peregrinus, he describes the subject of Christian worship as a crucified sophist.[17] The term in context is clearly meant disparagingly, but it is easy enough to see how it could be applied in a neutral or even complimentary way: Jesus Christ after all was during his lifetime a popular public speaker with an inner circle of disciples. And if Christ could be perceived as a sophist, then the tools of sophistic could be all the more readily rendered accessible to Christians. At the end of Antiquity we can still see the two cultural pressures at work within Christianity: on the one hand we find in the age of Constantine an illiterate St Antony in the Egyptian desert, exercising spiritual authority over men and demons alike without any benefit of a formal education. Or, on the other hand, a century later we can find Augustine drawing on the Biblical past as a justification for exploiting the pagan classics in education: as the Israelites spoiled the Egyptians before the flight from Egypt, so the Christians are entitled to take what is valuable from the heritage of paganism.[18] In short the arguments were available to allow anyone with serious educational aspirations to import these into their Christianity, and in the event this was clearly done.

In the period of Christian apologetic in the second and third centuries, sharp rhetorical reflexes were required if Christians were to speak to the gentile world as soon as possible in terms of a *paideia* it would recognise. Clement of Alexandria's Προτρεπτικὸς πρὸς Ἕλληνας (Exhortation to the Greeks) leads quickly into a story of how the minstrel Eunomus was singing a song at Delphi in honour of the dead serpent; when a string on his lyre broke, a grasshopper praising God of its own accord settled on the lyre, and he adapted his music accordingly. The tale has the characteristics of the sort of fabulous story to be expected in a sophistic *prolalia*; the Christian apologist only requires to make the grasshopper sing to God rather than respond to Eunomus' plight.

Nor does a Christian littérateur need to draw the line at a paradoxical opening. Time and again we can recognise mixtures of material as typically sophistic, as in the following *ecphrasis* of the wonders of nature:

But I ask you to be amazed at the natural instinct of even irrational creatures, and offer a rationale for it if you can.

How do birds cultivate nests, rocks, trees and reed roofs both for protection and adornment, and to furnish the needs of their nestlings? To what do bees and spiders owe their devotion to labour and art, through which the former weave their honeycombs, and fuse them together by hexagonal tubes that match, and lay a foundation for them by partitioning and alternating angles with straight lines – and all this in such dark hives and blind honey-combs? While as for the spiders, they weave their complicated webs by stretching such light and almost airy threads in all manner of patterns, and all this from imperceptible beginnings into both a prestigious palace and a trap for the weak and the enjoyment of nurture? What sort of Euclid imitated these, while conducting philosophical investigations with imaginary lines and struggling with his proofs? What Palamedes designed the tactics, so to speak, and the configuration of cranes, or taught them how to manoeuvre in ranks and adopt varied flight-patterns? What sort of Phidiases and Zeuxises and Aglaophons who knew how to draw and mould such amazingly beautiful things? What Cretan chorus of Daed-alus, moving in harmony, worked with female grace to new horizons of beauty? Or what Cretan labyrinth, difficult of exit and unravelling as poets say and continually crossing itself through the sophisms of its art?[19]

This could easily pass for a meditation on the subject-matter of Aelian's *Historia Animalium*: it is sophistically enriched paradox-ography. But in fact the basic topos certainly did have scriptural counterpart: 'Behold the fowls of the air, how they sow not, neither do they spin . . . consider the lilies of the field . . . and yet Solomon in all his glory was not arrayed like one of these.'[20] But here the parade of Greek engineering and artistic feats gives a strongly Hellenophile flavour. As so often, it is the combination of highly wrought rhetoric and 'Hellenic' subject-matter that offers the high road to 'sophistic'.

Even the general argument of a whole treatise can take on a sophistic flavour at a relatively early stage in the history of Christian letters. In the *de Pallio* Tertullian[21] argues for a change of dress for the inhabitants of Carthage: the toga is of Augustan date there and is worn by disreputable characters;

where the pallium is worn by professionals – grammarians, rhetors, sophists and other artists of repute. And, better still, it is now worn by Christians, practitioners of a divine philosophy. Here one recognises a number of sophistic traits, of a kind we should not have been surprised to find in some of the political speeches of Dio Chrysostom, for example. The speaker addresses a city whose morals he is setting out to 'correct' through their outward appearance. He is appealing to archaic practice: Cato among others wore the pallium. And there is room for the whole apparatus of secular learning: changing of clothes is a cue for Achilles as a girl on Scyros, or Hercules changing clothes with Omphale; there is scope for a 'rogues' gallery' of reprobates from the Late Republic and beyond, including Nero and Antony; and for secular philosophers such as Epicurus and Zeno as advocates of withdrawal from public life.[22] One notes that the real subject, the adoption of Christianity, seems almost incidental to some much more trivial matter of appearance. This is very much in tune with the technique of a Dio; one is reminded too of how the sophist Herodes presumed to change the ceremonial dress of the Athenians from black to white.[23] And a Christian writer has already acquired the techniques of the *adoxon*.

The Constantinian revolution in effect established Christianity as the official religion of the Roman Empire, and the brief reign of the pagan Julian failed to reverse the gradual Christianisation of the Empire and its institutions. But Christianity still tended to tolerate pagan culture for what it could offer. In the case of the remarkable trio of Cappadocian Fathers[24] in the latter part of the fourth century, we are well aware of a sophistic background: Gregory of Nazianzus' studies culminated in Athens under Prohaeresius and Himerius; his fellow-student in Athens, Basil of Caesarea,[25] and the latter's brother, Gregory of Nyssa,[26] had a rhetorician father. John Chrysostom, himself a native of Antioch, was a pupil of Libanius. Basil himself provides a theoretical basis for coming to terms with the resources of an essentially pagan rhetorical system in his short treatise Πρὸς τοὺς νέους, ὅπως ἂν ἐξ Ἑλληνικῶν ὠφέλοιντο λόγων ('To the young, on the benefits of Greek literature'), which offers a useful illustration of how, and how easily, Christian youths could exploit the heritage of paganism. The author advises against complete devotion to 'attending teachers and keeping company with the famous men of the ancients through the words they have left behind them'.[27] But the alternative is expressed in all too familiar terms:

> Now to this [other] life the Holy Scriptures lead us, educating us by means of mysteries. But while it is not possible for you because of your age to understand the depth of their meaning, nonetheless by means of other things not entirely dissimilar, we provide, as if in shadows and reflections, a preliminary training to the eye of the soul, imitating those who drill in military tactics: these men, after gaining experience through gymnastics and dance-steps, enjoy the benefit under genuine combat conditions of their training.[28]

Basil has no difficulty in 'latching' his pagan materials to Christian ends. One must prepare for the contest 'and must associate with poets and prose-writers and orators and all men from whom there is any likelihood of benefit with a view to the care of our soul',[29] which 'has to be processed with *paideumata* just as garments have to be processed before being dyed'[30] – not without a flourish of familiar Platonic phraseology even in the manifesto itself. Hence, Basil continues, one ought to avoid wicked deeds in the poets, as Odysseus avoided the songs of the Sirens,[31] or when they narrate the amours of the gods, especially Zeus – once more as argued by Plato, in *Republic* 2. And the Christian will be like the eclectic bee, getting honey for the soul as well as fragrance and colour from pagan literature (and adapting a celebrated simile of Pindar in the process).[32] It is not too long before Basil falls back on the *Allegory of Prodicus*: first its Hesiodic original, then Homer's poetry as an encomium of virtue. Even the scene with Nausicaa and Odysseus is pressed into service, with Odysseus improbably representing the life of virtue; although naked he is more honoured than the Phaeacians.[33] The painting and theatre similes are then displayed on cue,[34] as Basil continues to run through the repertoire.

Moreover, Christian users of a sophistic education were not prevented from being as equivocal about it as Plato or the general run of pagan philosophers had been. Gregory of Nazianzus rebukes a young Christian friend, Ablabius, for his yearnings in this direction:

I hear that you are a devotee of 'sophistic' and that it seems marvellous to you to speak impressively, to have a lofty expression, to stride in a high and mighty fashion, to wander off in your imagination to Marathon and Salamis, those aesthetic paradises of yours; to have no thought of anything but people like Miltiades, Cynagirus, Calli-machus, or Telemachos; to have everything presented in a sophistic manner as closely as possible to your inclination ... You must be aware that while amusing yourself for a short time with such childish pastimes, you will see what a fool you have made of yourself when at last you attain to discretion.[35]

Such a warning could have come almost verbatim from Lucian's *Rhetorum Praeceptor* some two centuries previously. As assiduously as a Christian ascetic could denigrate sophists, so could he apply the title to the enemies of orthodoxy. The Arian controversy in particular could give rise to the accusation of sophistry within the church itself. Gregory of Nazianzus can look back to the time

when this excessive, tongue-twisting and involved theology had not yet made its way into the divinity schools, but playing with pebbles which deceive the eye by the speed of their changes, or dancing in front of an audience with all sorts of effeminate contortions – such actions were re-garded as tantamount to speaking or hearing of God in a novel and fussy manner ... but since the Sextuses and Pyrrhos, and the antithetical style of speaking, like some dreadful and malignant disease, have infected our churches, and talking nonsense has gained the reputation of culture, we spend our time in nothing else, but, as the Book of Acts says of the Athenians, 'either in saying or hearing something new'.[36]

As in the case of secular sophists, we can note how invective may serve to draw out the most dramatic and striking images. The Arian controversy prompts Basil to a fully developed *ecphrasis-cum-syncrisis* of orthodox and heretic as opposing battle-fleets joining in a naval engagement:

On top of all this imagine a confused and meaningless din setting upon the sea at that point, from the noise of winds whistling round, and the ships colliding, the seething of the surge, the cries of the combatants hurling all kinds of sounds because of their wounds, so that neither the captain's nor the steersman's voice can he heard, but there is dreadful disorder and chaos and all too much evil as people despair of life and are driven to desperate criminal acts. Add to this some incurable disease, a mad lust for glory, so that as the ship already careers to the bottom the fighters do not give up their struggle for supremacy.[37]

Similarly, Gregory of Nazianzus launches out into a presentation of the Arian Bishop George of Cappadocia with the characteristic resources of sophistic invective:

Some Cappadocian monster, surging from the furthest parts of our land, or dreadful race and still more dreadful intent, not even wholly free, but of mixed descent as we observe the mule to be. First the servant of another's table, and a buyer of corn, having learned to say and do everything for the sake of his belly, at last he has infiltrated the state, and entrusted with its highest office, he rose to become receiver of the pork by which the army is fed; then he proved untrustworthy and pursued a policy dictated by his gluttony; since only his body was left to him, he contemplated flight, and changing territory and city as runaways do, at last he seized Alexandria, to the detriment of the common good of the church, like some Egyptian plague. There he put an end to his wandering and began his villainy. And in all other respects he was worthless, since he had no share in liberal education, and was not affable in conversation.[38]

As far as a sophistic outlook is concerned, the heretic must be a Philistine as well.

But there were other less overt routes by which a fair proportion of classical culture could be incorporated into the texture of Christian rhetoric, by way of such figures as *paraleipsis*: while affecting to dismiss a topic one actually incorporates it and affords it added prominence. Hence Gregory of Nazianzus will comment on his own omission of standard topics of panegyric ('the task of praising the country and family of our departed one I leave to another more scrupulous in adhering to the rules of eulogy').[39] Or he will make negative comparisons with classical material, as when he praises Basil's education under the latter's own father:

> [He did not boast] of some Thessalian mountain cave as the workshop of his virtue, nor of some boastful centaur, the teacher of the heroes of his day; nor was he taught by such a tutor to shoot hares, and run down fawns or hunt stags, or to excel in war, or in breaking in colts with the same person as teacher and horse.[40]

The fruits of a sophistic education had social nuances among the Christians no less than in their original pagan context. A revealing light on the ethos of personal relations is shown by the bulk of letters exchanged between educated Christian leaders in the late fourth century. In general, sophistic repertoire is kept out of purely doctrinal questions: where so much depends on clarity and verbal precision it is always one's opponent who resorts to sophistic tricks and equivocations. One's own sophistic reflexes tend to be reserved for self-consciously cultured relaxation either between highly educated Christians or between Christians and pagans of similar sophistication as a channel of cultural communication. In such a context Gregory of Nazianzus can produce a letter of friendship not unlike some of Fronto's examples, saying practically nothing more than that writing to the recipient is the next best thing to talking to him.[41] And we can expect flourishes of typically Platonic *politesse*: 'to me you are a good plectrum, you have caused a well-tuned lyre to reside in my soul'.[42] Oxymoron and *adoxon* need never be far away:

> Keeping free from business is for me the greatest business. And to make you aware of one of my finer points, I value freedom from business so much that I think I might even be a norm to all men for this kind of magnanimity, and if all men imitated me the Churches would have no troubles.[43]

Stripped of his pompous wordplay, Gregory realises that the *pepaideumenos* at leisure is free from schism or heresy. Or he can adopt characteristic comparison with Odysseus at the table of Alcinous (when in reality he is suffering privations in Pontus),[44] or produce an ingenious compression of sophistic repertoire into a single melodramatic *epiphōnēma*: 'O earth and sun, air and virtue – for I will do a little bit of tragic acting not so that we may join the Hellespont, but so that we may level the mountain'.[45] Even a jocular request for vegetables for a visit by Basil can be a pretext for sophistic trifling, this time a none too tasteful joke (when Ozizaleans die of hunger, they smell sweet because of the flowers at their funerals).[46] Amid such flosculi it is only a matter of time before the eucharist itself is manipulated into sophistic paradox: 'Do not cease to pray and plead on my behalf whenever you draw down the Word by your word, whenever with a bloodless incision you cut the Body and Blood of the Lord with your voice as a sword.'[47]

However, there was an opposite current: far simpler resources are available to Christian letters, so that when Basil writes a consolation for a young student who has died,[48] the resources are conventional enough. The victim does not leave a wife or children, nor did he submit to lusts; yet Basil ends with the simplest of Biblical tags: Ὁ Κύριος ἔδωκεν, ὁ Κύριος ἀφείλετο· ὡς τῷ Κυρίῳ, οὕτω καὶ ἐγένετο ('The Lord gave, the Lord took away; as it seemed good to the Lord, so it came to pass').[49]

But the highest-flown style of the *pepaideumenos* is also called forth in dealings with state officials and in requests for patronage. Gregory of Nazianzus begins a commendation of his nephew-in-law Nicobulus with flattery that Sophronius, prefect of Constantinople, has a disposition unchanged by promotion – like gold,[50] no matter what its uses or transformation into ornaments.[51] He himself is meanwhile under no illusion as to his own power: 'I have the power of words, and of heralding your goodness, at least to the best of my ability, even if I fall far short of doing you justice.'[52] And as usual with sophists, the benefits are not all one way: Gregory himself has to seek the protection of the same Sophronius over the problems besetting his late brother Caesarius' estate;[53] or he can begin a request for exemption for the deacon Euthalius with the Pindaric tag χρυσέας ὑπόστησον εὐτειχεῖ θαλάμῳ κίονας ('Have golden columns support a well-built hall').[54] Christianity and sophistic *paideia* converge to face bureaucracy with a flourish.

A PAGAN POSTSCRIPT

Christians, then, had free access to the sophistic heritage. It will serve as a suitable postscript to note at least one of the last responses of the sophists' world to the effects of Christian-isation: the speech of Libanius *pro Templis* ('on behalf of the Temples').[55] The speech cannot have been written too long before the final destruction of the Serapeum at Alexandria in 391; and it must rank among the last known examples by a pagan sophist acting as ambassador. Even if the eventual outcome of events proved to be beyond Libanius' control, the author's technique cannot be lightly dismissed.

One notes that even in what proved to be the twilight of paganism the traditional Homeric frame of reference for argu-ments is still firmly in place: it was sacrifice that had ensured the triumphant return of Agamemnon, as it had Heracles' previous sack of Troy:[56]

> Besides the glory of Marathon is not due to the Ten Thousand Athenians, but to Heracles and Pan, and the miracle of Salamis is not due to the Greek fleet, but to the allies from Eleusis, who arrived for the naval battle to the sound of their own sacred hymn.[57]

Much else too of the characteristic armoury of sophistic is still recognisable: forced converts are compared to the tyrants in tragedies who only wear their masks for the length of the performance;[58] enemies

> sweep through the field like rivers in spate, and by spoiling the temples they spoil the estates, for wherever they knock out a temple from an estate that estate is blinded and lies exposed and is dead. Temples, my lord, are the soul of the countryside.[59]

Philostratus might have cherished the boldness of these last metaphors; the repertoire itself had not changed any since Nicetes.

The traditional reflexes of the *psogos* are not lacking either: the Christian monks (traditionally acknowledged only in para-phrase) are alluded to as 'these men in the black robes, who eat more than elephants, and by the quantities they drink are a burden to those who accompany their drinking with hymns –

the men who conceal their excesses under their artificial pallor';[60] they are seen in almost identical terms to those in which Lucian could have viewed Cynics well over two centuries before.

Yet the overall tenor of the speech is well-calculated: Libanius keeps his temper and manoeuvres his arguments in much the same way as the Christian apologists of the second century: it is the temple-breakers who are breaking the law; the sacrifices foster the well-being of the Empire; and the Emperor himself is fair and tolerant.

Nor were fourth-century *pepaideumenoi* at a loss to find pagan precedent even for Christian charity. Julian can still remonstrate from the *Odyssey*:

> For it is disgraceful that, if none of the Jews needs to beg, and the impious Galileans support our own poor in addition to theirs, our people are seen to go without aid from us . . . You must accustom the Hellenists to do good works of this kind by teaching them that this was our practice long ago. At any rate Homer had made Eumaeus say, 'Stranger, it is not right for me, not even if a worse man than yourself should arrive, to fail to honour a stranger. For all strangers and beggars are sent from Zeus. And a gift is precious, even if it is only a small one.'[61]

Like the scriptural tags of the Christians themselves, Homeric holy writ can still be used to 'prove' just about anything.

The connexions between Sophistic and holiness will not surprise us. Sophists were ambitious men, and religious sublimity was something that fell comfortably within their domain; if religious sincerity was quite another matter, sophistic techniques could scarcely preclude it. But the sophists' techniques and versatility ensured an easy cultural continuity in late antiquity; and in East and West alike one finds that the Sophistic was too closely linked with pagan Hellenism and its institutions to survive comfortably. Otherwise we should have heard much more of Moses debating whether to cross the Red Sea on foot, or Isaac pleading to be sacrificed with even more aphorisms.

11

Sophistic self-presentation: four studies

In the pursuit of their professional activities sophists had frequent recourse to talking about themselves and projecting their personalities in the direction of their fellow-men. It is revealing to notice the kind of contexts in which these first-person activities can be presented. From a relatively wide field I have chosen four texts[1] which seem to me symptomatic of sophistic attitudes. The first narrates at first hand an exotic journey that inevitably finds Hellenism in a far-flung outpost; the second projects its author into a fictitious dialogue on a stroll from the Piraeus to Athens, perhaps the most familiar course from which a sophist might review the follies of his fellow-men; a third text serves to remind us that sophists had to and could defend their vital interests in the envious litigation to which they were so readily prone; while the fourth surveys an entire sophistic lifespan at the most critical period for Hellenic culture and its transmission. The object of assembling them together is to stress the difference of approach of four individualists revealing themselves against four different sophistic backgrounds.

A WANDERING SOPHIST AT WORK: DIO'S *BORYSTHENITICUS*

Dio Chrysostom narrates to an audience in his home town of Prusa an account of a stay in Borysthenes, a Greek outpost on the north-western coast of the Black Sea.[2] Outside the city he encounters a youth called Callistratus, questions him about Homer and tries to introduce him to the work of the gnomic poet Phocylides; they gather an audience and go to the space in

216

front of the temple of Zeus. Dio begins to discourse about the constituents of a mortal city, but is soon interrupted with a request for a description of the heavenly one. He develops this latter concept as that of a harmony between men and gods; to this he appends a purportedly Iranian myth of the magi, stating how the four horses controlling the universe bring about first universal conflagration, then re-creation.

In summary and out of context such an ensemble might seem merely arbitrary or eccentric, or both. Yet it provides not only a suitable transition from our previous topic but an excellent pot pourri of sophistic preoccupations. Dio begins in a low key, with an account of the Hypanis–Borysthenes estuary. Since the lower reaches of the river are a wide marsh, there is no great temptation to indulge in either *ecphrasis* or paradoxography, though Dio does point out that trees in the marsh have misled navigators into supposing they were other ships.[3] He moves quickly on to the fortunes and state of the city itself: after frequent barbarian pressures its defences are crudely improvised from the ruins, while its statues and tombs have been mutilated. Callistratus' dress does nothing to relieve the picture; he wears trousers and the rest of a Scythian costume, including a black cape.[4] But his somewhat Ionian appearance, his bravery against the Sarmatians and his enthusiasm for oratory and philosophy, as well as his homosexual orientation, mark him out as a Greek. The last feature, Dio remarks, has been taken over from Borysthenes' metropolis (Miletus).[5] Despite their no longer speaking Greek clearly because of living among barbarians, the Borysthenites do know their Homer, either because of their constant warfare or because of their devotion to the cult of Achilles. The picture now begins to make sense in sophistic terms: the sage Dio has 'discovered' Greek culture persistent in the face of adversity even in the most far-flung outpost: one thinks especially of Apollonius of Tyana's discovery of traces of an Eretrian Greek community in Parthia.[6]

The narrator now begins a cultural diversion. Which poet does Callistratus prefer, Homer or Phocylides? (A couplet of the latter is cited as a political *gnomē*.)[7] But the Borysthenites have a cult of Achilles,[8] amply attested from archaeological evidence[9] and hold Homer next to the gods. However, Dio gathers an improvised audience at the temple of Zeus; a philosopher would have been very pleased indeed at the sight as they all looked like the ancient Greeks as described by Homer, with long hair and flowing beards;[10] only one Romanophile was clean-shaven, and ridiculed accordingly.[11]

Dio now launches forth on the nature of cities, as befitting an audience both ancient and Greek; in turn they recognise the speaker as almost a divine stranger from Achilles' Isle.[12] One of the few Platonists among them warms to the subject of the perfect city which can only be divine,[13] and Dio accedes to the invitation with a typically sophistic flourish:[14]

> If you had told me yesterday when the enemy had made their attack on you to take up arms and fight like Achilles, I should have obeyed the first half of your injunction, and tried to come to the defence of my friends; but the second half, I fancy, I should not have been able to do, however much I should have wished to, to fight like Achilles. So now too I will fulfil the first half of your request – I will be glad to tell my story to the best of my ability in my own way: 'But I shall not want to strive with men of old, whether Plato or Homer . . .'.[14]

Dio is able to offer a philosophic view of the universe compared to a city, in that it embraces all rational creatures and a union of human and divine. There is discernible convergence here between the Platonic notion of a heavenly city-pattern and the Stoic image of the world-state,[15] but Dio is not too long in turning to the poets and in finding suitable literary metaphors for their part in the scene, as attendants at rites:

> It is natural to suppose that not only do those who are concerned near some ritual, at the entrance to the sanctuary, gain so much inkling of what is going on within, when either a single mystic expression is uttered aloud, or fire is seen above the shrine, but also that sometimes there has come something to the poets – the very archaic ones I mean – some brief snatch from the Muses and I suppose some inspiration of divine truth, like the light of some fire shining from the invisible, as in the case of Homer and Hesiod, even if others since have been less holy; yet all make the universe the home or city of Zeus.[16]

Dio has in effect retreated deftly from theology into literary colouring; and now Stoic metaphor is in turn invoked to make

Zeus King of the universe as a city: 'a good and humane community of gods and men which gives a share in law and citizenship, not to just any living creatures, but only to those who have a share in reason and intellect'.[17] The sophist selects a world-view that coincides neatly with the élite urban community in which he himself was so eager to participate in his native Prusa.

At this point he subjoins a myth 'which excites awe when sung in their secret rites by the Magi'. This concerns a chariot of Zeus, greater even than the chariot of Helios, revealed by Zoroaster after his experience on a mountain of fire. The magi have the universe travelling in unceasing cycles of time; the heavenly bodies are marks on the horse of Zeus, the highest of the team of horses; other horses are named after Hera, Poseidon and Hestia, with appropriately different characteristics: the last horse, while harnessed to the chariot of Zeus, is immovable. A fire from the first horse engulfs the whole – hence the Greek myth of Phaethon; the horse sacred to Poseidon by contrast causes flood. Sometimes too the horses of their own accord fuse into one, the soul of the charioteer: this effects a sacred marriage as of Zeus and Hera, the source and harmony of creation. Dio apologises for the inconsistencies in the myth: it is to be blamed on the barbarian nature of its originators, and on the insistence of the Borysthenites who had pressed him to speak.[18]

It is tempting to see the final myth as a sophistic *plasma* and nothing else:[19] one is instinctively suspicious of a myth quoted from the Persians to the Borysthenites and transferred as it were from one exotic fringe of the Greek world to another.[20] The nearness of the detail of the horses and charioteer to Socrates' presentation of the soul's charioteer and its horses in the *Phaedrus*[21] would certainly have been a sufficient inspiration for Dio, who has only to add another horse and an additional touch of Stoic colouring by way of the theory of *Ekpurōsis*, cyclic conflagration.[22] None the less there are at least some touches of authenticity: the preoccupation in the myth with fire, and with an interest in time-cycles, seems plausibly Zoroastrian.[23] And the supposed friendship of Dio with Apollonius of Tyana, who purported to have visited the magi, would suggest at least a plausible channel of communication.[24] We might also be tempted to see an element of genuine use of local culture:[25] the

Borysthenites are not indeed so very far removed from the northernmost fringe of the Zoroastrian world, and Dio may have been accommodating himself to local interest. It might also be argued that the clumsiness of imagery in the immobile horse and the fusion of the charioteer myth with sacred marriage is more probably explained if Dio is using at least a kernel of authentic material.

Altogether the *Borystheniticus* offers a wide cross-section of the sophistic interests and values we have already noted. In particular its prevailing atmosphere is that of the paradoxical placing of Hellenism in an unlikely place – and of a sophistic performance on a sacred subject. The philosophical materials are used moreover to an end which is sophistic enough: to give the *polis* a cosmic significance.

SOPHISTIC DAY-DREAMING: LUCIAN'S *NAVIGIUM*

In Dio's contrast of earthly and heavenly states one might detect something of the contrast of states in the latter stages of Plato's *Republic*. A very different approach to the same text can be found in Lucian's dialogue *Navigium*, which also illustrates the capacity of one writer to present the cultural thought-world of the Second Sophistic in fairly short compass.[26] In fact the overall theme is familiar from the repertoire of satire and indeed from popular literature in general as 'the vanity of human wishes'. But a simple moralising cliché and folktale device has been cleverly rearranged into a delightful and characteristically sophistic fantasy.

The scene is carefully set as a perambulation from the Piraeus to the Dipylon, and so moves towards the very centre of 'Attic' geography. Lycinus, a suitably 'atticised' Lucian, is looking with two friends for the errant lover Adimantus, in love with a young crew-member of a newly arrived Egyptian ship. But the décor of Platonic dialogue is not far away: we are assured that 'so many good-looking young men in Athens follow him around, all freeborn, always talking, and breathing wrestling-schools' (παλ-αίστρας ἀποπνέοντες).[27] There is nothing to stop audience or reader from reading the dialogue in the present; but it is clear enough that the present is a timeless Platonic one.

The company admires the *Isis*, a grain-carrying ship diverted to Athens by a storm; this provides the opportunity for *ecphrasis* of both vessel and storm. And once more realistic ethos can be happily merged with *mimēsis*:[28] the key figure in the storm narrative is that stock Platonic figure, the ship's pilot. It is proposed that each of the company should tell a wish to while away the journey. Adimantus is at one and the same time the *nouveau-riche* of diatribe tradition[29] and the typical urban philanthropist and benefactor (*euergetēs*) of a second-century city:

> [I will have] theatres and baths for the people, to beautify the city, and have the sea brought up to the Dipylon, and a harbour there supplied by a deep canal, so that my ship can anchor beside it in full view of the Ceramicus.[30]

Inevitably one must think in an Athenian context of Herodes Atticus,[31] though Lucian is circumspect enough to avoid direct attack, just as he does elsewhere when hinting at Herodes' estates at Marathon. Lycinus is able to demolish this little scenario without too much difficulty, ultimately by reminding Adimantus that he may not live to enjoy it. Again one senses that Cynic moralising would have gone hand in hand with the traditional rhetorical exercise of encomium and *psogos* or *anaskeuē* and *kataskeuē*.[32]

Samippus now tries his hand, once more with a neat convergence of past and present. He has dreams of re-enacting the conquests of Alexander. Not only is the theme a characteristic landmark in the Greek past,[33] the ridicule of it in itself pokes fun at the Alexander-mania of the present, which had either already given rise, or shortly would, to Arrian's *Anabasis Alexandri*.[34] The re-enaction of a battle would have been second nature to a sophistic rhetorician:[35] it is as if we have a live demonstration of Plutarch's *de Fortuna Alexandri*. And Samippus has to sustain an obligatory wound to keep up with Alexander.

The third panel is devoted to a dreamer who outdoes the other two. Timolaus uses the ring of Gyges to play at being providence itself, and turn human life into his own plaything; Lucian uses the Myth of Gyges, again straight from the *Republic*, and multiplies the rings the foolish dreamer craves for himself:

> Any amazing sights in India or the land of the Hyperboreans, any precious possession, anything nice to eat or drink, I should not send away for them, but fly there in person and enjoy every one of them all I liked. And the

winged griffin or the Phoenix in India that no-one else has
seen, I would see even that. I alone would have found the
source of the Nile and how much of the earth is uninhabit-
able and whether there are people living upside-down on
the underside half of the world . . . all in all I should make
human life my plaything; everything would be mine and
everyone else would think me a god.[36]

There is perhaps here too an element of Alexander, at least of
the fantasies of the *Alexander-Romance*.[37] These are cleverly
deflated by Lycinus:

did you see among all the different tribes you flew over any
other man already old and so far gone in his mind, carried
aloft by a tiny ring and able to move whole mountains with
a finger-tip, and loved by everyone even though he was
bald and snub-nosed?[38]

Timolaus has suddenly been presented not as a young blood
with the youth of a Gyges or Alexander, but rather as wearing
the characteristic uniform of Socrates, which he is quick to
disgrace.

So much for the second-century *Republic*. Lucian has gone for
a picturesque Plato, leaving out the elaborate texture of philosophical argument or mathematical demonstration. Lastly, one
is left wondering what it is that Lycinus can wish for: the
suspense is deflated by his announcing that he does not need to
wish, since the travellers have now reached their destination,
the Dipylon, and so killed the time available (nor does he wish
to share the foolishness of his fellow-travellers).[39]

It is hard to resist a comparison with the real world of
Philostratus, who tells us that Herodes Atticus was driving to
Corinth with his friend Ctesidemus sitting beside him; when
they arrived at the Isthmus he had cried: 'Poseidon, I want to do
it, but no one will agree to it!' Of course Ctesidemus was
surprised at this outburst and asked him the reason for it. And
so Herodes explained: 'For a long time I have been struggling
to bequeath to posterity some symbol of a mind that reveals me
for the man I am, and I do not yet consider that I have
established this.' Whereupon Ctesidemus rehearsed the compliments his speeches had won, as well as his matchless achievements. But Herodes replied:

What you mention is destined to perish and time will overtake it; and others will pillage my speeches and one will find fault with one thing, another with something else. But the cutting of the Isthmus is an immortal undertaking and a superhuman task, for I consider that to cut through the Isthmus requires Poseidon rather than a man.[40]

Herodes did not actually have in mind Lucian's canal from the sea to the Dipylon; but, as we have noted, he himself had presided aboard the Sacred Ship that brought the ceremonial robe of Athena from the Dipylon to the Pythium by means of underground machinery. Lucian's satire may well have alluded to both Herodes' real role and his still unfulfilled ambition. The dividing line between sophistic fantasy and the genuine aspiration of a real sophistic megalomaniac could be a fine one.

SOPHISTIC SELF-DEFENCE: APULEIUS' *APOLOGIA*

The *Apologia de Magia*[41] of Apuleius might seem a bizarre choice as a typical work of the Second Sophistic. But one of its many interests is the fact that it was a real speech on a real charge in the court of a real proconsul.[42] It is typical insofar as it suggests the amount of odium that a local feud could engender in a provincial African town, Oea, and it serves as a warning of how near a real speech and a real situation could come to what we might otherwise dismiss as the fantasy world of sophists. The situation in itself was complicated enough: Apuleius had been encouraged to marry the rich widow Pudentilla by her son, his old friend Sicinius Pontianus, in order to safeguard the prospective inheritance of himself and his younger brother Sicinius Pudens. But the latter is prevailed upon after Pontianus' death by Herennius Rufinus, Pontianus' father-in-law, and Pudentilla's first husband's brother Sicinius Aemilianus, to bring an action against Apuleius. He is accused towards the end of the reign of Antoninus Pius, at a hearing in Sabrata some sixty miles to the west of Oea itself, of using sorcery to woo Pudentilla and gain control of her estate.

We might be tempted to phrase the accusation as follows: 'a philosopher Apuleius defends himself on the charge of using magical means to entice a rich widow into marriage, in order to obtain an inheritance.' The theme of magic as such was certainly no stranger to the world of the declaimers: Hadrian of Tyre had included the practices of magicians in his regular repertoire; while Hippodromus of Larissa impressed Megistias of Smyrna by extemporising on the theme of the magician who sees fit to die because he is unable to kill an adulterous fellow-magician.[43] And had Apuleius himself found a place in the *Lives of the Sophists*, he might well have attracted the attention of Philostratus to the circumstances of the trial. It might be supposed, moreover, that Aemilianus had no real basis for his accusation; no one could be made to swear that they had actually seen Apuleius engaged in the practice of magic, and as all of the circumstantial evidence offered is reasonably capable of more innocent explanation, Apuleius might have been felt to have had nothing to fear. But the practice of magic for noxious purposes was none the less a capital offence,[44] and the defendant could not have afforded to risk an ineffectual performance.

Apuleius affords special prominence to the first 'evidence' of magical practice, the acquisition of a fish.[45] Because he has a satisfactory alternative explanation – he wanted a rare specimen for dissection, not magical purposes – he can afford to play at great length with his opponent while he establishes his own *paideia*. By citing a few lines of Virgil on noxious materials (cf. *Aen.* 4.513ff.), he can produce a threefold antithesis; his accuser Tannonius Pudens is attributing to magicians charms

> not to be wiped from the foreheads of the newly-born, but to be cut out from scaly backs; not to be torn up from the farm, but to be dragged out from the deep; not to be reaped with sickles, but to be caught with hooks. [Virgil] mentions poison, you produce an hors-d'oeuvre; he mentions herbs and tender shoots, you speak of scales and bones; he culls the meadow, you scour the waves.[46]

The mere business of acquiring the fish has already afforded scope for levity;

> Why should I blame fishermen for acquiring a fish? So you would have this operation entrusted to gold-workers or joiners, and so that I can avoid your calumnies, they have to change their trades so that I should commission the carpenter to catch the fish, and have the fisherman in turn fell the timber?[47]

It comes easily to the Platonising Apuleius to make jokes on trade demarcation, so characteristic a feature of Socratic dialogue. And the accuser is then framed in an ingenious *aporon*:

> Is there something mysterious in fish and fish alone, hidden from all save sorcerers only? If you know what this is, then you too must be a magician. If you do not, you must acknowledge that you are accusing me of something you know nothing about.[48]

Whatever the defendant's own knowledge of magic, his mastery of sophistic equivocation is not in doubt.

Many of Apuleius' asides are aimed at the lack of *paideia* of his accusers: he does not know enough popular tales, let alone literature, to invent even plausible charges of magic; he could not even read a letter from Pudentilla, since it was written in Greek.[49] Not all of Apuleius' reasoning is to be trusted: he does not, and indeed cannot, prove that fish could not be put to magical use; and it is of course entirely specious to say that Pythagoras the magician would never have thrown fish back into the sea, or Homer would never have omitted the sea as the provider of Circe's drugs.[50]

One of the next two charges might have been more seriously related to magic: a boy had collapsed in the presence of Apuleius. The implication of bewitching and procuring him for divinatory purposes is there; Apuleius is able to refute it partly from the fact that divinatory sacrifice requires pure victims, whereas the boy was a diseased epileptic;[51] but à propos the examination of a second subject, a woman, he paraphrases Plato's *Timaeus* at length in order to account for the physiology of epilepsy, with Aristotle and Theophrastus as subsidiary authorities.[52] His point is that a philosopher is entitled in his own right to act as a consultant. There is perhaps here an anticipation of the art of the fourth-century 'iatrosophists' who fill out the pages of Eunapius.[53] But he is able to wind up this second section by treating his opponent too as an epileptic:

> But compare your madness with that of Thallus; you will find that there is not very much difference except that Thallus keeps his madness to himself, while you go mad against other people; Thallus twists his eyes, you twist the truth; Thallus convulses his hands, you convulse your

supporters; Thallus dashes himself against the pavement, you arm yourself against the bench of the court.[54]

The next charge is that Apuleius keeps something mysterious among the household gods in the house of Pontianus. Apart from flamboyantly exposing the ignorance of his accuser in asserting the magical nature of something he does not know, Apuleius is able to claim that his secret consists of emblems of the mysteries, and take the opportunity to denounce the impiety of his opponent Aemilianus.[55] He also takes the opportunity to remind the audience how he recounted the number of mysteries he knew in a speech in honour of Asclepius during his days at Oea:[56] Apuleius the sophist loses no opportunity to reassert himself in the eyes of the public; and once more we have a convenient flourish of sophistic piety.

After emphasising the flimsiness of individual charges of magic, Apuleius can afford to play on his audience as he pleases: at last we are offered something of a formal *narratio* of events, of Sicinius Pontianus' eagerness to provide Apuleius as a bridegroom for his widowed mother in order to safeguard her inheritance from the rest of the family. For the accuser Aemilianus, Pontianus' father-in-law, Apuleius reserves a whole repertoire of sophistic *psogos*:

> He is the contriver of every court-case, the abetter of every falsehood, the architect of every pretence, the seed-bed of every wickedness, the place of appetite and gluttony, a cesspit and a brothel, infamous already from his earliest years in all impropriety in boyhood; before he became as bald and ugly as you see he spent his time in the most unspeakable acts of child-abuse; as a young man he performed limp and flaccid as a dancer on the stage, but so I hear, amateur and vulgar even in effeminacy. For they say he had nothing of an actor's equipment except lack of modesty.[57]

The victim has to be presented as an immoral reprobate reduced to penury, so that his daughter has to be married to Pontianus in order to enable him to gain control of the estate.[58]
Other charges are easily set up to be knocked down: Pudentilla had been misquoted as calling Apuleius a sorcerer;[59] the context had been an instruction to Pontianus not to do so, and

anyway such evidence was scarcely admissible; Apuleius for his part is able to make great play of dealings with Lollianus Avitus, predecessor as proconsul of Africa to Claudius Maximus, the presiding judge.[60] Finally Apuleius' summing-up is worthy of Philostratus:

> *possum securus existimationem tuam revereri quam potestatem vereri quod minus grave et verendum mihi arbitror a proconsule damnari quam si a tam bono tamque emendato viro improber* ('I can be secure in revering your judgement rather than in fearing your power, because I think it a less weighty and fearful matter to be condemned by a proconsul than to be wronged by so good and correct a man').[61]

Apuleius' confidence was evidently well-placed; one *pepaideumenos* has adeptly recognised another.

The *Apology* contains its fair share of sophistic self-indulgence and verbal bizarrerie. But it also serves as a reminder of how easily the educated sophist could expect to run rings round an uneducated opponent, particularly in a place where he had already made an impression, and with appeal to a sympathetic judge. A reading of the *Apology* offers some insight into the omissions of Philostratus on the frequent involvements of sophists, and their resilience against most odds. How many other sophists had to fight themselves out of local and family intrigues in this way?

A SOPHIST'S SELF-PORTRAIT: LIBANIUS' *FIRST ORATION*[62]

If Apuleius happens to furnish us with one example of dealing with an intrigue, Libanius furnishes us with the narrative of a whole series, and in so doing offers us the nearest we have to the autobiography of a sophist. Yet the subject is not conceived as his life but rather his fortune, and this he has elected to treat antithetically from the very outset. Some consider him to be the happiest man alive because of the applause he enjoys as a rhetor, while others think him the least so because of his toils and pain.[63] And indeed the account in *Oration* 1 as a whole maintains the counterpoint between these two themes: Libanius is alternately elated by his successes as a declaimer and downcast by numerous setbacks and a variety of personal disasters.

The setting proper has the reflexes of panegyric: the excellences of Antioch and the fact that Libanius himself belongs among its most distinguished citizens. He has all the advantages which Bowersock's sophists could expect as normal: 'My family were the greatest in a great city in culture, wealth, the provision of public entertainments and games, and in the public speaking which set itself against the arrogance of governors.'[64] If the last point sounds typical of the fourth century rather than the second, we should remember the case of Philostratus' very first Imperial exhibit, Nicetes of Smyrna.[65] Libanius has immediately to counter a rumour that his great-grandfather had come from Italy: Hellenism is a keynote of his heritage, and he must rehearse the unfortunate fates of the previous generation of his family in relation to the city, by way of confiscation and execution. His great-grandfather's capacity for divination is also mentioned, not without significance.[66]

The beginning of Libanius' oratorical career is symptomatic. His maternal uncle foresees his success as a sophist; after early indolence ill-luck bedevils him in the death of a fine teacher; single-minded rejection of the instructors he sees as indifferent looks forward to that determined independence and confidence in one's own powers to which sophists were particularly prone.[67] The effects of a bolt of lightning produce long-term ill-health – Libanius was by no means the first sophist to have been so afflicted: Scopelian and Herodes Atticus both had tragic experiences reported by Philostratus.[68]

Libanius describes in detail his fascination with Athens, the life of its sophists and students and his desire to go there – not without much praise of his own youthful discretion and a suitable literary flourish ('I think that after the manner of Odysseus I would have rejected even marriage with a goddess for the sight of the smoke of Athens').[69] On arrival he finds himself conned into the clutches of an indifferent teacher, Diophantus, a fact which he has no little cause to regret:

> Though the applause that ensued was loud enough to deceive the first-time hearers, I was already becoming aware that I had arrived at nothing spectacular, for the control of students had been hijacked by men who were not much different from the students themselves.[70]

He avoids the partisanship and its attendant violence, and as due reward for his labours finds fortune offering him a chair in Athens itself at twenty-five, when a governor dismisses the existing professors as a result of rioting; when the affair blows over and they return to their posts, the atmosphere is predictably unhealthy.[71] At this point a characteristic unease set in:

> however adequate my ability might appear to others, I did not share their confidence in me, and I was tormented by the fear that the connoisseurs, who surrounded me everywhere, would want to find me out by any number of tests, so that I had still to keep up my research and continue to learn.[72]

After journeying to Asia in support of a colleague, he is pressured to remain as professor in Constantinople; but after a double journey back to Athens he finds the post already filled.[73] Yet in advancing his popularity he meets with conspicuous success, attracting over eighty students; he outwits and out-manoeuvres the cheapjack Bemarchius and his claque in open and public competition, thus giving rise to public disorder and imprisonments.[74] He then accepts an appointment at Nicomedia, where he could claim five years of satisfaction:

> However, the time I spent under the care of Demeter excels all the rest, and wins in every respect: my physical health and mental well-being, my frequent declamations and the standing ovations at every one of them, my throngs of students applying themselves, my studies during the night and labours during the day, the honours, goodwill and affection shown to me.[75]

The reader cannot fail to be struck by the extent to which fortune is credited for every adjustment of the writer's circumstances: 'from all those ills I was freed by Fortune'; 'Fortune contrived this and offered me it in the following way'; 'Now let me mention one more not contemptible proof that I was in the care of Fortune.'[76] Not a few of Libanius' journeys, especially sea-journeys, carry such a parenthesis ('that the weather for sailing in winter was no worse than in summer . . . was the gift of Fortune'; 'my prayers had some effect; the gods of the sea calmed it down, and all our miseries were rapidly over').[77] Particularly providential are the circumstances which wrested him away from what he saw as the unhappy fate of too long a stay in Athens ('I should certainly still be there, without being able to make use of the skills I had acquired . . . but something like this came about by the machinations of Fortune').[78] It is not that such protection is unknown in the world of Philostratus, who can casually claim that 'fate was preparing far ahead for Smyrna to be rebuilt through the efforts of such a man as Aristides.'[79] But Libanius is more persistent than most, as on the occasion of a wrangle over a colleague's wife's death, which came to a hearing before the governor at Nicaea:

> So then the population of Nicomedia mourned for us while we were still alive, as the Athenians did for the victims they sent to the Labyrinth. However, with the help of Fortune, my saviour was to be Heracles, son of Zeus, and in a dream he revealed to me his plans, and that he would quench the funeral pyre; for I dreamed that a disciple of Antisthenes sat on a great pyre in the centre of Nicaea and quenched it, and that his body prevailed over the flames.[80]

Much of Libanius' narrative sets out to catalogue how well he held his own against the treachery of others. He has no small satisfaction at having outmanoeuvred the Athenians, since in Nicomedia Bithynia kept students coming to him, and he now had firm friendships. But the affair before the governor was fomented by one of his rival's supporters, and eventually led to the flight of the rival himself.[81] Libanius is further accused of poaching a Phoenician's pupils, and charges of magic and murder are brought;[82] his teacher Zenobius offers to step down in his favour, then goes back on his offer, while a rival perverts Libanius' speech in honour of the prefect Strategius with alterations of his own.[83] Even the respite offered by Julian[84] is followed immediately by an assassination plot and more slander.[85]

It is hard to escape the impression that the ever-virtuous Libanius is always in the right, while spontaneously engendered hysteria seizes any rival or indeed anyone who so much as crosses him. One notes moreover at least three purported 'offers' of chairs which then fell through: one suspects that either Libanius is rewriting his curriculum vitae in a way that no one is at this stage going to be able to contradict; or that he had the degree of arrogance that enabled him to turn down the most attractive offers because he expected every door to open

before him. The narrative is embellished with the most tendentious literary analogues: we have already met him as Theseus,
ready to be rescued by Heracles; when he returns in triumph to
Antioch we are told that 'Agamemnon did not set eyes on a
sunnier day when he captured Troy than I looked on the day I
enjoyed such a reception as that.'[86] Later, 'like the son of
Peleus, I found idleness a burden and called myself "a burden
to the earth"'.[87] 'I was as elated at this compliment as Lycurgus
when Apollo greeted him';[88] 'For as Thrasybulus used to cut off
the tallest ears of corn, so did Fortune rob me of my best
pupils.'[89] And like the no less tendentious Aristides he had a
strong streak of career superstition:

> I was the last to compete, for the Emperor himself had
> contrived that I should have the largest possible audience,
> and it was rumoured that Hermes was taking care of his
> servant, and excited everyone in the audience with his
> wand, so that no single word of mine should be without its
> share of awe.[90]

It is not just that the texture of Libanius' account is prone to
posturing and sophistic decoration. One suspects that he is
not now content with the temptation to remodel his life on
those of Achilles, Odysseus or the fourth-century political
orators: two detailed episodes bear an uncomfortable resemblance to parts of the life of the celebrated sophist Aelius
Aristides. Libanius records an episode in which Julian, visiting
Antioch, has to make a specific request to hear a performance
of Libanius, to which he himself assents with studied shyness
and reluctance. One wonders whether he would have made
quite so much of the situation if such a story had not been
told of Aristides' encounter with the Emperor Marcus Aurelius
over two centuries before.[91] And Libanius' accumulation of
illnesses seems to culminate in his putting himself into the
custody of none other than Asclepius, in a passage which
might as readily have figured in the *Hieroi Logoi* of Aristides
himself:[92] 'by each of three visions, two of them in broad
daylight, the god removed not a little of my malady, and
brought me to my present condition, which I pray may never
be taken away.'

The original version of the speech would have ended with a
prosōpopoiia of Fortune herself:

And so Fortune might take a speaking part as if in a play, and reply, 'Even although your art has been assailed with countless reverses, at least acknowledge this much: that you have had one thing from me that makes up for many: you have been so prolific in your orations and they have enjoyed such a reputation for excellence, that even in your own lifetime you have been the object of envy, since the copying arms of your scribes have still turned out to be too few to cope with the demand from so many admirers. And yet every rhetorical school proves that your works are in the hands of pupils and teachers alike.' For this, gentlemen, I owe a debt to Fortune, and I implore her that she may always make the future even better.[93]

Even at the climax of the most sincerely felt episode, the death of Julian, Libanius cannot resist paradox:

Then, as the envoys remounted, a spear cut the flank of our wisest of emperors, and with the blood of the victor it drenched the land of the vanquished, and it made the fugitive master of the pursuers.[94]

The final writing on the wall for the Second Sophistic begins with an epigram. But to the last Libanius' power to evoke his milieu is unimpaired:

And my success was secured in the previous speech, since some fortune, I am convinced, sent off to me people to shout 'encore' and lend me support, who found it to their advantage not to speak ill of my achievements. For the preceding speaker, since there was nobody there to praise him, praised himself, and so offered another reason for ridicule, and he did not stop abusing those who had been laughing at him, which made them laugh yet again. What he had gained by deceit was lost to him, though he would not have been found out if he had realised that he could have kept his ill-gotten reputation by keeping quiet.[95]

Libanius we must leave, then, wallowing in the applause sophists loved; though with hindsight we know that Fortune herself was soon to make her own final bow on the Antique stage.

Here, then, we have four different figures and four presenta-
tions of sophistic activity. Dio and Lucian put a sophistic
construction on different places: whether in Olbia or Athens,
there will be Hellenism to be dispensed. Apuleius and Libanius,
by contrast, give accounts of their lives: that in the real court-
case has a scarcely less tendentious panache than the *apologia*
for a sophist's whole life. Sophists as diverse as Dio and Libanius
will allow themselves to be compared, or will compare themselves, to Achilles; only Lucian will have a clear vision of the
vanity of it all, but his is still a testimony from within. We do not
have to look far for characteristic self-display, rhetorical overindulgence and a measure of sheer conceit; but there is also
conviction, real skill and not a little wit as well. We must now
prepare to weigh such competing impressions of sophistic
activity.

12

Conclusion: values and valuations

We can take our leave of the Second Sophistic with a scene which neatly embodies a glimpse of most of the perspectives employed so far. In Philostratus' enormous work on Apollonius of Tyana, the sage is in due course presented as sailing for Dicaearchia, with the risk of exposing himself to persecution by Domitian:

> He met Demetrius, who seemed to be boldest among the philosophers, because he lived not far from Rome; but Apollonius knew that Demetrius was in fact staying out of the tyrant's way, nevertheless he teased him: 'I have caught you,' he said, 'living in luxury, staying in the most blessed part of happy Italy, if happy is the right word, where Odysseus is said to have spent his time with Calypso, and to have forgotten the smoke of his home in Ithaca.' Demetrius embraced him, and after other expressions of acclaim exclaimed 'Ye gods, what will happen to philosophy if she risks the loss of a man like this?' 'And what risks does philosophy run?', Apollonius asked. 'Those you already knew about when you came here;' Demetrius answered, 'if I do not know what you are thinking, then I do not know my own thoughts either. But let us not talk here, but go where we can talk alone, with only Damis with us, a man, I swear by Heracles, who is the Iolaus of your labours.'
>
> And with that Demetrius took them to the house near the city where Cicero lived in olden times. As they sat under a plane tree the grasshoppers were chirruping to the whispering of the breeze, when Demetrius looked at them, and exclaimed: 'Blessed creatures and artlessly wise,

for the Muses I think have taught you a song which is not yet subject to lawcourt or libel; and they put you above all appetites, and settled you above the envy of mankind in these trees, where you sing in your happiness about your own and the Muses' powers of happiness.' Now Apollonius understood the drift of all this, but he took exception to it as too relaxed for a person of Demetrius' claims. 'In that case,' he said, 'although you only wanted to sing the praises of grasshoppers, you were not able to do it in the open, but ran here for cover, as if there were a civil law prohibiting anyone from praising grasshoppers.' 'My remarks,' Demetrius replied, 'were not in praise of grasshoppers, but to show that they are left free to make music in their concert halls, while we are not even given freedom to mutter; but wisdom has been found to be a cause of accusation. And while the accusation brought by Anytus and Meletus went, "Socrates does wrong by corrupting young men and introducing new cults," the indictment against us goes like this: "So and so does wrong by being wise and just and understanding the gods and men, and being expert in the laws." And as for you, since you are very much wiser than we are, all the more subtle is the indictment devised against you.'[1]

Apollonius' supposed conversation is presented through a number of sophistic prisms. It might be merely routine décor to present Demetrius as Odysseus, Apollonius as Heracles;[2] but the historical dimension is more subtle. The scene is set for defiance of a tyrant – itself the standard fare of historical declamation[3] – at a spot which would have evoked Cicero's defiance of Antony at the end of the Republic. There is ingenious convergence of Greek and Roman declamatory tradition here: Cicero's defiance too had been a school theme.[4] The indictment of Socrates is cited from Plato's *Apology* in such a way as to imply that Apollonius has far worse to face, and there is also a clever exercise in the revision of laws or decrees that harks back to the *progymnasmata*.[5] But the central feature is a new twist to the celebrated detail of the opening *ecphrasis* of the *Phaedrus*:[6] one is to envisage that tyranny is now so extreme that even praise of grasshoppers – again a likely theme of adoxography[7] – is banned. But underneath all the Platonic *politesse* is the imputation that Apollonius is brave, while Demetrius is a coward. Sophistic subtleties have been pressed, as so often, into the service of panegyric. It has been part of our task to accustom ourselves to detect sophistic ornamentation of this kind; we must now address ourselves to asking how much it mattered.

A CULTURAL PHENOMENON

It will be useful to recapitulate. We have seen that expert rhetoricians were as able to command media attention in the first four centuries AD as they had been in the fifth century BC, and with comparably elusive effect. Gorgias, Protagoras, Hippias or Prodicus could be seen or could present themselves as persons of consequence, and yet not everyone was impressed. In like manner Dio or Herodes Atticus could enjoy prestige tempered by controversy. Fifth-century sophists could attend on courts, assemblies or rulers; their successors enjoyed the same versatility and similarly varied fortunes. Consequently the political impact of the Second Sophistic remains difficult to assess. Sophists could certainly attain 'importance' in most of the ways we might care to define it. The patronage system was ready enough to accord recognition to the articulate man of letters with political ambition or potential. But we do well to see sophists as equivocal in their prominence. Some preferred their art and professional priorities to political prominence, and those that did not soon found themselves in a milieu where the techniques needed were not those of the *meletē*. Herodes' enemies were seldom his fellow-sophists, and it was his inherited wealth as much as his rhetorical reflexes that sped him from quarrel to quarrel. None the less Libanius' espousal of social causes in adverse conditions towards the end of his life shows the powers of the 'good man skilled in speaking' (*vir bonus dicendi peritus*) persisting right to the end of Antiquity. The kind of 'expertise in the arts of citizenship' which we associate with the original fifth-century sophists is never too far out of reach of their successors. We must not of course assume that if Rome had allowed them a freer hand in city politics than it did, then their attainments would always have been more creditable: the performances of their Republican counterparts such as Diodorus of Adramyttium and Aristion of Athens, one a sophist and the other a Peripatetic philosopher, demonstrate all too clearly the failure of intellectuals in power of which Plato had long ago been afraid, for both sided with Mithridates and emerged with blood on their hands. Nor must we assume that because the *Pax Romana* imposed peace for so much of the Imperial centuries that sophists were unable or unwilling to step into the breach. No one even in the Antonine Age had any right to assume that Rome would always be able to step in immediately in a crisis. Aristides might laud the pervasive presence of the ruling power; but he also had to lament a barbarian attack even on Eleusis. Dio Chrysostom too could make Trajan feel like a second Alexander; but he had arrived in a Black Sea city on the fringe of the Empire just after a barbarian raid and he himself had been able to intervene directly with soldiers in a succession crisis. One had always to be prepared for a situation in which fifth- and fourth-century skills of exhortation and diplomacy would be needed again.

The sophist maintained his position by means of skill: the culture he acquired and transmitted was as flexible and ambiguous as his social position. The cult of the rhetorical exercise was adopted for better or worse in the court, assembly, theatre, or the broader environment of literature as a whole. Curriculum exercises, curriculum authors and above all curriculum habits of thought produced generation after generation of intellectuals who cultivated a fluency of literary diction and literary decoration. It is difficult to arbitrate on the success of it all, since the criteria themselves are so elusive. But if the goal was to pretend to be in the fifth century BC, however contrived or perverse such an ideal might seem to us, then the Second Sophistic was well on the way to achieving it. If the aim was to invest present literature with a sense of continuity with the literature of the classical past, then again the illusion was largely successful. And we must not condemn rhetorical training and practice for their inherent mechanism: oral poetry is much more mechanical by nature; but its use did not after all prevent the emergence of the Homeric poems.

Sophistic influence and attainment are no less elusive in fields not directly related to rhetorical practice. We can suggest that the concept of sophistic historiography is difficult to press too far. Again, in responsible hands its results are no worse than at any other period; though at its worst it results in self-indulgent mannerist drivel, with frequently irritating embellishment in the hands of an indifferent historian. The two sets of 'sophistic biographies' mirror the problem that besets the writing of history itself. And Sophistic excursions into philosophy are open to similar criticism. No sophist that we know of succeeded in replicating Plato's unique balance of philosophical content and literary delight. Those that take up the challenge either sacrifice real philosophical substance, as Lucian all too often tends to do; or they abandon any pretensions to a sophistic idiom, as in the case of Plutarch and Arrian's Epictetus. There was nothing to prevent a sophist from moving effortlessly from the pose of philosopher to that of artistic connoisseur; he could present the world in a series of flamboyant tableaux and himself as the ultimate in verbal artistry – here is the man who will turn Phidias into a public speaker – while presenting himself as a verbal painter. Lucian or Philostratus can at least attain to a mannered charm in their presentation of pictorial myth. Yet it is perhaps on fiction that the Sophistic could be said to have made its most permanent mark. In the presophistic novelist Chariton we are still simply 'reading a story', even if the author does allow himself the occasional verbal flourish. But in Achilles, Heliodorus or Longus we are confronted with a trio of ambitious artistic ensembles. The variety of results once more mirrors the ambiguity of 'sophistic' attainments. Longus may have been able to produce a classic; he could arguably have done as well in any other age or idiom. Opinions still vacillate, not unreasonably, over Achilles and Heliodorus. But we are none the less obliged to respect the organisation of superb rhetorical skills in compositions of such length, by authors who go about their business with artistic conviction and achieve the results they set out to. One feels that if Achilles makes his readers squirm with displays of virtuoso bad taste it is because he wants to; similarly with Heliodorus, when he seems to set out to produce the longest literary maze known to us in antiquity. Perry was not far wrong to suggest that with Achilles the novel comes of age; it took over a millennium to regain its majority.

All three of these sophistic novelists seem to play with the literary and historical heritage at their disposal. The art of play should also be seen as an asset of sophistic writers in general. The very greatness of the fifth and fourth centuries BC produced a familiarity, and familiarity in turn allowed the mockery of pretensions. If sophistic littérateurs lack the forthrightness of

Old Comedy, they do have a wit of their own. The image of Lucian's Prometheus hanging in the Caucasus and delivering a sophistic declamation to his persecutors before the eagle arrives is not only subtle in itself but symptomatic: one thinks of the dying sophist Polemo exclaiming 'Give me a body and I will declaim!' It takes a thoroughly sophistic view of human affairs to produce the kind of tour de force of cultural topsy-turvydom embodied in Athenaeus' *Deipnosophistae*. But that same outlook can produce results with an appeal beyond the second century. In his fourth *Dialogue of the Dead* Lucian can have Cerberus reporting 'what really happened' over Socrates' martyrdom: no sooner had the hemlock worn off than he had to be dragged kicking and screaming into the Underworld for fear of death. But all such subversion of the heritage of Hellenism is still carried out with a passion for *paideia*.

The attitude of sophists to the divine represents another group of contrasts. There was no sense of incongruity in a sophist's seeing himself as a sacred functionary capable of performing encomia to the gods in prose, and in usurping the inspiration or even the frenzy of poets. Nor was there incongruity in educated Jews or Christians renewing and intensifying their elegance of presentation with sophistic techniques – or in a sophist's producing a confection such as the *Life of Apollonius of Tyana*. Aristides declaimed about Alexander the Great in the Asclepieion at Pergamum – as part of the god's own plan for his cure. Such a vignette is once more symptomatic of his age, and the way one sophist at least could view it.

On the whole it is arbitrary to epitomise the Imperial sophists in so narrow a range of texts as Dio's *Borystheniticus*, Lucian's *Navigium*, Apuleius' *Apology* and Libanius' *First Oration*. Yet it is hard to think of an aspect of sophistic outlook that is not at least implied in one or other of this strange quartet. The sophistic chameleon can adapt to any circumstances and accommodate his ego wherever he chooses; but that in itself betokens no lack of ability or potential for achievement.

Sophistic, then, promises an aura of smartness and lustre, just as it had done in the age of Gorgias: where there are sophists, there are admirers, marketable skills and Hellenic culture. But what did it all amount to? It has always been easy to despise the Greek literature of the Empire in terms of its failures rather than its successes, and in particular to dismiss individual achievement and denigrate what is 'typical'. At this stage we should at least try to make distinctions. In particular it seems misleading to try to put all the surviving material together, call it literature and impugn its quality on that account. For a start we ought to be able to put aside material that seems purely preparatory, such as Aelian's *Varia Historia*, or even for that matter Marcus Aurelius' *Meditations*, which are in the nature of an informal commonplace book. We ought then also to be able to put a very large proportion of the surviving material into a highly specialised category, as a literature of performance which requires almost as much of a *skēnē*, a stage-set, and a sense of audience and occasion as the dramatic genres. It is a pity that our appreciation of sophistic literature should so seldom take this living context into account. I can think of no better illustration of the ethos in which sophistic performance flourished than the opening of the Barcelona Olympic Games in 1992, complete with a spectacle commemorating the westward quest of Heracles to the site. The world-class local celebrities on that occasion were solo (operatic) performers, and parts of the proceedings were in Catalan: what a sophist would have been able to do would have been to improvise a speech suitable to the occasion ('Heracles debates whether to found Games at Barcelona or move on to establish the Pillars of Heracles . . .'); and of course, to have done so in Old Catalan for good measure.

What are we to make of sophistic 'influence' under the Empire? It is worthwhile to note a series of verdicts on the Sophistic, though in many cases these seem based not on the evidence we have considered, so much as on argument and environment tangential to sophists as such. Some scholars have treated the Sophistic in an influential way when their main concern was only one aspect of its output. Erwin Rohde in particular was responsible for a perspective which saw in the Second Sophistic some of the worst features of its supposed progeny, the Greek novel:

Rhetoric as such, despite all the rhetoricians' assurances that only the best man could be the best speaker, has absolutely nothing to do with the truth of its contents, with sincerity of opinion, or with authenticity of experience; these qualities, naturally highly essential requirements for a living rhetorical system, the rhetoric of an older period had simply taken for granted. They came with the concerns themselves, so long as these arose from real life and the rhetor's own interest. Once these concerns themselves had disappeared, and could only be conjured up through fantasy in accordance with an arbitrary act of will, the only surviving purely formal art of eloquence could not replace any of the ethical requirements of a genuine orator.[8]

Even long after this link between novel and sophistic had been shown to be false, we still find Wilhelm Schmid[9] and others taking up similar stances, and those not directly concerned with studying sophistic techniques of imitation tend to despise or attempt to circumvent them. The 1950s and early 1960s represented the low ebb in the evaluation of Imperial sophists, or at any rate their literature: first Perry, then van Groningen, reaffirmed the mediocrity of the age, with anything wholesome seen as exceptional:

The travelling sophists were acclaimed and worshipped by the public as film stars and sports matadors today; Radermacher very aptly called them 'Konzertredner'. People liked to speak well and people liked to listen. But the attention and the admiration were directed more towards the word, the sound, the rhythm than towards the ideas. The speakers wished above all to amaze and to dazzle. The ideas and emotions which they expressed had no other purpose than to make this striking form possible. No effort was demanded of the audience; neither originality of thought nor sincerity of feeling were pursued or expected. Time and again the same stale wine was offered in new, beautifully adorned cups; but it was incapable of quenching any real thirst for knowledge or understanding, had this thirst existed. The whole phenomenon strongly resembles a mesmeric trance, a soft delirium; speakers and listeners were hypnotized by an extravagant presentation of worthless contents. There was no longer a link with life as it is; people let themselves be roused up into a state of insincere pathos, in which the roar of strong words had to drown the deficiencies and the falsehoods of the contests.[10]

Such an evaluation is as one-sided as Plato's criticisms of the original sophists, or the lamentations of later Antiquity on the theme of the decline of oratory. It might be justified conceivably against Polemo's declamations on the aftermath of Marathon. But it carries a strong undertone of intolerance towards the preservation of a cultural and academic tradition, and a determination to isolate it from 'the real world'. The cultural life of the Empire is being insidiously written off because it was still in essence devoted to producing an articulate élite capable of maintaining a vital link with its past, rather than to the priorities that would have produced another Plotinus, for example. However, such an approach is as wanting as the caricature it is trying to discredit. Not all sophists and not all declamations were alike; and the system they fostered did not in the end limit creativity.

Among more recent commentators, Reardon and Bowersock polarise literary and historical views. Bowersock[11] tends to approve sophists for the sort of company they kept and the social status that some of them either had for other reasons or sought; but he remains at best neutral on their literary attainments. Reardon by contrast tends to confine his examination to the literary aspect which forms the core of any sophist's work,[12] while he warms rather to the fringe of littérateurs who abandon the *meletē* for 'rhétorique appliquée'. Both perspectives are essential for any balanced appreciation of sophistic activity in its context. The sophists are an important and characteristic part of the Greek urban aristocracies, and a symbol of their resilience, though acknowledgement as a sophist was not in itself necessary to attain recognition in a Roman dimension: Herodes might have acquired his social éclat through his fortunes, his benefactions and his early friendship with the future Marcus Aurelius, without ever having exerted himself to emulate the canon of the Ten Attic Orators. At the same time, acknowledgement as a sophist was not in itself a passport to literary attainment: we read Plutarch or Lucian, neither of whom can be regarded as more than marginal to the central activities of sophists, and avoid Aristides, whose skill and vanity conspire to stifle any real literary attainment, in spite of the verdict of later Antiquity. Moreover, Aristides' own refusal to improvise at once makes him less than typical of standard sophistic practice.[13] Yet the educational system of which sophists were the most accomplished embodiment also provided the cultural ecology for all such figures.

From yet another perspective we can choose to emphasise the role of sophists in the cultural continuity of Hellenism from the classical to the Byzantine world:

> Behind Dio and his History lies an important phenom-enon which has not yet found its historian – the Renais-sance of the Greek cities and Greek cultural life which appears in the latter half of the first century, continues into the third, and reappears in the fourth. The peaceful and prosperous life of the Greek Near East under Roman rule represents the most complete development of Greek civilisation in antiquity; more than that, it provides the vital cultural and economic link between the Hellenistic world and the Byzantine Empire and is thus one of the basic elements in the history of the ancient world.[14]

That is indeed the historical context in which the Second Sophistic has to be seen. It does not coincide exactly with what sophists were or did, but it does include them, and they provide in large measure the vision that operates it:

> Neither the orators and writers of the Second Sophistic nor their audiences would have recognised themselves in the modern convictions of their 'sterility' and emptiness; far from being marginalised into 'mere rhetoric', their oratory was an integral part of civilised life with a definite and public role to play.[15]

But this kind of cultural empathy has also to be treated carefully: the mere fact of public speaking as a cultural activity does not tell us anything about the quality of either. Civic speeches could undoubtedly be useful as well as merely ornamental: the sophist who could hint to Trajan about Alexander would still use his oratory when required to suppress a military revolt or civic unrest directed at himself; or the sophist who presented his neurotic superstition as pious acceptance of Fortune could still intercede for a city against the wrath of an Emperor.

One issue tends to underlie a good many of these contrasting viewpoints without ever coming clearly to the surface. How one regards sophists tends to rely on one's instinctive view of affectation: the very title 'Second Sophistic' is itself an elegant turn of phrase which reflects a borrowed glory from the fifth century BC to the early centuries AD; and many of the postures of sophists in their social and political relationships, as well as their writings, could be regarded in the same light. If we regard affectation as clever, elegant, ethically neutral and based on serious scholarly effort, then we are well on the way to sympathising and even empathising with sophists; if we equate affectation with dishonesty then we are unlikely to be able to come to terms with a basic facet of Imperial cultural history. The distinction is a fine one, and not all sophists themselves recognised it all of the time.

We can now hope to stand far enough back from the Second Sophistic to attempt both to characterise its influence and to evaluate it. I hope to have suggested at least something of the extent of influence involved. Throughout the Imperial period rhetoric itself enjoyed a paramount prestige and those who stood at the top of the rhetoricians' profession could expect a paramount influence over the education and literature they themselves did so much to condition. Rhetorical education produced sophistic flourish both in the curriculum exercises and well beyond them. Lucian and the novelists represent the potential of sophistic literature outside the schools. Harnessed to *ingenium*, sophistic *ars* can produce effective literature. Lucian and Apuleius are capable of using obviously sophistic techniques to produce literary masterpieces, while Achilles shows at least the dangers of sophistic mannerism for its own sake. In the smaller forms in particular, sophistic sketches on 'unreal or artificial' themes are again easily capable of generating literature in their own right. Dio Chrysostom is perhaps the best illustration of an all-round personality with a significantly sophistic formation. He is not all verbiage, though at times there is no lack of it. He possesses charm, independence and individuality, and a sophist's equipment is pressed into the service of such qualities.

The world of the sophists, then, was not a curious and sterile cultural irrelevance. It could add to a living heritage without necessarily being weighed down by it; and its practitioners could indeed contribute significantly to civic and Imperial service. The word sophist promised real versatility as well as mannered equivocation. But the whole business did run the constant risk of being institutionalised: whatever can be taught runs the risk of being reduced to stereotype. And sophists ran the risk of refining the tools of extempore rhetoric to the point where they could only produce extempore rhetors. In the end it is probably as difficult to come to a decision about those who affected the term sophist in the Empire as it still is for the sophists of the fifth century BC. One acknowledges their skill, not just rhetorical but diplomatic as well; one acknowledges their part in a complex social fabric and cultural heritage, subjective as the latter may ultimately have been. At the same time one must acknowledge the limitations of any rhetorician: he may be a genuine artist, or an overindulgent dabbler. In acknowledging the real strengths of sophists and the system of which they were in a sense the culmination, we should not remain blind to their flaws: they could all too easily produce words without substance and adopt an overdeveloped sense of their own importance. But they did keep alive a heritage to which they themselves felt able to contribute from the inside. Marathon still mattered, because one could still fight there and the messenger had still not reached Athens with the news of victory; Xerxes was to be on his way before too long, with Philip's intrigues not far behind him; audiences Greek and Roman alike were still waiting to admire one's response to Philip.

In conclusion it seems appropriate to turn back to the point where we first noticed the beginnings of sophistic training. We left our very first *progymnasma* in mid-flow, with the wise old monkey pointing out the advantages of not living in walled cities. It might not be inappropriate to suggest how he could have continued on the matter of sophists:

And furthermore, gentlemen of the monkeys, I must tell you about a tribe especially found in cities, the *pithecosophistae* ('monkey-sophists'). How much these creatures know and how often they are prepared to talk about it, I am too amazed to tell you. I must not call them new, because they say they are old. Some argue that they are a race of satyrs, as superior to mortal men as donkeys are to horses, and many applaud this view; others claim that they are related to men, and that that is why they imitate them; but all are agreed that our ancestors were known not as pithēkoi, but as *peithēkooi* ('hearers of persuasion'). This fact has a twofold significance, as Pan is my witness; it explains why you all believe me and proves that in origin the monkeys belong to the Hellenic race. I do not doubt

245

that association with such persons must be profitable; some enjoy the favour of the Emperor of the Romans, M. Antoninus Porphyropithecus. I have also heard however that they are vain and contentious and may be formidable in lawsuits and assemblies, though many spend most of their time in classrooms teaching little monkeys. Yet I have also heard that they are lovers of truth, and I myself know for certain that they worship Paideia in a grove where cicadas sing all day long; that is why I believe that *paideuein* ('teach') and *paizein* ('joke') are really the same, and the performances of many sophists confirms it. And this I know above all: when they chatter in Attic, their noblest form of utterance, the citizens of cities are seized with such madness that they will always be inspired to terrify the barbarians; at least I have heard a prophecy that some of their speeches, and many of their names, will outlast the Empire of the Romans.

If nothing else, such a speech will serve as a reminder of how much about sophists is complex and ambiguous, and why it is likely to remain so.

Notes and references

INTRODUCTION

1 Tacitus, *Annales* 4.55; Philostratus, *Vitae Sophistarum* (*VS*) 548.
2 For the Greek city, O. Murray and S. Price, *The Greek City from Homer to Alexander* (Oxford, 1990); for our period, A.H.M. Jones, *The Cities of the Eastern Roman Provinces* (Oxford, 1937); A.H.M. Jones, *The Greek City from Alexander to Justinian* (Oxford, 1940).
3 Useful summary in F. Millar, *The Roman Empire and its Neighbours* (2nd edn, London, 1981), 81–103.
4 For the hierarchy of cities, A.N. Sherwin-White, *The Roman Citizenship* (2nd edn, Oxford, 1973), 251–263 and passim.
5 For Athens in the early Empire, P. Graindor, *Athènes sur Hadrien* (Cairo, 1930); S. Follet, *Athènes au IIe et au IIIe siècle* (Paris, 1976); D.J. Geagan, 'Roman Athens: Some Aspects of Life and Culture I: 86 BC–AD 267', *ANRW* 2.7.1 (1979), 371–437; J.H. Oliver, *The Civic Tradition and Roman Athens* (Baltimore, Md, 1983).
6 Useful synthesis on the Hadrianic contribution to the Greek world in M.T. Boatwright, *Hadrian and the City of Rome* (Princeton, NJ, 1987), 202–212.
7 For Herodes, W. Ameling, *Herodes Atticus* (2 vols, Hildesheim, 1983) usefully updates the standard portrait of P. Graindor: *Un milliardaire antique: Hérode Atticus et sa famille* (Cairo, 1930).
8 For an important crisis in the third century, the Gothic invasion of 267, F. Millar: 'P. Herennius Dexippus: The Greek World and the Third-Century Invasions', *JRS* 59 (1969), 12–29.
9 For Libanius and Antioch, J.W. Liebeschütz, *Antioch: City and Imperial Administration in the Later Roman Empire* (Oxford, 1972).
10 See now G.M. Rogers, *The Sacred Identity of Ephesos: Foundation Myths of a Roman City* (London, 1991). For a lucid conspectus of urban life in the whole area, see A.D. Macro, 'The Cities of Asia Minor under the Roman *Imperium*', *ANRW* 2.7.2 (1980), 658–697.
11 Useful discussion of the political speeches in C.P. Jones, *The Roman World of Dio Chrysostom* (Cambridge, Mass., 1978).
12 *Ep.* 10.81, 10.82.
13 *Ep.* 10.37–40.

14 E.g. *P.Rainer* 20.1 (among much similar evidence).
15 For the case of the Smyrna earthquake under Marcus Aurelius, below 27.
16 For Pausanias, C. Habicht, *Pausanias' Guide to Ancient Greece* (Berkeley, Calif., 1985).
17 W.L. MacDonald, *The Architecture of the Roman Empire* vol. II: *An Urban Appraisal* (New Haven, Conn., 1986), 131.
18 Citizenship: Sherwin-White 1973; Senate: H. Halfmann, *Die Senatoren aus dem östlichen Teil des Imperium Romanum bis zur Ende des zweiten Jahrhunderts* (Göttingen, 1979).
19 *Acts* 25.11; cf. 22.25.
20 For the complex political background, E. Champlin, *Fronto and Antonine Rome* (Cambridge, Mass., 1980), 63f., 104f.
21 G.W. Bowersock, *Greek Sophists in the Roman Empire* (Oxford, 1969), 43–58.
22 Boatwright (1987), 202–212.
23 J.H. Oliver, 'Marcus Aurelius: aspects of civic and cultural policy in the East', *Hesperia* Suppl. 13 (1970).
24 Dio 69.4.1–5.
25 Philostratus, *VS* 582f.
26 Pausanias 8.43.1.
27 Pliny *Ep.* 8.24.
28 Horace, *Ep.* 2.1.156: *Graecia capta ferum victorem cepit.*
29 On Dio's Alexander speeches, C.P. Jones (1978a), 116–121.
30 For a collection of 'Renaissances', W.E. Treadgold (ed.), *Renaissances before the Renaissance: Cultural Revivals of Late Antiquity and the Middle Ages* (Stanford, Calif., 1984).
31 Pace S. Swain, 'The reliability of Philostratus's *Lives of the Sophists*', *CA* 10 (1991), 149; Macro (1980), 693. We can easily enough of course say that the two trends were concomitant and convergent, and agree with Swain that in the Empire at least sophistic preoccupations were a leisure industry; but the mere existence of sophistic statesmen in the late Republic (below 18f.) means that it was not always exclusively so.
32 On *paideia*, W. Jaeger, (tr. G. Highet), *Paideia: the Ideals of Greek Culture* (Oxford, 1939–44). In its Second Sophistic context, B.P. Reardon, *Courants littéraires grecs des IIe et IIIe siècles après J.-C.* (Paris, 1971), 3–11 and passim.
33 Contrasting images in C.P. Jones, *Plutarch and Rome* (Oxford, 1971), and D.A. Russell, *Plutarch* (London, 1972).
34 For Galen's society, Bowersock (1969) 59–75; for the new treatise, below ch. 1, n. 76.
35 Contrasting views in C.P. Jones, *Culture and Society in Lucian* (Cambridge, Mass., 1986), and Anderson, 'Lucian: Tradition versus Reality', *ANRW* 2.34.2 forthcoming.
36 Good brief conspectus in Reardon (1971), 180–185, 226f.
37 For the novel, below ch. 8.
38 D.A. Russell (ed.), *Antonine Literature* (Oxford, 1990), 1–17.
39 Bowersock (1969); Reardon (1971); E.L. Bowie, 'Greeks and their

past in the Second Sophistic', *Past and Present* 46 (1970), 3–41, revised in M.I. Finley, *Studies in Ancient Society* (London, 1974); Swain (1991), 148–163.

40 Reardon in Treadgold (1984), 23, 35; A. Cameron and S. Walker, *The Greek Renaissance in the Roman Empire* (London, 1989).

41 G. Anderson, *Philostratus: Biography and Belles-Lettres in the Third Century AD* (London, 1986); G. Anderson, 'The *Pepaideumenos* in Action: Sophists and their Outlook in the Early Empire', *ANRW* 2.33.1 (1989), 79–208.

42 *Noctes Atticae* 1.2.

1 SOPHISTS IN SOCIETY

1 For Philostratus' context, *VS* 481. No single work sets out to treat any more than a limited range of aspects of the Second Sophistic, nor is there any treatment of monograph length devoted to it; the major *élan* to its study in the late nineteenth century was the section devoted to it in Erwin Rohde's *Der griechische Roman* (1st edn 1876, 3rd edn 1914; I follow the latter's pagination), 310–387. Wilhelm Schmid surveyed the individual authors in encyclopaedic but necessarily superficial fashion in Schmid-Christ, *Geschichte der griechische Litteratur* (6th edn 2.2 (1924), 688–828; 985–1050), still invaluable for older bibliography. Boulanger's study of Aelius Aristides (Paris, 1923) is one among several early twentieth-century efforts to place individual authors against the background of the period. The historical, or more narrowly the prosopographical background is well focused in Bowersock (1969), which however ignores any material after Philostratus himself. The literary background is sympathetically provided in B.P. Reardon (1971), whose chronological limits offer similar restriction. Two recent variorum works have substantial bearing on the period: J.J. Winkler and G. Williams (eds), *Later Greek Literature*, *YCS* 27 (1982), and D.A. Russell (ed.), *Antonine Literature* (Oxford, 1990). For a recent survey of later Graeco-Roman literature in general, A. Dihle, *Die griechische und lateinische Literatur der Kaiserzeit von Augustus bis Justinian* (Munich, 1989). On the more specific background to the Sophistic, G. Anderson, *Philostratus: Biography and Belles-Lettres in the Third Century A.D.*, (London, 1986); G. Anderson, 'The *Pepaideumenos* in action in the Early Empire', *ANRW* 2.33.1 (1989), 79–208.

2 For recent assessment of the fifth-century sophists, F. Solmsen, *Intellectual Experiments of the Greek Enlightenment* (Princeton, NJ, 1975); G. Kerferd, *The Sophistic Movement* (Cambridge, 1981).

3 *VS* 481f.; 492f.

4 *VS* 535, 533, 538.

5 *VS* 481 (by implication).

6 For other discussions of the term 'sophistic', e.g. Bowersock (1969), 12ff.; Anderson (1989), 87f.; G. Anderson, 'The Second Sophistic: Some Problems of Perspective', in Russell (1990), 92ff.

7 For this superiority of sophists, cf. Lucian, *Rhetorum Praeceptor* 1: Ἐρωτᾷς ... ὅπως ἂν ῥήτωρ γένοιο καὶ τὸ σεμνότατον τοῦτο καὶ πάντιμον ὄνομα σοφιστὴς εἶναι δόξαις ('You ask ... how to become a rhetor and seem to be a sophist, this most august and prestigious of titles'). Cf. Bowersock (1969), 13: 'a virtuoso rhetor with a big public reputation'.

8 The monograph by R.C. Burgess, *Epideictic Literature* (Chicago, 1902) is still useful.

9 *VS* 481, cf. 482.

10 *VS* 510f. (three otherwise unknown names in all!).

11 Passages collected by C. Brandstätter, *De notionum* politikos *et* sophistes *usu rhetorico, Leipziger Studien zur classischen Philologie* 15 (1894), 216.

12 Ibid., 231ff.

13 For this sense, e.g. *Phaedrus* 257D, cf. *Gorgias* 465C.

14 Individual biographies are usefully assembled by H. Bornecque, *Les Déclamations et les déclamateurs d'après Sénèque le père* (Lille, 1902), 143–201; cf. also Anderson (1986), 84–87.

15 Bornecque (1902), 172f.; 192.

16 E.g. *Contr.* 1.2.22; *Suas.* 1.6.

17 Bornecque (1902), 139f. Cf. below 87–94.

18 *VS* 486.

19 *Vit. Ant.* 80.

20 *Fr. adesp.* 422 Nauck.

21 *VS* 510ff. On Nicetes (Sacerdos), Tacitus *Dialogus* 15.7; Pliny *Ep.* 6.6.3.

22 *VS* 512. For the identification, J.C. Fant, 'The choleric Roman official of Philostratus *Vitae Sophistarum* p. 512', *Historia* 30 (1981), 240–243, rightly following Jüttner's reading of the emperor as Nero, not Nerva.

23 For the label, below 90.

24 *VS* 512ff.; Pliny *Ep.* 2.3; see P. Grimal, 'Deux figures de la Correspondance de Pline: le philosophe Euphrates et le rhéteur Isée', *Latomus* 14 (1955), 370–383 at 383ff.

25 *VS* 486ff., cf. 492.

26 On Dio's civic speeches, see now C.P. Jones, (1978a), 19–44, 65–114. Also P. Desideri, *Dione di prusa. Un intellettuale greco nell' impero romano* (Messina, 1978).

27 Von Arnim's picture of Dio as a sophist, *Leben und Werke des Dio von Prusa* (Berlin, 1898), 115–222, is vitiated by schematised chronology, but remains the standard presentation of this aspect of his activities.

28 E.g. *Or.* 33.4f.; *Or.* 35.8ff.

29 Bowersock (1969) passim; for inventory, Bowersock (1974), 35–40; for Philostratus' general presentation, Anderson (1986), 23–120.

30 On Polemo, H. Jüttner, *De Polemonis rhetoris vita operibus arte* (Breslau, 1898); W. Stegemann, *Antonius Polemon, der Hauptvertreter des zweiten Sophistik* (Stuttgart, 1942); Stegemann, s.v. Polemon 10, *RE* 21.2 (1952), cols 1320–1357.

31 On Herodes, P. Graindor, *Athènes sur Hadrien* (Cairo, 1930); W. Ameling, *Herodes Atticus* (2 vols, Hildesheim, 1983).
32 *VS* 614.
33 *VS* 518, 531.
34 *VS* 613.
35 *VS* 619.
36 *VS* 564. For this kind of acclamation ritual, cf. Lucian, *Rhetorum Praeceptor* 21 (comparison with Demosthenes).
37 For the Clepsydrion, *VS* 585f. and 594. A further member, Amphicles (585), is also attested epigraphically: C.P. Jones, 'The teacher of Plutarch', *HSCPh* 74 (1970), 242f. on *IG* 12.9.1179.
38 *VS* 587.
39 *VS* 523.
40 *VS* 529. Herodes' pupils were similarly resourceful in obtaining copies of Philagrus' pretended improvisation, *VS* 579.
41 *VS* 586.
42 *VS* 567f., 571.
43 *VS* 578f.
44 *VS* 583. For a dream of Aristides along similar lines, *Or.* 51.45.
45 *VS* 587f. For a possible link with the book-collector of Lucian's *adversus Indoctum*, G. Anderson, 'Lucian: tradition versus reality', *ANRW* 2.34.2 forthcoming.
46 *VS* 614.
47 See below 42f.
48 *VS* 526.
49 *VS* 591.
50 *VS* 617. For a similar effect by Hadrian of Tyre in Rome, *VS* 589.
51 *VS* 591 (Chrestus of Byzantium).
52 *VS* 591f. (Chrestus against Diogenes of Amastris).
53 *VS* 617 (Hippodromus of Larissa against an admirer of Heraclides).
54 *VS* 613.
55 Bowersock (1969), 17–29. The urban context is also emphasised in Boulanger (1923). On rhetoric at Alexandria, neglected by Philostratus, R.W. Smith, *Rhetoric at Alexandria: its theory and practice in the Ancient World* (The Hague, 1974); for Antioch, cf. below 25.
56 Bowersock (1969), 17f. For epigraphical evidence of sophists at Ephesus, J. Keil, 'Vertreter der zweiten Sophistik in Ephesos', *JöAL* (1953), 5–26. But I am not sure that the epigraphic use of the title *sophistes* entitles us to say that 'Damianus misled Philostratus about Soterus' (pace S. Swain, 1991, 162): considerable subjectivity was natural in the application of so flexible a title.
57 *VS* 511, 516, 530ff., 582.
58 Bowersock (1969), 18.
59 *VS* 605 (as ἀθύρματα τῶν Ἑλλήνων).
60 *VS* 605, 605f.
61 See e.g. Libanius *Or.* 1.31–36 (intrigues to fill a sophistic chair); cf. Bowersock (1969), 20.
62 Libanius, *Or.* 1 passim; P. Petit, *Libanius et la vie municipale à Antioche au IVe siècle après J.-C.* (Paris, 1955); Liebeschütz (1972).

63 Dio's *Borystheniticus* (*Or.* 36), below ch. 11; for Lucian, E.L. Bowie, 'Lucian at Philippopolis', *Mitteilungen des Bulgarischen Forschunginstitutes in Österreich* 3.1 (1980), 53–60.

64 *VS* 529. For the nature of these traditional inter-city quarrels, C.P. Jones (1978a); cf. Bowie (1970/74).

65 *VS* 526. For this post, also held by Philostratus, D.J. Geagan, 'The Athenian constitution after Sulla', *Hesperia* Suppl. 12 (1967), 18–31.

66 *VS* 519, 518.

67 *VS* 512; for the official's identity as Verginius Rufus, above 20. As he was acting in Smyrna as an auditor, Nicetes' own building projects and their finances may well have come under scrutiny: cf. Fant, 'The choleric Roman official', 243.

68 E.g. *Or.* 1.25, 35, 62–72.

69 *VS* 616.

70 *VS* 531f. For the two-edged nature of these interventions, Anderson (1989), 151.

71 *VS* 532.

72 *VS* 531, 533, 540f. Cf. below 30–35.

73 For Herodes and the Athenians, *VS* 549, 558, 559ff.

74 *VS* 548; Lucian, *de Morte Peregrini* 19, cf. Frazer's edn of Pausanias, vol. 4 (London, 1898), 72–75.

75 *VS* 549; Anderson (1986), 108, 110f.

76 *VS* 559. Herodes' grief evidently became a grand obsession in itself, amply confirmed archaeologically: see e.g. L. Robert, 'Deux Inscriptions de l'époque impériale en Attique II: un concours et Hérode Atticus', *AJPh* 100 (1979), 160–165.

77 For the Demostratus conspiracy, *VS* 559ff. For the new Galen, A.Z. Iskandar, *Galen on Examination by Which the Best Physicians are Recognised*, *CMG Supplementum Orientale* 4 (Berlin, 1988), 9.19. Cf. V. Nutton, 'The Patient's Choice: a New Treatise by Galen', *CQ* N.S. 40 (1990), 236–257.

78 *VS* 566; *VS* 568.

79 *VS* 582, *Or.* 19.3K; *VS* 596.

80 *VS* 600.

81 *VS* 603.

82 For this phenomemon, Bowersock (1969), 34–41.

83 Cf. Bowie, 'The importance of sophists,' *YCS* 27 (1982), 53: 'that in all roles except that of *ab epistulis* the sophist should be seen as a species of the genus Greek aristocrat and that his membership of that genus is the greatest factor contributing to his success'.

84 *VS* 605f.

85 *VS* 531, 533.

86 For the details, C.P. Jones (1978a), 111–114.

87 *VS* 582.

88 It is conceivable that Nicetes' gateway for Smyrna (Philostratus, *VS* 511) was the result of fund-raising rather than largesse; but we might infer Nicetes' own wealth from the social preeminence of his descendant Euodianus (*VS* 596).

89 *Vita Apollonii* 1.34.
90 Cf. Anderson (1989), 181–184.
91 Plato *Gorgias* 447AB; *Protagoras* 310B-311A; *Euthydemus* 271A–272A.
92 *VS* 571ff., 578ff.
93 *VS* 535, 586f.; cf. Alexander Peloplaton, below 57ff.
94 *VS* 532 (cf. 533, 540ff.). For similarly notorious extravagance, perhaps on the part of Hadrian of Tyre, cf. Lucian, *Pseudologista* 21.
95 *VS* 532.
96 Ibid. For Polemo as companion of Hadrian, Bowersock (1969), 120–123.
97 *VS* 596.
98 E.g. *VS* 534f. (Polemo at the Olympic Games); Antipater 607 (Olympic and Panathenaic orations); 616 (Hippodromus at the Amphictyonic Games); 539 (Herodes at the Olympic Games).
99 *VS* 529, 618f.
100 *Or.* 13.11ff.; cf. *VS* 488.
101 *VS* 520, 537, 529f., 570.
102 *VS* 524ff. (for an exorbitant fee).
103 *VS* 512.
104 *VS* 581f. Swain (1991, 160) speaks of 'the requirement to travel widely'; this seems overprescriptive.
105 *VS* 625.
106 *Or.* 1.11–101.
107 Bowersock (1969), 120–123; *VS* 571; *VA* 1.3. Cf. Bowie (1982), 50.
108 Jerome, *Chronicle* at AD 88.
109 *VS* 526.
110 *VS* 566.
111 *VS* 526; for a useful summary of the problem, J.A. Hall, *Lucian's Satire* (New York, 1981), 396–402, after C. Bargaballo, *Lo Stato e l'Istruzione Pubblica nell' Impero Romano* (Catania, 1911), 147–152).
112 E.g. *VS* 589, 594 (Pausanias).
113 E.g. Marcus, *VS* 588f., Hadrian of Tyre, in response to a complaint); Caracalla, 622f. (Philiscus, in revenge for supposed sharp practice over a liturgy).
114 E.g. Libanius *Or.* 1.25, 82f., 106 (with Norman ad 25).
115 *VS* 580. Rothe's commentary (1989) is specifically devoted to the chair-holders; note also I. Avotins, 'The holders of the chairs of rhetoric at Athens', *HSCPh* 79 (1975), 313–324.
116 *VS* 591.
117 *VS* 594. For the kind of criticism the consequent metrical false quantities would have occasioned, cf. ch. 4 below.
118 *VS* 592f.
119 *VS* 596f.
120 *VS* 613.
121 *VS* 621ff. See below 33ff.
122 *VS* 627. Perhaps at the expense of the Lemnian Philostratus, though it is not quite clear what the biographer wishes to imply.
123 Suet. *Tiberius* 11.5f.

124 Fronto *ad M. Caes.* 2.5.1 (vol. 1, 116 Haines = 2.7.1. van den Hout): *omnia ad usum magis quam ad voluptatem.*

125 *VS* 582f., in spite of his known association with the father of the discredited Avidius Cassius, as pointed out by F. Gasco, 'The meeting between Aelius Aristides and Marcus Aurelius in Smyrna', *AJPh* 110 (1989), 471–478.

126 *VS* 577, 588f. I cannot see why Bowersock posits a later audience with Marcus for Hermocrates.

127 *VS* 593.

128 *VS* 601, 614.

129 *VS* 625f. Bowie (1980), 60 plausibly guesses that Lucian's stay at Philippopolis to deliver the *Fugitivi* could have been occasioned by embassy business.

130 *VS* 570f., 622f. For the former mannerisms as characteristic of sophists, cf. Lucian, *Rhetorum Praeceptor* 11f.

131 *VS* 607; Dio Cassius 69.3.3f. Cf. Fronto's rather discreetly expressed awkwardness *vis-à-vis* Hadrian, *ad M. Caes.* 2.1.1. (vol. 1, 110ff. Haines = 24ff. van den Hout).

132 *VS* 524.

133 Dio Cassius 69.3.6.

134 Fronto *ad M. Caes.* 3.3 (vol. 1, 64ff. Haines = 37ff. van den Hout).

135 *VS* 512.

136 *Ep.* 10.82. Cf. Sherwin-White, *The Letters of Pliny* (Oxford, 1966) ad 81f. for the overall situation.

137 *VS* 533, 534.

138 *VS* 561.

139 *VS* ibid. For this complex situation, see J.H. Oliver, 'Marcus Aurelius: aspects of civic and cultural policy in the East' (*Hesperia* Suppl. 13, (1970), 80–83; F. Millar, *The Emperor in the Roman World* (London, 1977), 4ff.; Anderson (1986), 111f.; Anderson (1989), 199ff.

140 *VS* 622f.

141 Bowersock (1969), 40f.

142 *VS* 623.

143 For sophists and emperors in general, Bowersock (1969), 43–58; Millar (1977) 91f., 138, 281, 468.

144 For the post *ab epistolis* as a special case naturally accessible to sophists, Bowie (1982), 43–47, 57ff.

145 Bowersock (1969), 89–100. In fact few of the quarrels he describes need have been professional in the strictest sense.

146 *VS* 579, 599.

147 *VS* 515. This may also have been a hit at overscrupulous Atticists. Cf. ch. 4 below.

148 *VS* 513. For disapproval of intoned recitation, below 60f.

149 *VS* 514, 590.

150 *VS* 583.

151 *VS* 574.

152 *VS* 583, 614. Cf. the new evidence of Galen for a failure of Herodes, above 27.

153 *VS* 595f., 542. On the problems surrounding the application of *stasis* theory, D.A. Russell (1983), 40–73.

154 *VS* 588; for Nicetes as ignoring these boundaries, *VS* 511.

155 *VS* 604. For fourth-century practice in schools, Walden (1909), 296–333.

156 *VS* 591ff. He was not alone in his superstition. Cf. the evidence for Libanius' gullibility over career anxieties, below 229–232.

157 *VS* 591.

158 *VS* 573, 586.

159 *VS* 617.

160 *VS* 535 and passim, 534.

161 *VS* 512.

162 E.g. *VS* 534 (Polemo). Philostratus himself acknowledges that Sophistic is a τέχνη φίλαυτὸς τε καὶ ἀλαζών: 'a profession given to egotism and pretension' (*VS* 616).

163 *VS* 582, 578.

164 E.g. *VS* 601 (Apollonius of Athens and Heraclides of Lycia); cf. 617 (pressure for a contest between Hippodromus of Larissa and Philostratus the Lemnian).

165 *VS* 615, 625, 617. Cf. Lucian's extant satire *Rhetorum Praeceptor*.

166 *VS* 578ff.

167 *VS* 605. And Soterus at least was accorded more dignified commemoration by his own pupils: for the inscription, Keil, 'Vertreter der zweiten Sophistik' 15–18.

168 *VS* 566.

169 Cf. Oliver, 'Marcus Aurelius', 80–83.

170 Ibid.

171 *VS* 566. He had evidently co-operated in the speech of Demostratus against Herodes. It is not uncharacteristic of Philostratus to condemn the action while admiring the speech itself.

172 *Or.* 51.29f.K.

173 For a possible identity (Ptolemy of Naucratis), C. Behr, *Aelius Aristides and the Sacred Tales* (Amsterdam, 1968), 105 and n. 34.

174 *VS* 555, 560f.

175 *VS* 516ff.

176 Lucian, *Rhetorum Praeceptor* 23; Aulus Gellius, *Noctes Atticae* 1.5.1.

177 *VS* 601, 613.

178 *VS* 616, 607.

179 *VS* 602f. On other sophists' attempts to avoid it, Bowersock (1969), 34–42.

180 *VS* 601, 626, 623.

181 *VS* 628. There are considerable omissions in Philostratus' roll-call, notably Lesbonax, on whom see Aulitsky *RE* 12 (1925), 2103–2106; Swain (1991, 162 n. 74).

182 For the date, Russell-Wilson (1981), xxxix–xl.

183 2.415 (Russell-Wilson, 164).

184 On Malchion, Eusebius *HE* 7.29.2 (a nominative *sophistes* seems to have been subject to genitival attraction, but the overall sense is hardly in doubt). For the circumstances, F. Millar, 'Paul of

Samosata, Zenobia and Aurelian', *JRS* 61 (1971), 1–17 at 14–17. On Longinus, Schmid-Christ, *Geschichte der griechische Litteratur*, 2.2.889ff.

185 Correspondence with Porphyry, *Vita Plotini* 19; appointment and death, *SHA* Aurelian 30.3; cf. Zosimus 1.56.

186 Cf. below ch. 6.

187 On Dexippus, F. Millar, 'P. Herennius Dexippus: the Greek world and the third-century invasions', *JRS* 59 (1969), 12–29.

188 For Eunapius, below 109–113; 129–132.

189 On whom see the massive monograph by B. Schouler, *La Tradition Héllénique chez Libanios*, 2 vols (Paris, 1984).

190 See especially P. Petit (1956).

191 Below 206–213.

192 Cf. Libanius' reaction, below 43f.

193 E.g. *Or.* 1 passim.

194 *Or.* 1.156.

195 Cf. Liebeschütz (1972), 256–265 for the institutional changes in Libanius' own city.

196 *Or.* 1.19.

197 *Or.* 2 Förster.

198 *Or.* 2.14.

199 Ibid. 15.

200 *Or.* 1.118f.

201 *Ep.* 36.422Cf.

202 Ed. A. Colonna (Rome, 1950). For an attempt at chronology, T.D. Barnes, 'Himerius and the fourth century', *CPh* 82 (1987), 206–225.

203 Ed. G. Downey and F.A. Norman (Teubner, 1951–74). For the omission of Themistius from Eunapius' *Lives*, R.J. Penella, *Greek Philosophers and Sophists in the Fourth Century AD* (Leeds, 1990), 134–137.

204 For sophistic influence on Julian, W.C. Wright, *The Emperor Julian's relation to the New Sophistic and Neo-Platonism* (London, 1896); P. Athanassiadi-Fowden, *Julian and Hellenism* (Oxford, 1981).

205 For a guide to individuals, Penella (1990), 79–117.

206 On the latter, Wright (1896), 38–66; Athanassiadi-Fowden (1981), 120–160 and passim.

207 *Or.* 1.2f.

208 Ibid. 120.

209 For Themistius' political loyalties, Imperial rather than civil, G. Dagron, 'L'Empire romain d'orient au IVe siècle et les traditions politiques de l'héllénisme: le témoignage de Themistios', *Travaux et mémoires* 3 (1968), 1–214; and now Averil Cameron, *Christianity and the Rhetoric of Empire*, (Berkeley, Calif., 1991), 131ff. For sophists and governors in the fourth century, cf. A.F. Norman, 'Teachers and administrators', inaugural lecture, University of Hull (Hull, 1969), 11.

210 *Or.* 19, 20.

211 *Or.* 50, 47.

212 See above 25–28.
213 Text of Choricius by R. Förster and E. Richsteig (Leipzig, 1929). For a brief roll-call of other late antique figures, as they emerged from Libanius' letters, Eunapius, or through the Suda from Hesychius, Schmid-Christ, *Geschichte der griechische Litteratur,* 1027. It is unfortunate that Bowersock's *Hellenism in Late Antiquity* (Cambridge, 1990) affords no place in its index for such figures, shadowy as they are.
214 *SEG* 31 (1981), 169.
215 *SEG* 28 (1978), 1022.
216 Procopius, *Secret History* 26.5f.
217 *Code* 1.2.7.1–42, 12.15.
218 See e.g. I. Ševčenko, 'A shadow outline of virtue: the classical heritage of Greek Christian literature (second to seventh century)', in K. Weitzmann (ed.), *The Age of Spirituality: a Symposium,* New York, 1980 (= *Ideology, Letters and Culture in the Byzantine World* (London, 1982)), 63.
219 See now R. Beaton, *The Medieval Greek Romance* (Cambridge, 1989), 49–66.

2 PREPARATION, PRELUDE, PERFORMANCE

1 On sophistic rhetoric in general, E. Rohde (1914), 310–387; E. Norden, *Die antike Kunstprosa von VI. Jahrhundert v. Chr. bis in die Zeit der Renaissance* I (Berlin, 1915), 346–416; G. Kennedy, *The Art of Rhetoric in the Roman World, 300 BC–300 AD* (Princeton, NJ, 1972), 553–641; G. Kennedy, 'The sophists as declaimers', in Bowersock (1974), 17–22; G. Kennedy, *Greek Rhetoric under Christian Emperors* (Princeton, NJ, 1983); Russell (1983); G. Anderson, *Philostratus* (London, 1986), 23–120 passim; Anderson (1989), 89–104.
2 E.g. *VS* 518 (Scopelian), 565 (Herodes), 583 (Aristides).
3 *Rhetorum Praeceptor* 14–19.
4 For the role of *progymnasmata* in education, Bompaire (1958), 36ff. and passim; S.F. Bonner, *Education in Ancient Rome* (London, 1977), 250–276; D.A. Russell, 'Rhetoric and criticism', *GR* N.S. 14 (1967), 130–144; Reardon 75f. On the *Chreia*, R.F. Hock and E.N. O'Neill, *The* Chreia *in Ancient Rhetoric* I: The *Progymnasmata* (Atlanta, Ga., 1986).
5 Vol. 8 Förster.
6 'Hermogenes' (Spengel vol. 2, 3f.).
7 Ibid.
8 Plato, *Protagoras* 320C-322D.
9 'Hermogenes' (Spengel vol. 2, 5).
10 Ibid. (Spengel vol. 2, 6f.).
11 Ibid. (Spengel vol. 2, 6).
12 Diomedes 1.310 Keil; Stobaeus 3.29.90 (Hense, 655).
13 'Hermogenes' (Spengel vol. 2, 5).
14 Aphthonius (Spengel vol. 2, 23).

15 'Hermogenes' (Spengel vol. 2, 9).
16 Dio, *Or.* 11.
17 'Hermogenes' (Spengel vol. 2, 12f.).
18 Ibid. (Spengel vol. 2, 13, cf. Theon ibid., 110f.).
19 *Or.* 19. 5ff.
20 *Encomium* 4 (vol. 8, 243–251 Förster).
21 Frr. 11, 11a Diels-Kranz (8th edn, 1956).
22 Aphthonius (Spengel vol. 2, 43f.).
23 Cf. Libanius, *Encomia* 3f. (vol. 8, 235–251 Förster).
24 Demosthenes *de Corona* 18.265.
25 Dio *Or.* 1.66–83; Lucian, *Somnium* 5–14.
26 Achilles 2.35.2–38.5.
27 'Hermogenes' (Spengel vol. 2, 15).
28 Ibid.
29 Ibid.; Apthonius (Spengel vol. 2, 45).
30 Libanius *Ēthopoiia* 14 (vol. 8, 405–408 Förster).
31 Fronto *ad M. Caes.* 3.15 (vol.1, 100 Haines = 3.16, 48 van den Hout); Philostratus, *Ep.* 73; Philostratus, *VS* 522.
32 Theon (Spengel vol. 2, 123ff.).
33 Theon (Spengel vol. 2, 120ff.).
34 Theon (Spengel vol. 2, 121).
35 *Or.* 7, ed. D.A. Russell (Cambridge, 1992).
36 *Or.* 7.1–15.
37 *Or.* 7.27–40.
38 *Or.* 7.53–59.
39 *Or.* 7.81–103.
40 On the *prolaliae*, A. Stock, *De prolaliarum usu rhetorico* (Diss. Königsberg, 1911); K. Mras, 'Die *prolalia* bei den griechischen Schriftstellern', *WS* 64 (1940), 71–81; K. Mras, 'Apuleius' *Florida* im Rahmen ähnlicher Literatur' (*Anzeiger der phil.-hist. Klasse der österreichischen Akademie der Wissenschaften* 12 (Vienna, 1949); G. Anderson, 'Patterns in Lucian's *prolaliae*', *Philologus* 121 (1977), 313ff.; R.B. Branham, 'Introducing a Sophist: Lucian's prologues', *TAPhA* 115 (1985), 237–243; H.G. Nesselrath, 'Lucian's introductions' in Russell (1990), 111–140. Both the latter wrongly seem to assume that this author is dismissive of the form.
41 For the latter, e.g. Dio, *Or.* 1 (discussed below) and *Or.* 13. The proem of Longus might also be argued to owe something to the form.
42 Lucian, *Herodotus seu Aetion* 1f., 4ff.
43 Ibid. 8. For a visit of Lucian to Thrace, Bowie (1980), 58ff.
44 Lucian, *Herodotus seu Aetion*, 7, 3.
45 Ibid. 5.
46 Dio, *Or.* 1.1f.
47 Ibid. 2.
48 Ibid. 6.
49 *Prometheus es in verbis* 1ff., 7.
50 *Heracles* 7.
51 *Scytha* 9f.

52 *Zeuxis* 12.
53 E.g. *Florida* 13; cf. also 9, 20. For the *Florida* in general, Mras (1949).
54 *VS* 519f.
55 Lucian, *Rhetorum praeceptor* 18ff. For comparisons with Philostratus, J. A. Hall, *Lucian's Satire* (New York, 1981), 267–278.
56 *VS* 571–574; cf. also Russell (1983), 84ff.
57 For the identity of this building as the Odeion, see H.A. Thompson, 'The Odeion in the Athenian agora', *Hesperia* 19 (1950), 89.
58 For this form, above 53ff.
59 *VS* 572.
60 On the 'Scythian' repertoire, Bompaire (1958), 677–689.
61 For sophistic *variatio* in general, G. Anderson, *Lucian: Theme and Variation in the Second Sophistic* (Leyden, 1976), passim.
62 *VS* 573.
63 *VS* 574; for similar gestures, *VS* 586 (Hadrian of Tyre on Herodes), *VS* 539 (Herodes on Polemo).
64 *VS* 573.
65 Lucian, *Pseudologista* 5ff. For a likely identitiy, C.P. Jones (1972), 478–487.
66 Himerius, *Or.* 5.
67 Ibid. 5.3.
68 Ibid. 5.6.
69 P. 5 Hinck.
70 Lucian, *Phalaris* 1.3.
71 C.P. Jones (1978a), 65–70.
72 *Or.* 35.13–17; cf. Ps.-Menander *peri Epideiktikōn* I (Russell-Wilson, Oxford, 58–74).
73 *Or.* 35.1–4, cf. 11f.
74 In Synesius' *Praise of Baldness* (vol. 2, 190–195 Terzaghi).
75 Dio, *Or.* 35.18–24, cf. Lucian, *Gallus* 16.
76 Fronto *ad M. Caes.* 3.6 (vol. 1, 70 Haines = 39f. van den Hout).
77 Philostratus, *VS* 555.
78 Achilles 5.17.9–8.8.14.
79 Ibid. 8.8.3.
80 Ibid. 8.8.5.
81 Ibid. 8.8.11, 13.
82 Cf. Anderson (1982a), 30.
83 *VS* 542.
84 On alternatives to the *meletē*, Reardon (1971), 120–232 passim.
85 Cf. below chs 8, 5, 6.
86 Philostratus, *VS* 579.
87 *Or.* 28.2.
88 For aspects of this unusual piece, below 117–120.
89 For the medium, below ch. 9 passim.
90 For the nature of the *de Dea Syria*, G. Anderson, *Studies in Lucian's Comic Fiction* (Leyden, 1976), 68–72; commentary by R.A. Oden (Missoula, Mont., 1977).

3 COMMUNING WITH THE CLASSICS

1 Aristides, *Or.* 50.57K.
2 *Ep. graec.* 8 (vol. 1, 20 Haines = *Epistula Acephala* 234 van den Hout).
3 The classic treatment of the doctrine of *mimēsis* is Bompaire (1958), 13–154; see also D.A. Russell in D. West and A. Woodman (eds), *Creative Imitation and Latin Literature* (Cambridge, 1979), 1–16.
4 For limitations, cf. F. Norman, 'The library of Libanius', *RhM* 107 (1964), 158–175; and F.W. Householder, *Literary Quotation and Allusion in Lucian* (Columbia, Ohio, 1941).
5 See especially J.F. Kindstrand, *Homer in der Zweiten Sophistik* (Uppsala, 1973).
6 Cf. Norman (1964), 162–165.
7 Ibid. 161f.
8 *Or.* 18.6–17.
9 *VS* 518, 539.
10 *VS* 524.
11 Lollianus, *VS* 527; cf. Apollonius of Athens and Heraclides, *VS* 601; Marcus of Byzantium, *VS* 528; Herodes Atticus, *VS* 574.
12 *VS* 620.
13 Ibid. For the writing of verse by sophists, no more surprising than for example the Younger Pliny's efforts, see now E.L. Bowie, 'Greek sophists and Greek poetry in the Second Sophistic', *ANRW* 2.33.1 (1989), 209–258; for the broader background of verse-composition in the Empire, E.L Bowie, 'Greek poetry in the Antonine age', in Russell (1990), 53–90; E.L. Bowie, 'Poetry and poets in Asia and Achaia', in Cameron and Walker (1989), 198–205.
14 *Orr.* 16, 5f.
15 *Ep. graec.* 8 (vol. 1, 20–30 Haines = *Epistula Acephala*, 234–239 van den Hout).
16 *Ēthopoiiae* 3 (vol. 8, 379ff. Förster, cf. *Il.* 18.316–342); 15 (vol. 8, 408–411 Förster, cf. *Il.* 1.334–344).
17 *Ēthopoiiai* 5f. (vol. 8, 384–391 Förster); Lucian, *D. Mort.* 23.
18 *Piscator* 1–5, 22, 26. On Lucian's *mimēsis*, Bompaire (1958), 123–154 and 157–735 passim, esp. 737–744; cf. Anderson (1976a); 'Lucian, a sophist's sophist', *YCS* (1982), 74–78; 'Some sources of Lucian, *Icaromenippus* 25f.', *Philologus* 124 (1980), 159–161.
19 For Maximus see now M. Szarmach, *Maximos von Tyros, eine literarische Monographie* (Toruń, 1985).
20 Lucian, *Symposium* 12–47. On the Symposium form, J. Martin, *Symposion: die Geschichte einer liter. Form* (Paderborn, 1931); Bompaire (1958), 314–320.
21 Alciphron, *Ep.* 3.19. The precise relationship with Lucian here remains conjectural; it is clear that Alciphron also borrows extensively from comedy.
22 Below 176–179. On Athenaeus see now A. Lukinovich, 'The Play of Reflections between Literary Form and the Sympotic Theme in the *Deipnosophistae* of Athenaeus' in O. Murray (ed.), *Sympotica* (Oxford, 1990), 263–271.

23 Lucian, *Lexiphanes* 1, 2–15.
24 Lucian, *D. Mar.* 1 Macleod.
25 *D.Mar.* 1.1f.; cf. Theocr. 11.25–33.
26 Whiteness, *D. Mar.* 1.2, Theocr. 11.19f.; cheese and milk, *D. Mar.* 1.2, Theocr. 11.19f., cf. 35f.
27 *D.Mar.* 1.4.
28 *D.Mar.* 1.5.
29 E.g. Philostr., *VA* 1.30, 5.21.
30 *D.Mar.* 1.1f.; Theocr. 11.77ff.
31 On the latter transposition, Bompaire (1958), 562–584.
32 *Or.* 57.1; Il. 1.260–268, 273f.
33 Who must be Trajan in this case, C.P. Jones (1978a), 137.
34 *Or.* 57.4.
35 Aristides, *Or.*16 Lenz-Behr; Kindstrand (1973), 215–219.
36 *Il.* 9.225–306, 434–605.
37 *Or.* 16.8.
38 *Or.* 16.18–21.
39 *Or.* 16.2.
40 On Odysseus in Aristides, H.O. Schröder, 'Das Odysseusbild des Aelius Aristides', *RhM* 130 (1987), 350–356.
41 Ps.-Menander *Peri Epideiktikōn* 2.15 (Russell-Wilson, Oxford 1981, 194); *Od.* 13.69–72, 13.38–41.
42 *Od.* 6.149–185; Max. Tyr. *Or.* 14.5c.
43 *Od.* 18.74: οἵην ἐκ ῥακέων ὁ γέρων ἐπιγουνίδα φαίνει; *Od.* 22.1: αὐτὰρ ὁ γυμνώθη ῥακέων πολύμητις Ὀδυσσεύς (Lucian, *Heracles* 8; Philostr., *VA* 488).
44 Libanius, *Ēthopoiiai* 23 (vol. 8, 425–429 Förster).
45 Ibid. 24 (vol. 8, 429–431 Förster).
46 *D. Mar.* 2.1 Macleod.
47 Ibid. 2.2.
48 Ibid. 2.3f.
49 Ibid. 2.4.
50 *Pseudolog.* 27.
51 Achilles Tatius 2.23.3; *Priapeia* 68.25f.
52 Lucian, *Verae Historiae* 2.29, 2.35f.
53 *Heroicus* 195ff. For the hostile image of Odysseus in general, W.B. Stanford, *The Ulysses Theme* (Oxford, 1954), 90–158.
54 For a more traditional treatment of Odysseus and Palamedes, cf. Dio's ambitious paraphrase of the *mise en scène* of Euripides' *Philoctetes*, *Or.* 59.
55 *Phaedr.* 230B–D. On the influence of the *Phaedrus* on sophistic literature, see now M.B. Trapp (1990).
56 *Phaedr.* 230E–234C, 237A–241D.
57 *Phaedr.* 243E–257B.
58 *Phaedr.* 257C–279B.
59 Fronto, *Ep. Graec.* 8 (vol. 1, 20–30 Haines = *Epistula Acephala*, 234–239 van den Hout).
60 On quotation in general, Bompaire (1958), 382–404.
61 Aristides *Or.* 28.

THE SECOND SOPHISTIC

62 Lucian, *Adversus indoctum* 27.
63 E.g. G. Anderson, 'Lucian's quotations: some shortcuts to culture', *BICS* 23 (1976), 59–68; 'Patterns in Lucian's quotations', *BICS* 26 (1978), 97–100.
64 *Dem. Enc.* 5. For the pairs, cf. *Il.* 1.225/Dem. *Ol.* 2.18; *Il.*12.243/ Dem. *de Corona* 97; *Il.* 7.125/Dem. *in Aristocraten* 210; *de Corona* 136/ *Il.*3.222; *Il.*12.322ff./*de Corona* 97.
65 *VS* 526. Cf. Aristophanes, *Plut.* 1002, Anacreon fr. 426 Page.
66 *VS* 544. Cf. Hesiod, *Opera* 25, with ῥήτορι for τέκτονι.
67 *VS* 594. Cf. Euripides, *Hercules Furens* 1406 with πόλιν for τέκνα.
68 *VS* 558. Cf. *Od.* 4.498 with μωρὸς for ζωὸς, καταλείπεται for κατερύκεται; οἴκῳ for πόντῳ.
69 Lucian, *Iuppiter Tragoedus* 15; cf. Demosthenes, *Ol.* 1.1.
70 *VS* 511.
71 Fronto *ad M. Caes.* 3.15.2 (vol. 1, 102 Haines = 3.16.2: 48 van den Hout); Plato, *Resp.* 560C.
72 *Suas.* 1.13 (Musa): *quid ibi potest esse salvi ubi ipsum mare perit?*
73 *Pseudologista* 6.
74 See further M. Kokolakis, *The Dramatic Simile of Life* (Athens, 1960).
75 For its place in Lucian, Bompaire (1958), 436ff.; O. Schmidt, *Metapher und Gleichnis in den Schriften Lukians* (Diss. Zurich, Wintherthur 1897), 56–68; M. Kokolakis, 'Lucian and the tragic performances of his time', *Platon* 12 (1960), 67–109.
76 P. Louis, *Les Métaphores de Platon* (Paris, 1945), 209f.
77 E.g. Lucian, *Navig.* 46.
78 E.g. Lucian, *Nigrinus* 11, *Saturnalia* 28; cf. *Gallus* 11.
79 Lucian, *Necyomantia* 16, cf. *adversus Indoctum* 8ff. (the latter presented as anecdote).
80 Plato *Resp.* 6.488A–489C.
81 Lucian, *J. Trag.* 46–49; Max. Tyr. *Or.* 30 Hobein.
82 For the theme in ancient literature as a whole, J. Alpers, *Hercules in bivio* (Diss. Göttingen, 1912); cf. also Bompaire (1958), 258–264.
83 Xen., *Mem.* 2.1.21–33.
84 Sen., *Suas.* 2.19.
85 *Hist. Consc.* 26.
86 Bowie (1970/74), 197.
87 E.g. Lucian, *Verae Historiae* 2.19f.
88 For Lucian's 'typical' geography, Bompaire (1958), 221–235.
89 Cf. Lucian, *Navigium*, 39, 44.
90 Philostratus, *VA* 5.1, 5.5.
91 For this sort of fantasy, cf. Anderson (1989), 170–175, cf. eundem (1990), 110.
92 For *eidōlopoiia*, above 00.
93 For *ecphrasis* of Thermopylae, e.g. Seneca, *Suas.* 2; for Calypso's cave, cf. Lucian, *Verae Historiae* 2.36.
94 For *encomium, psogos*, above 50f.
95 Particularly against Leptines: cf. Philostr., *VS* 527, cf. 601.
96 Cf. Anderson (1976a), 109–112.
97 E.g. *Phaedr.* 237AB, 238CD; *Symp.* 174D.

98 Philostr., *VA* 4.15; Lucian, *Icaromenippus* 1ff., *Necyomantia* 1f.; *Nigrinus* 1–12.

99 E.g. Philostr., *VS* 537 (Polemo): withdrawal from the crowd, rising up to speak, leaping up at climaxes, thigh-slapping.

100 See Anderson (1986), 241f., cf. eundem (1976a), 109–112.

101 Philostr., *VS* 552ff.; cf. J. Kindstrand, 'Sostratus–Hercules–Agathion, the rise of a legend', *Annales Societatis Litterarum Humanarum Upsaliensis* (1979–80), 50–79.

102 *Or.* 1.52–84.

103 *Or.* 11.37–43; *Timaeus* 21E–25D.

104 *Or.* 12.19f.

4 ATTICISM AND ANTAGONISM

1 Lucian, *Iudicium Vocalium* 6.

2 Philostr., *VS* 579.

3 Athenaeus, *Deipnosophistae* 3.99C.

4 On the language of sophists, the fundamental contributions are mainly those of the last century: E. Rohde, 'Die asianische Rhetorik und die zweite Sophistik', *RhM* 41 (1886), 170–190 (= *Kleine Schriften* 2, 1901, 75–97); G. Kaibel, 'Dionysios von Halikarnass und die Sophistik', *Hermes* 20 (1885), 497–513; Wilamowitz, 'Asianismus und Atticismus', *Hermes* 35 (1900), 1–52 (*Kleine Schriften* 3) (Berlin, 1969), 223–272. The phenomenon of Atticism was examined on a magisterial scale, but in diffuse and opaque fashion, by Wilhelm Schmid, *Der Atticismus in seinen Hauptvertretern von Dionysius von Halikarnass bis auf den zweiten Philostrat* I–IV (Stuttgart, 1887–96); cf. also Norden (1898), 344–416. But the daunting scale of Schmid in particular should not blind us to the fact that the linguistic map of the second century AD, for example, is still far from complete. It is disconcerting to be confronted with the hundreds of words in Galen unreported in *LSJ*, for example: see R.J. Durling, 'Lexicographical notes on Galen's pharmacological writings' 1–3 , *Glotta* 57 (1979), 218–224; ibid. 59 (1981), 108–116; ibid. 60 (1982), 236–244).

5 *Or.* 1 Lenz-Behr 322, 325–328.

6 *VS* 585.

7 Boulanger (1923), 401.

8 Ibid.

9 Ibid. 401, 402.

10 Ibid. 402, 403.

11 Ibid. 404–407.

12 Ibid. 395–399.

13 *VS* 512.

14 *VS* 523f.

15 Phrynichus, *Eklogē* 231, 371 Fischer. For a plausible case that the *Philetairos* was the work of Cornelianus in question, S. Argyle, 'A new Greek grammarian', *CQ* 39 (1989), 524–535.

16 Phrynichus, *Eklogē* 236 Fischer (κεφαλαιωδέστατον).

17 For Caecilius, Kennedy (1972), 364–369. The characterisation of sophistic rhetoric in general has never been straightforward. Rohde argued for a 'sophistic' of Asianist inspiration, Kaibel for a development from Isocrates through Dionysius of Halicarnassus. Schmid (1887–96), 1.27ff. stressed the importance of Herodes Atticus as a turning point. For various formulations from Rohde to Wilamowitz, Boulanger (1923), 60–69; cf. V.A. Sirago, 'La seconda sofistica come espressione culturale della classe dirigente del II sec.', *ANRW* 2.33.1 (1990), 43–56. Reardon's view well summarises the general impression of what is really a non-problem: 'Mais en réalité l'Asianisme et l'Atticisme ne sont guère que des mots' (1971, 94 and n. 118).

18 *VS* 564.

19 E.g. *VS* 600 (Apollonius of Naucratis); cf. 598 (Onomarchus). Cf. Reardon (1971), 92f., after Boulanger (1923), 106.

20 Reardon (1971), 82–86.

21 M.J. Higgins, 'The Renaissance of the First Century and the Origins of Standard Late Greek', *Traditio* 3 (1945), 49–100.

22 G. Anlauf, *Standard Late Greek oder Attizismus? Eine Studie zum Optativgebrauch in nachklassischen Griechisch* (Diss. Cologne, 1960).

23 Philostr., *VS* 553.

24 M. Nächster, *De Pollucis et Phrynichi controversiis* (Diss. Leipzig, 1908).

25 For modern discussion, E. Fischer's edn of the *Eklogē*, (Berlin, 1974), pp. 43–47.

26 Cf. 592f.

27 Lucian, *Rhetorum Praeceptor* 17.

28 *Ecl.* 170 Fischer.

29 Ibid. 157.

30 Ibid. 218.

31 Ibid. 236.

32 E.g. διδοῦσιν for διδόασιν (Favorinus, *Ecl.* 215); υἱέα for υἱόν (Peloplaton, *Ecl.* 234); νῆας for ναῦς (Lollianus, *Ecl.* 140).

33 Sixteen in all: see Barigazzi's edition (Florence, 1966) on frr. 7,8,25, 129–141.

34 So ἀφιερῶσαι, *Ecl.* 163; σταθερός used of persons, *Ecl.* 185; doubled superlative, κορυφαιότατον, *Ecl.* 213.

35 And in Aristotle, pace *Ecl.* 207 (417); also Aristotelian is Dio's πιοῦμαι for πίομαι, *Ecl.* 22.

36 In the *corpus Hippocraticum*, cf. *Ecl.* 422.

37 In Diphilus, pace *Ecl.* 172.

38 *Rhet. Prec.* 16f.; Philostr., *VS* 592.

39 *Rhet. Prec.* 16f. The grotesque English equivalents are Harmon's. For Philagrus claiming himself as authority, above 35.

40 *Moralia* 42DE.

41 *Deipn.* 3.97CD.

42 *Deipn.* 3.97DE.

43 *Deipn.* 3.98B.

44 Phrynichus 396, cf. Chr. Habicht. *Altertümer von Pergamon 8.3: Die Inschriften des Asklepieions* (Berlin, 1969), 33: 75f.

45 *NA* 10.1.7.
46 See Harmon's notes ad *Pseudolog.* 1, 16.
47 Fr. 309K.
48 E.g. *VS* 572 (Alexander Peloplaton); *VS* 589 (Hadrian of Tyre); 602 (Apollonius of Athens).
49 *VS* 574.
50 Boulanger (1923), 431–434.
51 Barigazzi's edn (1966), 72.
52 Cf. Jüttner (1898), 112.
53 Boulanger (1923), 429–434.
54 Norden (1915) I.413–416.
55 Boulanger (1923), 430.
56 E.g. *VS* 598ff. analysed by Norden (1915), I.414f., where only two cola out of twenty-one exactly correspond.
57 Hence the difficulty of classifying the practice of such a writer as Longus, on which see now B.D. MacQueen, *Myth, Rhetoric and Fiction: A Reading of Longus' Daphnis and Chloe* (Lincoln, Neb., 1990), 239 n.6.
58 E.g. Philostratus *VS* 519 (Scopelian); cf. 568 (Aristocles); 568f. (Antiochus).
59 For characteristics of the *apheleis*, e.g. Schmid (1887–96) 4.8f. (on Philostratus).
60 Cf. Hunter (1983), 84–98 passim; Anderson (1984), 54.
61 *VS* 522.
62 *VS* 598f.
63 Philostratus, *Imag.* 1.11.1.
64 E.g. *Or.* 2 Lenz-Behr, cf. Boulanger (1923), 211–225.
65 *VS* 582.
66 *Peri Politeias* 25f.
67 Neither J.S. Morrison, 'Meno of Pharsalus, Polycrates and Ismenias', *CQ* 36 (1942), 68–74 nor Wade-Gery, 'Critias and Herodes', *CQ* 39 (1945), 19–33 succeeds in proving that the *peri Politeias* must belong to the 5th century BC, though they have no difficulty in disposing of any attempt to establish second-century origin on linguistic grounds. In the end there seems no reason why Herodes should not have succeeded in attaining an ideal.
68 *Editio princeps* by B.P. Grenfell and A.S. Hunt, *Oxyrhynchus Papyri* 3 (London, 1903), 26–31.
69 W. Rhys Roberts, *CR* 18 (1904), 18ff.
70 *Pseudologista* 30. For Lucian's enemy's identity, C.P. Jones, 'Two enemies of Lucian', *GRBS* 13 (1972), 478–86, plausibly suggests Hadrian of Tyre. For caution, Anderson (1976a), 71 n. 40.

5 HELLENIC PAST, GRAECO-ROMAN PRESENT

1 L. Robert, 'Documents d'Asie Mineure', *BCH* 101 (1977), 120–129; also A.J. Spawforth and S. Walker, 'The world of the Panhellenion II: three Dorian cities', *JHS* 76 (1986), 88–105 at 103.

2 The standard treatment of archaism on the Greek side is Bowie (1970/74); some reservations in Anderson (1989), 137–145 passim. For archaism on the Latin side, R. Marache, *La Critique littéraire de langue latine et le développement du goût archaisant au IIe siècle de notre ère* (Rennes, 1952); L. Holford-Strevens, *Aulus Gellius* (London, 1988), passim.

3 *Ep.* 8.24.2ff.

4 *Praecepta gerendae reipublicae* 813D.

5 *Or.* 50.60f. For other dreams of a similar nature, *Or.* 50.57 (Plato); *Or.* 50.49 (to share a tomb with Alexander the Great!).

6 E.g. Bowie (1970/74), 170–174.

7 For the resemblance of the sophists' own highly coloured lives to some of these, Anderson (1986), 58ff.

8 Dio *Or.* 2, *Or.* 4. Cf. C.P. Jones (1978a), 119, 120f.

9 *FGrH* 93 Jacoby (Bowie 1970/74, 177).

10 Bowie (ibid. 178) notes only one, that of Jason of Argos, ending in 322, once Charax of Pergamum (*FGrH* 103) is set aside as too vaguely known.

11 E.g. that Athenaeus is third-century, others pro-Roman, or that Josephus is outside the mainstream (cf. Bowie 1970/74, 179f.).

12 *FGrH* 277.

13 Ibid. 505.

14 For the Salutaris Foundation and a new text of its inscription, *IE* 27, G.M. Rogers, *The Sacred Identity of Ephesos: Foundation Myths of a Roman City* (London, 1991), whose interpretation I follow.

15 Pausanias 7.9–97. On Pausanias' antiquarianism in general, Chr. Habicht, *Pausanias' Guide to Greece* (Berkeley, Calif., 1985).

16 Ibid. 1.20.3f.

17 On this similarity, Bowie (1970/74), 191–195; for general fantasising along such lines, cf. Anderson (1990), 175–179.

18 *Diss.* 3.23.

19 Philostr. *VS* 487.

20 Ibid. 607.

21 Ibid. 570. For epigraphic evidence, Robert, (1977), 120–129.

22 1. 22.4.

23 For the limitations of Cassius Dio, F. Millar, *A Study of Cassius Dio* (Oxford, 1964), 171ff.; cf. Reardon (1971), 206–209.

24 Ibid. 209.

25 On the case of Philiscus, Millar (1964), 49f. (tentative).

26 Dio 52.14–40.

27 For a generally less scathing assessment of Herodian than the conventional condemnation, see C.R. Whittaker's unusually detailed introduction to vol. 1 of his *LCL* (Cambridge, Mass., 1969, ix–lxxxii); and for the reign of Elagabalus, where he is arguably superior to Dio in respect of first-hand knowledge, Bowersock, 'Herodian and Elagabalus', *YCS* 24 (1975), 229–238.

28 Herodian 4.3.6.

29 Ibid. 4.3.8.

30 For Lucian's treatise, commentary by H. Homeyer (Munich, 1965);

for the sources of the precepts, G. Avenarius, *Lukians Schrift zur Geschichtsschreibung* (Meisenheim am Glan, 1956).

31 *Hist. Conscr.* 15.

32 Ibid. 15, cf. 21.

33 Ibid. 14.

34 Ibid. 28, 19.

35 Ibid. 14.

36 Ibid. 31.

37 For reservations, Anderson (1976a), 77–80.

38 See B. Baldwin, *Studies in Lucian* (Toronto, 1973); C.P. Jones (1986), 59–67; P.V. Cova, *I* principia historiae *e le idee storiographiche di Frontone* (Naples, 1970); E. Champlin *Fronto and Antonine Rome* (Cambridge, Mass., 1980), 55.

39 Fronto, *Principia Historiae* 12f. (vol. 2, 208f. Haines = 2.12f., 196f. van den Hout).

40 *Ad Verum Imp.* 2.3. (vol. 2, 196 Haines = 125 van den Hout).

41 Fragments with introduction and brief commentary in R.C. Blockley, *The Fragmentary Classicizing Historians of the later Roman Empire* vol. II (Liverpool, 1983).

42 For his shortcomings in general, R.C. Blockley, *The Fragmentary Classicizing Historians of the Later Roman Empire*, vol. 1 (Liverpool, 1981), 25f.

43 Book 1 fr. 1 (1.1) = *Excerpta de Sententiis* 1 (Blockley II, 8).

44 Ibid. (Blockley II, 8).

45 Ibid. (Blockley II, 10).

46 1.14 = *Exc. de Sent.* 4 (Blockley II, 18).

47 1.17 = *Exc. de Sent.* 7 (Blockley II, 22).

48 3.18.4 = *Exc. de Sent.* 10 (Blockley II, 24).

49 3.21.3 = *Exc. de Sent.* 14 (Blockley II, 32).

50 3.23.3 = *Exc. de Sent.* 17 (Blockley II, 34).

51 Cf. Athanassiadi-Fowden (1981), 22 for Julian's attitude.

52 5.27.1 = *Exc. de Sent.* 20 (Blockley II, 38).

53 5.27.6 = *Exc. de Sent.* 23 (Blockley II, 40).

54 2.15 = *Exc. de Sent.* 5 (Blockley II, 20).

55 3.21.1f. = Eunapius *VPS* 476, 498 (Blockley II, 32).

56 3.18.6. = *Exc. de Legibus gentium* 1 (Blockley II, 26).

57 9.72.1 = *Exc. de Sent.* 79 (Blockley II, 116ff.).

58 For the character of Arrian's achievement, P. Stadter, *Arrian of Nicomedia* (Chapel Hill, NC, 1980), 164–169; cf. Bowie (1970/74), 191–195. Against, Reardon (1971), 209–216; and especially A.B. Bosworth, Commentary on *Anabasis* I–III (Oxford, 1980) passim; A.B. Bosworth, *From Arrian to Alexander, Studies in Historical Interpretation* (Oxford, 1988).

59 Cf. Stadter (1980), 164–169; Reardon (1971), 213.

60 Cf. *Anab.* 1.12.1–5; for Arrian as Xenophon, Bowie (1970/74), 192ff.

61 *Anab.* 7.28ff.

62 Bosworth (1988), 135–156.

63 *Anab.* 5.25–28.

64 Bosworth (1988), 123–134.
65 Seneca, *Suasoriae* 1 ('Alexander debates whether to sail the Ocean').
66 Contra, Bosworth (1988), 127–132.
67 Boulanger (1923), 275–279; Bompaire, 'Le Décor Sicilien dans le Roman Grec', *REG* 90 (1977), 55–68. On the whole subject of 'declaimers' history', Russell (1983), 106–128.
68 L. Pernot (commentary, New York, 1981), 44f.
69 Thuc. 6.8–24; 7.10–16.
70 Pernot 48f.; Aristides *Or.* 5.40f., 6.50ff., cf. Thuc. 8.1.2, 8.26.1.
71 Pernot 52ff.
72 *Or.* 5.32.
73 On the *De Fortuna* see J. R. Hamilton's commentary on Plutarch's *Alexander* (Oxford, 1969), 23–33.
74 *De Fortuna* 326EF.
75 Ibid. 327AB. For the topos, cf. Petronius, *Satyrica* 1.1.
76 Ibid. 327C–E.
77 Ibid. 327E–328A.
78 Ibid. 328C–E.
79 Ibid.
80 Ibid. 329EF.
81 Ibid. 330F–331A.
82 For this bizarre work, A. Baur, *Lukians Demosthenous Enkomion* (Diss. Paderborn, 1914); B. Baldwin, 'The Authorship and Purpose of Lucian's *Demosthenis Encomium*', *Antichthon* 3 (1969), 54–62; Hall (1981), 324–331.
83 *Dem. Enc.* 1f.
84 Ibid. 4.21.
85 Ibid. 29–50.
86 Ibid. 33f.
87 Ibid. 49.
88 E.g. Seneca *Suasoriae* 7.
89 For Marathon to the declaimer, cf. Polemon, ed. Hinck (1873).
90 Vol. 2, 20–30 Haines = 206–211 van den Hout.
91 Ibid. 1 (vol. 2, 20 Haines = 206 van den Hout).
92 Ibid. 2f. (vol. 2, 20ff. Haines = 206f. van den Hout).
93 Ibid. 4–6 (vol. 2, 22–26 Haines = 207ff. van den Hout).
94 Ibid. 7 (vol. 2, 26 Haines = 209 van den Hout).
95 Ibid. 7ff. (vol. 2, 26ff. Haines = 209f. van den Hout).
96 Ibid. 10 (vol. 2, 30 Haines = 210 van den Hout).
97 Ibid.
98 On the subject of Graeco-Roman relations in general in the Empire, J. Palm, *Rom, Römertum und Imperium in griechische Literatur der Kaiserzeit* (Lund, 1959); H. Fuchs, *Der geistige Widerstand gegen Rom in der antiken Welt* (Berlin, 1938). For the political realities relating to sophists, Bowersock (1969), passim; cf. Bowie (1982), 29–59. For Rome in Plutarch and Dio, C.P. Jones (1971, 1978a). For a brief conspectus of the shifting literary balance even in the Antonine decades alone, Russell (1990), 1–17.
99 On the Roman view of loss of freedom, e.g. C. Wirzubski, *Libertas*

as a Political Ideal at Rome during the Late Republic and Early Empire (Cambridge, 1950); R. MacMullen, *Enemies of the Roman Order* (New Haven, Conn., 1966), 1–94 passim.

100 Cf. H. Last in *CAH* 11 (1936), 446.

101 Ps.-Lucian *Demosthenis Encomium* 10.

102 *Panathenaicus* (*Or.* 1 Lenz-Behr), 332.

103 Ibid. 335. For the five-empires theory, J.H. Oliver, *The Civilizing Power: A Study of the Panathenaic Discourse of Aelius Aristides against the Background of Literature and Cultural Conflict* (Philadelphia, 1968), 143.

104 *Or.* 31.116; for Rhodes and Athens, C.P. Jones (1978a), 31f.

105 *Or.* 31 ibid.

106 *Or.* 31 ibid. (but cf. Pausanias 2.8.6, attributing the negotiation to recover Salamis to Aratus of Sicyon); 121.

107 For the nature of the *de Fortuna*, above 115ff.

108 *De Fortuna* 317C–E.

109 Aelian, *VH* 3.22.

110 Numa, *VH* 2.17, *Pseudologista* 8, Bompaire (1958), 189; Augustus, *pro Lapsu* 18; Italy, *Navigium* 44.

111 Fronto, *Ep. graec.* 1.5 (vol. 1, 136 Haines = *ad M. Caes.* 10.5, 23 van den Hout).

112 Pausanias 7.17.2; Plato, *Resp.* 491E.

113 Philostr., *VA* 4.38.

114 On this aspect of Favorinus' activity see now L. Holford-Strevens (1988), 83–91.

115 Pindar and Virgil, *NA* 17.10; barbarisms 8.2 (lost); colour-words, 2.26; words for winds, 2.22.

116 Plautine authenticity, *NA* 3.3.6; Plato and Lysias, 2.5.

117 Apuleius, *Florida* 18; 26 (= *de deo Socratis praef.*).

118 Lucian, *Demonax* 40.

119 *Ep. Apoll.* 71 (with Penella's commentary); *VA* 4.5.

120 Lucian, *Nigrinus* 15–34 passim. One notes that Latin writers could of course put these criticisms just as readily: see Tacitus, *Ann.* 15.44; Juvenal 3 passim.

121 *Or.* 26.4ff.

122 *Il.* 16.214ff.

123 *Or.* 26.84.

124 For the geography of Imperial residences, Millar (1977), 15–57.

125 *Ep.* 28.

126 Ibid. 407B–E.

127 Ibid. 408D.

128 Ibid. 409D.

129 *Hymn to Helios* (4), 152D–153A.

130 For Philostratus in general, the study of evidence for the family of Philostratus by K. Münscher, 'Die Philostrate', *Philologus* Suppl. 10 (1907), 469–558, is still invaluable, as is the excellent article by F. Solmsen, *RE* 20.1 (1941), cols. 124–177 (s.v. Philostratos 9–12). For an overall view, Anderson (1986).

131 *VS* 602f.

132 As hoplite general. For his biography, Anderson (1986), 3–7.
133 For the problem of such a circle, Bowersock (1969), 101–109.
134 For his identity, still inconclusive, Anderson (1986), 297f.
135 *VS* 479f.
136 For Philostratus' idiosyncrasies, C.P. Jones in Bowersock (1974), 11–16; Anderson (1986), 23–41, 77–96 and passim; Swain (1991).
137 *VS* 615–20.
138 *VS* 480; for his attitude to parentage, Anderson (1986), 79f.
139 *VS* 616.
140 *VS* 616 (*Od.* 16.187).
141 *VS* 617. On the peacock as a subject for *ecphrasis*, Bompaire (1958), 718–721.
142 *VS* 617.
143 Cf. Libanius' observation that he had educated pupils for Hades, *Or.* 1.153.
144 *VS* 617.
145 Ibid.
146 On both, Anderson (1986), 106–114; on the *Life* of Herodes, the dissertation by I. Avotins (Harvard, microfilm 1968) is still excellent except where superseded by the publication of the new Roman Agora Inscription). For the question 'Which Gordian?', Anderson (1986), 297f.
147 Cf. Anderson (1986), 77–120.
148 Ed. G. Giangrande (Rome, 1956). Penella (1990) in essence supplies the background to Eunapius that Bowersock has supplied for Philostratus. For the shortcomings of the *Histories*, Blockley (vol. I, 1981), 15f.; cf. above 109–113.
149 *VPS* 454.
150 *VPS* 493f.
151 *VPS* 483ff.
152 *VPS* 460.
153 *VPS* ibid.
154 *VPS* 462.
155 *VPS* 452f.
156 *VPS* 453.
157 *VPS* 482–485; Penella (1990), 79–83.
158 *VPS* 482; Lucian, *Rhetorum Praeceptor* 19.
159 *VPS* 482.
160 *VPS* ibid.
161 *VPS* 483.
162 *VPS* ibid. Cf. the experience of Libanius *Or.* 1.19ff.; Himerius *Or.* 4.9, *Or.* 19.
163 *VPS* 483ff.
164 *VPS* 484.

6 COOKERY AND CONFECTION: SOPHISTIC PHILOSOPHY, PHILOSOPHIC SOPHISTRY

1 On the philosophical schools of the Early Empire, J.-M. André, 'Les Écoles philosophiques aux deux premiers siècles de l'Empire', *ANRW* 2.36.1 (1987), 5–77; J. Whittaker, 'Platonic philosophy in the early centuries of the Empire', *ANRW* 2.36.1, 81–123. On the traditional struggles between rhetoric and philosophy, see still J. von Arnim, *Dio von Prusa* (Berlin, 1898), 4–114; and now B. Vickers, *In Defence of Rhetoric* (Oxford, 1988), 83–213. For the general philosophical interest of later Greek literature, Reardon (1971), 31–40, 200–205. On the privileges accorded to philosophers, Bowersock (1969), 32f. The whole subject of the philosopher in society is opened up by J. Hahn, *Der Philosoph und die Gesellschaft* (Stuttgart 1989), especially useful on the tendentiousness of Philostratus' testimony (46–53).

2 For the overlap, G.R. Stanton, 'Rhetors and philosophers: problems of classification', *AJPh* 94 (1973), 350–364.

3 Lucian's 'conversion' to philosophy (strictly speaking his change from rhetoric to dialogue): *Bis Accusatus* 30ff.; *Nigrinus* 1–5 and passim (though here he is not identified in person).

4 *VS* 567 (Aristocles turns from Peripatetic philosophy to the sophists); cf. Isaeus' conversion from riotous living to (sophistic) self-discipline, *VS* 513. On Herodes and Lucius, *VS* 556ff. (for the latter's identity, Anderson, 1989, 168ff.); for Polemo and Timocrates, *VS* 535f.

5 For these two sides, E. Champlin, *Fronto and Antonine Rome* (Cambridge, Mass., 1980), 56f., 107f., 121–126; R.B. Rutherford, *The Meditations of Marcus Aurelius: a Study* (Oxford, 1989), 137–147 and passim.

6 For the latter, see in particular *Or.* 21 (vol. 2, 17–49 Downey-Norman).

7 Cf. Plato, *Protagoras* 318E–319B; *Gorgias* 451D.

8 Esp. Plato, *Phaedrus* 259E–262C.

9 As *vir bonus dicendi peritus* (Cato apud Quintilian 12.1.1., cf. Isocrates, *Nicocles* 7).

10 See P. De Lacy, 'Plato and the intellectual life of the second century AD' in Bowersock (1974), 4–10.

11 Lucian, *Vita Demonactis* 14; the style is not unlike that of Maximus of Tyre.

12 *Mor.* 48E–74E.

13 *Mor.* 49C.

14 *Mor.* 49B, 49CD, 49DE, 50AB.

15 *Mor.* 50E, 51A.

16 *Mor.* 511CD, cf. Plato, *Gorgias* 465B.

17 *Mor.* 51D, cf. Theognis 215.

18 *Mor.* 51E, 52 BC, 52F, 53D. On Plutarch's imagery in general, F. Fuhrmann, *Les Images de Plutarque* (Paris, 1964).

19 Fronto *de eloquentia* 1.15f. (vol. 2, 66ff. Haines = 1.17f., 140 van den Hout).

20 Ibid. 1.1f. (vol. 2, 52ff. Haines = 2.1f., 133f. van den Hout).
21 Plutarch *de gloria Atheniensium, Mor.* 350DE.
22 *Or.*3; *Orr.* 8f. Hobein.
23 *Or.* 17; *Orr.* 18–21; *Or.* 26.
24 *Orr.* 23ff.; *Orr.* 30f.
25 *Or.* 37.
26 *Or.* 37.1.
27 *Or.* 37.2e.
28 *Or.* 37.3c.
29 *Or.* 37.4.
30 *Or.* 1.7d–8a.
31 On Apuleius' profile as a philosopher, see now B.L. Hijmans Jr., 'Apuleius, *philosophus Platonicus*', *ANRW* 2.36.1 (1987), 396–475.
32 *Florida* 18 (Helm, 34).
33 Ibid.
34 Ibid. (Helm, 35).
35 Ibid. (Helm, 36f.).
36 Ibid. (Helm, 37f.).
37 *Or.* 2 Lenz-Behr.
38 *Or.* 2.22, Plato, *Gorgias* 463A–465C.
39 *Or.* 2.24.
40 *Or.* 2.35–49.
41 *Or.* 2.50, cf. 41; cf. *Legg.* 245B, *Resp.* 540C; madness, *Or.* 2.52.
42 *Or.* 2.59, 2.78.
43 *Or.* 2.86f.
44 *Hermotimus* 67. R. Joly, 'La Réfutation des analogies dans l'Hermotime de Lucien', *AC* 50 (1981), 417–426, claims that Lucian's techniques in refuting analogies were ahead of his time; but much of the point of the piece is the literary display of highly Platonising analogies themselves; cf. Anderson (1976a), 121.
45 On this still not altogether intelligible piece, cf. Bompaire (1958), 509f.; Anderson (1976a) 85–89; G. Anderson, 'Lucian's Nigrinus: the problem of form', *GRBS* 19 (1978), 367–374; C.P. Jones (1986), 84–87.
46 On the *Demonax*, C.P. Jones (1986), 90–98; Anderson *ANRW* 2.34.2/3 (forthcoming).
47 For three very different interpretations of the work as a whole, Bowie, 'Apollonius of Tyana: tradition and reality', *ANRW* 2.16.2.(1978), 1652–1699; Anderson (1986), 121–239; M. Dielska, *Apollonius of Tyana in Legend and History* (Rome, 1986).
48 Anderson (1986), 121–153.
49 E.g. *VA* 4.44 (Tigellinus); 8.3ff. (Domitian); 1.31ff. (King of 'Babylon'); 3.28f. (King of North India).
50 For this phenomenon see now D.J. O'Meara, *Pythagoras Revived: Mathematics and Philosophy in Late Antiquity* (Oxford, 1989).
51 Eunapius, *VPS* 485.
52 Ibid. 475.
53 Libanius, *Decl.* 1 (vol. 5, 13–121 Förster); Maximus, *Or.* 3.

7 SOME SOPHISTIC SCENE-PAINTING

1 Philostratus, *VS* 548–551; cf. 551; Damascius: Photius *Bibl.*242.
2 *VA* 8.1.
3 Theon (Spengel vol. 2, 118, 119ff.).
4 On *Ecphrasis* in general, J. Palm, 'Bemerkungen zur Ekphrase der griechischen Literatur', *Kungliga Humanistika Vetenskapssamfundet i Uppsala* 1 (1965), 108–211. For specific authors, H. Piot, *Les Procédés littéraires de la IIe Sophistique chez Lucien: l'ecphrasis* (Rennes, 1914); Bompaire (1958), 707–735; S. Bartsch, *Decoding the Ancient Novel* (Princeton, NJ, 1989) (Achilles, Heliodorus); Anderson (1986), 259–268. For a new look at the relationship between description and narration, see now D.P. Fowler, 'Narrate and describe: the problem of ekphrasis', *JRS* 81 (1991), 25–35.
5 Herodotus 7.129.
6 Aelian, *Varia Historia* 3.1.
7 Lucian, *Historia Conscribenda* 19.
8 Fronto, *Principia Historiae* 10–14 (vol. 2, 106–212 Haines = 196ff. van den Hout).
9 Commentary by E. Kalinka and O.Schönberger (Munich, 1968); also Anderson (1986), 259–268.
10 Most readily accessible (with the two Philostrati) in A. Fairbanks' *LCL* (1931).
11 Vol. 8, 460–546 Förster. See also the important study of later *ecphrasis*, L. Friedlaender, *Johannes von Gaza, Paulus Silentiarius und Prokopios von Gaza* (Leipzig, 1912).
12 *Imag.* 2.2.
13 Pan, Dionysus: *Imag.* 1.18ff., 2.11; unusual births: 1.26, 2.3, 2.27; collections of little people: 1.5f., 2.22; paradoxography: passim.
14 Philostr., *Imag.* 2.2; Philostr. junior 1.
15 Philostr., *Imag.* 1.19; *Hom. Hymn to Dionysus* (7) 53.
16 Philostr., *Imag.* 1.19.2. For similar humour, Lucian, *Bacchus* 1f.
17 Philostr., *Imag.* 1.19.3f. For a further Bacchic ship, Lucian *VH* 2.41.
18 (Libanius) *Imag.* 19.5 (Förster, 512).
19 Ibid. 14 (Förster, 515).
20 Achilles Tatius 3.8.
21 Seneca *Contr.* 10.5.
22 *Or.* 4.
23 *Eth.* 11.
24 Lucian, *Zeuxis* 3–6; Philostr., *Imag.* 2.3.
25 Philostr., 2.3.1.
26 Lucian, *Zeuxis* 6.
27 Philostr., 2.3.2.
28 Lucian, *Zeuxis* 6.
29 Philostr., 2.3.1; 2.3.2. For this tendency, cf. below ch. 9.
30 Often paradoxographical in emphasis: cf. Philostratus *Imag.* 1.9.6 on amorous palm trees; also Achilles Tatius 1.17.3ff.
31 On Plato's own use of painting, E. Keuls, 'Plato on painting', *AJPh* 95 (1974), 100–127.

32 For Philostratus' use of Platonic material, E. Birmelin, 'Die kunsttheoretischen Gedanken in Philostrats Apollonius', *Philologus* 88
(1933), 149–80, 392–414.
33 *VA* 6.19.
34 Plato, *Resp.* 9.588B–E.
35 Lucian, *Imagines* 7f.
36 Aelian, *Varia Historia* 9.11, 4.12.
37 Ibid. 2.3.
38 Plato, *Resp.* 596C.
39 Dio, *Or.* 12.55–83 at 62.
40 Achilles 2.3.2.

8 *LOGOS ERŌTIKOS*: THE SOPHIST AS STORYTELLER

1 *VS* 590.
2 Mark 5.38–42.
3 Apuleius *Florida* 19.
4 There are several recent characterisations of the ancient novel: e.g.
Bowie, *CHCL* 1.683–699; T. Hägg, *The Novel in Antiquity* (Oxford,
Basil Blackwell, 1983); Anderson, *Ancient Fiction* (London, 1984);
N. Holzberg, *Der antike Roman, Eine Einführung* (Munich, 1986).
Positions up to the 1960s are considered by B.E. Perry, *The Ancient
Romances* (Berkeley, Calif., 1967), and Reardon (1971), 309–403.
Three new titles attest to the continued vitality of a subject which is
far from commanding total agreement: M. Fusillo, *Il Romanzo greco.
Polifonia ed Eros* (Venice, 1989); A. Billault, *La Création romanesque
dans la littérature grecque à l'époque impériale* (Paris, 1991), and
Reardon, *The Form of Greek Romance* (Princeton, NJ, 1991); as do the
four *Groningen Colloquia* volumes so far published (ed. H. Hofmann,
Groningen 1988–92). For the specific subject in question here, see
also Reardon, 'The Second Sophistic and the novel' in Bowersock
(1974), 23–29; for love and learning in the novel, cf. Anderson
(1984), 43–61.
5 Achilles 5.27.4; Longus 4.18.1.
6 Chariton 5.8.4f.
7 Achilles 8.1.2–8.2.3.
8 Menander *peri Epideiktikōn* 2.7. (*peri kateunastikou*), 148ff. Russell-
Wilson.
9 On this text see still R. Bloch (Strasbourg, 1907).
10 *Amores* 17f. (with direct mention of shade and cicadas, 18).
11 *Amores* 14f.
12 *Amores* 53f.
13 On the vexed question of readership, see now B. Wesseling, 'The
audience of the ancient novel', in Hofmann (1988), 67–79.
14 Achilles 1.8.3f.
15 Heliodorus 1.19.6–1.21.1.
16 Achilles 2.37.5 (as far as having experience of prostitutes).

17 Ibid. 2.35–38. On the material, F. Wilhelm, 'Zu Achilles Tatius', *RhM* 57 (1902), 55–75.

18 On pictorial *ecphrasis* in Achilles see now Bartsch (1989), 48–79; (overingenious however in forging the prefigurement by *ecphrasis* of action).

19 Achilles 1.1.1. (Sidon); 5.1 (Alexandria).

20 Ibid. 1.1.2–13 (Europa); 3.6ff. (Andromeda, Prometheus); 5.3.4–8 (Philomela).

21 E.g. Achilles 1.16.2–18.5.

22 Ibid. 1.6. and passim; cf. Anderson (1982a), 24.

23 Note also the *ei gameteon* by the homosexual Clinias, 1.8.1–9.

24 For this once-popular view, e.g. Rohde (1914), 511–514; cf. S.L. Wolff, *The Greek Romances in Elizabethan Prose Fiction* (New York, 1912), 202–208 (descriptions as 'irrelevances' of various kinds).

25 Achilles 4.11.3–12.4.9 (at 12.1).

26 Ibid. 4.12.4–8, 4.13.1–14.7.

27 Ibid. 4.14.8; cf. Anderson (1982a), 27.

28 Ibid. 4.14.1–7 (at 1–3).

29 Ibid. 4.3.2–4.5.3.

30 Ibid. 1.16.2–1.18.5.

31 Ibid. 1.4.4f.

32 Ibid. 3.4.4f.

33 Heliodorus 4.12f./2.30ff. On Calasiris' technique in general, J.J. Winkler, 'The mendacity of Calasiris and the narrative strategy of Heliodorus' *Aithiopika*', *YCS* 27 (1982), 93–158.

34 Heliodorus 3.7.2–8.2, cf. Plutarch, *Quaest. Symp.* 680Cff.

35 Heliodorus 2.34.5ff.

36 On the latter, Anderson (1986), 268–272.

37 Bartsch (1989); treatment of spectacles, ibid. 109–143.

38 Heliodorus 7.6.4–7.7.2.

39 See J.H.W. Walden, 'Stage-terms in Heliodorus' *Aethiopica*', *HSCPh* 5 (1909), 1–43.

40 *Il.* 22.136ff., with the notes of Rattenbury, Lumb and Maillon ad 7.6.3ff.

41 *Od.* 18.66–74.

42 Hel. 7.6.5, πολλὰ μὲν ἀνατλάντα καὶ πάντα μηχανησάμενον, Cf. *Od.* 1.1f. Ἄνδρα μοι ἔννεπε, Μοῦσα, πολύτροπον, ὅς μάλα πολλὰ/ πλάγχθη.

43 See below 195f.

44 Good characterisation in Hunter (1983); J.-R. Viellefond's introduction to the revised Budé (1987), cix–ccxxi; and now B.D. MacQueen, *Myth, Rhetoric and Fiction: A Reading of Longus' Daphnis and Chloe*, (Lincoln, Neb. 1990).

45 For this aspect, cf. Anderson (1982a), 42, 45.

46 Longus 4.17.3–7.

47 Ibid. 4.18.1.

48 Ibid. 2.39.2–6.

9 *ADOXA PARADOXA*: **THE** *PEPAIDEUMENOS* **AT PLAY**

1 Philostratus, *VA* 4.30. For sophistic lightness of touch in fiction, Anderson (1982a), passim; in declamatory literature, especially Libanius, Russell (1983), passim. But the subject has scarcely been approached at all.
2 For the mode, A.S. Pease, 'Things without honor', *CPh* 21 (1926), 27–42.
3 Synesius, *phalakrās encomium*, (vol. 2, 190–232 Terzaghi), including Dio's *Praise of Hair*, ibid. 190–195.
4 *Muscae Encomium.*
5 Sleep: *de feriis Alsiniensibus* 3.8–13 (vol. 2, 12–18 Haines = 216ff. van den Hout); smoke and dust: vol. 1, 38–44 Haines = 201ff. van den Hout; negligence: vol. 1, 44–48 Haines = 203ff. van den Hout.
6 Gellius, *NA* 17.12.3ff.
7 Regarding Dio's encomium of a parrot, *VS* 487, cf. Apuleius, *Florida* 12.
8 Fronto, *Laudes fumi et pulveris* 3 (vol. 1, 40ff. Haines = 201 van den Hout).
9 *Georg.* 4.67–87.
10 For the date, H. Wolke, *Untersuchungen zur Batrachomyomachia* (Meisenheim am Glan, 1978), 46–70.
11 *Imag.* 2.22.3.
12 Ibid.
13 *Imag.* 2.22.4.
14 Philostr., *VS* 490; Lucian, *VH* 1.1.
15 *Lysis* 209DE.
16 Cf. above ch. 2.
17 Apuleius, *Florida* 12, 14, 15, 6, 18, 4, 16.
18 On paradoxography in general, below 185–188 and passim.
19 For Homer in the Second Sophistic, Kindstrand (1973).
20 Cf. *Phaedr.* 278BC.
21 *Od.* 11.543f., 549f., 563f.
22 Lucian, *D.Mort.* 23.1.
23 Cf. Heliodorus 3.14.2f., 15.1; Anderson, 'Two notes on Heliodorus', *JHS* 99 (1979), 149.
24 *Or.* 11; Kindstrand (1973), 141–162.
25 *Or.* 11.53, 11.96, 11.123.
26 Ed. L. de Lannoy, (Teubner, 1977); Anderson (1986), 243–247.
27 At *Heroicus* 136 (de Lannoy 7), Protesilaus is claimed to know not only all the Homeric material, but much of Greek and Persian history as well, to the extent of holding views on Xerxes' expedition.
28 *Or.* 61.
29 *Il.* 14.1; Athen. 10.433BC.
30 *Od.* 7.216; Athen. 10.412BC (as proof of Odysseus' gluttony).
31 For the symposium as a theme for imitation, cf. above 72.
32 For Athenaeus, Reardon (1971), 226f.; Lukinovitch (1990), 263–271.
33 *Deipn.* 11.481E, cf. 11.461CD.

34 *Deipn.* 4.153E–154B.
35 *Deipn.* 13.590AB; 13.610CD.
36 *Deipn.* 14.648C, cf. 647C, 648B.
37 Plato *Conv.* 176A–E; 175B.
38 Ibid. 175B.
39 *Deipn.* 12.516C.
40 E.g. *Deipn.* 3.111E–112C (though even Archestratus is unaware that the best breadmakers are Cappadocian, 112C; as is Hesiod, 3.101f.).
41 *Deipn.* 3.116A–D.
42 *Deipn.* 3.107DE (Alexis, Kock 2.335).
43 *Deipn.* 3.101F., 3.102B (Damoxenus, Kock 3.349).
44 *Deipn.* 5.203C–209F.
45 *Deipn.* 13.610B.
46 *Deipn.* 14.622E–623C.
47 *Deipn.* 6.270B; 4.159E.
48 *Deipn.* 2.40F–46E, 3.83B, 14.616C.
49 *Deipn.* 3.112DE.
50 See especially Antiphanes, *Carians* (Kock 2.55), *Deipn.* 4.134BC.
51 *Deipn.* 5.186CD (*Bacch.* 1129).
52 *Deipn.* 4.162C (there seems no need to emend with Kaibel to exclude Socrates; the whole tenor of Athenaeus' work is to include the 'scandal of the great').
53 *Deipn.* 13.610E–611B.
54 Plato *Conv.* 194E–197E.
55 E.g. *Deipn.* 3.96F–100B, and cf. above ch.4.
56 *Deipn.* 4.134D–137C.
57 *Deipn.* 10.420F/*Il.* 2.38.
58 Alexandrian dinners, *Deipn.* 10.420E; those of Philip, Mnesimachus (Kock 2.441), *Deipn.* 10.421BC; Phoenix of Colophon, *Deipn.* 421D.
59 *Deipn.* 1.2C (cf. *Il.* 21.140ff.).
60 Lucian, *VH* 2.14–18, 2.17.
61 Philostr. *VA* 3.32.
62 *Or.* 30.29–44; for a 'festival of life' in Alexis' *Tarentinoi* (Kock 2.377), *Deipn.* 11.463C–E.
63 *Or.* 30.31, 30.
64 Especially *Deipn.* 11.504E–509E passim.
65 *Deipn.* 11.507BC.
66 *Deipn.* 11.507E.
67 Bowie (1970/74) passim. Above, ch. 5.
68 Lucian, *Quomodo historia conscribenda sit* 38.
69 *Deipn.* 9.407A (it was Hegemon of Thasos' *Gigantomachy*).
70 *Deipn.* 10.418F.
71 *VS* 485 (attr. to Leon); Athenaeus, *Deipn.* 12.550F.
72 *Deipn.* 12.550F.
73 Aelian, *VH* 11.4.
74 Athenaeus, *Deipn.* 10.435D.
75 Aelian, *VH* 12.17.
76 Lucian, *Adv. Ind.* 15.

77 Id. *de Parasito* 34.
78 Athenaeus, *Deipn.* 3.98D.
79 Ibid. 6.249E–250D, 10.435E.
80 *Deipn.* 2.48.
81 *Deipn.* 10.416A.
82 *Deipn.* 4.138Bff.; cf. 4.148Dff., of the Thebans.
83 Aelian *VH* 3.8, 13.48.
84 *Deipn.* 10.435BC.
85 Herod. 1.17, *Deipn.* 12.517A.
86 Aelian *VH* 7.14; (Socrates says that those who best honour the gods in dances are also best in war, *Deipn.* 14.628EF).
87 *Deipn.* 5.215C–216C.
88 Aelian *VH* 3.9.
89 *Deipn.* 12.534E, 535C.
90 *Deipn.* 12.520CD.
91 *Deipn.* 10.434 A–D, 12.535A, 13.603B.
92 *Deipn.* 10.434F.
93 *Deipn.* 12.537D.
94 *Deipn.* 12.537D–540A; 538E–539A.
95 *Deipn.* 6.250F–251A, 251C.
96 Lucian *pro Imag.* 9.
97 *Deipn.* 13.591D.
98 Plut. *Mor.* 328A, C.
99 *Mor.* 332B.
100 *Mor.* 326E.
101 *Mor.* 327AB.
102 Aelian *VH* 13.24.
103 Lucian, *D. Mort.* 25.5.
104 Cf. Bowie's explanation for archaism as a whole (1970/74), 204–209.
105 Above 154.
106 *VS* 557.
107 Cf. Bompaire (1958), 203–221 passim ('les types psychologiques').
108 Xen. *Mem.* 3.11.
109 *Menexenus* 235E–249C.
110 *Deipn.* 14.614D.
111 *Deipn.* 6.246F, 246C.
112 *Deipn.* 6.236BC (Diphilus, Kock 2.561).
113 *Deipn.* 6.236CD, *Il.* 17.575ff., 237f. (Timocles' Dracontium, Kock 2.454).
114 *De Parasito* 10, 34 (ed. H. Nesselrath, Berlin, 1985).
115 *Deipn.* 13. 588B–589D.
116 *Deipn.* 4.157A–158A.
117 *Ep.* 4.7.4–7, cf. Athenaeus, *Deipn.* 13.584A (Stilpo's eristic versus Glycera's erotic).
118 *Deipn.* 13.588C–589C.
119 *Deipn.* 13.590A.
120 *Deipn.* 13.597DE.
121 Alciphron, *Ep.* 3.1; for conjecture on the source, A.S. Gratwick,

'Sundials, Parasites and Girls from Boeotia', *CQ* N.S. 29 (1979), 308–323.

122 Alciphron, *Ep.* 3.1.3.

123 *Ep.* 3.7.3.f., 3.38.2f.

124 On Anacharsis, Bompaire (1958), 678–682; R.B. Branham, *Unruly Eloquence: Lucian and the Comedy of Traditions*, (Cambridge, Mass., 1989), 82–104 passim.

125 Longus 2.7.2.

126 Philostr., *VS* 554.

127 Lucian, *Bis Accusatus* 11.

128 For the repertoire, A. Oltramare, *Les Origines de la diatribe Romaine* (Lausanne, 1926).

129 Philostr., *VA* 5.15.

130 Philostr., *Imag.* 1.3.2.

131 Apuleius, *Florida* 12.

132 Ar. *Nub.* 156–166; Achilles Tatius 2.22.3.

133 *Conv. Sept Sap., Mor.* 149C–E.

134 *Conv. Sept. Sap., Mor.* 150AB, EF.

135 Hermogenes (Spengel vol. 2, 3f.).

136 Achilles Tatius 2.22.

137 *Conv. Sept. Sap.* 162B.

138 Ibid. 162C–163A; Lucian, *D. Mar.* 5.1.

139 *Mor.* 986C; Lucian, *Gallus* 17.

140 Aelian, *Natura Animalium* 10.8.

141 *Or.* 32.63–66.

142 Lucian, *Piscator* 36; Greg. Nyss., *PG* 46. 240C–241A; cf. Claudian, *Eutr.* 1.300–308.

143 *Deipn.* 12.518F.

144 Aelian *NA* 5.17.

145 Achilles 3.25.7.

146 Philostr. *VA* 2.15f.

147 *Or.* 2.8–10.

148 *Or.* 2.11f.

149 *Or.* 2.14ff.

150 *Or.* 58.

151 *Or.* 2.18.

152 *Or.* 2.19f.

153 *Or.* 2.23.

154 *Or.* 2.30f., 2.47.

155 On the latter category, I. Sykoutris, *RE* Suppl. 5 s.v. Epistolographie, cols. 208–216; Bompaire (1958), 295ff.; Reardon (1971), 180–185 (Alciphron).

156 E.g. in *Daphnis and Chloe* 1.16 (*syncrisis*): and notably the miniature *ecphrasis* in Heliodorus 5.14 (pastoral scene as intaglio on a ring).

157 Reardon (1971), 182.

158 E.g. Bowie, *CHCL* 1 (1985), 680.

159 Aelian, *Ep. Rust.* 20.

160 Ibid. 7f.; Alciphron, *Epp.* 4.18f.

161 Lucian, *D. Deor.* 20, 23.

162 *D. Mort.* 12, 13, 25.
163 Aelian, *Ep. Rust.* 6 (Demosthenes 55.18, 1, 6, 33, 32 and Hesiod, *Opera* 346).
164 Alciphron, *Ep.* 4.7.1–3.
165 Xenophon, *Mem.* 3.11.
166 Alciphron, *Ep.* 4.7.4–6.
167 Ibid. 4.7.6ff.
168 Ibid. 4.7.8.
169 Alciphron, *Ep.* 2.38.
170 *Nub.* 92–118 and passim; the context is clearly alluded to, e.g. at *Ep.* 2.11 (*Nub.* 102f.); *Ep.* 2.6, cf. *Nub.* 46–52.
171 E.g. *Fugit.* 12–21.
172 See D.R. Dudley, *A History of Cynicism* (London, 1937), 17–58.
173 Dio, *Or.* 58.
174 Ibid. 1–3.
175 Ibid. 4.
176 Ibid. 4–6.
177 Ibid. 2.
178 *D. Mort.* 25. See now B. Baldwin, 'Alexander, Hannibal and Scipio in Lucian', *Emerita* 58 (1990), 51–60.
179 *D. Mort.* 25.2; 4f.
180 25.2ff.
181 25.7.
182 Cf. Livy 35.14, Appian 11.10; Plutarch *Flamininus* 21.3; *Pyrrhus* 8.2.
183 *Ran.* 757–1523; Anderson (1976a), 98.
184 Cf. 115ff. above.
185 For this aspect, cf. also Anderson (1982a), 41–49.
186 E.g. *praef.* 1, 1.1, 3.12f.
187 Longus 3.2.5.
188 Ibid. 1.26.3, 2.1.4.
189 Ibid. 2.33.2f., 2.35.1.
190 Ibid. 2.7.1f.
191 Only Lucian's contributions to this area have received much attention: Bompaire (1958), 657–705; Anderson (1976a), 23–40.
192 For the private fantasy world evoked by sophistic *paideia*, cf. Anderson (1989), 170–184.
193 Libanius, *Decl.* 28 (vol. 6, 573–588 Förster).
194 *VS* 513.
195 Iamblichus fr. 101 Habrich.
196 Lucian, *Tyrannicida* 22.
197 Bompaire (1958), 677–689.
198 Lucian, *Rhet. Prec.* 18.
199 Dio, *Or.* 32.44, cf. **Lucian**, *Anacharsis* 1.5. On the latter see now Branham (1989), 88f.
200 *Charon* 1.
201 For the range, above 52.
202 *Charon* 3–7.
203 *Charon* 3.7; Aelian, *VH* 13.22.
204 *Charon* 10ff., Herod. 1.30–33; *Charon* 13, Herod. 1.214; 2.1–3.66

passim; *Charon* 14, Herod. 3.39–43, 120–125.
205 *Charon* 15f.; 20f.
206 Especially *Pinax* 27; for the strings, Marcus Aurelius 7.3, cf. 6.10.
207 *VH* 2.20.

10 PIETY AND *PAIDEIA*: THE SOPHIST AND HIS GODS

1 Philostr., *VS* 533, 535. For an inscription of Polemo in honour of Asclepius, Habicht, (1969) 75f. n. 33, cf. Phrynichus, *Eklogē* 396.
2 *VS* 568; 101 above.
3 *VS* 549.
4 *Or.* 50.69K.
5 *Or.* 50.14–18.
6 *Metamorphoses* 11.28.6, 11.30.2 (Lucius' career is by this point made to converge with Apuleius' own). For the implication of this idea for the rest of the work, Anderson (1982a), 83.
7 For the form, Reardon (1971), 143–148; Russell (1990), 199–219.
8 Ps.-Menander 1.333–344 (Russell-Wilson, 6–28).
9 For the problem of religious motivation in Heliodorus, Reardon (1971), 385f.; Anderson (1982a), 33ff.; cf. Bowie in *CHCL* (I, 1985), 695f.
10 Heliodorus 3.1–5.
11 For comparison with Philostratus' *Life of Apollonius*, Anderson (1986), 230f.
12 *Legatio ad Gaium* 12.86–90.
13 Philo, *Vita Iosephi* 23ff.
14 Ibid. 61f.
15 On Christian *paideia*, W. Jaeger, *Early Christianity and Greek Paideia* (Cambridge, Mass., 1961); M.L.W. Laistner, *Christianity and Pagan Culture in the Later Roman Empire* (Ithaca, NY, 1951); and now G. Kennedy, *Greek Rhetoric under Christian Emperors* (Princeton, NJ, 1983); G. Kennedy, *Classical Rhetoric and its Christian and Secular Tradition from Ancient to Modern Times* (Chapel Hill, NC, 1980, 120–160).
16 E.g. *Cor.* 1.1.21.
17 *Acts* 17.28; *Peregrinus* 13.
18 Athanasius, *Vita Antoni* 73; Augustine, *de Doctrina Christiana* 2.40.60.
19 Gregory Nazianzenus *Or.* 28.25 (PG 36.60C–61A). For Gregory in general, see R.R. Rüther, *Gregory of Nazianzus, Rhetor and Philosopher* (Oxford, 1969).
20 Matt. 6.26. For a similar *ecphrasis* on the theme of the divine vine (cf. John 15.5), M. Richard, *Asterii Sophistae Commentaria* (Oslo, 1956), *Homily* 14, 105f.
21 For Tertullian's rhetoric, R.D. Sider, *Ancient Rhetoric and the Art of Tertullian* (Oxford, 1971); T.D. Barnes, *Tertullian: A Historical and Literary Study* (2nd edn, Oxford, 1987); on the *de Pallio*, Barnes 230ff.
22 Wearers: *De Pallio, PL* 2.1050AB. Archaic practice: ibid. 1039B–1040A. Secular learning: ibid. 1040B–1041B. Rogues' gallery: ibid.

1047B. Secular philosophers: ibid. 1049A.
23 Ibid. 1050AB; Philostr., *VS* 550.
24 For a good short discussion of the often ambivalent humanism of the Cappadocian Fathers, Ševčenko (1980), 57–61.
25 For Basil, J.M. Campbell, *The Influence of the Second Sophistic on the Style of the Sermons of St. Basil the Great* (Washington, DC, 1922); G.L. Kustas, 'St. Basil and the Rhetorical Tradition', in P.J. Fedwick (ed.), *Basil of Caesarea: Christian, Humanist, Ascetic'* (Toronto, 1981), 221–279.
26 For Gregory of Nyssa, L. Méridier, *L'Influence de la seconde sophistique sur l'oeuvre de Grégoire de Nysse* (Paris, 1906); E.C.E. Owen, 'St. Gregory of Nyssa, Grammar, Vocabulary and Style', *JThS* (1925), 64–71; C. Klock, *Untersuchungen zu Stil und Rythmus bei Gregor von Nyssa* (Meisenheim, 1987).
27 Commentary by N.G. Wilson, *St. Basil on Greek Literature*, (London, 1975), 4.
28 Ibid. 2.5.
29 Ibid. 2.8.
30 Ibid.
31 Ibid. 4.1–5.
32 Ibid. 4.7f. For this cliché of classical poetry, Wilson compares Plut. *Mor.* 79CD. For its general place in Christian writing, cf. Ševčenko (1980), 68 n. 43.
33 Basil, *Protrepticus* 5.2–14; Hesiod, *Erga* 287–292; *Od.* 6.135ff.
34 Painting and theatre, Basil, *Protrepticus* 6.2f.
35 Gregory Nazianzenus, *Ep.* 233 (*PG* 37.376BC).
36 Greg. Naz., *Or.* 21.12 (*PG* 35.1093C–1096A). The Arians could just as readily produce their own sophistic ammunition: for the fragments of Asterius, Richard, *Asterii Sophistae Commentaria, Homily* 14, 105ff.
37 Basil, *de spiritu sancto* 30 (*PG* 32.209D–211C).
38 Greg. Naz., *Or.* 21.16 (*PG* 35.1097C–1100A).
39 Greg. Naz., *Or.* 8.3 (*PG* 35.792D).
40 Greg. Naz., *Or.* 43.12 (*PG* 36.509B).
41 *Ep.* 66 (*PG* 37.129C, 131A).
42 *Ep.* 171 (*PG* 37.279C).
43 *Ep.* 49 (*PG* 37.101A).
44 *Epp.* 4, 5 (*PG* 37.24C–29B).
45 Ibid.
46 *Epp.* 25f., 27 (*PG* 37.60D–61C).
47 *Ep.* 171 (*PG* 37.280C–281A).
48 *Ep.* 5 (*PG* 32.240CD).
49 *Job* 1.21.
50 *Ep.* 21 (*PG* 37.56C).
51 For a variation on the gold imagery, *Ep.* 22 (*PG* 37.57A).
52 *Ep.* 21 (*PG* 37.56D).
53 *Ep.* 29 (*PG* 37.64A–65B).
54 *Ep.* 9 (*PG* 37.36B); Pindar *Ol.* 6.1.
55 *Or.* 30.

56 *Or.* 30.31.
57 *Or.* 30.32.
58 *Or.* 30.28.
59 *Or.* 30.9.
60 *Or.* 30.8.
61 *Ep.* 22, 431D; *Od.* 14.56ff.

11 SOPHISTIC SELF-PRESENTATION: FOUR STUDIES

1 For a similar group of 'typical texts', cf. Anderson (1989), 192–199 (Plutarch, *de genio Socratis*; Favorinus, *Corinthiacus*; Dio *Or.* 12 (*Olympicus*); Lucian, *de Astrologia*). The Philostratean *opuscula* might form a further such group within the (likely) output of a single author: Anderson (1986), 159–182.
2 *Or.* 36. For brief analysis of the *Realien*, C.P. Jones (1978a), 61ff.
3 *Or.* 36.2f. (ed. D.A. Russell, Cambridge, 1992).
4 For the sophistic interest in Graeco-Scythian fantasy, Bompaire (1958), 227–234, cf. 677–687.
5 *Or.* 36.8.
6 Philostr. *VA* 1.24.
7 *Or.* 36.13.
8 Ibid. 14. For the Achilles cult, cf. Philostratus, *Heroicus* 208f.
9 See G. Hedreen, 'The Cult of Achilles in the Euxine', *Hesperia* 60 (1991), 313–330 (at 314–319).
10 *Or.* 36.17. For the notion of an improvised audience, e.g. *Or.* 51.31ff.; *VS* 619 (Hippodromus of Larissa).
11 *Or.* 36.17. Cf. ch. 5 above.
12 For the sophist as holy man, cf. G. Anderson, *Sage, Saint and Sophist* (London, forthcoming).
13 *Or.* 36.26f.
14 *Or.* 36.28.
15 E.g. *Resp.* 592B; Cicero, *de Natura Deorum* 2.62 (154); Marcus Aurelius 4.4.
16 *Or.* 36.34f.
17 *Or.* 36.36ff.
18 *Or.* 36.39–61.
19 For 'invented' myth, cf. Theon (Spengel vol. 2,76).
20 For Lucian's *pseudos* in such areas, Anderson (1982b), 69–74.
21 *Phaedr.* 246AB; cf. Trapp (1990), 148–155.
22 Nock saw the myth as Dio's own creation, *Essays on Religion and the Ancient World* 2 (Oxford, 1972), 607. But it becomes a little too facile to attribute to forgery everything that is not directly attested, as the problems surrounding Apollonius of Tyana continue to suggest.
23 For Zoroaster in the Greek world, cf. A. Momigliano, *Alien Wisdom* (Cambridge, 1975), 141–149.
24 Cf. Anderson (1986), 183; for reservations, Bowie (1978), 1655–59, 1667–70.

25 For this dimension in Philostratus' *Heroicus*, T. Mantero, *Richerche sull' Heroikos di Filostrato* (Genoa, 1966), passim.
26 Commentary: G. Husson (Paris, 1970). Brief Studies: G. Anderson 'Some notes on Lucian's *Navigium*', *Mnemosyne* 30 (1977), 363–368; Anderson (1982b), 88–91.
27 *Navig.* 2.
28 On the voyage of the Isis, Anderson (1976a), 39f.; also G.W. Houston, 'Lucian's *Navigium* and the dimensions of the Isis', *AJPh* 108 (1987), 444–450.
29 For this figure, cf. Bompaire (1958), 210–213.
30 *Navigium* 24.
31 For the reference to Herodes, Husson ad loc. (missing however the allusion to the canal at the Isthmus, cf. below 222f.).
32 On the moral theme, cf. also Lucian, *Icaromenippus*, esp. 18; for the ship of fools, cf. *J.Trag.* 47ff., above 81.
33 Above 113–117; 182f.; 189f.; 194f.
34 Above 113ff.
35 For a possible reminiscence of Theophrastus, Anderson (1982b) 89 (*Char.* 23.3ff.); for sophistic battles, e.g. Libanius *Imag.* 1 (vol. 8: 460–464 Förster); cf. Iamblichus fr. 101 Habrich.
36 *Navig.* 42ff., cf. *Resp.* 359C–360C.
37 E.g. Ps.-Callisthenes, recension C 2.24–35.
38 *Navig.* 46.
39 Ibid.
40 Philostr., *VS* 552. W. Ameling, *Herodes Atticus* (2 vols, Hildesheim, 1983), I.87 n. 19 and Swain (1991), 163 n. 75 rightly resist Münscher's inclination to doubt the incident, *RE* 8 (1913), 933.
41 Commentary by H.E. Butler and A.S. Owen (0xford, 1914); also A. Abt, *Apuleius und die antike Zauberei* (Giessen, 1908). Note also R. Helm, 'Apuleius' *Apologie*– ein Meisterwerk der zweiten Sophistik', *Altertum* 1 (1955), 86–108; and now T.D. McCreight, 'Invective techniques in Apuleius' *Apology*', *Groningen Colloquia* 3 (1990), 35–62. For the difference between writing and actual delivery, T.N. Winter, 'The publication of Apuleius' *Apology*', *TAPhA* 100 (1969), 607–612.
42 Claudius Maximus, *PIR*^{2} C933.
43 *VS* 590, 619. Hadrian was regarded by many as a magician for his use of such material, *VS* 590; cf. J. de Romilly, *Magic and Rhetoric in Ancient Greece* (Cambridge, Mass., 1975), 83f.
44 For discussion of the legal aspects, F. Norden, *Apuleius von Madaura und das römische Privatrecht* (Leipzig, 1912), 24–56, esp. 54: 'dies Kunstwerk, das dem antiken Ideal der gerichtlichen Beredsamkeit so vollkommen wie möglich entspricht, seinem ganzen Tenor auch bei seinem Autor eine lange, gründliche, praktische Erfahrung *in forensibus* zur Voraussetzung hatte'.
45 *Apology* 29–41.
46 Ibid. 30. For Apuleius' style in general, L. Callebat, 'La Prose d'Apulée dans le De Magia: Eléments d'interprétation', *WS* 18 (1984), 143–167.

47 Ibid. 29.
48 Ibid. 30.
49 Ibid. For Apuleius' sustained use of the charge of ignorance against Aemilianus, McCreight (1990), 42.
50 *Apology* 31.
51 Ibid. 43f.
52 Ibid. 48–51.
53 Eunapius, *VPS* 497f.; Penella (1990), 109–117.
54 *Apology* 52.
55 Ibid. 55f.
56 Ibid. 55.
57 Ibid. 74ff.
58 Ibid. 78–84.
59 Ibid. 78–84.
60 Ibid. 94ff.
61 Ibid. 102f.
62 Edition: A.F. Norman (Hull, 1965). For Libanius' career, see also Liebeschütz (1972), 1–39 and cf. G. Misch, *A History of Autobiography in Antiquity*, (English transl. of 3rd edn, vol.2, London, 1950), 554–563.
63 *Or.* 1.1.
64 *Or.* 1.2; cf. especially Bowersock (1969), 17–29. For the priority of this topos, Norman, commentary (Hull, 1965) and Philostratus, *VS* passim.
65 Philostr., *VS* 512.
66 *Or.* 1.3.
67 *Or.* 1.5; 1.8. The first teacher was probably Ulpianus (Schemmel, *NJklAlt* 20, 1907, 52ff.; Eunapius, *VPS* 487).
68 *Or.* 1.9f.; Philostr., *VS* 515 (of Scopelian).
69 *Or.* 1.11f. For a similar picture of Athens, above 120; Norman commentary (Hull, 1965), 17.
70 *Or.* 1.16f. This sophist (Diophantus) is regarded as no more reputable by Eunapius, *VPS* 494, cf. 495. For the student–teacher rituals, Norman commentary (Hull, 1965), 16.
71 *Or.* 1.19–25.
72 *Or.* 1.26. For the sophistic pose, Norman compares Isocr., *Antidosis* 162f.; but rightly sees it here as 'a professional insurance policy'.
73 *Or.* 1.27–35. As Norman shrewdly implies, his stay was all the happier for his not becoming embroiled in politics as he was later to be in Antioch itself.
74 *Or.* 1.37–44. For competitive oratory prior to the fourth century, cf. Philostr., *VS* 601 (Apollonius of Athens v. Heraclides of Lycia).
75 *Or.* 1.51.
76 *Or.* 1.23, 1.24, 1.26.
77 Ibid. 18, 32, cf. 15.
78 *Or.* 1.27.
79 Philostr., *VS* 583.
80 *Or.* 1.67.
81 *Or.* 1.62–72.

82 *Or.* 1.90f.(accuser's identity still uncertain), 98, cf. 43, and of course Apuleius' own trial, above 223–227.
83 *Or.* 1.111ff.
84 *Or.* 1.118–133.
85 *Or.* 1.136ff. The original speech would have ended at 155, with piecemeal additions thereafter.
86 *Or.* 1.89.
87 *Or.* 1.101. For sophists posing as Achilles, Philostratus, *VS* 521 (Polemo).
88 *Or.* 1.131.
89 *Or.* 1.152.
90 *Or.* 1.129.
91 *Or.* 1.120–131; Philostr., *VS* 582f.; R.A. Pack, 'Two Sophists and Two Emperors', *CPh* 42 (1947), 17–20.
92 *Or.* 1.139–143; cf. Aristides, Pack (1947) 19f.
93 *Or.* 1.155. For the theatrical metaphor, above 80f.
94 *Or.* 1.133.
95 *Or.* 1.128f.

12 CONCLUSION: VALUES AND VALUATIONS

1 *VA* 7.10f.
2 For the former role, above 75ff.; the Cynic Demetrius naturally pays Apollonius the compliment of assimilation to the Cynic arch-hero Heracles.
3 Cf. Bompaire (1958), 338ff.
4 E.g. Seneca, *Suas.* 6.7; cf. also Juvenal 10.114–126.
5 In particular the *nomou eisphora*, e.g. Hermogenes (Spengel vol. 2, 18), Apthonius (ibid., 53–56), Theon (ibid., 128ff.).
6 Cf. Trapp (1990), 145ff. Note the association of Cicero's Tusculan villa with the *Phaedrus* passage itself at Brutus 6.24 (Trapp 1990, 146).
7 Cf. Lucian, *Muscae Encomium*; Clitarchus on the wasp, Demetrius, *de Elocutione* 304.
8 Erwin Rohde, *Der griechische Roman* (3rd edn, Leipzig, 1914), 348f.
9 E.g. Schmid-Christ, *Geschichte der griechische Litteratur,* (6th edn, 1924), II.ii.667.
10 Van Groningen,'General literary tendencies in the second century AD', *Mnemosyne*, 4th series 18 (1965), 47. Cf. also B.E. Perry, 'Literature in the second century', *CJ* 50 (1955), 295–298; *Ancient Romances* 231. The latter passage in particular seems to characterise the whole ethos of the period in terms that particularly describe the *Zeitgeist* of Apuleius' *Metamorphoses*; but this is only a limited part of the picture. For sensible modification of Perry, Reardon (1984), 33–41 passim.
11 Bowersock (1969), 1. For Bowersock it is almost as if the (assumed) literary mediocrity of sophists is somehow redeemed by their social *éclat*: 'Such works (over-elaborated productions on unreal, un-

important or traditional themes) were rhetorical showpieces, whose authors, highly trained in oral presentation, were showmen. Yet this fact does not preclude composition for important persons and occasions'.

12 Reardon (1971), 407f. Epideictic rhetoric is seen as 'a quite esoteric art, but not without interest or value'; while Lucian, Alciphron and Philostratus are responsible for 'a very varied minor literature, a literature of occasion and diversion in prose, which, though of unequal quality, represents altogether a new stage in the history of Greek literature'. The sophistic phase of the Greek novel is seen as 'a form of major importance in late Greek literature'. There are also some useful correctives to the general picture in Reardon (1984), 23–41.

13 Bowersock's controversial suggestion (1969, 58) 'it could be argued without apology that the Second Sophistic has more importance in Roman History than it has in Greek literature' is at best an oversimplification: sophists are an important part of the social and intellectual fabric of the Empire, though one suspects that they were inclined to exaggerate it when they could; and they were undoubtedly an important influence on literature, but essentially of a neutral kind: bad or indifferent writing will be the more so for misuse of rhetorical resources; but outstanding literature can still use sophistic textures to its own ends.

14 Millar (1964), 174.

15 Cameron (1991), 82.

Select bibliography

EDITIONS, TRANSLATIONS, COMMENTARIES

Achilles Tatius: A. Vilborg, I–II (Stockholm, 1955–62); K. Plepelits (Stuttgart, 1980); Y. Yamanolakis (Athens, 1990); S. Gaselee (rev. B.H. Warmington), *LCL* 1968; J.-Ph. Garnaud (Budé, 1991)

Aelian: *De Natura Animalium*, R. Hercher, I–II (Teubner, 1864); A.F. Scholfield I–III, *LCL* 1958–59. *Epistulae, Fragmenta*, R. Hercher (Teubner, 1870); *Varia Historia*, M.R. Dilts, (Teubner, 1974); *Epistulae*, A.R. Benner and F.H. Fobes, with the *Letters* of Alciphron and Philostratus), *LCL* 1949

Aelius Aristides, F. Lenz and C. Behr, *Orr.* 1–16 (Leiden, 1976–80); *Orr.* 17–53, B. Keil, Berlin, 1898; tr. C. Behr I–II (Leiden, 1986, 1981)

Alciphron: M.A. Schepers (Teubner, 1905); A.R. Benner and F.H. Fobes, *LCL* 1949 (with Aelian and Philostratus, *Letters*)

Apuleius: R. Helm and P. Thomas (Teubner, 1955–69). *Metamorphoses*, D.S. Robertson and P. Valette (Budé, 1956–65); S. Gaselee, *LCL* 1915; J.A. Hanson I–II, *LCL* 1989. *Apologia*, H.E. Butler (Oxford, 1914); P. Vallette (Budé, 1924)

Athenaeus: G. Kaibel I–III (Teubner, 1887–90); S.P. Peppink I–III (Leiden, 1936–39); C.B. Gulick I–VII, *LCL* 1927–41. A.M. Desrousseaux and C. Astuc (Budé 1956–).

S. Basil, *Letters*, R.J. Deferrari I–IV, *LCL* 1928–34; Y. Courtonne I–III (Budé, 1957–66); *Saint Basil on Greek Literature*, N.G. Wilson (London, 1975)

Dio Cassius, U.P. Boissevain, I–V (Berlin, 1895–1931); J. Melber (Teubner, 1890–1928); E. Cary I–IX, *LCL* 1914–26

Dio Chrysostom, J. von Arnim I–II (Berlin, 1893–1896); J.W. Cohoon I–V, *LCL* 1932–1964; D.A. Russell, *Orr.* 7, 12, 36 (Cambridge, 1992)

Favorinus, A. Barigazzi (Florence, 1966); E. Mensching, *Testimonia, Omnigena Historia* (Berlin, 1963)

Fronto, C.R. Haines, *LCL* I–II; M.P.J. van den Hout (Leiden, 1954, 2nd edn 1988)

Gellius, P.K. Marshall I–II, *OCT* 1968; J.C. Rolfe I–III, *LCL* 1927

Heliodorus, R.M. Rattenbury and T.W. Lumb (tr. Maillon) I–III (Budé, 1935–43)

SELECT BIBLIOGRAPHY

Herodes Atticus: *Peri Politeias*, U. Albini (Florence, 1968)
Herodian, ed. K. Stavenhagen (Teubner, 1922); C.R. Whittaker I–II, *LCL* 1969–70
Himerius, A. Colonna (Rome, 1950)
Julianus Apostata, J. Bidez and F. Cumont, *OCT* 1922; J. Bidez, G. Rochefort, C. Lacombrade, I–IV (Budé 1924–64; W.C. Wright I–III, *LCL* 1913–23
Libanius, R. Förster I–XII (Teubner, 1903–27); J. Martin and P. Petit, *Or.* I (Budé, 1979); J. Martin, *Orr.* II–X, 1988; F. Norman, Select Orations, *LCL* I–II, 1969, 1977; F. Norman, *Or.* I (Hull, 1969); *Autobiography and Select Letters, LCL* I—II, 1992
Longus, M.D. Reeve (Teubner, 1982); J.R. Viellefond (Budé, 1987); commentary by O. Schoenberger (3rd edn, Berlin, 1988)
Lucian, A.M. Harmon, K. F. Kilburn and M.D. Macleod, I–VIII, *LCL* 1913–67; M.D. Macleod I–IV, *OCT* 1972–1987; *Historia conscribenda*, H. Homeyer (Munich, 1967); *Navigium*, G.Husson (Paris, 1970); *de Parasito*, H. Nesselrath, (Berlin, 1985)
Maximus Tyrius, H. Hobein (Teubner, 1909)
Philostratus, C.L. Kayser, (*editio minor*, Teubner 1870), *Vitae Sophistarum LCL* 1922 (with Eunapius, *Lives*); *Vita Apollonii*, F.C. Conybeare I–II (*LCL* 1912); *Imagines* A. Fairbanks (with Philostratus junior and Callistratus), *LCL* 1931; A. Kalinka and O. Schoenberger (Munich, 1968); *Heroicus*, L. de Lannoy, (Teubner, 1977); *Gymnasticus* J. Juethner (Berlin, 1909)
Polemo, H. Hinck (Teubner, 1873)
Themistius, *Orationes* I–III G. Downey and A.F. Norman (Teubner, 1951–74)

SECONDARY WORKS

Abt, A.: *Apuleius und die antike Zauberei* (Giessen, 1908)
Alpers, J.: *Hercules in bivio* (Diss. Göttingen, 1912).
Anderson, G.: *Lucian, Theme and Variation in the Second Sophistic* (Leyden 1976a)
—— *Studies in Lucian's Comic Fiction* (Leyden, 1976b)
—— 'Lucian's quotations: some short cuts to culture', *BICS* 23 (1976), 59–68
—— 'Some notes on Lucian's Navigium', *Mnemosyne*, 4th series 30 (1977), 363–368
—— 'Putting pressure on Plutarch: Philostratus *Ep.* 73', *CPh* 72 (1977), 43ff.
—— 'Patterns in Lucian's Quotations', *BICS* 26 (1978), 97–100
—— 'Lucian's Nigrinus: the problem of form', *GRBS* 19 (1979), 367–374
—— 'Two notes on Heliodorus', *JHS* 99 (1979), 149
—— Eros Sophistes: *Ancient Novelists at Play* (Chico, Calif. 1982a)
—— 'Lucian: a sophist's sophist', *YCS* 27 (1982b), 61–92
—— *Ancient Fiction: The Novel in the Graeco-Roman World* (London, 1984)

289

—— *Philostratus: Biography and Belles-Lettres in the Third Century* AD (London, 1986)

—— 'The *Pepaideumenos* in action: sophists and their outlook in the Early Empire', *ANRW* 2.33.1 (1989), 79–208.

—— 'The Second Sophistic: some problems of perspective', in Russell (1990), 91–100

—— 'Lucian: tradition versus reality', *ANRW* 2.34.2 forthcoming

—— 'Aulus Gellius: a miscellanist and his world', ibid.

André, J.-M. 'Les écoles philosophiques aux deux premiers siècles de l'Empire', *ANRW* 2.32.1 (1987), 5–77

Anlauf, G.: *Standard Late Greek oder Attizismus? Eine Studie zum Optativsgebrauch im nachklassischen Griechisch*, (Diss. Cologne, 1960).

Argyle, S.: 'A new Greek grammarian', *CQ* 39 (1989), 524–535

Athanassiadi, P.: 'A contribution to Mithraic theology: the Emperor Julian's Hymn to King Helios', *JThS* 28 (1977), 360–371

Athanassiadi-Fowden, P.: *Julian and Hellenism, an Intellectual Biography* (Oxford, 1981)

Avotins, I: 'Prosopographical and chronological notes on some Greek sophists of the empire', *CSCPh* 4 (1971), 67–80

—— 'The holders of the chair of rhetoric at Athens', *HSCPh* 79 (1975), 313–324

Baldini, A.: *Ricerche sulla storia di Eunapio di Sardi, Problemi di storiografia tardopagana* (Bologna, 1984)

Baldwin, B.: *Studies in Lucian* (Toronto, 1973)

—— 'Alexander, Hannibal and Scipio in Lucian', *Emerita* 58 (1990), 51–60

Barnes, T.D.: *Tertullian, A Literary and Historical Study* (2nd edn, Oxford, 1987)

—— 'Himerius and the fourth century', *CPh* 82 (1987), 206–225

Bartsch, S.: *Decoding the Ancient Novel: The Reader and the Role of Description in Heliodorus and Achilles Tatius* (Princeton, NJ, 1989)

Billault, A.: *La Création romanesque dans la littérature grecque à l'époque impériale* (Paris, 1991)

Birley, A.R.: *Marcus Aurelius, a Biography* (2nd edn, London, 1987)

—— *Septimius Severus, the African Emperor* (2nd edn, London, 1988)

Birmelin, E.: 'Die kunsttheoretischen Gedanken in Philostrats Apollonius', *Philologus* 88 (1933), 149–80, 392–414

Boatwright, M.T.: *Hadrian and the City of Rome* (Princeton, NJ, 1987)

Bompaire, J.: *Lucien écrivain, Imitation et création* (Paris, 1958)

Bornecque, H.: *Les Déclamations et les déclamateurs d'après Sénèque le pere* (Lille, 1902)

Bosworth, A.B.: *From Arrian to Alexander* (Oxford, 1988)

Boulanger, A.: *Aelius Aristide et la Sophistique dans la province d'Asie au IIe siècle de notre ère* (Paris, 1923)

Bowersock, G.W.: *Augustus and the Greek World* (Oxford, 1965)

—— *Greek Sophists and the Roman Empire* (Oxford, 1969)

—— *Approaches to the Second Sophistic: Papers presented at the 105th Annual Meeting of the American Philological Association* (University Park, Pennsylvania, 1974)

—— 'Herodian and Elagabalus', *YCS* 24 (1975), 229–238

—— *Hellenism in Late Antiquity* (Cambridge, 1990)

Bowie, E.L.: 'Greeks and their past in the Second Sophistic', *Past and Present* 46 (1970), 3–41 (revised in *Studies in Ancient Society*, ed. M.I. Finley (London, 1974, 166–209)

—— 'Apollonius of Tyana: tradition and reality', *ANRW* 2.16.2 (1978), 1652–1699

—— 'Lucian at Philippopolis', *Mitteilungen des Bulgarischen Forschungsinstitutes in Österreich* 3.1 (1980), 53–60

—— 'Poetry and poets in Asia and Achaia', in Cameron and Walker (1989), 198–205

—— 'Greek poetry in the Antonine age', in Russell (1990), 53–90

—— 'Greek sophists and Greek poetry', *ANRW* 2.33.1 (1990), 209–258

Brancacci, A.: Rhētorikē philosophousa: *Dione Crisostomo nella cultura antica e bizantina* (Naples, 1985)

Brandstätter, C.: 'De notionum *politikos* et *sophistes* usu rhetorico', *Leipziger Studien zur classischen Philologie* 15 (1894), 129–273

Branham, R.B.: 'Introducing a sophist: Lucian's prologues', *TAPhA* 115 (1985), 237–243

—— *Unruly Eloquence: Lucian and the Comedy of Traditions* (Cambridge, Mass., 1989)

Brock, M.D.: *Studies in Fronto and his Age* (Cambridge, 1911)

Brown, P.R.L.: *The Making of late Antiquity* (Cambridge, Mass.,1978)

Brunt, P.A.: 'Aspects of the social thought of Dio Chrysostom and the Stoics', *PCPhS* 19 (1975), 9–34

—— 'The Romanization of the local ruling classes in the Roman Empire', in *Assimilation et résistance à la culture gréco-romaine dans le monde ancien* (1976), (= *Roman Imperial Themes* (Oxford, 1990), 267–281).

Callebat, L.: 'La Prose d'Apulée dans le De Magia: éléments d'interprétation', *WS* 18 (1984), 143–167

Cameron, Averil: *Christianity and the Rhetoric of Empire: the Development of Christian Discourse* (Berkeley, Calif., 1991)

Cameron, A., and Walker, S. (eds), *The Greek Renaissance in the Roman Empire* (London, 1989)

Campbell, J.M.: *The Influence of the Second Sophistic on the Style of the Sermons of St. Basil the Great* (Washington, DC, 1922)

Crawford, M.H.: 'Greek intellectuals and the Roman aristocracy in the first century BC', in *Imperialism in the Ancient World*, P.D. Garnsey and C.R. Whittaker (eds) (Cambridge, 1978, 193–207, 330–338)

De Lacy, P.: 'Plato and the method of the arts adopted by Galen', in *The Classical Tradition: Literary and Historical Studies in honor of H.Caplan*, ed. L. Wallach, (Ithaca, NY, 1966), 123–132

—— 'Galen's Platonism', *AJPh* 93 (1972), 27–39

—— 'Plato and the intellectual life of the second century AD', in Bowersock (1974), 4–10

Desideri, P.: *Dione di Prusa. Un intellettuale greco nell' impero romano* (Messina, 1878)

Dihle, A.: 'Der Beginn des Atticismus', *Antike und Abendland* (1978), 162–177

—— *Die griechische und lateinische Literatur der Kaiserzeit von Augustus bis Justinian* (Munich, 1989)

Dodds, E.R.: *Pagan and Christian in an Age of Anxiety* (Cambridge, 1968)

Durling, R.J.: 'Lexicographical notes on Galens's pharmacological writings', *Glotta* 57 (1979), 218–224; ibid. 59 (1981), 108–116; ibid. 60 (1982), 236–244

Follet, S.:*Athènes au IIe et IIIe siècles* (Paris, 1976)

—— 'La Datation de l'archonte Dionysius (IG2 3968): ses conséquences archéologiques, littéraires et épigraphiques', *REG* 90 (1977), 47–54

Friedlaender, P.: *Johannes von Gaza, Paulus Silentiarius und Prokopios von Gaza* (Leipzig, 1912)

Fuchs, H.: *Der geistige Widerstand gegen Rom in der antiken Welt* (Berlin, 1938)

Fuhrmann, F.: *Les Images de Plutarque* (Paris, 1964)

Funk, K.: 'Untersuchungen über die Lucianische Vita Demonactis', *Philologus* suppl. 10 (1907), 558–674

Fusillo, M.: *Il Romanzo greco. Polifonia ed Eros* (Venice, 1989) (Fr. tr. as *Naissance du Roman*, Paris, 1991)

Gasco, F.: 'The meeting between Aelius Aristides and Marcus Aurelius in Smyrna', *AJPh* 110 (1989), 471–478

Geagan, D.J.: 'Roman Athens: some aspects of life and culture I: 86 BC – AD 267', *ANRW* 2.7 (1979), 371–437

Geffcken, J.: *Der Ausgang des griechisch-römischen Heidentums* (Heidelberg, 1929); tr. with revised footnes by S.G. MacCormack as *The Last Days of Greco-Roman Paganism* (Amsterdam, 1978)

Gigon, O.: 'Antike Erzählungen über die Berufung zur Philosophie', *MH* 3 (1946), 1–21.

Griffin, M. and Barnes, J. (eds), *Philosophia Togata, Essays on Philosophy and Roman Society* (Oxford, 1989).

Grimal, P.: 'Deux figures de la Correspondance de Pline: le philosophe Euphrates et le rhéteur Isée', *Latomus* 14 (1955), 370–383

Groningen. B.A. van: 'General literary tendencies in the second century AD', *Mnemosyne*, 4th series 18 (1965), 41–56

Habicht, Chr.: *Altertümer von Pergamon 8.3: Die Inschriften des Asklepieions* (Berlin, 1969)

—— *Pausanias' Guide to Ancient Greece* (Berkeley, Calif., 1985)

Hahn, J.: *Der Philosoph und die Gesellschaft: Selbstverständnis, öffentliches Auftreten und populäre Erwartungen in der Hohen Kaiserzeit* (Stuttgart, 1989).

Hall, J.A.: *Lucian's Satire* (New York, 1981)

Harris, B.F.: 'The Olympian oration of Dio Chrysostom', *JRH* 2 (1962), 85–97

Hedreen, G: 'The cult of Achilles in the Euxine', *Hesperia* 60 (1991), 313–330.

Helm, R.: 'Apuleius' *Apologie* – ein Meisterwerk der zweiten Sophistik', *Altertum* 1 (1955), 86–108

Higgins. M.J.: 'The renaissance of the first century and the origins of Standard Late Greek', *Traditio* 3 (1945), 49–100

Hirzel, R: *Der Dialog* I–II (Leipzig, 1895)

Hock, R., and O'Neill, E.: *The* Chreia *in Ancient Rhetoric, 1: The* Progymnasmata (Decatur, Ga, 1986)

Holford-Strevens, L.: *Aulus Gellius* (London, 1988)

Hunter, R.: *A Study of Daphnis and Chloe* (Cambridge, 1983)

Jaeger, W.: *Early Christianity and Greek Paideia* (Cambridge, Mass., 1961)

Joly, R.: 'La réfutation des analogies dans l'Hermotime de Lucien', *AC* 50 (1981), 417–426.

Jones, A.H.M.: *The Greek City from Alexander to Justinian* (Oxford, 1940)

—— *The Cities of the Eastern Roman Provinces* (Oxford, 1937)

Jones, C.P.: *Plutarch and Rome* (Oxford, 1971)

—— 'Two enemies of Lucian', *GRBS* 13 (1972), 475–487

—— 'The Reliability of Philostratus', in Bowersock (1974), 11–16

—— *The Roman World of Dio Chrysostom* (Cambridge, Mass., 1978a)

—— 'Three foreigners in Attica', *Phoenix* 33 (1978b), 222–234

—— *Culture and Society in Lucian* (Cambridge, Mass., 1986)

Kaibel, G.: 'Dionyios von Halikarnass und die Sophistik', *Hermes* 20 (1885), 497–513.

Kennedy, G.: *The Art of Persuasion in Greece* (Princeton, NJ, 1963)

—— *The Art of Rhetoric in the Roman World, 300 BC*–300 AD, (Princeton, NJ, 1972)

—— 'The sophists as declaimers', in Bowersock (1974), 17–22.

—— *Classical Rhetoric and its Christian and Secular Tradition from Ancient to Modern Times* (Chapel Hill, NC, 1980)

—— *Greek Rhetoric under Christian Emperors* (Princeton, NJ, 1983)

Kindstrand, J.F.: *Homer in der Zweiten Sophistik, Studia graeca Upsaliensia* 7 (Uppsala, 1973)

Kokolakis, M.: *The Dramatic Simile of Life* (Athens, 1960)

Kustas, G.L.: 'St. Basil and the rhetorical tradition' in P.J. Fedwick (ed.), *Basil of Caesarea: Christian, Humanist, Ascetic* (Toronto, 1981), 221–279

Liebeschütz, J.H.W.G.: *Antioch: City and Imperial Administration in the Later Roman Empire* (Oxford, 1972)

Lukinovich, A.: 'The play of reflections between literary form and the sympotic theme in the *Deipnosophistae* of Athenaeus, in O. Murray (ed.), *Sympotica* (Oxford, 1990)

McCreight, T.D.: 'Invective techniques in Apuleius' *Apology*, in H. Hofmann (ed.), *Groningen Colloquia on the Novel* 3 (1990), 35–62

Macleod, M.D.: "AN with the Future in Lucian and the Solecist', *CQ* N.S. 6 (1956), 102–111.

—— 'Syntactical variation in Lucian', *Glotta* 55 (1977), 215–22

MacQueen, B.D.: *Myth, Rhetoric and Fiction: A Reading of Longus' Daphnis and Chloe* (Lincoln, Neb. 1990)

Macro, A.D.: 'The Cities of Asia Minor under the Roman *Imperium*', *ANRW* 2.7.2 (1980), 658–697.

Marincola, J. M.: 'Some suggestions on the proem and "second preface" of Arrian's *Anabasis*', *JHS* 109 (1989), 186–189

Mazzarino, S.: 'Prima cathedra', *Mélanges d'archéologie et d'histoire offerts à Andre Piganiol* (Paris 1966), 1660f.

Méridier, L.: *L'Influence de la IIe Sophistique sur l'oeuvre de Grégoire de Nysse* (Rennes, 1906)

Millar, F.: *A Study of Cassius Dio* (Oxford, 1964)

—— 'Epictetus and the imperial court', *JRS* 55 (1965), 141–148

—— 'P. Herennius Dexippus: the Greek world and the third-century invasions', *JRS* 59 (1969), 12–29

—— 'Paul of Samosata, Zenobia and Aurelian', *JRS* 61 (1971), 1–17

—— *The Emperor in the Roman World* (London, 1977)

Misch, G.: *A History of Autobiography in Antiquity* (English transl. of 3rd edn, London, 1950)

Moles, J.L.: 'The career and conversion of Dio Chrysostom', *JHS* 98 (1978), 79–100

Momigliano, A.: *Alien Wisdom: The Limits of Hellenization*, (Cambridge, 1975)

Morrison, J.S.: 'Meno of Pharsalus, Polycrates and Ismenias', *CQ* 36 (1942), 68–74

Mras, K.: 'Die *prolaliai* bei den griechischen Schriftstellern', *WS* 64 (1940), 71–81

—— 'Apuleius' *Florida* in Rahmen ähnlicher Literatur', *Anzeiger der phil.-hist. Klasse der österreichischen Akademie der Wissenschaften* 12 (Vienna, 1949)

Nächster, M.: *De Pollucis et Phrynichi controversiis* (Diss. Leipzig, 1908)

Nesselrath, H.: *Lukians Parasitendialog* (Berlin, 1985)

—— 'Lucian's introductions' in Russell (1990), 111–140

Norden, E.: *Die antike Kunstprosa vom VI. Jahrhundert v. Chr. bis in die Zeit der Renaissance* I–II (Berlin, 1915)

Norman, A.F.: 'Libanius' library', *RhM* 107 (1964), 158–175

—— 'Teachers and administrators', inaugural lecture, University of Hull (Hull, 1969)

Nutton, V.: 'Galen and medical autobiography', *PCPhS* 18 (1972), 50–62

—— *Galen: Problems and Prospects* (London, 1981)

—— 'The patient's choice: a new treatise by Galen', *CQ* N.S. 40 (1990), 236–257.

Oliver, J.H.: *The Civic Tradition and Roman Athens*, (Baltimore, Md, 1983).

Owen, E.C.E.: 'St. Gregory of Nyssa, grammar, vocabulary and style', *JThS* 26 (1925), 64–71

Pack, R.: 'Two sophists and two emperors', *CPh* 42 (1947), 17–20

Palm, J.: *Rom, Römertum und Imperium in der griechischen Literatur der Kaiserzeit* (Lund, 1959)

Papalas, A.J.: 'Lucius Verus and the hospitality of Herodes Atticus', *Athenaeum* N.S. 56 (1978), 182–185.

—— 'Marcus Aurelius and three sophists', *Aevum* 53 (1979), 88–93.

Pease, A.S.: 'Things without Honor', *CPh* 21 (1926), 27–42

Penella, R.J.: 'Philostratus' letter to Julia Domna', *Hermes* (1979), 161–168

—— *Greek Philosophers and Sophists in the Fourth Century AD: Studies in Eunapius of Sardis* (Leeds, 1990)

Perry, B.E.: 'Literature in the second century', *CJ* 50 (1955), 295–298

—— *The Ancient Romances* (Berkeley, Calif., 1967)
Petit, P.: *Les étudiants de Libanius* (Paris, 1957).
Pouilloux, J.: 'Une famille de sophistes thessaliens à Delphes au IIe s. ap. J.-C.' *REG* 80 (1967), 379–384
Prächter, K.: 'Skeptisches bei Lukian', *Philologus* 51 (1892), 284–293
Previale, L. 'L'Epistolario di Alciphrone', *MC* 2 (1932), 38–71
Rawson, E.: *Intellectual Life in the Late Roman Republic*, (London, 1985)
Reardon, B.P.: *Courants littéraires grecs des IIe et IIIe siècles après J.-C.* (Paris, 1971)
—— 'The Second Sophistic', in W.E. Treadgold (ed.), *Renaissances before the Renaissance. Cultural Revivals of Late Antiquity and the Middle Ages* (Stanford, Calif., 1984), 23–41.
—— *The Form of Greek Romance* (Princeton, NJ, 1991)
Robert, L.: 'Documents d'Asie Mineure', *BCH* 101 (1977), 43–132
—— 'Deux Inscriptions de l'époque impériale en Attique II: un concours et Hérode Atticus', *AJPh* 100 (1979), 160–165
Rogers, G.M.: *The Sacred Identity of Ephesos: Foundation Myths of a Roman City* (London, 1991)
Rohde, E.: 'Die asianische Rhetorik und die zweite Sophistik', *RhM* 41 (1886), 170–190 (*Kleine Schriften* 2, Tübingen 1901, 75–97)
—— *Der griechische Roman und seine Verläufer* (3rd edn, Leipzig 1914)
Romilly, J. de: *Magic and Rhetoric in the Ancient World*, (Cambridge, Mass., 1975)
Rüther, R.R.: *Gregory Nazianzus, Rhetor and Philosopher* (Oxford, 1969)
Russell, D.A.: 'Rhetoric and criticism', *GR* N.S. 14 (1967), 130–144
—— *Plutarch* (London, 1972)
—— *Greek Declamation* (Cambridge, 1983)
—— (ed.) *Antonine Literature* (Oxford, 1990)
—— 'Introduction: Greek and Latin in Antonine literature', ibid., 1–17
—— 'Aristides and the prose hymn', ibid. 199–216
Schmid, W.: *Der Atticismus in seinen Hauptvertretern von Dionyius von Halikarnass bis auf den zweiten Philostrat* I–IV (Stuttgart, 1887–96)
Schröder, H.O.: 'Das Odysseusbild des Aelius Aristides', *RhM* 130 (1987), 350–356
Ševčenko, I.: 'A shadow outline of virtue: the classical heritage of Greek Christian literature (second to seventh century)', in K. Weitzmann (ed.), *The Age of Spirituality, a Symposium* (New York, 1980), 53–73 (*Ideology, letters and culture in the Byzantine World*, paper 2 [London, 1982])
Sider, R.D.: *Ancient Rhetoric and the Art of Tertullian* (Oxford, 1971)
Spawforth, A.J. and Walker, S.: 'The world of the Panhellenion I: Athens and Eleusis', *JHS* 75 (1985), 78–104; and 'II: Dorian Cities', *JHS* 76 (1986), 88–105
Stadter, P.A.: 'Flavius Arrianus, the new Xenophon', *GRBS* 8 (1967), 151–161
—— 'Xenophon in Arrian's Cynegeticus', *GRBS* 17 (1976), 157–167
—— 'The *Ars Tactica* of Arrian: Tradition and Originality', *CPh* 73 (1978), 117–128

—— *Arrian of Nicomedia* (Chapel Hill, NC, 1980)

Stanton, G.R.: 'Sophists and Philosophers: problems of classification', *AJPh* 94 (1973), 350–364

Steinmetz, P.: *Untersuchungen zur römischen Literatur des Zweiten Jahrhunderts nach Christi Geburt* (Wiesbaden, 1982)

Swain, S.: 'The reliability of Philostratus' *Lives of the Sophists*', *CA* 10 (1991), 148–163

Šzarmach, M.: *Maximos von Tyros, eine literarische Monographie* (Toruń, 1985)

Thompson, H.A.: 'The Odeion in the Athenian agora', *Hesperia* 19 (1950), 31–141

Trapp, M.B.: 'Plato's *Phaedrus* in second-century Greek literature', in Russell (1990), 141–174

Viljamaa, T.: 'From Grammar to Rhetoric. First exercises in composition according to Quintilian *Inst.* 1,9', *Arctos* 22 (1988), 179–201

Wade-Gery, H.T.: 'Critias and Herodes', *CQ* 39 (1945), 19–33

Walden, J.W.H.: *The Universities of Ancient Greece* (New York, 1909)

Whittaker, J.: 'Platonic philosophy in the early centuries of the empire', *ANRW* 2.36.1 (1987), 81–123

Wilamowitz-Möllendorff, U. von: 'Asianismus und Atticismus', *Hermes* 30 (1900), 1–52

Winkler, J.J. and Williams, G.: *Later Greek Literature*, *YCS* 27 (Cambridge, 1982)

Winter, T.N.: 'The publication of Apuleius' *Apology*', *TAPhA* 100 (1969), 607–612.

Wright, W.C.: *The Emperor Julian's Relation to the New Sophistic and Neo-Platonism* (London, 1896)

Index

The following is intended as a select index of persons and topics. Nominal and adjectival forms are not distinguished.